A WOMAN'S PLACE

A WOMAN'S PLACE

Rhetoric and Readings for Composing
Yourself and Your Prose

SHIRLEY MORAHAN

Northeast Missouri State University

State University of New York Press

ALBANY

Published by State University of New York Press, Albany

For information, address State University of New York Press, State University Plaza, Albany, N.Y., 12246

Library of Congress Cataloging in Publication Data

Morahan, Shirley, 1945–
A Woman's Place
Bibliography: p. 303
Includes index.

1. English language—Rhetoric. 2. College readers. I. Title.
PE1417.M618   808'.042   81-4802
ISBN 0-87395-488-2 (pbk.)   AACR2
0-87395-549-8 (hbk.)

**Dedicated to my mother
and to all my sisters**

Contents

Preface

This textbook was developed from three major assumptions: writing is a process and not just a product; collaborative learning can improve a writing classroom; thinking and writing focused on a cluster of shared themes can facilitate invention, research, composing, revising and reperceiving. I am adapting what could be labeled a "pedagogy for liberation" to the introductory composition course. This textbook combines the inquiry about and practice of basic writing and thinking skills with the raising of consciousness about men and women in a changing world, about their senses of self, and about their experiences.

The discussion of rhetoric—the art of speaking and writing—found in this textbook could be found in other writing textbooks. The focus on writing as process informs most new textbooks. However, the readings of this textbook are presented both as writing models and as representative readings in the area of "women's studies." They range from a discussion of "writing as re-vision" and the way words work to an essay that asks what would have happened had Shakespeare had a sister, from a comparison of non-aggressive male cultures with American culture to an argument about "female chauvinism." Writings by students, from composition courses which used these textbook materials, are included. These themes you address in your lives. Through reflection upon them, you can study, talk about, write, re-vise and express again your ideas and feelings. You can learn how better to "compose yourself."

I wish to acknowledge and to thank several friends and colleagues who helped me with the inventing, composing and revising of this textbook. Three mentors at the University of Massachusetts—Dr. Jane Blankenship, Charles Kay Smith and Dr. John Weston—offered incisive advice, helpful criticisms and encouragement. Other "mentors" have been those students with whom I worked at the University of Massachusetts and at Northeast Missouri State University. Some of them are cited specifically in the formal acknowledgments; many of them remain anonymous but have certainly helped me think through and practice what I set to view in this textbook.

Annye Camara has helped me through her careful reading and criticism of the manuscript; Dr. Orlee Holder, Dr. Carey Kaplan and Maria Larsen have encouraged me in revising the text. I thank all these friends and colleagues.

I wish to thank Ann Baird, Phyllis Bell, Dr. Edwin Carpenter, and Maureen Stickles for assistance with the typing. For proofreading of the drafts of the textbook, I am grateful for the assistance of Victoria Amador, Dr. Kay Blair, Pat Cottey, Donna Crawford, Julie Farrar, Loring Ivanick, Dr. Nancy Kiger, Dr. Connie Sutherland, Mary Ann Templeton, Tamsen Wassell and Ed Zeiser.

Acknowledgments

James Agee, excerpt on page 270, from "Knoxville: Summer 1919" from *A Death in the Family* by James Agee. © 1957 by The James Agee Trust. Published by Grosset and Dunlap, Inc., New York, N.Y. Reprinted by permission of the publisher.

Maya Angelou, excerpt on pages 80–82, from *I Know Why the Caged Bird Sings* by Maya Angelou. © 1969 by Maya Angelou. Reprinted by permission of Random House, Inc., New York, N.Y.

Hannah Arendt, excerpt on page 211, from *Origins of Totalitarianism* by Hannah Arendt. © 1966 by Hannah Arendt. Reprinted by permission of Harcourt, Brace, Jovanovich, Inc., New York, N.Y.

Claude Brown, excerpt on page 270, from *Manchild in the Promised Land* by Claude Brown. © 1965 by Claude Brown. Reprinted by permission from Macmillan Company, New York, N.Y.

Edward Hallett Carr, excerpt on pages 77 and 78, from "What is History?" by Edward Hallett Carr. © 1961 by Edward Hallett Carr. Reprinted by permission of Alfred A. Knopf, Inc., New York, N.Y. and Macmillan, London and Basingstroke.

Bruce Castle, excerpt on page 52. Published by permission of the writer.

Beth Caurant, excerpt on page 52. Published by permission of the writer.

Joan Didion, "On Self-Respect" from *Slouching Towards Bethlehem* by Joan Didion. © 1961, 1968 by Joan Didion. Reprinted by permission of Farrar, Strauss and Giroux, New York, N.Y.

Kitti Carriker Eastman, "Work Break." Published by permission of the writer.

Riley D. Ellerbusch, excerpt on page 267. Published by permission of the writer.

Patricia Ewart, excerpt on page 35. Published by permission of the writer.

Paolo Freire, excerpt on page 149, from *Pedagogy of the Oppressed* by Paolo Freire; © 1970 by Paolo Freire. Reprinted by permission of Seabury Press, New York, N.Y.

Elloise Gard, excerpt on page 53. Published by permission of the writer.

Leslie Beatty Gibson, excerpt on page 52. Published by permission of the writer.

Patricia Glynn, excerpt on page 53. Published by permission of the writer.

Alma Graham, "The Making of a Nonsexist Dictionary" from *Ms.* (December, 1973). © 1973, *Ms.* Magazine. Reprinted by permission of *Ms.* Foundation for Education and Communication, Inc., New York, N.Y.

Sharon Hanrahan, excerpt on page 78. Published by permission of the writer.

Tessie Harper, excerpt on page 52. Published by permission of the writer.

Kim Hill, excerpt on page 263. Published by permission of the writer.

Marybeth Joyce, excerpt on page 263. Published by permission of the writer.

Maura Kelley, excerpts on pages 259 and 260. Published by permission of the writer.

Barbara Lawrence, "Four Letter Words Can Hurt You" from *The New York Times* (October 27, 1973). © by the New York Times Company. Reprinted by permission of the New York Times Company, New York, N.Y.

Doris Lessing, excerpt on page 269, from *Children of Violence — A Proper Marriage* by Doris Lessing. © 1964 by Doris Lessing. Reprinted by permission of Simon & Schuster, a Division of Gulf and Western Corporation.

Kathleen Lindsey, excerpt on page 267. Published by permission of the writer.

Suzanne Leroux Lindsey, excerpt on page 53. Published by permission of the writer.

Margaret Mead, "A Co-operative Society" from *Sex and Temperament in Three Primitive Societies.* © 1935 by Margaret Mead. Reprinted by permission of William Morrow and Company, New York, N.Y.

Lisa Methfessel, excerpt on page 53. Published by permission of the writer.

Anne Moody, excerpt on pages 269 and 270, from *Coming of Age in Mississippi* by Anne Moody. © 1968 by Anne Moody. Reprinted by permission of Dial Press, New York, N.Y.

Iris Murdoch, excerpt on page 2, from "Salvation by Words" from *The New York Review of Books* (June 15, 1972). © by Iris Murdoch. Reprinted by permission of *The New York Review of Books,* New York, N.Y.

Karen Olsen, "A Critical Look at *Language and Woman's Place* or Who Says I'm Polite?" Published by permission of the writer.

Oxford English Dictionary. © 1971. Reprinted by Permission of the Oxford University Press, New York, N.Y.

Tillie Olsen, "Silences" from *Silences* by Tillie Olsen. © 1978 by Tillie Olsen. Reprinted by permission of Delacorte Press/Seymour Lawrence, New York, N.Y.

Jo Goodwin Parker, "What is Poverty?" from *America's Other Children: Public Schools Outside Suburbia,* edited by George Henderson. © 1971 by the University of Oklahoma Press. Reprinted by permission of the University of Oklahoma Press, Norman, Oklahoma.

Debbie Picciato, excerpt on page 264. Published by permission of the writer.

Sylvia Plath, "Morning Song" from *Ariel.* © 1966 by Ted Hughes. Reprinted by permission of Harper and Row, New York, N.Y.

Barbara Quigley, excerpt on pages 79 and 80. Published by permission of the writer.

Adrienne Rich, "When We Dead Awaken: Writing as Re-vision." © 1972 by Adrienne Rich. © 1972 by W. W. Norton. Reprinted by permission of W. W. Norton, New York, New York.

Anne Roiphe, "Confessions of a Female Chauvinist Sow" from *New York* Magazine (October 30, 1972). © 1972 by Anne Roiphe. Reprinted by permission from Brandt and Brandt.

Kathy San Antonio, excerpt on page 296. Published by permission of the writer.

Muriel Schulz, "The Semantic Derogation of Women" from *Language and Sex: Difference and Dominance,* edited by Barrie Thorne and Nancy Henley. © 1975 by Newbury House Publishers. Reprinted by permission of Newbury House Publishers Inc., Rowley, Massachusetts.

Marcia Seligson, excerpt on page 112, from *The Eternal Bliss Machine* by Marcia Seligson. © 1973 by Marcia Seligson. Reprinted by permission of William Morrow and Company, New York, N.Y.

Debbie Snyder, excerpt on page 52. Published by permission of the writer.

Karen Soltesz, excerpt on page 52. Published by permission of the writer.

Una Stannard, "The Mask of Beauty" from *Woman in Sexist Society* edited by Vivian Gornick and Barbara Moran. © 1971 by Basic Books.

Reprinted by permission of Basic Books, New York, N.Y.

Judy Syfers, "I Want a Wife" from *Ms*. Magazine (December, 1971). © 1971, by Judy Syfers. Reprinted by permission of the writer.

Sasha Tranquili, excerpt on pages 105 and 106. Published by permission of the writer.

Elaine Tufts, excerpt on page 35. Published by permission of the writer.

John Updike, excerpt on page 269, from "A Sense of Shelter" from *Pigeon Feathers* by John Updike. © 1962 by John Updike. Reprinted by permission of Alfred A. Knopf, Inc., New York, N.Y.

Evelyn Waugh, excerpt on page 269, from *Brideshead Revisited* by Evelyn Waugh. © 1945 by Evelyn Waugh. Reprinted by permission of Little, Brown and Company, Boston, Massachusetts.

Naomi Weisstein, "Psychology Constructs the Female." © 1969, by Naomi Weisstein. Reprinted by permission of the writer.

Virginia Woolf, excerpt on pages 1 and 2, from *Death of the Moth and Other Essays* by Virginia Woolf. © 1942 by Harcourt, Brace and World; © 1970 by Marjorie Parsons, executrix. Reprinted by permission of the author's literary estate, The Hogarth Press and Harcourt, Brace Jovanovich Inc. Excerpt on pages 189–199, from *A Room of One's Own* by Virginia Woolf, © 1929 by Harcourt, Brace and World; © 1957 by Leonard Woolf. Reprinted by permission of the author's literary estate, the Hogarth Press and Harcourt, Brace Jovanovich.

A WOMAN'S PLACE

CHAPTER ONE

Introduction

Welcome to a community of practicing writers. You are well come to the process of freeing your ideas and feelings through written and oral expression. During this course, you will be shaping the flux of our surrounding reality into symbols which can present to other persons your ordering of that changing world.

We will begin our task with definitions. First, I will borrow some words from other writers. Then I will add my words about words. Always as you read these words, talk back to them, converse with them, maintain a dialogue about their power and process. We work at this task of composition communally.

Lewis Carroll through the character of Humpty Dumpty defined words as tokens of power. When Alice wanders through the looking glass, she meets an egg-shaped pundit who defines words by rules Alice has never heard and who tricks her by shifting from syntactic to semantic quibbles. When Alice questions whether he *can* define the term "glory" as "a nice knock-down argument," Humpty Dumpty insists he can use words as he chooses:

> "When I use a word," said Humpty Dumpty in rather a scornful tone, "it means just what I choose it to mean—neither more nor less."
>
> "The question is," said Alice, "whether you can make words mean so many different things."
>
> "The question is," said Humpty Dumpty, "which is to be master—that's all."

Virginia Woolf, a twentieth-century writer who helped shape the traditions of the modern novel and biography, wrote about the multiple powers of words in *The Death of the Moth*. Woolf wrote many essays about what happens when we write and when we read. She defines words this way:

> Words...are the wildest, freest, most irresponsible, most unteachable of all things. Of course, you can catch them and sort them and place them in alphabetical order in dictionaries. But words do not live in dictionaries; they

live in the mind ... Thus to lay down any laws for such irreclaimable vagabonds is worse than useless. A few trifling rules of grammar and spelling are
all the constraint we can put on them. All we can say about them, as we peer at
them over the edge of that deep, dark and only fitfully illuminated cavern in
which they live—the mind—all we can say about them is that they seem to like
people to think and to feel before they use them, but to think and to feel not
about them, but about something different. They are highly sensitive, easily
made self-conscious. They do not like to have their purity or impurity discussed... Nor do they like being lifted out on the point of a pen and examined
separately. They hang together, in sentences, in paragraphs, sometimes for
whole pages at a time. They hate being useful; they hate making money; they
hate being lectured about in public. In short, they hate anything that stamps
them with one meaning or confines them to one attitude, for it is their nature
to change.

In this short passage, Virginia Woolf describes words the way she might
describe her relatives. Do you find these words personable? Does she
persuade you that you could be good friends?

When Iris Murdoch, a contemporary novelist and Oxford Don, accepted in 1972 the Blashfield Award for Letters, she also defined words.
When she discusses the "purity" of words, she is not quibbling over
standards of usage like those people to whom Woolf alludes. Murdoch is
defining the virginal energy and the possibilities to make new worlds
which she finds in a language. Woolf intimates that words are as various,
gregarious, idealistic, and unpredictable as people. Murdoch asserts that
words are the very wellsprings of human variety, community, idealism
and ingenuity. Her lecture titled "Salvation by Words" further describes
for us the significance of the writing process to our everyday lives:

Words constitute the ultimate texture and stuff of our moral being, since
they are the most refined and delicate and detailed, as well as the most
universally used and understood of the symbolisms whereby we express
ourselves into existence. We become spiritual animals when we become
verbal animals. The *fundamental* distinctions can only be made in words.
Words are spirit. Of course eloquence is no guarantee of goodness, and an
inarticulate man can be virtuous. But the quality of a civilization depends
upon its ability to discern and reveal truth, and this depends upon the scope
and purity of its language.

Iris Murdoch and Virginia Woolf both define words as life forces whose
power to change makes them more spiritual beings than nonspiritual
artifacts. Iris Murdoch insists that the ability to shape with words is the
essential human activity and that this ability *makes* us human. She might
even paraphrase the French philosopher and writer Jean-Paul Sartre and

say that, "People are nothing more than what they make of themselves through words." Certainly, she defines human struggle as those processes of thinking, choosing, inventing, playing, rethinking, and naming—which we call language.

When we use words, we engage in a process which helps to shape our very selves. If we too define words as the means whereby we express the self into being, and if we additionally define writing as this existential and moral activity, we do not restrict our definitions to those writings which are most "personal" like journal entries, letters home, and autobiographic statements. Rather, we describe *all* writing activity as a process of self-definition. We will not make a distinction between writing in an English class and what we do with pencils, pens, and typewriters for another class or for our jobs or hobbies. Every writing activity is a process by which we further shape who we are, how we see things, why we define them, when we change, and where we live. In defining writing, we include the formal research paper written for a sociology class, the essay-exam for physics, the statistical abstract for economics, the report for abnormal psychology, and the exercises for freshman composition.

When we define writing as a process of shaping the self, we assume that the ways we write express into being the ways that we feel and the ways that we think. We do not divorce the process of writing from the process of thinking. We assume that writing is a survival skill for use in a complex society, and we assume that writing provides tools for crafting complicated responses and ideas. We assume more. We assert that writing is the process whereby we "name" the world about us and gain control over that world through making meaning of it. When we engage in the process of writing, we demonstrate that we will not be mastered by words and we inquire further into needs for and uses of power.

In a college composition course, goals are multiple. Our primary goal in this course will be that we consciously perceive and use writing as thinking, that we diligently reflect upon and act through this process of cognition. What this complex goal means, you will understand more fully at the end of the course than today. We will write and think and write again and think anew about the subject matter of men and women in a changing society. We begin an inquiry — linguistic, experiential, communal, and aesthetic—into woman's and man's sense of self in contemporary society, into the character of "woman's language" and the models of writings about women and men, into the roles of women and men in the past, present and future. No learner is prohibited from this inquiry. All persons are encouraged to research in their own minds and in the artifacts of their culture, to examine in their own lives and in the behaviors of their companions, and to promote in their own experience and in the experiences of their communities, the making of a life with guarantees of respect, equality and opportunity for women and for men.

I suggest that such inquiry is as necessary as any inquiry into ways of liberating ourselves from antiecologic behavior, from fear of technology, from intimidation by bureaucracy, and from ethnocentric and racist assumptions. We can free ourselves from servitude to nonhumane and nonhealthy patterns of life through the careful play of mind and language upon, about, under and through these patterns. Such play of mind and language can result in new assumptions about the possibilities of human growth, new models for describing and arguing for such growth, and new criteria for maintaining ourselves ever in the process of perceiving, naming, evaluating, reperceiving, renaming: that is, growing. These important human activities we can initiate through our study and practice of words, sentences, paragraphs, essays, books.

This textbook is so organized that you will be identifying, practicing, analyzing, and evaluating patterns of writing which embody patterns of perception. Some of the writing exercises may look too easy to practice; others may seem too complicated to attempt. All the activities in this book have been practiced and played with by learners in college writing classrooms. All the skills involved—from the basic skills of recalling facts and listing assumptions which underly the readings to the needed skills of analyzing the interplay of subject and style and of evaluating the relationships between ideas to the vital skills of seeing and defining and reperceiving and redefining—are skills which you can and, I believe, must acquire to become free.

All the writing and thinking activities of the textbook are based on the assumption that the processes of recognition, analysis, evaluation, definition, description, persuasion, rewriting and reperception that we engage in while practicing the "elements of writing"—while crafting sentences, paragraphs and essays—are the very processes we engage in while writing at length and while working to solve problems. The sentence you write functions as a holograph. What you do when you write an effective and eloquent sentence "images forth" what you do when you solve a problem.

Holograph? Back to definitions. For years, the dictionary defined *holograph* as "a document wholly in the handwriting of the purported writer." Yes, of course, the sentence *can* be this literal "manuscript." But I use the term *holograph* as it is most frequently used today and in a manner not yet recorded in the dictionary. (More about dictionaries in Chapter Three.)

I mean by *holograph* the product, artifact, or image which results from projecting a coherent beam of light through one point of a picture. Both the negative and positive components of that photograph are projected into a three-dimensional image. Any point of the photograph can be used and each part which is used reproduces the *entire* image. This happens because any point upon the spectrum contains all the light waves, although in varying degrees of resolution. Holography then is the projection of the whole image by beaming light through one point of the original.

Just as light beamed through one point will create the entire picture, your sentence can "image forth" an entire pattern of thinking. This sentence you write is one component of the holistic system called writing. We can easily describe and practice the linear sequence of the basic sentence in English prose: Subject—Verb—Object. Do you remember the primer's use of this pattern? Jane sees Spot. Dick climbs trees. Dick and Jane eat apples.

In such a sequence of S-V-O we move from the Subject or Agent (We) to the Verb or the Acting (can ... describe and practice) to the Object or the Acted Upon (... sequence). We organize the sentence in this particular sequence because we assume that much of our behavior proceeds in a linear fashion. The same assumption of linearity which causes this basic model of a sentence underlies much of our thinking about how reality is organized. The sentence you wrote is thus a holograph for the way you perceive.

We have available to us alternative sentence models. These include compound-complex sentences, periodic sentences, and elliptical sentences. We'll be noting them as we use them and read them. What would you call this sentence with this question mark? Each alternative model can function as a holograph to an alternative model of perception. Consequently, practicing various patterns of sentencing will be an important activity for learning to practice various models of organization, various models of response, various models of perception. These writing activities are not so elementary as they may seem. The limits of time will often restrict us to practicing components and mastering components, but the skill acquired from writing "perfect" small units will transfer to the entire intellectual task of complicated problem-solving.

Because grammar is part of our human psychology and part of our very processes of thinking, we have at hand models from which we can produce new models without ever having seen them or heard them. Watch any child at age thirty months as he or she shapes a phrase that has not been stated by parents, by television, by neighborhood children, by babysitters, by Good Humor salespeople. Watch that child as he or she creates a sentence that you recognize as "correct," as using a sequencing of words which coheres.

We can understand new words, new sentences, new ideas and new systems of thinking when we hear them codified. We can produce our own new words, new sentences, new ideas and new systems of thinking which others will understand. Because we have grammar, we can generate new and unrecorded words by combining the sounds and syntax we have at hand. We can generate new and unrecorded sentences by using sentence kernels we already own. We can generate new and unrecorded ideas from combinations of structures, assumptions, and conventions of thinking.

By learning and practicing alternative grammatical structures, alternative methods of organization, alternative modes of expression, and alternative patterns of reasoning, we can generate new ways to describe the social changes which we witness daily. We are freed through our perceptions of whole systems from conventional and static responses to systems. We are freed so that we can respond afresh. We can respond afresh through the process of reflecting upon language and through our activity of writing. What we will do through these writing activities Adrienne Rich describes in this lyric:

> What we see, we see
> And seeing is changing.

A course in composition with multiple goals requires multiple approaches to writing. The writing activities suggested in this textbook are sequenced to assist you as an individual to dust off old skills and to pack in new skills. The activities will assist you as a group member to collaborate in learning and practicing writing and rewriting skills.

Learning writing is much more than a linear process. We come to our task from differing levels of consciousness about how language works, with varying beliefs about the world about us, for diverse personal and intellectual motives. You may need to pick up skills you somehow leapfrogged over. Perhaps you need to learn how to give concrete examples of the abstractions you describe to your audience. You may desire to speed up the rate at which you can move from specific data to generalizations. Perhaps you want to learn how to conclude an essay by synthesizing research and interpretation. You may decide to pause longer in your prose so your reader can hear more. Perhaps you will choose to learn how to use stylistic devices like parallelisms and repetition to underline your ideas for your audience. Our writing and thinking tasks will be as multiple as our needs, beliefs, experiences, and identities. For that reason, the book includes more writing suggestions than every learner can follow but enough for any one learner to use.

There are no "rhetorical questions" in this text. There *are* many questions. I ask you so many questions because I do want you to think about what I am asking and to respond and to define for yourself the several ideas and feelings and skills I ask about. I'm not fancying myself the Grand Inquisitor. What I want is that you and have the only kind of dialogue possible to us through the medium of this textbook.

I will try to imagine how you might respond—based largely on how I might respond, how my friends have responded, and how the students in my courses have responded. Unfortunately, I will not be able to share the unique and novel response you do make. But I will ask you many questions to anticipate the moments when you would ask me "Come again?" if we were chatting face to face.

Often I will ask you questions that I could answer but which I want you to answer so that you can have the fun and excitement of discovering that thing I enjoyed discovering. Sometimes I will ask you questions which puzzle me. I hope you can find some answers to these questions which my generation hasn't been able to answer.

I expect you to quarrel with some of my questions. I expect you to formulate questions that are more pertinent or more meaningful to you because, of course, you can see things I can't and hear things I don't. I hope you can use some of these questions to make yourself question.

When Gertrude Stein, an American writer who played with conventions in her imaginative writing, lay on her deathbed, she heard her grief-crazed friend Alice B. Toklas mutter over and over: "What's the answer? What's the answer?" Gertrude Stein changed the question with her last words. She asked: "What's the question?"

I suggest that the more you can ask of yourself, and of the people whom you read and hear, "What is the question?", the more you will recognize and identify and name and reperceive and transform your world. Asking questions is essential to the imaginative and free play of the mind. We must ask questions to make life out of muddle. When you come across my questions in this textbook, make them your questions.

You may find in the text words new to you; many were new to me last year. Even though you will be able to understand most from context, I hope that you will research them, play with their possible usage, and become master of them.

I would also suggest that you save your writing drafts and finished products all semester. You will need the materials again. You might use them for some other paper. You might discover some stylistic pattern characteristic of your writing which you'd like to practice. I recommend that you keep a file of materials or keep a working journal or keep both. I encourage you to generate your own assignments. Use the resources of the classroom — the expertise of the instructor and other learners, the several audiences within the classroom, the editors and "literary critics," the community of practicing writers. You will grow as a writer if you write frequently and rewrite more frequently, if you define and redefine.

Defining Our Task

From the finite structures of our language and our persons, we can make an infinity of new words and new worlds. From our limited examinations of the interrelationships of language and culture, we can help make unlimited options for human growth for every person.

Let us begin again with definitions.

Writing task one: Define yourself as a writer now. Take thirty minutes and tell the instructor anything which she or he needs to know to work with you as a writer. Identify if you can your particular strengths as a writer and any weaknesses as a writer.

Writing task two: Define in the manner and length that seems most appropriate to you the term *woman*. After you have defined this term, choose three terms from the list which follows and define them in the way which seems most appropriate to you. Education, youth, collaboration, holism, art, truth, age, language, existentialism, man, friendship, success, cognition, beauty, failure, racism, philosophy, community, rhetoric, motherhood, ethnocentrism, patriarchy, democracy, freedom, assumption, androgyny. We will use these materials now and later: save your drafts and finished versions.

Let us look now at an extended definition by the contemporary poet Adrienne Rich of her progress and process as a writer. She describes the particular events which led her to an essay titled "When We Dead Awaken: Writing as Re-vision."

While you read the essay and when you read it a second time, ask yourself these questions: How does she describe our tasks as writers? Does she propose the same tasks for men writers and for women writers? What does she mean by "re-vision?" Does this word, which she seems to have coined, effectively define the process she describes? What does she mean by "writing as re-vision?" How do we "re-vise" when we write if she means something *more* than proofreading, editing and polishing a piece of prose? How does she organize the essay to demonstrate the process of "re-vision" which she encourages? How are the poems cited connected to the thesis of the essay? Can you remember any time when you suddenly discovered, in the process of doing something, another way of proceeding which was new and exciting? Was that an instance of "re-vision?" Is this essay effective in arguing its thesis? What might be audience response to the essay? What is your response to the essay?

When We Dead Awaken: Writing As Re-vision

Adrienne Rich

Ibsen's *When We Dead Awaken* is a play about the use that the male artist and thinker—in the process of creating culture as we know it—has made of women, in his life and in his work; and about a woman's slow struggling awakening to the use to which her life has been put. Bernard Shaw wrote in 1900 of this play:

> [Ibsen] shows us that no degradation ever devized or permitted is as disastrous as this degradation; that through it women can die into luxuries for men and yet can kill them; that men and women are becoming conscious of this; and that what remains to be seen as perhaps the most interesting of all imminent social developments is what will happen "when we dead awaken."[1]

It's exhilarating to be alive in a time of awakening consciousness; it can also be confusing, disorienting, and painful. This awakening of dead or sleeping consciousness has already affected the lives of millions of women, even those who don't know it yet. It is also affecting the lives of men, even those who deny its claims upon them. The argument will go on whether an oppressive economic class system is responsible for the oppressive nature of male/female relations, or whether, in fact, patriarchy—the domination of males—is the original model of oppression on which all others are based. But in the last few years the women's movement has drawn inescapable and illuminating connections between our sexual lives and our political institutions.T he sleepwalkers are coming awake, and for the first time this awakening has a collective reality; it is no longer such a lonely thing to open one's eyes.

Re-vision—the act of looking back, of seeing with fresh eyes, of entering an old text from a new critical direction—is for women more than a chapter in cultural history: it is an act of survival. Until we can understand the assumptions in which we are drenched we cannot know ourselves. And this drive to self-knowledge, for women, is more than a search for identity: it is part of our refusal of the self-destructiveness of male-dominated society. A radical critique of literature, feminist in its impulse, would take the work first of all as a clue to how we live, how we have been living, how we have been led to imagine ourselves, how our language has trapped as well as liberated us, how the very act of naming has been till now a male prerogative, and how we can begin to see and name—and therefore live—afresh. A change in the concept of sexual identity is essential if we are not going to see the old political order reassert itself in every new revolution. We need to know the writing of the past, and know it differently than we have ever known it; not to pass on a tradition but to break its hold over us.

For writers, and at this moment for women writers in particular, there is the challenge and promise of a whole new psychic geography to be explored. But there is also a difficult and dangerous walking on the ice, as we try to find language and images for a consciousness we are must coming into, and with little in the past to support us. I want to talk about some aspects of this difficulty and this danger.

Jane Harrison, the great classical anthropologist, wrote in 1914 in a letter to her friend Gilbert Murray:

> By the by, about "Women," it has bothered me often—why do women never want to write poetry about Man as a sex—why is Woman a dream and a terror to man and not the other way around? ... Is it mere convention and propriety, or something deeper?[2]

I think Jane Harrison's question cuts deep into the myth-making tradition, the romantic tradition; deep into what women and men have been to each other; and deep into the psyche of the woman writer. Thinking about that question, I began thinking of the work of two twentieth-century women poets, Sylvia Plath and Diane Wakoski. It strikes me that in the work of both Man appears as, if not a dream, a fascination and a terror; and that the source of the fascination and the terror is, simply, Man's power — to dominate, tyrannize, choose, or reject the woman. The charisma of Man seems to come purely from his power over her and his control of the world by force, not from anything fertile or life-giving in him. And, in the work of both these poets, it is finally the woman's sense of *herself*—embattled, possessed—that gives the poetry its dynamic charge, its rhythms of struggle, need, will, and female energy. Until recently this female anger and this furious awareness of the Man's power over her were not available materials to the female poet, who tended to write of Love as the source of her suffering, and to view that victimization by Love as an almost inevitable fate. Or, like Marianne Moore and Elizabeth Bishop, she kept sexuality at a measured and chiseled distance in her poems.

One answer to Jane Harrison's question has to be that historically men and women have played very different parts in each others' lives. Where woman has been a luxury for man, and has served as the painter's model and the poet's muse, but also as comforter, nurse, cook, bearer of his seed, secretarial assistant, and copyist of manuscripts, man has played a quite different role for the female artist. Henry James repeats an incident which the writer Prosper Mérimée described, of how, while he was living with George Sand, he once opened his eyes, in the raw winter dawn, to see his companion, in a dressing-gown, on her knees before the domestic hearth, a candlestick beside her and a red *madras* round her head, making bravely, with her own hands the fire that was to enable her to sit down betimes to urgent pen and paper. The story represents him as having felt that the spectacle chilled his ardor and tried his taste; her appearance was unfortunate, her occupation an inconsequence, and her industry a reproof—the result of all which was a lively irritation and an early rupture.[3]

The specter of this kind of male judgment, along with the misnaming and thwarting of her needs by a culture controlled by males, has created problems for the woman writer: problems of contact with herself, problems of language and style, problems of energy and survival.

In rereading Virginia Woolf's *A Room of One's Own* (1929) for the first time in some years, I was astonished at the sense of effort, of pains taken, of dogged tentativeness, in the tone of that essay. And I recognized that tone. I had heard it often enough, in myself and in other women. It is the tone of a woman almost in touch with her anger, who is determined not to appear angry, who is *willing* herself to be calm, detached, and even charming in a roomful of men where things have been said which are attacks on her very integrity. Virginia Woolf is addressing an audience of women, but she is acutely conscious — as she always was — of being overheard by men: by Morgan and Lytton and Maynard Keynes and for that matter by her father, Leslie Stephen.[4] She drew the language out into an exacerbated thread in her determination to have her own sensibility yet protect it from those masculine presences. Only at rare moments in that essay do you hear the passion in her voice; she was trying to sound as cool as Jane Austen, as Olympian as Shakespeare, because that is the way the men of the culture thought a writer should sound.

No male writer has written primarily or even largely for women, or with the sense of women's criticism as a consideration when he chooses his materials, his theme, his language. But to a lesser or greater extent, every woman writer has written for men even when, like Virginia Woolf, she was supposed to be addressing women. If we have come to the point when this balance might begin to change, when women can stop being haunted, not only by "convention and propriety" but by internalized fears of being and saying themselves, then it is an extraordinary moment for the woman writer —and reader.

I have hesitated to do what I am going to do now, which is to use myself as an illustration. For one thing, it's a lot easier and less dangerous to talk about other women writers. But there is something else. Like Virginia Woolf, I am aware of the women who are not with us here because they are washing the dishes and looking after the children. Nearly fifty years after she spoke, that fact remains largely unchanged. And I am thinking also of women whom she left out of the picture altogether—women who are washing other people's dishes and caring for other people's children, not to mention women who went on the streets last night in order to feed their children. We seem to be special women here, we have liked to think of ourselves as special, and we have known that men would tolerate, even romanticize us as special, as long as our words and actions didn't threaten their privilege of tolerating or rejecting us and our work according to *their* ideas of what a special woman ought to be. An important insight of the radical women's movement has been how divisive and how ultimately destructive is this myth of the special woman, who is also the token woman. Every one of us here in this room has had great luck—we are teachers, writers, academicians; our own gifts could not have been enough, for we all know women whose gifts are buried or aborted. Our struggles can have meaning and our privileges — however precarious under patriarchy—can be justified only if they can help to change the lives of women whose gifts — and whose very being — continue to be thwarted and silenced.

My own luck was being born white and middle-class into a house full of books, with a father who encouraged me to read and write. So for about twenty years I wrote for a particular man, who criticized and praised me and made me feel I was indeed "special." The obverse side of this, of course, was that I tried for a long time to please him, or rather, not to displease him. And then of course there were other men—writers, teachers—the Man, who was not a terror or a dream but a literary master and a master in other ways less easy to acknowledge. And there were all those poems about women, written by men: it seemed to be a given that men wrote poems and women frequently inhabited them. These women were almost always beautiful, but threatened with the loss of beauty, the loss of youth — the fate worse than death. Or, they were beautiful and died young, like Lucy and Lenore. Or, the woman was like Maud Gonne, cruel and disastrously mistaken, and the poem reproached her because she had refused to become a luxury for the poet.

A lot is being said today about the influence that the myths and images of women have on all of us who are products of culture. I think it has been a peculiar confusion to the girl or woman who tries to write because she is peculiarly susceptible to language. She goes to poetry or fiction looking for *her* way of being in the world, since she too has been putting words and images together; she is looking eagerly for guides, maps, possibilities; and over and over in the "words' masculine persuasive force" of literature she comes up against something that negates everything she is about: she meets the image of Woman in books written by men. She finds a terror and a dream, she finds a beautiful pale face, she find La Belle Dame Sans Merci, she finds

Juliet or Tess or Salomé, but precisely what she does not find is that absorbed, drudging, puzzled, sometimes inspired creature, herself, who sits at a desk trying to put words together.

So what does she do? What did I do? I read the older women poets with their peculiar keenness and ambivalence: Sappho, Christina Rossetti, Emily Dickinson, Elinor Wylie, Edna Millay, H. D. I discovered that the woman poet most admired at the time (by men) was Marianne Moore, who was maidenly, elegant, intellectual, discreet. But even in reading these women I was looking in them for the same things I had found in the poetry of men, because I wanted women poets to be the equals of men, and to be equal was still confused with sounding the same.

I know that my style was formed first by male poets: by the men I was reading as an undergraduate—Frost, Dylan Thomas, Donne, Auden, Mac-Niece, Stevens, Yeats. What I chiefly learned from them was craft.[5] But poems are like dreams: in them you put what you don't know you know. Looking back at poems I wrote before I was twenty-one, I'm startled because beneath the conscious craft are glimpses of the split I even then experienced between the girl who wrote poems, who defined herself in writing poems, and the girl who was to define herself by her relationships with men. "Aunt Jennifer's Tigers" (1951), written while I was a student, looks with deliberate detachment at this split.[6]

> Aunt Jennifer's tigers stride across a screen,
> Bright topaz denizens of a world of green.
> They do not fear the men beneath the tree;
> They pace in sleek chivalric certainty.
>
> Aunt Jennifer's fingers fluttering through her wool
> Find even the ivory needle hard to pull.
> The massive weight of Uncle's wedding band
> Sits heavily upon Aunt Jennifer's hand.
>
> When Aunt is dead, her terrified hands will lie
> Still ringed with ordeals she was mastered by.
> The tigers in the panel that she made
> Will go on striding, proud and unafraid.

In writing this poem, composed and apparently cool as it is, I thought I was creating a portrait of an imaginary woman. But this woman suffers from the opposition of her imagination, worked out in tapestry, and her life-style, "ringed with ordeals she was mastered by." It was important to me that Aunt Jennifer was a person as distinct from myself as possible—distanced by the formalism of the poem, by its objective, observant tone—even by putting the woman in a different generation.

In those years formalism was part of the strategy—like asbestos gloves, it allowed me to handle materials I couldn't pick up barehanded. A later strategy was to use the persona of a man, as I did in "The Loser" (1958):

A man thinks of the woman he once loved: first, after her wedding, and then nearly a decade later.

.

I

I kissed you, bride and lost, and went
home from that bourgeois sacrament,
your cheek still tasting cold upon
my lips that gave you benison
with all the swagger that they knew—
as losers somehow learn to do.

Your wedding made my eyes ache; soon
the world would be worse off for one
more golden apple dropped to ground
without the least protesting sound,
and you would windfall lie, and we
forget your shimmer on the tree.

Beauty is always wasted: if
not Mignon's song sung to the deaf,
at all events to the unmoved.
A face like yours cannot be loved
long or seriously enough.
Almost, we seem to hold it off.

II

Well, you are tougher than I thought.
Now when the wash with ice hangs taut
this morning of St. Valentine,
I see you strip the squeaking line,
your body weighed against the load,
and all my groans can do no good.

Because you are still beautiful,
though squared and stiffened by the pull
of what nine windy years have done.
You have three daughters, lost a son.
I see all your intelligence
flung into that unwearied stance.

My envy is of no avail.
I turn my head and wish him well

who chafed your beauty into use
and lives forever in a house
lit by the friction of your mind.
You stagger in against the wind.

I finished college, published my first book by a fluke, as it seemed to me, and broke off a love affair. I took a job, lived alone, went on writing, fell in love. I was young, full of energy, and the book seemed to mean that others agreed I was a poet. Because I was also determined to prove that as a woman poet I could also have what was then defined as a "full" woman's life, I plunged in my early twenties into marriage and had three children before I was thirty. There was nothing overt in the environment to warn me: these were the fifties, and in reaction to the earlier wave of feminism, middle-class women were making careers of domestic perfection, working to send their husbands through professional schools, then retiring to raise large families. People were moving out to the suburbs, technology was going to be the answer to everything, even sex; the family was in its glory. Life was extremely private; women were isolated from each other by the loyalties of marriage. I have a sense that women didn't talk to each other much in the fifties—not about their secret emptinesses, their frustrations. I went on trying to write; my second book and first child appeared in the same month. But by the time that book came out I was already dissatisfied with those poems, which seemed to me mere exercises for poems I hadn't written. The book was praised, however, for its "gracefulness"; I had a marriage and a child. If there were doubts, if there were periods of null depression or active despairing, these could only mean that I was ungrateful, insatiable, perhaps a monster.

About the time my third child was born, I felt that I had either to consider myself a failed woman and a failed poet, or to try to find some synthesis by which to understand what was happening to me. What frightened me most was the sense of drift, of being pulled along on a current which called itself my destiny, but in which I seemed to be losing touch with whoever I had been, with the girl who had experienced her own will and energy almost ecstatically at times, walking around a city or riding a train at night or typing in a student room. In a poem about my grandmother I wrote (of myself): "A young girl, thought sleeping, is certified dead" ("Halfway"). I was writing very little, partly from fatigue, that female fatigue of suppressed anger and loss of contact with my own being; partly from the discontinuity of female life with its attention to small chores, errands, work that others constantly undo, small children's constant needs. What I did write was unconvincing to me; my anger and frustration were hard to acknowledge in or out of poems because in fact I cared a great deal about my husband and my children. Trying to look back and understand that time, I have tried to analyze the real nature of the conflict. Most, if not all, human lives are full of fantasy—passive day-dreaming which need not be acted on. But to write poetry or fiction, or even to think well, is not to fantasize, or to put fantasies on paper. For a poem to coalesce, for a character or an action to take shape, there has to be an imaginative transformation of reality which is in no way passive. And a certain freedom of the mind is needed—freedom to press on, to enter the currents of your thought like a glider pilot, knowing that your motion can be sustained, that the buoyancy of your attention will not be suddenly snatched away. Moreover, if the imagination is to transcend and transform experience, it has to question, to challenge, to conceive of alternatives, perhaps to the very life you are living at that moment. You have to be free to play around with the notion that day might be night, love might be hate; nothing can be too sacred for the imagination to turn into its opposite or to call experimentally by another name. For writing is re-naming. Now, to be maternally with small children all day in the old way, to be with a man in the old way of marriage, requires a holding-back, a putting-aside of that imaginative activity, and demands instead a kind of conservatism. I want to make it clear that I am *not* saying that in order to write well, or think well, it is necessary to become unavailable to others, or to become a devouring ego. This has been the myth of the masculine artist and thinker; and I do not accept it. But to be a female human being trying to fulfill traditional female functions in a traditional way *is* in direct conflict with the subversive function of the imagination. The word traditional is important here. There must be ways, and we will be finding out more and more about them, in which the energy of creation and the energy of relation can be united. But in those years I always felt the conflict as a failure of love in myself. I had thought I was choosing a full life: the life available to most men, in which sexuality, work, and parenthood could coexist. But I felt, at twenty-nine, guilt toward the people closest to me, and guilty toward my own being.

I wanted, then, more than anything, the one thing of which there was never enough: time to think, time to write. The fifties and early sixties were years of rapid revelations: the sit-ins and marches in the South, the Bay of Pigs, the early antiwar movement, raised large questions — questions for which the masculine world of the academy around me seemed to have expert and fluent answers. But I needed to think for myself—about pacifism and dissent and violence, about poetry and society, and about my own relationship to all these things. For about ten years I was reading in fierce snatches, scribbling in notebooks, writing poetry in fragments; I was looking desperately for clues, because if there were no clues then I thought I might be insane. I wrote in a notebook about this time:

> Paralyzed by the sense that there exists a mesh of relationships—e.g., between my anger at the children, my sensual life, pacifism, sex (I mean sex in its broadest significance, not merely sexual desire)—an interconnectedness which, if I could

see it, make it valid, would give me back myself, make it possible to function lucidly and passionately. Yet I grope in and out among these dark webs.

I think I began at this point to feel that politics was not something "out there" but something "in here" and of the essence of my condition.

In the late fifties I was able to write, for the first time, directly about experiencing myself as a woman. The poem was jotted in fragments during children's naps, brief hours in a library, or at 3:00 A.M. after rising with a wakeful child. I despaired of doing any continuous work at this time. Yet I began to feel that my fragments and scraps had a common consciousness and a common theme, one which I would have been very unwilling to put on paper at an earlier time because I had been taught that poetry should be "universal," which meant, of course, nonfemale. Until then I had tried very much *not* to identify myself as a female poet. Over two years I wrote a ten-part poem called "Snapshots of a Daughter-in-Law" (1958–1960), in a longer looser mode than I'd ever trusted myself with before. It was an extraordinary relief to write that poem. It strikes me now as too literary; too dependent on allusion; I hadn't found the courage yet to do without authorities, or even to use the pronoun "I"—the woman in the poem is always "she." One section of it, No. 2, concerns a woman who thinks she is going mad; she is haunted by voices telling her to resist and rebel, voices which she can hear but not obey.

> 2.
> Banging the coffee-pot into the sink
> she hears the angels chiding, and looks out
> past the raked gardens to the sloppy sky.
> Only a week since They said: *Have no patience.*
>
> The next time it was: *Be insatiable.*
> Then: *Save yourself; others you cannot save.*
> Sometimes she's let the tapstream scald her arm,
> a match burn to her thumbnail,
>
> or held her hand above the kettle's snout
> right in the woolly steam. They are probably angels,
> since nothing hurts her anymore, except
> each morning's grit blowing into her eyes.

The poem "Orion," written five years later, is a poem of reconnection with a part of myself I had felt I was losing—the active principle, the energetic imagination, the "half-brother" whom I projected, as I had for many years, into the constellation Orion. It's no accident that the words "cold and egotistical" appear in this poem, and are applied to myself.

Far back when I went zig-zagging
through tamarack pastures
you were my genius, you
my cast-iron Viking, my helmed
lion-heart king in prison.
Years later now you're young

my fierce half-brother, staring
down from that simplified west
your breast open, your belt dragged down
by an oldfashioned thing, a sword
the last bravado you won't give over
though it weighs you down as you stride

and the stars in it are dim
and maybe have stopped burning.
But you burn, and I know it;
as I throw back my head to take you in
an old transfusion happens again:
divine astronomy is nothing to it.

Indoors I bruise and blunder,
break faith, leave ill enough
alone, a dead child born in the dark.
Night cracks up over the chimney,
pieces of time, frozen geodes
come showering down in the grate.

A man reaches behind my eyes
and finds them empty
a woman's head turns away
from my head in the mirror
children are dying my death
and eating crumbs of my life.

Pity is not your forte.
Calmly you ache up there
pinned aloft in your crow's nest,
my speechless pirate!
You take it all for granted
and when I look you back

it's with a starlike eye
shooting its cold and egotistical spear
where it can do least damage.
Breathe deep! No hurt, no pardon

out here in the cold with you
you with your back to the wall.

The choice still seemed to be between "love" — womanly, maternal love, altruistic love—a love defined and ruled by the weight of an entire culture; and egotism—a force directed by men into creation, achievement, ambition, often at the expense of others, but justifiably so. For weren't they men, and wasn't that their destiny as womanly, selfless love was ours? We know now that the alternatives are false ones—that the word "love" is itself in need of re-vision.

There is a companion poem to "Orion," written three years later, in which at last the woman in the poem and the woman writing the poem become the same person. It is called "Planetarium," and it was written after a visit to a real planetarium, where I read an account of the work of Caroline Herschel, the astronomer, who worked with her brother William, but whose name remained obscure, as his did not.

Thinking of Caroline Herschel, 1750 – 1848, astronomer, sister of William; and others

A woman in the shape of a monster
a monster in the shape of a woman
the skies are full of them

a woman   "in the snow
among the Clocks and instruments
or measuring the ground with poles"

in her 98 years to discover
8 comets

she whom the moon ruled
like us
levitating into the night sky
riding the polished lenses

Galaxies of women, there
doing penance for impetuousness
ribs chilled
in those spaces   of the mind

An eye,
        "virile, precise and absolutely certain"
        from the mad webs of Uranisborg
                              encountering the NOVA

every impulse of light exploding
from the core
as life flies out of us

Tycho whispering at last
"Let me not seem to have lived in vain"

What we see, we see
and seeing is changing

the light that shrivels a mountain
and leaves a man alive

Heartbeat of the pulsar
heart sweating through my body

The radio impulse
pouring in from Taurus

I am bombarded yet   I stand

I have been standing all my life in the
direct path of a battery of signals
the most accurately transmitted most
untranslateable language in the universe
I am a galactic cloud so deep   so invo-
luted that a light wave could take 15
years to travel through me   And has
taken   I am an instrument in the shape
of a woman trying to translate pulsations
into images   for the relief of the body
and the reconstruction of the mind.

In closing I want to tell you about a dream I had last summer. I dreamed I was asked to read my poetry at a mass women's meeting, but when I began to read, what came out were the lyrics of a blues song. I share this dream with you because it seemed to me to say something about the problems and the future of the woman writer, and probably of women in general. The awakening of consciousness is not like the crossing of a frontier—one step and you are in another country. Much of woman's poetry has been of the nature of the blues song: a cry of pain, of victimization, or a lyric of seduction.[7] And today, much poetry by women—and prose for that matter—is charged with anger. I think we need to go through that anger, and we will betray our own reality if we try, as Virginia Woolf was trying, for an objectivity, a detachment, that would make us sound more like Jane Austen or Shakespeare. We know more than Jane Austen or Shakespeare knew: more than Jane Austen because our lives are more complex, more than Shakespeare because we know more about the lives of women—Jane Austen and Virginia Woolf included.

Both the victimization and the anger experienced by women are real, and have real sources, everywhere in the environment, built into society, language, the structures of thought. They will go on being tapped and explored by poets, among others. We can neither deny them, nor will we rest there. A new generation of women poets is already working out of the psychic energy released when women begin to move out towards what the feminist philosopher Mary Daly has described as the "new space" on the boundaries of patriarchy.[8] Women are speaking to and of women in these poems, out of a newly released courage to name, to love each other, to share risk and grief and celebration.

To the eye of a feminist, the work of Western male poets now writing reveals a deep, fatalistic pessimism as to the possibilities of change, whether societal or personal, along with a familiar and threadbare use of women (and nature) as redemptive on the one hand, threatening on the other; and a new tide of phallocentric sadism and overt woman-hating which matches the sexual brutality of recent films. "Political" poetry by men remains stranded amid the struggles for power among male groups; in condemning U.S. imperialism or the Chilean junta the poet can claim to speak for the oppressed while remaining, as male, part of a system of sexual oppression. The enemy is always outside the self, the struggle somewhere else. The mood of isolation, self-pity, and self-imitation that pervades "nonpolitical" poetry suggests that a profound change in masculine consciousness will have to precede any new male poetic—or other—inspiration. The creative energy of patriarchy is fast running out; what remains is its self-generating energy for destruction. As women, we have our work cut out for us.

Notes

[1] G. B. Shaw, *The Quintessence of Ibsenism* (New York: Hill & Wang, 1922), p. 139.

[2] J. G. Stewart, *Jane Ellen Harrison: A Portrait from Letters* (London: Merlin, 1959), p. 140.

[3] Henry James, "Notes on Novelists," in *Selected Literary Criticism of Henry James*, Morris Shapira, ed. (London: Heinemann, 1963), pp. 157–58.

[4] *A. R., 1978:* This institution of mine was corroborated when, early in 1978, I read the correspondence between Woolf and Dame Ethel Smyth (Henry W. and Albert A. Berg Collection, The New York Public Library, Astor, Lenox and Tilden Foundations); in a letter dated June 8, 1933, Woolf speaks of having kept her own personality out of *A Room of One's Own* lest she not be taken seriously: " ... how personal, so will they say, rubbing their hands with glee, women always are; *I even hear them as I write.*" (Italics mine.)

[5] *A. R., 1978:* Yet I spent months, at sixteen, memorizing and writing imitations of Millay's sonnets; and in notebooks of that period I find what are obviously attempts to imitate Dickinson's metrics and verbal compression. I knew H. D. only through anthologized lyrics; her epic poetry was not then available to me.

[6]A. R., 1978: Texts of poetry quoted herein can be found in A. R., *Poems Selected and New: 1950–1974* (New York: Norton, 1975).

[7]A. R., 1978: When I dreamed that dream, was I wholly ignorant of the tradition of Bessie Smith and other women's blues lyrics which transcended victimization to sing of resistance and independence?

[8]Mary Daly, *Beyond God the Father: Towards a Philosophy of Women's Liberation* (Boston: Beacon, 1973).

We will make frequent reference back to this essay as we move through the textbook. In fact, you should approach each reading in a less linear way than you might be accustomed to doing in most textbooks. Examples and readings will anticipate later examples and readings or ricochet off earlier examples and readings. We are defining an area of study that is both conventional and new. It is important that as writers and thinkers and citizens of the world we draw connections between all the characteristics of a system. Most of our definition of ourselves as writers will be an incremental process. We will be frequently entering a piece of writing from one direction and then reentering the writing from a new critical perspective so that we can become more skilled at "re-vision."

Adrienne Rich directed these remarks to a group of literature instructors at a professional meeting, but her larger audience includes all practicing writers. In the essay, she uses terms which may be new to you and which have certainly been stipulated or redefined during the 1960s. You will come across many of these terms in other readings and will perhaps use them in your own classroom discussions. Many of the terms you understood by meeting them in context. Many you may need to research further before you can comfortably add them to your word-hoard. With each of these terms you might ask yourself whether you can explain how Rich uses the word. It would be a good practice to write out—in your journal or in your class notes—how you would define the words and how you would use them next week. What do you mean by *consciousness, tone, persona, pacificism, dissent, Sisyphean, transcendence, transformation, egotis, love, the special woman, the token woman, feminism*?

Adrienne Rich makes several assumptions which may also be new or not familiar to you. In fact, she's packed the essay with ideas which could provoke, and which have provoked, long and spirited discussion. These ideas will recur in other readings and you will have time to investigate the assumptions. The idea of an "awakening consciousness" is central to this course. Other assumptions which we will note here and discuss later include the "collective reality" of this consciousness, the myth of the special woman, the fact of the token woman, the description of the "female fatigue of suppressed anger," the allusion to the discontinuity of female life, the assumption of male dominance, the speculation about a new masculine consciousness and the assertion that "love is itself in need of re-vision."

Today, however, we will focus on that assumption which Rich shares with us: writing is a process of re-naming. Rich describes the process early in the essay. She compares it carefully and deliberately with the process of becoming aware of the self. She indicates that self-definition and honest writing are the same processes. Did you notice how she played with metaphors of death, sleep, waking up, and opening the eyes to describe both a change of consciousness and the task of writing?

Such metaphors are familiar to us, but here the writer uses them in a new way when she connects physical alertness and health with moral alertness and the health of improved, "re-vised" writing. All these states of alertness are described by her pattern of metaphor. In paragraphs one and two, she equates acts of living with acts of understanding. We watch the process when we read this sequence of metaphors: "slow struggling awakening . . . 'when we dead awaken' . . . awakening of dead or sleeping consciousness . . . illuminating . . . The sleepwalkers are coming awake, and for the first time this awakening has a collective reality; it is no longer such a lonely thing to open one's eyes."

Then, she defines for us our task as writers. She uses the metaphor of sight and fresh sight.

Re-vision—the act of looking back, of seeing with fresh eyes, of entering an old text from a new critical direction—is for us more than a chapter in cultural history: it is an act of survival. Until we can understand the assumptions in which we are drenched we cannot know ourselves. And this drive to self-knowledge, for woman, is more than a search for identity: it is part of her refusal of the self-destructiveness of male-dominated society. A radical critique of literature, feminist in its impulse, would take the work first of all as a clue to how we live, how we have been living, how we have been led to imagine ourselves, how our language has trapped as well as liberated us, how the very act of naming has been until now a male prerogative; and how we can begin to see—and therefore live—afresh.

I suggest that we should use this definition as a major objective in our work in a composition course. I propose that we set ourselves to the business of "re-vision." We must see the assumptions that shape our identities and worlds, name them, see them again by questioning and evaluating them, see them with new eyes and rename them. We must maintain ourselves at this level of consciousness if we are to be the alert, articulate and able writers which we aspire to be.

Recommended Reading

In each chapter, I'll list a few books that you might want to read because you've enjoyed reading the "other work by" in the chapter. At the end of the textbook, you'll also find a selected bibliography.

I recommend that you read more by Adrienne Rich, a major contemporary poet. *Selected Poems* (London: Chatto and Windus, 1967) is a fine introduction to the early poems; *Leaflets, Poems 1965–1968* (New York: W. W. Norton, 1969), *Diving into the Wreck: Poems 1971–1972* (New York: W. W. Norton, 1973), and *The Dream of a Common Language* (New York: W. W. Norton, 1978) all show the poetry which she described in this essay as the poetry with *her* voice.

Rich also has two volumes of prose which will provoke you to new ideas and feelings. *Of Woman Born: Motherhood as Experience and Institution* (New York: W. W. Norton, 1976) is a book Rich explains in her preface that she wrote "for the young woman I once was, divided between body and mind, wanting to give her the book she was seeking, a perspective which would clarify the past and open ways of thinking and changing for the future." The book expands themes which Rich identified in "When We Dead Awaken: Writing as Re-vision." *On Lies, Secrets and Silence: Selected Prose 1966–1978* (New York: W. W. Norton, 1979) is an intellectual biography and shows the writer defining herself.

CHAPTER TWO

Language and Culture

Through words, we name our worlds. With words, we codify flux. We shape chaos into meaningful patterns. We adapt or redefine our worlds when older namings no longer fit. The codifications or language which we use — whether Hopi or English or Gaelic or Efik — share certain characteristics. We can say of every language that it is a system of rules, but a system with infinite possibilities for change. We can say that every language combines the conventional and the creative to produce a culture.

From the past, each speaker of a language inherits linguistic conventions. In the present, each speaker selects from among those conventions. The speaker uses old patterns to create new patterns which both serve the speaker's present needs and reshape the tradition of the language. When the speaker synthesizes the past with the present through the process of revision, the speaker moves into a future realm of new thought and action. To talk about the interconnectedness of experience and the language which shapes the experience, we need to talk about the interplay of language and culture. We need to define the conventional and the creative aspects of language and to question how these forces inform culture.

Language: Conventions

The patterns used by most speakers of a language are called conventions. So that we can communicate with each other, we have made tacit but public agreements to name certain things certain ways, to pronounce certain groups of sounds certain ways, to arrange certain units of phrasing in certain orders. Conventions shape a language so that it is collective and shared. We have agreed, rather arbitrarily, as English speakers to designate a young human being below the age of puberty as *child*. Spanish speakers have agreed, also arbitrarily, to say *niño*.

Should you decide to learn Spanish, you would identify and acquire the conventions for the Spanish language. Through learning such conventions, you can move from being confused by sounds and phrasings which seem perfectly random to you to recognition of patterns in the sounds and

25

finally to acceptance and use of those patterns. The more you understand the conventions and the assumptions of the language, the more fluent you become in Spanish.

Because the conventions of any language are arbitrary and multiple, we must often specify which conventions we are following at specific moments. If I follow a convention which describes an object by function, and you follow one which describes an object by shape, we might not agree that a cardboard box is a wastebasket. As a writer, I must know your conventions so that I can persuade you to accept my terms and conventions for a while. As writers, we need to know the conventions of our language system — the morphology (sounding), orthography (spelling), and grammar (patterning of meaning units) — both to make connections with others through the shared conventions and to also be able to combine and recombine conventions to invent new patterns of thinking.

Language is arbitrary. Nothing about the nature or the essence of the object we describe makes us choose those words which we do choose for description. Some people mistake the name for the thing and think that there exists a real or natural or inevitable name for a thing. Children particularly will act as if they believe that names are things. When you ask a small child why she calls her truck *truck,* she's likely to answer "Because that's what it is."

Some cultures teach that words and things are identical and share power. The Yahi Indians of California would not speak their names lest the power of the name be lost through speaking. In 1911, the last member of this tribe was discovered, frightened and crouching in a corral. Theodora Kroeber, one of the anthropologists who cared for the man, later described the process of learning to communicate with Ishi. When they had learned enough Yahi, the anthropologists named the Indian *Ishi* or man. Once Ishi learned that the symbol *Ishi* meant his name, he never again spoke the name *Ishi*; he didn't want to give up any power.

You might argue that language is not arbitrary and point out words which clearly imitate the very sound they describe. You tell me: "Listen to these words. Pop! Splash! Meow! Crackle! Don't you hear them say what they are? How can they be arbitrary if their being pronounced echoes the object?"

I tell you that these echoic terms (a poetry anthology will label this language convention *onomatopoeia) seem* to prove a natural and immediate connection between the word and what the word means. When a dog barks, it does say *bow-wow.* It also says *woof-woof.* As English speakers, we most often describe the sound as *bow-wow.* When that dog barks in Japan, the sound is described as *wung-wung*; in Germany *wau-wau*; in France *gnaf-gnaf.* The only nonarbitrary factor here is the agreement by speakers of each language to group echoic words together as a special class which *seems* to show identity of word and thing. In each language, the speakers have agreed upon describing this linguistic behavior as *onomatopoeia*.

Yet we still act as if words were things. How chary are you that no one misspells or mispronounces your name? How often do you substitute less offensive words for more offensive words? When we correct someone who misspelled our names or when we say *pass away* rather than *die*, we show that for us some words seem more real and less arbitrary than others. Think about all the taboo words which you would not use in "polite company." When you use *perspire* for *sweat* or *unpleasant odor* for *stink*, you are being polite and you may also be saying that you or your audience still believes that words are the objects they name. However, when we use the language most precisely and honestly, we know that words have the power we *give* them, not a power which resides in the object they name. We know that what we call a rose—whether *rose* or *borogove*—doesn't stop the rose from smelling sweet. We understand that we follow a linguistic convention of euphemism because as English speakers we have agreed to do so, not because English is something more than an arbitrary symbol system.

Because language is arbitrary, each person could be locked into a language system he or she devised. In fact, one characteristic of schizophrenic behavior is the use of private language which makes no concessions to the patterns used by the majority. For a good example of a language invented by a schizophrenic and a language coherent only to that disturbed person, you could read Hannah Greene's novel *I Never Promised You a Rose Garden*. People escape the cages of their own symbols and definitions by sharing language conventions. From multiple languages with multiple and arbitrary patterns, certain patterns are acknowledged as communal and are used to structure one language for a group of people.

Language: Creativity

Language changes. Conventions are amended and ratified anew by new groups of speakers. Every component of a language system can change. Sounds might disappear from pronunciation although they remain in spelling. Middle English speakers enunciated the *k* of *knave* and both the *k* and *gh* (a harsh sound you make in your throat) of *knight*.

Inflections or endings may become simpler. Old English had a series of inflections which changed how a word ended according to its gender, person, number, function, and place in the sentence. The genitive inflection—what we call the possessive—was a suffix which did not resemble the nominative suffix. Today we use either the preposition *of* or *'s* to show possession. We do not show through the way the word ends that it stands at the front of the sentence (what we call the nominative).

Functions vary. The noun *female* can also modify another noun and become an adjective: *female trucker.* Have you ever used a noun as a verb? You can see this change in the expression "they jetted south."

Meanings alter. In the fifteenth century, people used both *rouge* and *harlot* to describe wandering male entertainers. By the eighteenth century, *rogue* was specialized to mean a man of rascal tendencies and *harolot* was specialized to mean a woman who worked as a prostitute. Usage changes. Words which were once labeled nonstandard or colloquial usage like *ain't* and *damn* now are used with less censure.

Words become new. They are invented; they are rediscovered; they are generated from preexisting structures. Modern English speakers talk about supersonic transports, birth control, boycotts, generation gaps, tripping, television, rip-offs, toxic shock syndrome, skyjacks, and the women's movement. You have heard and seen language changing around you. You have played with words and patterns of words and made your own vocabulary. What are some of those new words which you have changed? What new terms do you use for new ideas? What new meanings have you given to conventional terms? How do you use an old word in new ways?

> **Writing task one:** Take a word which you know has changed and write a paragraph or two describing the moment when you first realized the word had become something new. How had you previously seen that word? How did you see it fresh? How did you come upon the word? How was it used? How do you now use it? These examples might help you think of some other examples: laid back, the pill, brainwash, grok, quadraphonic, bliss out, tape deck, trashing.

Language can be changed in so many ways they cannot all be counted. From fewer than one hundred verbal units, you can combine and recombine without cease. You can combine phonemes (the smallest sound units available; for example, /s/) and morphemes (the smallest meaning units available; for example, [mean] and [ing]) into hundreds of thousands of words. These words you can combine and recombine using grammatical patterns or "rules" to create hundreds of thousands of sentences.

Remember *Jabberwocky?* In this poem, Lewis Carroll combines phonemes which are familiar to us with morphemes whose meanings we guess from their resemblance to those we know. He sets these new words into sentence patterns that are conventional to English literature. What does this poem mean?

Jabberwocky

Lewis Carroll

'Twas brillig and the slithy toves
Did gyre and gimble in the wabe:
All mimsy were the borogoves
And the momeraths outgrabe.

"Beware the Jabberwock, my son:
The jaws that bite, the claws that catch:
Beware the Jubjub bird, and shun
The frumious Bandersnatch!"

He took his vorpal sword in hand:
Long time the manxome foe he sought—
So rested he by the Tumtum tree,
And stood a while in thought.

And as in uffish thought he stood,
The Jabberwock, with eyes of flame,
Came whiffling through the tulgey wood
And burbled as it came!

One, two! One, two! And through and through
The vorpal sword went snicker-snack!
He left it dead, and with its head
He went gallumphing back.

"And hast thou slain the Jabberwock?
Come to my arms, my beamish boy!
Oh frabjous day! Callooh! Callay!"
He chortled in his joy.

'Twas brillig and the slithy toves
Did gyre and gimble in the wabe:
All mimsy were the borogoves
And the momeraths outgrabe.

How is it that you can tell me what this poem means if you don't know what the many new words mean? You have read this poem and "understood" it by using your language conventions and your imagination. You have spotted the patterns of plot and character and you filled in the patterns with your own words. You will find that whenever you name the underlying conventions, your interpretation of the poem will be very much like your roommate's.

Although you might need to write down definitions for *slithy, wabe* and *borogove,* you could do that because you could speculate meaning from what you know of how language works and from what resemblances you find between your language and this language. Humpty Dumpty explains to Alice that *slithy* means both *lithe* and *slimy* because "it's like a portmanteau—there are two meanings packed up in one term." You could define *wabe* and *borogove* by explaining what cross-structures you see of the conventional and the creative aspects of language.

> **Writing task two:** Play with the new words in *Jabberwocky*. Quickly describe what you think happens in the poem. Then take several new words from the poem and finish a short essay by stipulating a meaning for each and speculating about what preexisting parts of language have been structured together to make these words. The words in the first four lines have been explicated for us by Alice and Humpty Dumpty in Chapter 6 of *Through the Looking Glass*. You might want to read that adventure before playing with your own definitions.

Within any language the combining and recombining possibilities are multiple and mathematically immense. Every language has a many-layered structure of sounds, meanings, grammar, usages and invention. You have recognized this open-ended structure most often in your use of standard American English, but when you study any other language you will also find an adaptable, complex structure.

You might learn, for example, that one American Indian language uses long and intricately complicated words and subtle nuances of grammar. The Hopi, for example, can distinguish carefully between several kinds of information by using what in English are "tenses." The Hopi language, however, does not describe in terms of time or duration. When the Hopi use a verb form that we can only translate with our future tense, they might also be using the verb to refer to past events.

In Hopi the verb form marks not by time but by an assertion of an expected or anticipated situation. In a narrative, the verb form would mean something like "begins to." The Hopi use a form like our present tense to report a historical fact of a situation: "I see it fresh; he saw it; she is seeing it." They use a third form to offer a general statement: "They write essays; rain comes from clouds; aerosol sprays deplete ozone layers." The Hopi can make such distinctions because their language *too* is a finite system with infinite possibilities.

Language: Culture

This language which is arbitrary yet precise, which is conventional and creative, which changes in myriad ways yet stays firm through its many conventions, comes to each speaker through culture. Each speaker learns a set of linguistic conventions from parents and playmates who had learned them in turn from their parents and playmates. We begin to learn our language when we are infants. Much language learning occurs between ages one and six. As we change and grow, our language changes and grows. We learn more about how the system functions and about how to make it function optimally. We see and then see again with fresh eyes. We learn our language; we learn our culture.

Language and culture are interrelated and symbiotic. Some linguists and anthropologists would even say that language *is* culture. Others are more cautious and describe language and culture as "related." Perhaps the central problem for us in discussing the interrelatedness of language and culture would be to question whether and how extensively our acquisition and practice of language with its conventions for defining a world have focused our attention on *only* that world conventionally defined.

We should consider these questions. How does language affect the way we think? Can our language determine the way we perceive reality? How much are we influenced to act in, for example, racist ways because our language has fossilized in it patterns which describe other races as monstrous, as dullwitted, as devious, as somehow unlike and therefore inferior to our race? To what extent does our language past lock us into ways of thinking and feeling and acting toward others which are not appropriate to nor creative in our present and which cannot free us for our futures? How much does a linguistic convention determine a convention of our culture?

We should shift the terms a minute. How much does our language only *reflect,* in patterns of insult, prior racist assumptions about the supremacy of one race and the inferiority of another? Does language only transmit the patterns of culture? Does culture shape language? Does language shape culture? Could there be other ways to describe the interrelatedness of language and culture? Does social change precede linguistic change? Does linguistic change determine social change? Are there other ways of describing the interrelatedness of linguistic and social change?

These questions are central to our task of defining our selves and defining our worlds. It may be that we cannot answer them completely, but we can certainly begin responding to them in our essays and in our talking.

Writing task three: Begin your response by asking yourself whether your language determines the way you think. Think about some occasion when you were aware or became aware that a certain phrasing or a certain term influenced you to act in a particular way. Describe as carefully as possible the occasion and your behavior. Analyze the incident from the question: Did language determine my thinking, feeling, and acting? Such an essay is not easily written; remember that *essay* itself means "an initial tentative effort" as well as "an analytic and interpretative literary composition." Such an essay will be helpful to you in playing with questions about language and culture. If you need some suggestions, you might think about whether any of these terms influenced you to act in a particular way that a synonymous term might not have caused. Think about gook, chick, redneck, "If you're not with us, you're against us," twirp, cool, gay, Number 10.

One noted—some claim notorious—response to the questions "Does language determine thinking?" and "Does language determine culture?" would be the Sapir-Whorf hypothesis. Both men were twentieth-century linguists who concluded from their careful study of many language systems that each individual language gives its speakers patterns of expression which vary markedly from the patterns available in other languages. This concept they tagged "linguistic relativity."

Benjamin Whorf further hypothesized that patterns of language habitual to a language could predispose the speaker to see the world in already-fashioned patterns. He speculated that linguistic patterns, particularly the pattern of grammar, influence users to see their world in ways very distinct from the perspectives of nonusers. Whorf suggested that the Hopi whom he studied name and see their worlds in ways very unlike the Navajo or the Chinese or the English-speaking peoples.

One experiment designed to test the Sapir-Whorf hypothesis studied the responses and the namings of bilingual Japanese women married to servicemen in San Francisco. When these women shopped and when they talked with their husbands and children, they spoke English. When they visited with other Japanese friends to talk about times past, news from Japan, and mutual friends, they spoke Japanese. A bilingual Japanese interviewer met with each woman two times. During the first interview, they spoke in Japanese. During the second, they talked about the same topics in English. In this sample of the interview, you can see that the responses of the women changed according to which language they used to answer questions:

"Real friends should....
    Japanese   .... help each other."
    English   .... be frank."

"When my wishes conflict with my family's. . . .
 Japanese   . . . . it is a time of unhappiness for me."
 English   . . . . I do what I want."

It seems that when speakers take up a language, they also take upon themselves the conventions of perceiving of the culture which the language serves.

The anthropologist Dorothy Lee describes patterns of perception among people living in the Trobriand Islands that are almost radically unlike our own. How would you see the world about you if we removed from our language any reference to line? In an essay "Codifications of Reality," Dorothy Lee describes the linguistic conventions of the Trobriand and cites the absence of linear assumptions or linear figures of speech. She suggests that the Trobrianders see the world in ways unlike the time and space punctuations of the world which we see as Western thinkers.

Lee points out that we frequently use metaphors like "course of action," "drawing conclusions," and "line of thought" which indicate that we understand the world "to happen" in a linear way. She moves from that data to suggest that these metaphors reveal our habit of thinking which assumes cause-effect relationships and which assumes chronology or a sequence of events. In fact, if she read this paragraph, she would say that my use of "points out," "moves from," and the adjectival clauses "which indicate . . . " and "which assume . . . " demonstrates again the persistence of line in our language and thinking. Do you remember diagramming sentences on a chalkboard? Can you see that we must assume line in our world to be able to represent our sentences or codifications of reality with a series of straight, perpendicular and slanted lines?

If you tried to diagram a Trobriand sentence, you would need to invent new diagrams — maybe spirals or circles superimposed on circles. The Trobriand Islanders place value on events and name events not because they lead to other events and have climax but because they are "foreordained of old." Trobrianders value most what has been, what is, and what always will be. They describe ritualized actions and they focus on repeated activities and similarities.

If you tried to step out of your skin and into that of a Trobriander, you would find yourself lost at first. You would also quickly realize how much you rely upon the conventions of English to give shape to your world. How, for example, would you write an autobiographic statement for a job résumé if you assumed nonlinearity as a major value for the statement? You wouldn't talk about your "lineage" nor even trace the chronology of your schooling and previous work experience. What new information would you be giving the employer which could help that employer decide whether you would be the best candidate?

Consider this example. Many older women who have raised families and now seek to begin a new career must hurdle immediately a popular belief that "time out" from a sequence of public jobs disqualifies them from working. Often they must learn ways to define the complexity of raising a family and running a home which will demonstrate the range of skills they have and which they can transfer to a new work employment.

But let's say that you have been translated into a Trobriand Islander. You do not use any linguistic patterns which show an aim or a goal. How then do you describe your residence at this college? If you are not here to "finish a degree and get a better job," why are you here? What is it about college which makes value in your nonlinear life? If you did not have in your vocabulary words and phrases which define line, what would you define and perhaps see fresh?

As a Trobriand Islander, you would use the following linguistic conventions: You would use no copulative verbs (*is* and family) nor any verbs of becoming. You would use only the present tense and describe all activity as a present process. What would change in *your* thinking and experiencing if you used these patterns?

You would not distinguish one object from another with adjectives. You would have in your word-hoard, or you would invent, a separate noun for each separate thing. You wouldn't talk about a blue sky and a grey sky as you do in English. You would have one word to mean *blue sky* and another to mean *grey sky* and they would not be connected to each other by the substantive *sky*. Perhaps you would say *blueskyness* and *greycover*.

You would not compare objects by marking degrees. *More* and *most* would disappear. If you have no comparatives or superlatives, how could you compete with another person for the highest test grade or the best lab report or the wittiest classroom retort? What might happen in your relationships with other learners? How would you see and experience your world anew?

If your new language uses no temporal adverbs like *after, before,* or *when,* how would you have to rethink history? If you could not use directional prepositions like *to, up, from, before, above,* and *on,* how could you continue to see a hierarchy in which some people stand above others? How could you continue to define man as above woman? In what new ways might you define the relationships of men and women?

In Trobriandesque, you describe some recurring activity in which you participate. You do not describe it with our Western conventions of plot or chronology. You do not see or name any cause-effect relationships. How then do you have science?

Are you persuaded that language influences us to focus on some parts of our world and to ignore others? When thinking about Trobriand codifications of reality, do you notice the possibilities for describing ideas and feelings that you might not remember to describe because our language conventions direct us to other descriptions? Did you find any of the Trobriand conventions puzzling? Did any seem oppressive? Did any seem to set your thoughts free of their usual routine?

When I have asked learners to try to write using Trobriand conventions, they insisted that the task couldn't be done. However, when they completed the task, they learned how much they are tied to the conventions of English for patterning their ideas. They learned that by denying those English conventions, they found their world at first less safe and less coherent. Once they relaxed and played with the new patterns, they learned how they might stretch their thinking about their world. They learned that unexamined conventions of thinking and writing had locked them into patterns of behavior that might be unfulfilling.

These two writings were attempts by learners to use Trobriand language habits. Each writer describes some recurring activity which each perceives and values as a ritual. How successfully have the writers used Trobriand conventions? What aspects of the writings would have been left out had they used English conventions?

1. Waking up.

Brazzzzzzzzle! Bedsoftness. Room yawns.
Eyes cross. Sleep. Br . . . Sun teases eyes.
Burrow. Darkness creeps. Foot stretches
coldness. Brazzle! Sleep. Ticks. Clicks.
Pillow yawns. Darkness hides. Brazzle?
Burrow. Eyes squeeze sun. Bedsoftness.
Bright brazzle.

Patricia Ewart

2. Walking the woods.

Two. Phoebes fly. We walk two. We walk one.
We walk. Our feet touch tar. Mosquitoes
swarm. Skyprettiness. Squirrels scold. Roads
fork. Roads blend. Barbara smiles talk.
Roads pass. Chipmunks screech. Leaves
slither. We walk two. I talk. Sun sinks.
Feet kick stones. Sun warms. We walk two.

Elaine Tufts

Writing task four: Try writing about some contemporary subject using the language system described below. Remember that Trobriand Islanders would be most likely to talk about a recurrent social activity and would cluster their ideas and feelings about that activity in terms of the ongoingness of what has been. Organization: Avoid plot and space-time sequencing.
Avoid cause and effect structures.

Conventions   Use no metaphors which show line.
of style: Use no connectives like *because, since, then, and.*
                Use no directional prepositions.
                Use no adverbs of time.
                Use no adjectives.
                Use no verbs of becoming; use no copulative verbs.
                Use only the present tense.

Does the absence of habital codifications of linearity mean that Tro-brianders do not experience line or never behave in linear ways? Does the absence of nonlinear behavior in your habits mean that you never experience life in a nonlinear fashion? Does the schedule of classes, meals, meetings, and recreations which you post on your bulletin board so you can remember your schedule mean that you do nothing spontaneously?

We can assume that we share basic life experiences with the Trobriand Islanders. We are born. We age. We die. We reap a harvest from sowings. We travel from place to place. Our languages, however, demonstrate that we may not share the same ways of valuing and codifying those experiences. We may not value the same aspects of those experiences. We may not perceive them in the same ways. The ways that we think about reality and the ways we describe that reality may be dissimilar from culture to culture and may even be dissimilar from group to group within one culture. Recent study indicates that in the English language there may be a "woman's language" which names things in patterns that may not be shared by all those who speak this English language which we usually describe as "one." We will explore this idea more in Chapter Nine.

Languages are created to meet the felt needs of a group. A Trobriander lives in a semitropical area where basic needs of food and shelter can be easily met. An Eskimo, however, may need for survival some codifications of reality that will permit a careful ranking of kinds of snow and the effects of each kind upon the terrain. Accordingly, Eskimos may need some of the language patterns which the Trobriand Islanders do not have.

To say that the Trobriand Islander does not name the world in linear ways does not mean that the Islander is linguistically determined not to perceive and experience line. Although language marks the necessary and the valuable through conventions, we always can choose to create new markings and new values. We can choose to combine the conventional and creative components of a language system and set ourselves free. Although our past seems to determine our present, we have through language the power to use that past in new ways to shape *our own* present and to move into a future which we determine and redetermine. We can synthesize a new culture from the dialectic of language.

Often we find it easier to stay within the grooves for defining that our language has worn into its system of sounds and structures. We can, however, discard those grooves and cut new paths around or alongside them. To rename, to reperceive, to grow, we need to recognize and analyze our present conventions and grooves of thought. We need to reflect carefully upon our conventional assumptions and behaviors. We need to compare our namings with other namings to learn new ways to name.

Recent cross-cultural, cross-linguistic comparisons gave us a new way of defining a language behavior that educators and citizens had long labeled "nonstandard" and "inferior." The dialect characteristic of inner-city blacks had been scorned as "poor folks' talk." Often teachers would circle this speech in essays and describe it as "bad English" with "faulty grammar" and "sloppy pronunciation." They would insist that students not talk that way and that they "learn to talk right."

Linguists now agree that no dialect can be considered good or bad. They have demonstrated that Black English is a complicated dialect with a form and structure all its own. Like any dialect, it has a rigid system of speech patterns with specialized sounds and vocabulary. Black English is not a careless practice of Standard American English (SAE). Black English is not defective talk; it is only different talk.

Everybody who tries to learn a new language is influenced by the conventions of the native language. Black speakers brought to American English the sounds and structures of their native languages, mostly West African dialects. Learners often substitute sounds from the first language if they find those sounds missing from the second. For example, the German language does not have /th/ but it has a sound /d/ which approximates to German-trained ears the English sound. German immigrants would often substitute /d/ for the /th/ in American English. In like manner, West African dialects do not feature /th/ and speakers carried over the pronunciation /d/ to *this* and *that* and made the new words *dis* and *dat*.

Black English differs from Standard American English (SAE) both in sounds and structures. Ways of marking tense, for example, differ from the tense markers of SAE. "To be" is used in SAE to show varying tenses: I will *be* collating; she has *been* collating. Black English speakers, however, use *be* to indicate an habitual tense common to most West African languages. This tense expresses an action that is always happening. A sentence like "She be praying" could translate to SAE as "She's always praying" or "She usually prays" or "She has been praying."

Black English speakers have taken components from two dialects—the particular West African dialect of their home and the particular American English dialect of their new dwelling—and structured a new dialect which shares features of both. Black English synthesizes language conventions from two traditions into a new living language. Recognition of this fact forces educators to revise their definitions of black speech. Rather than assume that the speaker is deficient in one dialect, the educator must understand that the speaker is asked to be bidialectal and to exercise more linguistic versatility than the person who uses only Standard American English.

The repeated demonstration this century of separate but equal languages has prompted sociolinguists and psycholinguists to question what effects the English language has on the way our society works and on the ways our psyches are shaped. They research the role of language in shaping and transmitting culture. The changed consciousness of women and men about how woman *is* defined, how she *could* be defined, how she *will* be defined, prompted new inquiry into the ways that language affects a culture's perceptions of women and of men. Those questions I posed earlier return.

How much does our language affect the way we think about each other? Can our language determine the ways we perceive the reality of men and women? How much are we influenced to act in sexist ways because our language has fossilized in it patterns which describe women or men as monstrous, as dullwitted, as devious, as somehow unlike and inferior to the other sex?

We must shift terms again. How much does our language only reflect, in patterns of insult, prior sexist assumptions about the supremacy of one sex and the inferiority of another? How are we to describe the interrelatedness of sexist language and sexist culture? Does social change precede linguistic change? Does linguistic change determine social change? What alternative definitions might we generate for the interrelatedness of linguistic and social change? How are we to use a conventional language creatively to get us into a present and future world of equality and optimal fulfillment for both sexes? These questions will come up again and again in our work. They are large, complicated, and necessary questions. We need to begin to respond to them.

In the essay which follows, the educator Muriel Schulz describes a pattern of insult, of semantic derogation of women, which has become a convention in the English language. You will have many reactions to this essay; you may be surprised, angered, annoyed, and incredulous. You will see conventions for describing *women* which may influence the present ways that we treat each other. While you read, ask yourself what conventions which derogate women you use, consciously or unconsciously. Think about what new patterns of description you can create so that your future language is not abusive.

The Semantic Derogation of Woman

Muriel R. Schulz

The question of whether or not language affects the thought and culture of the people who use it remains to be answered. Even if we were to agree that it does, we would have difficulty calculating the extent to which the language we use influences our society. There is no doubt, on the other hand, that a language reflects the thoughts, attitudes, and culture of the people who make it and use it. A rich vocabulary on a given subject reveals an area of concern of the society whose language is being studied. The choice between positive and negative terms for any given concept (as, for example, in the choice between *freedom fighter* and *terrorist*) reveals the presence or absence of prejudicial feelings toward the subject. The presence of taboo reveals underlying fears and superstitions of a society. The occurrence of euphemism *(passed away)* or dysphemism *(croaked)* reveals areas which the society finds distasteful or alarming. To this extent, at least, analysis of a language tells us a great deal about the interests, achievements, obsessions, hopes, fears, and prejudices of the people who created the language.

Who are the people who created English? Largely men—at least until the present generation. Stuart Flexner (1960: xii) points out that it is mostly males who create and use slang, and he explains why. A woman's life has been largely restricted to the home and family, while men have lived in a larger world, belonged to many sub-groups, and had acquaintances who belonged to many other sub-groups. That men are the primary creators and users of the English language generally follows from the primary role they have traditionally played in English-speaking cultures. They have created our art, literature, science, philosophy, and education, as well as the language which describes and manipulates these areas of culture.

An analysis of the language used by men to discuss and describe women reveals something about male attitudes, fears, and prejudices concerning the female sex. Again and again in the history of the language, one finds that a perfectly innocent term designating a girl or woman may begin with totally neutral or even positive connotations, but that gradually it acquires negative implications, at first perhaps only slightly disparaging, but after a period of time becoming abusive and ending as a sexual slur.

That disparagement gravitates more toward terms for women than for men is evident from some matched pairs designating males and females. Compare, for example, the connotations of *bachelor* with those of *spinster* or *old maid*. Or compare the innocuousness of *warlock* with the insinuations of *witch. Geezer,"* an eccentric, queer old man,"[1] and *codger,"* a mildly derogatory, affectionate term for an old man," carry little of the opprobium of such corresponding terms for old women as *trot, hen, heifer, warhorse, crone, hag, beldam,* and *frump.* Furthermore, if terms designating men are used to denote a woman, there is usually no affront. On the other hand, use a term generally applied to women to designate a man, and you have probably delivered an insult. You may call a woman a *bachelor* without implying abuse, but if you call a man a *spinster* or an *old maid,* you are saying that he is "a prim, nervous person who frets over inconsequential details." If you speak of a woman as being a *warlock,* you may be corrected; if you say a man is a *witch,* he is presumed to have a vile temper. Or call a woman an *old man* and you have simply made an error of identification. Call a man an *old woman* or a *granny* and you have insulted him.

The term used to denote a semantic change whereby a word acquires debased or obscene reference is *pejoration,* and its opposite is *amelioration.* It is the purpose of this paper to study the pejoration of terms designating women in English and to trace the pattern whereby virtually every originally neutral word for women has at some point in its existence acquired debased connotations or obscene reference, or both.

The mildest form of debasement is a democratic leveling, whereby a word once reserved for persons in high places is generalized to refer to people in all levels of society. Even this mild form of derogation is more likely to occur with titles of women than with titles of men. *Lord,* for example, is still reserved as a title for deities and certain Englishmen, but any woman may call herself a *lady.* Only a few are entitled to be called *Baronet* and only a few wish to be called *Dame,* since as a general term, *dame* is opprobrious. Although *governor* degenerated briefly in nineteenth-century Cockney slang, the term still refers to men who "exercise a sovereign authority in a colony, territory, or state." A *governess,* on the other hand, is chiefly "a nursemaid," operating in a realm much diminished from that of Queen Elizabeth I, who was acknowledged to be "the supreme majesty and governess of all persons" (OED). We might conceivably, and without affront, call the Queen's Equerry a *courtier,* but would we dare refer to her lady-in-waiting as a *courtesan? Sir* and *Master* seem to have come down through time as titles of courtesy without taint. However, *Madam, Miss,* and *Mistress* have all derogated, becoming euphemisms respectively for "a mistress of a brothel," "a prostitute," and "a woman with whom a man habitually fornicates."

The latter titles illustrate the most frequent course followed by pejorated terms designating women. In their downhill slide, they slip past respectable women and settle upon prostitutes and mistresses. When *abbey, academy,* and *nunnery* became euphemisms for "brothel," *abbess* acquired the meaning "keeper of a brothel," *academician,* "a harlot," and *nun,* "a courtesan." (Here, at last, one male title also pejorated. *Abbott* at the same time came to mean "the husband, or preferred male of a brothel keeper.") Although technically *queen* has withstood pejoration in English (*princess* has not), a thinly veiled homonym has existed side-by-side with it since Anglo-Saxon times. The Queen is "the consort of the king" or "a female sovereign" whereas queen means "prostitute." Spelling has kept the two terms apart visually (both derived from the same Old English root, *cwen* "woman"), but as homonyms they have long provided writers with material for puns. Thus, in *Piers Plowman* (IX, 46) we are told that in the grave one cannot tell "a knight from a knave, or a queen from a queen," and Byron calls Catherine the Great "the Queen of queens" (*Don Juan,* Canto 6, Stanza xcvi).

Female kinship terms have also been subject to a kind of derogation which leaves the corresponding male terms untouched. *Wife* was used as a euphemism for "a mistress" in the fifteenth century, as was *squaw* in America during World War II. *Niece* has been used as a euphemism for "a priest's illegitimate daughter or concubine," and surely Humbert Humbert was not the first man to hide his mistress behind the locution, *daughter.* Browning uses *cousin* as an evasive term for Lucrezia's lover in "Andrea del Sarto" (l. 200). As a term for a woman, it was cant for "a strumpet or trull" in the nineteenth century. And *aunt* was generalized first to mean "an old woman" and then "a bawd or a prostitute." It is the latter meaning which Shakespeare draws upon in the lines: "Summer songs for me and my aunts/As we lie tumbling in the hay." (*Winter's Tale,* IV, 3, 11–12). Even *mother* was used as a term for "a bawd" and *sister* as a term for "a disguised whore" in the seventeenth century.

Terms for domestics are also more subject to perjoration if they denote females. *Hussy* derives from Old English *huswif,* "housewife," and at one time meant simply "the female head of the house." Its degeneration was gradual. It declined in reference to mean "a rustic, rude woman"; then it was used as an opprobrious epithet for women in general; and finally it referred to "a lewd, brazen woman or a prostitute." In their original employment, a *laundress* made beds, a *needlewoman* came in to sew, a *spinster* tended the spinning wheel, and a *nurse* cared for the sick. But all apparently acquired secondary duties in some households, because all became euphemisms for

"a mistress" or "a prostitute" at some time during their existence.
One generally looks in vain for the operation of a similar pejoration of
terms referring to men. *King, prince, father, brother, uncle, nephew, foot-
man, yeoman,* or *squire,* for example, have failed to undergo the derogation
found in the history of their corresponding feminine designations. Words
indicating the station, relationship, or occupation of men have remained
untainted over the years. Those identifying women have repeatedly suffered
the indignity of degeneration, many of them becoming sexually abusive. It is
clearly not the women themselves who have coined and used these terms as
epithets for each other. One sees today that it is men who describe and
discuss women in sexual terms and insult them with sexual slurs, and the
wealth of derogatory terms for women reveals something of their hostility.

If the derogation of terms denoting women marks out an area of our
culture found contemptible by men, the terms they use as endearments
should tell us who or what they esteem. Strangely enough, in English the
endearments men use for women have been just as susceptible to pejoration
as have the terms identifying the supposedly beloved object itself.[2] *Dolly,
Kitty, Biddy, Gill* (or *Jill*), and *Polly* all began as pet names derived from
nicknames. All underwent derogation and eventually acquired the meaning
of "a slattern," "a mistress," or "a prostitute." *Jug* and *Pug,* both originally
terms of endearment, degenerated to apply contemptuously to "a mistress or
a whore." *Mopsy,* a term of endearment still found in Beatrix Potter's *Peter
Rabbit,* for centuries also meant "a slatternly, untidy woman," as well.
Mouse began as a playful endearment, but came to mean "a harlot, especially one arrested for brawling or assault." Even *sweetheart* meant "one
loved illicitly" in the seventeenth century, although it has ameliorated since.
Duncan MacDougald (1961:594) describes the course all of these endearments seem to have followed: *Tart,* referring to a small pie or pastry, was
first applied to a young woman as a term of endearment, next to young
women who were sexually desirable, then to women who were careless in
their morals, and finally—more recently—to women of the street."

If endearments for young girls have undergone pejoration, so have terms
denoting girls and young women. *Doll,* "a small-scale figure of a human
being," referred first to "a young woman with a pretty babyish face," then
became an insulting epithet for women generally, and finally acquired the
meaning of "a paramour." *Minx* originally meant "a pert, young girl," and
this meaning exists today, despite its pejoration to "a lewd or wanton
woman: a harlot." *Nymph* and *nymphet* both referred to beautiful young
girls, or women. *Nymph* became a euphemism in such phrases as "nymph
of the pave" and "nymph of darkness," while *nymphet* acquired the derogated meaning of "a sexually precocious girl; a loose young woman."
Peach is an enduring metaphor for "a luscious, attractive girl or woman,"

but around 1900 it, too, degenerated to mean "a promiscuous woman." *Broad* was originally used with no offensive connotations for "a young woman or girl" (Wentworth and Flexner, 1960), but it acquired the suggestion of "a promiscuous woman" or "a prostitute." *Floozie,* first "an attractive but uncultivated girl," pejorated to mean "an undisciplined, promiscuous, flirtatious young woman; cynical, calculating." *Girl,* itself, has a long history of specialization and pejoration. It meant originally "a child of either sex"; then it was specialized to mean "a female child"; later it meant "a serving girl or maidservant"; and eventually it acquired the meanings "a prostitute," "a mistress," or "the female sex — or that part of it given to unchastity." Today *girl* has ameliorated (but *girlie* has sexual undertones), and we can call a female child, a *sweetheart,* or even a woman a *girl* without insult (although the emcee who jollies along the middle-aged "girls" in the audience is plainly talking down to them).

That emcee has a problem, though. There just aren't many terms in English for middle-aged or older women,[3] and those which have occurred have inevitably taken on unpleasant connotations. Even a relatively innocuous term like *dowager* is stigmatized. *Beldam* is worse. Formed by combining the English usage of *dam,* "mother," with *bel* indicating the relationship of a grandparent, it simply meant "grandmother" in its earliest usage. It was later generalized to refer to any "woman of advanced age," and, as so frequently happens with words indicating "old woman," it pejorated to signify "a loathsome old woman; a hag." *Hag,* itself, originally meant simply "a witch" and was later generalized as a derisive term for "an ugly old woman," often with the implication of viciousness or maliciousness. Julia Stanley (1973) records it as a synonym for "a prostitute." *Bat* followed the opposite course. Originally a metaphor for "prostitute" (a "night bird"), it has become a generalized form of abuse meaning simply "an unpleasant woman, unattractive." It still bears the taint of its earlier metaphoric use, however, and is banned on TV as an epithet for a woman (Wentworth and Flexner, 1960). *Bag* meant "a middle-aged or elderly slattern" or "a pregnant woman" before it came to mean "a slatternly prostitute" or "a part-time prostitute" in the late nineteenth century. In the U.S., it has ameliorated slightly and refers (still derisively) to "an unattractive, ugly girl; an old shrew."

To be fat and sloppy is just as unforgivable in a woman as is being old, and the language has many terms designating such a person (are there any designating slovenly men?) — terms which have undergone pejoration and acquired sexual overtones at one time or another.[4] A *cow,* "a clumsy, obese, coarse, or otherwise unpleasant person," became specialized to refer chiefly to women and then acquired the additional sense of "a degraded woman" and eventually "a prostitute." *Drab* (also occurring as *drap*) originally referred to "a dirty, untidy woman," but was further pejorated to refer to "a harlot or prostitute." Both *slut* and *slattern* were first used to designate "a person, especially a woman, who is negligent of his appearance." Both acquired the more derogatory meaning "a woman of loose character or a prostitute," and both are currently polysemantic, meaning concurrently "a sloppy woman" or "a prostitute." *Trollop,* another word for "an unkempt woman," extended to mean "a loose woman," and eventually, "a hedge whore." *Mab,* first "a slattern" and then "a woman of loose character" seems to have withstood the third logical step pf degeneration in England. In the U.S., however, it is used as an epithet for "a prostitute," as well.

Horse metaphors used to denote women have also undergone sexual derogation. *Harridan,* "a worn-out horse," seems to have originally been used as a metaphor for "a gaunt woman," then "a disagreeable old woman," and later "a decayed strumpet" or "a half-whore, half-bawd." A *jade* was originally "a broken-down, vicious or worthless horse," or else such man as is illustrated in the lines from *The Taming of the Shrew*: "Gremio: What! This gentleman will outtalk us all./Lucentio: Sir. Give him head. I know he'll prove a jade" (I, 2, 249). It became a contemptuous epithet for women, however, and was eventually another synonym for "whore." A *hackney* (or *hack*) was first "a common riding horse, often available for hire." Its meaning was extended to encompass, with derogatory connotations, anyone who hires himself out (hence *hack writer*), but when used for women it acquired sexual overtones as a metaphor for "a woman who hires out as a prostitute" or for "a bawd." A *tit* referred either to "a small horse" or "a small girl," but degenerated to mean "a harlot." There is in all of these horse metaphors, perhaps, the sense of a woman as being a *mount,* a term used indifferently for "a wife" or "a mistress" in the nineteenth century.[5]

All these terms originated as positive designations for women and gradually degenerated to become negative in the milder instances and abusive in the extremes. A degeneration of endearments into insulting terms for men has not occurred. Words denoting boys and young men have failed to undergo the pejoration so common with terms for women. *Boy, youth, stripling, lad, fellow, puppy,* and *whelp,* for example, have been spared denigration. As for terms for slovenly, obese, or elderly men, the language has managed with very few of them. A similar sexual difference is evident in terms which originated as words denoting either sex. Often, when they began to undergo pejoration they specialized to refer solely to women in derogatory terms. Later they frequently underwent further degeneration and became sexual terms of abuse. *Whore* is a well-known example of the process. Latin *carus,* "dear," is a derivative of the same Indo-European root. It was probably at one time a polite term (Bloomfield, 1933: 401). Originally it seems to have referred to "a lover of either sex," but eventually it specialized to refer solely to women. Later it degenerated to meaning "a prostitute," and it became a term occurring only in "coarse, abusive speech" (OED). A *harlot* was originally "a fellow of either sex," referring more to men than to women in Middle English and characterizing them as "riffraff." It degenerated further, and Shakespeare's *harlot King (Winter's Tale* II, 3, 4) was characterized as "lewd." However, after Elizabethan times the word was specialized for women only, meaning first "a disreputable woman" and later, specifically, "a prostitute." *Bawd,* similarly, originally referred to a "go-between or panderer of either sex," but after 1700 it was used only for women, either as "a keeper of a brothel" or "a prostitute." *Wench,* "a child of either sex," has sufficient prestige to appear in *Piers Plowman* in the phrase *Goddess Wench,* "the Virgin Mary" (l. 336). Later it was specialized to refer to a "rustic or working woman." As do so many terms referring to rustics, male or female (compare *villain, boor, peasant, churl,* for example), the term degenerated. Then it acquired sexual undertones, coming to refer first to "a lewd woman" and finally to "a wanton." *Wench* has been rehabilitated and has lost its stigma. Today it can be used to refer to a woman without suggesting wantonness. Another term which specialized to refer to women, then degenerated to the point of abusiveness, and later ameliorated is *cat.* Originally it was a term of contempt for "any human being who scratches like a cat." Later it was specialized to refer to "a spiteful, backbiting woman" (a usage which survives). For a period it meant "a prostitute," but this sexual taint was lost in the nineteenth century, and only the less denigrating (but still pejorative) sense of "spiteful woman" remains.

A comparison of the metaphors *cat* and *dog* illustrates the difference evident in many terms designating male and female humans. The term for the female is more likely to become pejorative, more likely to acquire sexual suggestions, and less likely to be transferrable to a male. *Cat* originally meant "any spiteful person," but specialized to refer only to women. It remains an abusive term for women. *Dog* is only "sometimes used contemptuously for males." More frequently it is used "in half-serious chiding" (Farmer and Henley, 1965) as in *He's a sly dog,* or to mean "a gay, jovial, gallant fellow" (OED), as in *Oh, you're a clever dog!* However, *dog* has recently been transferred to women, and it occurs in totally negative contexts, meaning either "a woman inferior in looks, character, or accomplishments" or "a prostitute." Or compare the use of *bitch.* It is an abusive term when applied to a woman, meaning either "a malicious, spiteful, domineering woman" or "a lewd or immoral woman." When applied to a man it is "less opprobrious and somewhat whimsical, like the modern use of *dog*" (OED). *Pig,* applied contemptuously to men, means "a person who has sloppy morals." *Sow* is not transferrable to men. It is an abusive metaphor for "a fat, slovenly woman" which in the U.S. has acquired the additional sense of "a promiscuous young woman or a prostitute."

Robin Lakoff (1973) has pointed out that metaphors and labels are likely to have wide reference when applied to men, whereas metaphors for women are likely to be narrower and to include sexual reference. She uses as an example the term *professional*. If you say that a man is a *professional*, you suggest that he is a member of one of the respected professions. If you call a woman a *professional*, you imply that she follows "the oldest profession." In a similar way, if you call a man a *tramp* you simply communicate that he is "a drifter." Call a woman a *tramp* and you imply that she is "a prostitute." Historically, terms like *game, natural, jay, plover,* and *Jude* have meant merely "simpleton or dupe" when applied to men, but "loose woman or prostitute" when applied to women. A male *pirate* is "one who infringes on the rights of others or commits robbery on the high seas," whereas a female *pirate* is "an adultress who chases other women's men."[6]

What is the cause of the degeneration of terms designating women? Stephen Ullman (1967: 231–32) suggests three origins for pejoration: association with a contaminating concept, euphemism, and prejudice. As for the first possibility, there is some evidence that contamination is a factor. Men tend to think of women in sexual terms whatever the context, and consequently any term denoting woman carries sexual suggestiveness to the male speaker. The subtle operation of this kind of contamination is seen in the fortunes of such words as *female, lady,* and *woman. Woman* was avoided in the last century, probably as a Victorian sexual taboo, since it had acquired the meaning "paramour or mistress" or the sense of intercourse with women when used in plural as in *Wine, Women, and Song*. It was replaced by *female,* but this term also came to be considered degrading and indelicate. Freyer (1963:69) tells that "When the Vassar Female College was founded in 1861, Mrs. Sarah Josepha Hale, editor of *Godey's Lady's Book,* spent six years in securing the removal of the offending adjective from the college sign. The OED recorded *female* as a synonym "avoided by writers," and the Third identifies it as a disparaging term when used for women. It was replaced in the 19th century by *lady,* which Mencken (1963: 350) called "the English euphemism-of-all-work." *Lady* also vulgarized, however, and by the time Mencken wrote, it was already being replaced by *woman,* newly rehabilitated. Even so neutral a term as *person,* when it was used as a substitute for *woman,* suffered contamination which Greenough and Kittredge found amusing (1901: 326): "It has been more or less employed as a substitute for *woman* by those who did not wish to countenance the vulgar abuse of *lady* and yet shrank from giving offense. The result has been to give a comically slighting connotation to one of the most innocent words imaginable."

Despite this repeated contamination of terms designating women, we cannot accept the belief that there is a quality inherent in the concept of *woman* which taints any word associated with it. Indeed, the facts argue against this interpretation. Women are generally acknowledged to be—for whatever reasons—the more continent of the two sexes, the least promiscuous, and the more monogamous. Nevertheless, the largest category of words designating humans in sexual terms are those for women — especially for loose women. I have located roughly a thousand words and phrases describing women in sexually derogatory ways.[7] There is nothing approaching this multitude for describing men. Farmer and Henley (1965), for example, have over five hundred terms (in English alone) which are synonyms for *prostitute*. They have only sixty-five synonyms for *whoremonger*.

As for the second possibility, one must acknowledge that many terms for "women of the night" have arisen from euphemism—a reluctance to name the profession outright. The majority of terms, however, are dysphemistic, not euphemistic. For example, the bulk of terms cited by Farmer and Henley (1965) as synonyms for *prostitute* are clearly derogatory: *broadtail, carrion, cleaver, cocktail, flagger, guttersnipe, mutton, moonlighter, omnibus, pinchprick, tail trader, tickletail, twofer,* and *underwear* are just a few.

The third possibility—prejudice—is the most likely source for pejorative terms for women. They illustrate what Gordon Allport calls (1954: 179) "the labels of primary potency" with which an in-group stereotypes an out-group. Certain symbols, identifying a member of an out-group, blind the prejudiced speaker to any qualities the minority person may have which contradict the stereotype. "Most people are unaware of this basic law of language—that every label applied to a given person refers properly only to one aspect of his nature. You may correctly say that a certain person is *human, a philanthropist, a Chinese, a physician, an athlete.* A given person may be all of these but the chances are that Chinese stands out in your mind as the symbol of primary potency. Yet neither this nor any other classificatory label can refer to the whole of a man's nature." Antifeminism, he points out, contains the two basic ingredients of prejudice: denigration and gross overgeneralization (p. 34).

Derogatory terms for women illustrate both qualities which Allport attributes to prejudice. And what is the source or cause of the prejudice? Several writers have suggested that it is fear, based on a supposed threat to the power of the male. Fry (1972: 131) says of male humor: "In man's jokes about sex can be found an answer as to why man is willing to forego to a large extent the satisfactions of a reality and equality relationship with his fellow mortal, woman. Part of this answer has to do with the question of control or power." He theorizes that power becomes a question because the male is biologically inferior to the female in several respects. Girls mature earlier than boys physically, sexually, and intellectually. Boys are biologically frailer in their first years of life than girls. At the other end of their life span, they also prove to be weaker. More men have heart attacks, gout, lung cancer, diabetes, and other degenerative diseases than women. Finally, they deteriorate biologically and die earlier than women. Fry (1972: 133) continues: "The jokes men tell about the relationships between the sexes—especially the frankly sexual jokes — reveal awareness and concern, even anxiety, about the general presence of these biologic disadvantages and frailties."[8] Grotjahn (1972: 53) concurs that anxiety prompts man's hostility, but he believes the source is fear of sexual inadequacy. A woman knows the truth about his potency; he cannot lie to her. Yet her own performance remains a secret, a mystery to him. Thus, man's fear of woman is basically sexual, which is perhaps the reason why so many of the derogatory terms for women take on sexual connotations.

I began with the acknowledgment that we cannot tell the extent to which any language influences the people who use it. This is certainly true for most of what we call *language*. However, words which are highly charged with emotion, taboo, or distaste do not only reflect the culture which uses them. They teach and perpetuate the attitudes which created them. To make the name of God taboo is to perpetuate the mystery, power, and awesomeness of the divine. To surround a concept with euphemisms, as Americans have done with the idea of death, is to render the reality of the concept virtually invisible. And to brand a class of persons as obscene is to taint them to the users of the language. As Mariana Birnbaum (1971: 248) points out, prejudicial language "always mirror[s] generalized tabloid thinking which contains prejudices and thus perpetuates discrimination." This circularity in itself is justification for bringing such linguistic denigration of women to a conscious level. The semantic change discussed here, by which terms designating women routinely undergo pejoration, both reflects and perpetuates derogatory attitudes toward women. They should be abjured.

Notes

[1]Citations are based upon, but are not necessarily direct quotations from, the *Oxford English Dictionary*, cited henceforth as (OED), *Webster's third international* (Third), the *Dictionary of American slang* (Wentworth and Flexner, 1960), *Slang and its analogues* (Farmer and Henley, 1965), *A dictionary of slang and unconventional English* (Partridge, 1961), and the *American thesaurus of slang* (Berrey and Van den Bark, 1952). Sources are only indicated if the source is other than one of the above, or if the citation contains unusual information.

[2]Endearments and terms for young women have undergone a similar pejoration in other languages, as well. Thass-Thienemann (1967: 336) cites *Metze* and *Dirne* from German, *fille* or *fille de joie* from French, *hetaira* and *pallakis* or *pallake* from Greek, and *puttana* from Italian as endearments which degenerated and become sexual slurs.

[3]There are few terms for old people of either sex in English, "senior citizen" being our current favorite euphemism. However, the few terms available to denote old men *(elder, oldster, codger, geezer, duffer)* are, as was mentioned above, less vituperative than are those denoting women.

[4]C. S. Lewis (1961), in discussing four-letter words, makes a point which is perhaps applicable to the tendency these words have to acquire sexual implications. He argues, with evidence from Sheffield and Montaigne, that four-letter words are not used in order to provoke desire. In fact, they have little to do with sexual arousal. They are used rather to express force and vituperation.

[5]Several bird names originating as metaphors for young girls have also become abusive epithets for them. *Columbine, quail, flapper, bird, chicken, hen,* and in this country *sea gull* all began affectionately but acquired the meaning "a prostitute."

[6]Several terms which originally applied to thieves, beggars, and their female accomplices have specialized and pejorated as terms for women: *badger, doxy, moll* (from *Mary*), *mollisher,* and *bulker,* for example. *Blowse* reversed the process. Denoting first "a prostitute," and then "a beggar's trull," it finally ameliorated slightly to mean "a slattern or a shrew." Other terms which originally designated either sex but came to refer only to women with the sense of "a prostitute" are *filth, morsel* (perhaps with the present sense of *piece*), *canary, rig,* and *rep.* The reverse has happened in a strange way with *fagot* (or *faggot*). It was first a term of abuse for women (sixteenth to nineteenth century) or a term for "a dummy soldier." Today it has transferred as an abusive term for "a male homosexual." Not all the terms specializing to women acquired sexual implications. *Potato* "ugly face," *prig, prude, termagant,* and *vixen* were all used in a general sense first and only later narrowed to refer specifically to women.

[7]I have restricted myself in this paper to terms which have undergone the process of pejoration or amelioration — terms which have not always been abusive. The majority of derogatory words for women, of course, were coined as dysphemisms and are, hence, outside the scope of my study. In Farmer and Henley (1965), the chief entry containing synonyms for "prostitute" is *tart,* while for "*whoremonger*" it is *mutton-monger.* There are, in addition to the English synonyms, over 200 French phrases used to refer to women in a derogatory and sexual way, and another extended listing occurs under the entry *barrack-hack.* Stanley (1973) lists 200, and I found another 100, culled chiefly from Fryer (1963), Sagarin (1962), Berrey and Van den Bark (1952), Partridge (1961), and Wentworth and Flexner (1960).

[8]Bettelheim and Janowitz (1950: 54–55) also cite anxiety as the source of prejudice. They argue that the prejudiced person "seeks relief through prejudice, which serves to reduce anxiety because prejudice facilitates the discharge of hostility, and if hostility is discharged anxiety is reduced. Prejudice reduces anxiety because it suggests to the person that he is better than others, hence does not need to feel so anxious."

References

Allport, Gordon W. (1954). *The nature of prejudice.* Cambridge, Mass.: Addison-Wesley.

Berrey, Lester V. & Van den Bark, Melvin. (1952). *The American thesaurus of slang.* New York: Thomas Y. Crowell.

Bettelheim, Bruno & Janowitz, Morris. (1950). *Dynamics of prejudice.* New York: Harper & Row.

Birnbaum, Mariana D. (1971). "On the language of prejudice," *Western Folklore,* 30, 241–68.

Bloomfield, Leonard. (1933). *Language.* New York: Henry Holt.

Farmer, J. S. & Henley, W. E. (1965). *Slang and its analogues.* Repr. of 7 vols, publ. 1890–1904. New York: Kraus Reprint Corp.

Flexner, Stuart. (1960). Preface to Harold Wentworth and Stuart Flexner (eds.), *Dictionary of American slang.* New York: Thomas Y. Crowell.

Fry, William P. (1972). "Psychodynamics of sexual humor: man's view of sex." *Medical Aspects of Human Sexuality,* 6, 128–34.

Fryer, Peter, (1963). *Mrs. Grundy: studies in English prudery.* London: Dennis Dobson.

Gove, Philip (ed.). (1971). *Webster's third new international dictionary.* Springfield, Mass.: G. & C. Merriam.

Greenough, James Bradstreet & Kittredge, George Lyman. (1901). *Words and their ways in English speech.* New York: Macmillan.

Grotjahn, Martin. (1972). "Sexuality and humor. Don't laugh!" *Psychology Today,* 6, 51–53.

Lakoff, Robin. (1973). "Language and woman's place." *Language in Society,* 2, 45–80.

Lewis, C. S. (1961). "Four-letter words." *Critical Quarterly,* 3, 118–22.

MacDougald, Duncan, Jr. (1961). Language and sex. In Albert Ellis & Albert Abarbanel (eds.), *The encyclopedia of sexual behavior.* London: Hawthorne Books, Vol. II.

Mencken, H. L. (1963). *The American language. The fourth edition and the two supplements.* Abridged and ed. by Raven I. McDavid, Jr. New York: Knopf.

Oxford English Dictionary. (1933). Oxford: Clarendon Press.

Partridge, Eric. (ed.). (1961). *A dictionary of slang and unconventional English.* 5th ed. New York: Macmillan.

Sagarin, Edward, (1962). *The anatomy of dirty words.* New York: Lyle Stuart.

Stanley, Julia. (1973). The metaphors some people live by. Unpublished mimeo.

Thass-Thienemann, Theodore. (1967). *The subconscious language.* New York: Washington Square Press.

Ullman, Stephen. (1967). *Semantics. An introduction to the science of meaning.* New York: Barnes & Noble.

Wentworth, Harold & Flexner, Stuart Berg. (eds.). (1960). *Dictionary of American slang.* New York: Thomas Y. Crowell.

Why do you think semantic derogation happens? How much of semantic derogation is an unconscious and careless use of unexamined assumptions? How much of semantic derogation results from an assumption that woman is inferior? How comfortable are you with the continued use of language conventions which oppress people? What instances of semantic derogation of some other group do you remember from your own experience? Why did semantic derogation happen? How can we change this behavior?

Suggested Group Writing and Discussing Activities

1. Describe in a few paragraphs some situation in which you were aware of semantic derogation. Define what you mean by semantic derogation, and describe the instance of insult carefully and completely. After the narrative, analyze *why* the semantic derogation occurred, both in that instance and as a repeated pattern.

2. In group discussion, draw up a list of terms which derogate men. Can you discern a pattern of insult for men? Are sexual slurs as frequent and as negative? What do you conclude about any pattern of semantic derogation of

men? Summarize your findings in one paragraph which could introduce a long paper.

Recommended Reading

Peter Farb. *Word Play: What Happens when People Talk.* New York: Alfred Knopf, 1973.

Casey Miller and Kate Swift. *Words and Women: New Language for New Times.* New York: Anchor Press/Doubleday, 1976.

Benjamin Whorf. *Language, Thought* and *Reality.* Edited by John Carroll. Cambridge, MA: M I T Press, Massachusetts Institute of Technology, 1962.

CHAPTER THREE

Definition

How did you define *woman?*
I asked you in Chapter I to define *woman* "in the manner and length that seems most appropriate to you." I also asked writers in an introductory composition course to do the same. They were all students new to the study of rhetoric; their ages ranged from seventeen to twenty-eight. All had used the word for a long time. Certainly, they all knew what it meant. *Woman* is a common term in our language. Their definitions will help us begin to analyze and practice several methods of defining. You'll notice at once that even opinions about "appropriate manner and length" vary a great deal.

I asked the writers: "What is woman? How do you define woman?" They replied:

A woman is the female human being in this world. There is no one definition of woman, because each woman is different from others of her sex. — Tessie Harper

Woman is the member of the human race who bears children. — Leslie Beatty Gibson

When I think of the word woman, I think of a mother bearing children because that is the task for women since the beginning of time. But she has progressed rapidly in the last ten years or so. Today a woman has many more responsibilities than she used to have. She is now thought to be more than just a potential mother. She has a solid head on her shoulders, and can equal and can even sometimes surpass her male counterpart. — Debby Snyder

wom•an/ 'wum-on/n, pl wom•en/ 'wim-n/ME, fr. OE *wifman,* fr. wif woman, wife & man human being, man 1: an adult female person. 2: WOMANKIND 3: distinctively feminine nature: WOMANLINESS 4: a female servant or personal attendant 5: MISTRESS syn see FEMALE — Bruce Castle

Woman is the second sex, often treated as "other" and less authentic. — Beth Caurant

A woman is a person, a human being. — Karen Soltesz

52

A woman is the female human being with anatomical characteristics of uterus and ovaries and with a renal system that is unlike that of the male. —Elloise Gard

A woman is an individual whose ideas are new, fresh and all her own. She is warm sometimes, cold other times, tender at times, rough at times. But she does not want to be characterized one way or the other. She wants to be free to express her feelings outside the realm of a fixed category. Above all a woman is a person, a human being placed on this earth to respect others for what they are and to be respected for what she is—a person, not an object. — Suzanne Leroux Lindsey

Woman — an adult female; a wife, a female attendant. The female sex. Feminine nature (Webster's Dictionary). A person of the female sex, usually able to bear children. A person with maturity and understanding, intelligence and compassion. Strong in body and mind. A member of the human race. Independent and respected. A woman is many things in the eyes of many people. My image of a woman is a person capable of being herself and of living according to her own principles. —Lisa Methfessel

Woman is possibility. This is a time of discovery and actualization, for many women, of dormant talent and abilities. Woman has been, traditionally, mother, wife, teacher, nurse, seamstress, etc., and discouraged from participating in the more aggressive, competitive elements of her society, other than in supporting roles to men. She is changing, dissatisfied, demanding her right to be what her natural inclinations will lead her to be, demanding her right to govern her own body and mind, to learn her buried history and to make her own present and future. She is aware of the vastness of what has been denied her, and is becoming secure in the awareness of her potential. — Patricia Glynn

How, then, are we to define this term? Some based their definitions on role; some based them on physical make-up; some based them on psychological traits. Which definition is the correct definition?

I hope you winced at that question. Your wince shows me that you quarrel with the belief that *one* definition can catch an essence and fix it fast in words. My asking you for a "correct" definition asks you to make laws about what a word means and how people must use the word. It asks you to proscribe rather than to describe.

But we now know that defining is a process as various and capable of chance and "re-vision" as the process of language. We know that to judge a "correct" definition, we need first to decide what purpose we have for defining, then to evaluate what method would most aptly meet that purpose, and finally to consider the site and audience for the definition. When I ask which definition is correct, we know that the "correct answer" must be "that all depends."

In this chapter we will be defining words, ideas and feelings both fresh and familiar. We'll discover more about how and why the words we use can change our thinking and acting. We'll acquire alternative methods for defining and will assess advantages and disadvantages of each method. We'll examine the ways that definitions organize our thinking and writing.

Let's go back to those definitions of *woman*. Did you notice that two of the writers took their definitions from the dictionary? We'll begin, then, with the method of defining most familiar to us—dictionary definition.

Dictionaries

Did you, like those two writers, turn to the dictionary on your desk when you sat down to define *woman*? Did you pattern your definition on the single line entry you found there? When you talk about that book do you tend to call it THE DICTIONARY or do you call it "a dictionary"? When I say THE DICTIONARY I fall back into an old trap which you might share of thinking that somehow THE DICTIONARY is the final authority about language, that it commands me to accept its meaning for a word, to imitate its spelling and pronunciation, and to follow its usage. Because many of us have this habit of unduly respecting and deferring to the authority of the dictionary, let's look at a dictionary. How did a dictionary originate? What's a dictionary good for? Why is it so highly respected? How does it work? When should I use it?

Dictionaries are often more linguistically sophisticated than the individual writer who consults them. They have been carefully prepared by language experts who record, research, analyze, write and revise entries. They are frequently updated. They make available the conventions of the majority speakers of a language. They describe for us the habitual ways that a large group of people uses words. They are a valuable reference work for every practicing writer.

However, writers are often more linguistically imaginative than dictionaries suggest. Because language changes constantly, dictionaries can never record all the possible ways of using words. The written word always lags behind the spoken word and the dictionary always lags behind contemporary usage. Moreover, dictionaries are prepared by fallible humans who can make mistakes of fact and of judgment. They might select words for entry while wearing lenses which filter real usage through personal and societal biases. Dictionaries are not value-free and can't offer absolute accuracy or truth. In fact, by describing the language conventions of the majority speakers of English, they might affirm and perpetuate inhuman behaviors of racism, sexism, and ageism practiced by those majority speakers. With these advantages and disadvantages in mind, watch how the dictionary became an important reference tool and see what the dictionary can offer our community of writers.

Dictionaries (from the Middle Latin *dictio* for speaking) are rather recent inventions. Scholars and scribes of the Middle Ages traded word lists which gave Latin words with English translations. The first English words–English meanings list was published in 1603. Robert Cawdrey called his list *A Table Alphabetical* and gave synonyms for some 2,500 "hard words" he copied from earlier lists. He added words he had heard and not seen on lists. Since then most dictionary-makers have used his method of selecting terms from published lists and adding other words used by many speakers of the language. They copy but they revise and refine the words when they do so.

During the seventeenth century, compilers traced down histories of words and included those histories or etymologies in their definitions. At first they were only concerned with difficult words, often imports from other language, which readers might stumble over. Remember that these were a small group of gentlemen trained in the classics. However, when the compilers began competing with each other for drawing up the longest word lists, some began to include everyday terms. These words made lists helpful to a new audience; men and women with scant schooling but with knowledge of the common words could now use the alphabetical lists to become literate.

In the early eighteenth century, John Kersey decided that dictionaries should include common words and should be a representative sampling of the English language. He and Nathaniel Bailey were the first professional dictionary-makers or lexicographers. Their dictionaries were written to aid not only gentlemen versed in Latin and Greek but also the class which included "Young Scholars, Tradesmen, Artificers, and the Female Sex." One title page described the audience as "Ladies who have a turn for Reading and Gentlemen of no learned Profession." Another stated that it was "chiefly intended for more-knowing Women and less-knowing Men." Notice this change in the reading audience of the eighteenth century. You might say that the dictionary was a democratizing book.

Mid-eighteenth century, a major lexicographer published a work he had been seven years compiling. *A Dictionary of the English Language* by Samuel Johnson was a serious work which influenced many later writers in their word choices. If you have heard of this work, it's likely that someone has quoted a few of the witty or satiric or overly complicated definitions you can find in the book. Johnson defined *lexicographer* as "a harmless drudge" and *oats* as "A grain, which in England is generally given to horses, but in Scotland supports the people." He satirized contemporary politics when he described pension as "An allowance made to any one without an equivalent. In England it is generally understood to mean pay given to a state hireling for treason to his country." Johnson specified the common word *network* as "Any thing reticulated or decussated, at equal distances with interstices between the intersections." Readers who tried to learn the meaning of *reticulated* found "Made of network; formed with interstitial vacuities."

These definitions are amusing and cheer us up when we feel we're being run in circles by a dictionary. They are, however, only infrequent and whimsical and are scattered among the clear definitions which characterize Johnson's word-book. Johnson was the first to number meanings of a word and to indicate that the meanings settle into separate categories. He was the first to define contextually in a dictionary. From his extensive reading, he would cite a passage and make meanings clear by showing how words had actually been used in speaking and writing. He took his citations from the writers he considered finest—Shakespeare, Milton and Swift—and also from scientific writings of his day. Most of the entries in Johnson's dictionary offer the reader a regularized spelling (orthography), a pronunciation, a history (etymology), specific meanings, and passages showing words at work. Johnson's dictionary was called THE DICTIONARY and was used by British readers and writers into the twentieth century. Here's Johnson's entry for *woman:*

WOMAN. n.f. ʃipman, ʃimman, Saxon; whence we yet pronounce women in the plural, wimmin, Skinner.

1. The female of the human race.
    That man who hath a tongue is no man,
    If with his tongue he cannot win a woman.

    —Shakespeare

    Thou dotard, thou art woman-tir'd, unrooted
    by the dame Perlet here.

    —Shakespeare

    Women are soft, mild, pitiful and flexible;
    Thou stern, obdurate, flinty, rough, remorseless.

    —Shakespeare

    And Abimelah took men servants and women servants.

    —*Genesis*

    O woman, lovely woman, nature form'd thee
    To temper man: we had been brutes without thee.

    —Otway

Ceneus once a woman and once a man;
But ended in the sex the first began.

—Dryden

Women are made as they themselves would choose,
Too proud to ask, too humble to refuse.

—Garth

Women in their nature are much more gay and joyous than the man; whether it be that their blood is more refined, their fibres more delicate, and their animal spirits more light; vivacity is the gift of woman, gravity that of man.

—Addison

2. A female attendant on a person of rank.

I could not personally deliver to her what you commanded me; but by her woman I sent your message.

—Shakespeare

Writing task one: Take the words which you previously defined and write for each an entry that would look like Johnson's entry. You can find etymologies in a contemporary dictionary. You can find sentences to illustrate meaning by context by using *Bartlett's Quotations* or the *Oxford Dictionary of Quotations*.

Writing task two: In his preface to the dictionary, Johnson said he had been careful to find passages which would elucidate and educate. Consider that you are a reader consulting Johnson's dictionary for aid in understanding the term *woman*. What implied beliefs do you find in the passages which define the word? Select one passage and in a few paragraphs explain what additional meanings for the term other than the "female of the human race" you pick up from the quotation.

Although Johnson would have preferred that language be more fixed, he did not try to mold language or to legislate usage. If you have studied French, you would have learned that, in fact, the French Academy, which wrote a dictionary for French speakers at the same time that Johnson wrote his, decided that language should be regulated and controlled by some group of word experts. This tendency to proscribe how language will be used is not uncommon with writers. Many writers believe in some previous golden age when words were more powerful and were "pure." There's a reflection here of an assumption about reality which Plato first described.

In Plato's view, our physical reality is a shadow or an imperfect representation of an ideal reality. Words represent forms that are perfect but the words became tainted by humans who use them in imperfect worlds.

Have you heard this complaint about people destroying language? Perhaps your parents or some TV commentator or an English teacher have exclaimed that words have been corrupted. Know that some dictionary-makers hoped to keep language "pure" by putting it in reference books and that some people still regard the dictionary as a tabernacle for words.

Johnson knew that we could never make words stand still. He thought that the lexicographer had a duty to correct and proscribe only to aid readers who needed basic structures to learn to use the language. He believed that dictionary-makers should correct the "improprieties and absurdities" of a language. But he makes clear in the preface to the dictionary that, although he as a writer and an editor wanted to fix words fast, he knew language would always wriggle free of rules formulated by compilers who observed how language had been used.

Dictionaries: Proscription or Description

Johnson recognized the problem of proscribing and he described multiple meanings for words without insisting on any as most correct. Succeeding lexicographers have also been worried about proscribing meaning. However, their readers have been less worried about that problem and more willing to simply accept proscriptions. When Thomas Sheridan, a contemporary of Johnson's, drew up a guide for pronunciation which described the ways words were pronounced by his friends trained in theatre and public speaking, readers began to pronounce by the guide rather than by their own practice. Even today arguments over how a word should be spoken are settled by consulting the dictionary rather than by examining the regional dialect.

In America in the nineteenth century, Noah Webster proposed that spelling should be reformed and he published in 1806 a *Compendious Dictionary* which listed *color* for British *colour, center* for *centre, fether* for *feather* and *masheen* for *machine*. Although readers accepted few of his spelling reforms, they immediately accepted the authority of Webster's definitions. In 1828 he published *An American Dictionary of the English Language* which became THE DICTIONARY in America. We often use "Webster's" to mean a dictionary; remember the student writer who cited it when she defined *woman?*

Fierce competition among American dictionary publishers from the late 1800's through the early 1900's resulted in an increase of entries, in illustrations, gazetteers, geographical listings, essays on style, revised synonymies and lists of abbreviations. If you have a hardbound dictionary on your desk, you will find that it is a very useful tool.

While nineteenth-century American lexicographers improved the portable dictionary, British scholars were hard at work researching and writing the *Oxford English Dictionary on Historical Principles*. This dictionary runs to twenty volumes and lists definitions for approximately half the words in the English language. The OED was initiated by the Philological Society of England as a scientific attempt to produce a reliable and authoritative word-book. Scores of volunteers scavenged print to find citations. Over five million citations were culled from all existing English literature from before 1500 and from much of the writing published since 1500, including magazines, imaginative prose, poetry, drama, expository prose, cookbooks, newspapers, trade journals, and philosophical-religious penny tracts. From those, over one and one-half million citations were used in compiling the OED.

Entries in the OED give meanings and a series of citations which show how the words were used throughout history. Every word has its birth into the language, its changes, and sometimes its "death" of one meaning recorded. Twice this century, supplements to the OED have recorded new words, new meanings for old words, and new citations. Later in this chapter, you will be asked to use the OED to make "lexical definitions." In the following entry for the word *girl,* you can see described but not proscribed meanings for a word common to our speech (see figure 1).

Despite the example of the OED which describes usage, debate continues about whether a dictionary should proscribe word usage. Contemporary American dictionaries seem to agree that a dictionary must offer readers a comprehensive and accurate description of contemporary usage. They are led by the findings from the discipline of descriptive linguistics that language is an open system structured by human conventions and restructured by new human conventions and that usage is relative. These dictionaries try to set down as completely as possible what happens when native speakers use American English today.

Of course, many people still moan and grouse about dictionaries being irresponsible and becoming "polluted" by describing language without judging its quality or acceptability. Many people also complain about language changes, particularly deliberate changes which people make to avoid being racist, sexist, or ageist. Have you heard anyone making fun of the substitution of *person* for *man* in terms like *chairperson?* What seem to be their attitudes about language? What would you expect to be their attitude about dictionaries that are just dictionaries and not THE DICTIONARY?

Writing task three: List seven words which you would call "new" words and seven words which you would speculate were "new" words in the 1970's and

Girl (gɜ̄l), *sb.* Forms: 3 *gurle*, 4-6 *gerl(e*, 4-7 *girle*, *gyrle*, (6 *guirle*, *gierle*, *gyrll*, 7 *garle*), 9 *dial.* **gal**, **gell**, 7- **girl**. [Of obscure etymology.

A conjecture favoured by many scholars (Möller, Noreen, Luick) is that the word represents OE. *gyrela* masc., *gyrele* fem.:—OTeut. types *gurwilon-*, *-ôn-*, a dim. of *gurwejo-z*, *-jâ* found in LG. *gerr*, boy, girl:—Aryan *gh⁽ʳ⁾gh⁽ʷ⁾-*, presumed to be represented in Gr. *παρθένος* virgin. This involves some uncertain phonological assumptions, and the late appearance of the Teut. words gives additional ground for doubt, the ME. *gürle* being recorded only from the end of the 13th c., and the LG. *gerre* from the 17th c. It may be noted that *boy*, *lad*, *lass*, and the numerous synonyms in the mod. Scandinavian langs., are all of difficult etymology; probably most of them arose as jocular transferred uses of words that had originally a different meaning.]

† 1. A child or young person of either sex, a youth or maiden. Chiefly in *pl.*: Children, young people. *Knave girl*: a boy. *Gay girl*: applied to a young woman. *Obs.*

c **1290** *S. Eng. Leg.* I. 108/76 And suyþe gret prece of gurles and Men: comen hire al-a-boute. **13..** *K. Alis.* **2802** Men myghte ther y-seo hondis wrynge.. Women scrike, girles gredyng. *c* **1350** *Will. Palerne* 816 And whan þe gaye gerles were in-to þe gardin come, Faire floures þei founde. **1360** LANGL. *P. Pl.* A. xi. 131 Gramer for gurles I gon furste to write, And beot hem with a baleys but 3if thei wolde lernen. *c* **1386** CHAUCER *Prol.* 666 In daunger hadde he at his owne gyse The yonge girles of the diocyse, And knew hir counseil, and was al hir reed. *c* **1450** *Bk. Curtasye* 328 in *Babees Bk.* 308 Ne delf þou neuer none thyrle With thombe ne fyngur, as 3ong gyrle. *c* **1450** *Cov. Myst.* (Shaks. Soc.) 181 Here knave gerlys I xal steke.

2. A female child; commonly applied to all young unmarried women.

1530 PALSGR. 922 A gyrle [F. *garce*] havyng laughyng eyes. *c* **1530** REDFORDE *Play Wit & Sc.* (Shaks. Soc.) 17 *Idelnes.* Thow [Recreacion] art occacion, lo! of more evyll Then I, poore gerle, nay, more then the dyvyll! **1546** HEYWOOD *Prov.* (1874) 50 The boy thy husband, and thou the girle, his wife. **1591** SHAKS. *Two Gentl.* v. iv. 134, I hold him but a foole that will endanger His Body, for a Girle that loues him not. *a* **1652** BROME *Queene's Exch.* I. ii. Wks. 1873 III. 467 What's that my Girle? **1679** *Hatton Corr.* (1878) 197 *note*, One of his sisters .. announces the birth of a very lusty garle. **1709** STEELE *Tatler* No. 75 P 1 The Girl is a Girl of great Merit .. she converses with me .. like a Daughter. **1760** C. JOHNSTON *Chrysal* II. i. ii. 11, I will lay you, and you shall lose, my girl, if it was ten times as much. **1784** COWPER *Task* II. 227 As smooth And tender as a girl, all-essenced o'er With odours. **1855** BROWNING *Fra Lippo* 214 You should not take a fellow eight years old And make him swear to never kiss the girls. **1859** GEO. ELIOT *A. Bede* 62 To think of a gell o' your age wanting to go and sit with half-a-dozen men. **1863** LANDOR *Heroic Idylls, Theron & Zoe* 27 Girls often say More than they mean: men always do. **1894** H. GARDENER *Unoff. Patriot* 329 No girl is ever quite good enough to marry any mother's son.

Prov. **1683** TRYON *Way to Health* 628 The Proverb Is certainly true .. He that Marries a Girl, marrs a Woman.

¶ *Old girl*: Applied *colloq.* to a woman at any time of life, either disrespectfully or (occas.) as an endearing term of address. Also, to a mare, etc.

1837 DICKENS *Pickwick* xiv, 'Cheer up, old girl', said Tom, patting the bay mare on the neck..' Soho, old girl—gently'. **1848** C. BRONTE *J. Eyre* ii. (1890) 19 He called his mother 'old girl', too.

b. A maid-servant. Also in *girl-of-all-work.*

1668 PEPYS *Diary* 24 Aug., My wife is upon hanging the long chamber, where the girl lies, with the sad stuff that was in the best chamber. **1812** A. ADAMS in *J. Adams' Lett.* (1848) 409 Seven o'clock. Blockheads not out of bed. Girls in motion. Mean, when I hire another man-servant, that he shall come for one call. **1875** *Scribner's*

Mon'hly X. 287 But all this time we had no girl, and .. at last I determined to go and get a girl myself. So one day at lunch-time I went to an intelligence office in the city. **1880** MRS. ALEXANDER *Freres* I. ii. 19, I [a landlady] must look to it myself, for I never yet see a gurl I could trust with a hegg. **1883** S. C. HALL *Retrospect* II. 119 A dirty, slipshod girl-of-all-work bawled at me from the area.

c. A sweetheart, lady-love. Also (*U.S. colloq.* or *slang*) *best girl.*

1791 'G. GAMBADO' *Ann. Horsem.* vii. (1809) 9⁰, I may lose my dear girl for ever. *Mod. Pop. Song.* The girl I left behind me.

d. († More fully, *A girl about* or *of the town*, *a girl of case*): a prostitute. † *A kind girl*: a mistress.

1711 STEELE *Spect.* No. 187 P 2, I know not whether you have ever heard of the famous girl about Town called Kitty: This Creature .. was my Mistress. **1712** ADDISON *Ibid.* No. 486 P 1, I am very particularly acquainted with one who is under entire Submission to a kind Girl, as he calls her .. No longer than Tuesday last he took me with him to visit his Mistress. **1756** *Demi-Rep* 6 The Men of pleasure, and the Girls of ease. **1815** W. H. IRELAND *Scribbleomania* 141 Lewis, of monkish renown, Who tickled the fancies of girls of the town. **1851** MAYHEW *Lond. Labour* I. 477 The 'gals' are sure to be beaten cruelly .. by their 'chaps'.

† 3. A roebuck in its second year. *Obs.*

1486 *Bk. St. Albans* F vi b, The first yere he [the Roobucke] is a kyde .. The secunde yere he is a gerle .. The thirde yere an hemule. **1576** TURBERV. *Venerie* 236 A Rowe, the which is called the first yeare a Kidde, the second Gyrle, the third an Hemuse. **1660** HOWELL *Parley Beasts* 62 Those pretty Fawns, Prickets, Sorrells, Hemuses, and Girls .. which I [a Hinde] brought into the world. **1706** *Dict. Rust.* (ed. 3), *Girle* (among Hunters) a Roe-buck of 2 Years.

4. *attrib.* and *Comb.* **a.** appositive, indicating sex, as *girl-child*, *-friend*, *-graduate*, *-miser*, *-sculler*, *-sorter*, *-warrior*, *-widow*; or youthfulness, as *girl-mother*, *-queen*, *-widow*, *-wife*, *-woman*; **b.** simple attrib., as *girl-life*, *-nature*, *-tragedy*; **c.** objective, as *girl-confining* adj.; *girl-like* adj. and adv. Also *girl-boy*, ? a girlish boy.

1589 WARNER *Alb. Eng.* v. xxvi. (1597) 129 *Girle-boyes*, fauouring Ganimede. **1598** DRAYTON *Heroic. Ep.* 18/2 And in my place vpon this regal throne, To set that girle-boy wanton Gaueston. **1604** BLACK *Jud. Shaks.* ix. in *Harper's Mag.* Mar. 542/2 My father used to call him the girl-boy. **1886** LONGM. *Mag.* 646 A very great number of the *girl-*children of the State have found happy homes in Canada. **1798** SOTHEBY tr. *Wieland's Oberon* (1826) I. 55 The guardian of these *girl-confining* walls. **1896** *Westm. Gas.* 19 May 4/2 The 'Wedding March' was whistled by twelve *girl*-friends of the bride. **1847** TENNYSON *Princ.* Prol. 142 Sweet *girl-*graduates in their golden hair. **1808** *Athenæum* 26 May 659/3 A well meaning .. story of *girl-life.* **1851** ROCK *Ch. of Fathers* III. 1. 269 The *girl*-like maiden-mother bowed down before the crib. *a* **1868** T. WOOLNER *My Beautiful Lady* (1863) 124 Years before .. girllike she Adored a youth with sparkling genius graced. **1863** DICKENS *Mut. Fr.* I. vi, I saw you sitting there, like the ghost of a *girl-miser* in the dead of the night. *a* **1861** T. WOOLNER *My beautiful Lady* (1863) 95 What art thou whispering lowly to thy babe, O wan *girl-*mother? **1877** *Edin. Rev.* Oct. 393 The *girl-*mother of Amadis. **1876** BLACK *Madcap V.* xxvi. 242 Was it not true, he had to admit, that he knew nothing of *girl-*nature? **1880** J. H. BLUNT *Ref. Ch. Eng.* II. 189 The 'girl-' Queen'—she was only sixteen years of age. **1894** *Daily News* 28 Mar. 3/1, 10,000 notices of withdrawal .. are handed to a roomful of 'girl sorters'. **1876** GEO. ELIOT *Dan. Der.* I. xvii. 342 His mind glanced over the *girl*-tragedies that are going on in the world. **1894** *Dublin Rev.* Oct. 309 Leaders to whom the triumphs of the *girl*-warrior were a reproach. **1837** HAWTHORNE *Twice-Told T.* (1851) I. xix. 285 Inflamed to madness by the coquetry of the *girl-*widow. **1857** MRS. CARLYLE *Lett.* II. 321 The young *girl-wife* who lives there is very lovely. **1876** MISS BRADDON *Dead Men's Shoes* I. i. 1 A *girl-woman* alone on Battersea Bridge. **1885** *Tablet* 20 July 108 The *girl-workers* taking their wages home.

Figure 1

look them up in your desk dictionary. Then check the same list in three other hardbound dictionaries. What do you learn about the editorial policy of each dictionary from this research? Do all the dictionaries list all the words? Do all the dictionaries exclude the same words? Do they agree on the meanings of terms? In what other ways do these dictionaries agree and differ?

If in the 1980's we compiled a new dictionary, how would we decide what should and should not be listed? If you now believe that our language changes with incredible velocity, and if you believe that it is changing daily because of mind boggling changes in our thinking about ourselves and about the way we treat other persons, what words would you expect to find in a dictionary? What would you expect to find changed? More specifically, when a major segment of our population has become involved—wittingly or not—in changing racist and sexist behaviors, what changes would be described in this new dictionary?

Once again, we can examine the interconnectedness of linguistic and social change. In the essay which follows, Alma Graham, an associate editor of *The American Heritage Dictionary,* describes the task of making a new dictionary. This particular dictionary prides itself on listing new terms or new meanings for new terms more quickly than other dictionaries of its size. In fact, some parents have forced school boards or teachers to discontinue using this dictionary; those parents believe that they must censor the book because its objective description of the ways Americans use English might corrupt the minds of their children. Those parents clearly believe that a dictionary should proscribe.

Alma Graham describes the work of compiling a dictionary for use by younger Americans; the editorial policy states that the dictionary should describe. Notice while you read the essay that some of the lexicographic chores are the same as those of earlier lexicographers while some are unique to needs of contemporary speakers of American English. Ask yourself this question when you read: Is a dictionary which tries not to reinforce sexist biases — either in entry selections or in definitions — describing the current state of the language or proscribing an ideal state? Should we defer to the authority of this dictionary? How best could we use such a reference tool?

The Making of a Nonsexist Dictionary

Alma Graham

The first dictionary to define *sexism,* to include the phrase *liberated women,* and to recognize *Ms.* was a wordbook for children published in 1972 by American Heritage Publishing Company.

The American Heritage School Dictionary contains 35,000 entries, which were selected after an unprecedented analysis of 5 million words encountered by American children in their schoolbooks.

When the task of compilation began in 1969, we could not predict that the dictionary would be the first ever published in which lexicographers made a conscious effort to correct the sex biases that exist in English as it is commonly used. But the computer revealed a pattern that we who were editing the dictionary could not ignore: in schoolbooks, whether the subject is reading, mathematics, social studies, art, or science, males command center stage. Boys and girls may go to school in equal numbers; they may be graded for equal achievements; but the computer had tipped the scales on the side of male supremacy.

In some ways the American Heritage computer was no different from any other. It was stupid. Though it devoured reams of printed matter — 10,000 passages of 500 words each culled from 1,000 books and magazines — it couldn't read. To the computer the "lead" in flaking paint was no different from the "lead" in a play, and a "row" of cabbages was the same as a "row" between lovers. Fortunately, this lack of discrimination was unimportant, for in addition to alphabetizing all its words and ranking them by the frequency of their usage, the computer's unprecedented contribution was to deliver 700,000 citation slips, each of which showed a word in three lines of context. By using these slips, the editors could see each word as it is used in sentences that schoolchildren read and we could in turn write definitions that schoolchildren could comprehend.

The original objective in using a computer was this obvious one of gaining access to primary sources. Peter Davies, the editor-in-chief of the school dictionary, was the first to recognize what else the computer had delivered. To Davies, the vast body of words was a reflection of the culture talking to its children. He suspected that if imaginatively used, the computer could also supply a profile of what was being said between the lines.

For example, Davies noticed that when adults write for one another, they refer to young people as *children,* almost as often as they call them *boys* and *girls.* When writing books and stories for children, however, adults use the gender words *boy* and *girl* twice as often as the neutral words *child* and *children.* When the culture talks *to* its children, it is careful to distinguish them by sex. Moreover, no matter what the subject being taught, girls and women are always in a minority. Overall, the ratio in schoolbooks of *he* to *she, him* to *her,* and *his* to *hers* was almost four to one. Even in home economics, the traditional preserve of the female, the pronoun *he* predominated by nearly two to one.

If this new dictionary were to serve elementary students without showing favoritism to one sex or the other, an effort would have to be made to restore the gender balance. We would need more examples featuring females, and the examples would have to ascribe to girls and women the active, inventive, and adventurous human traits traditionally reserved for men and boys.

Our new archetypal woman took form gradually. Each of the dozen editors writing and reviewing word entries had special moments of insight and decision when we recognized her presence among us. Mine came at the word *brain,* where a computer citation asserted "he has *brains* and courage." In what seemed at the time an act of audacity, I changed the pronoun. "She has *brains* and courage."

As the number of word entries grew, the new woman made her way from example to example, establishing her priorities, aspirations, and tastes. She was "a woman of dedicated political *principles.*" She "made a *name* for herself" and "everyone *praised* her good sense and learning." When she "*plunged* into her work, her mind began to *percolate*" (not her coffee), and "she *prided* herself on her eloquence" (not on the sheen of her freshly waxed floors).

Her appearances in the dictionary were widely separated, of course. Her brothers and traditional sisters continued to surround and outnumber her, example for example. But she had arrived, and from A, where at *abridge* she quoted the 19th Amendment, to Z, when "she *zipped* down the hill on her sled," her spirit, character, and credentials were never in doubt.

As the feminists—male and female—who had brought her into the lexicon cheered her on, "her *determination* to win" was bolstered by our "*devout* wish for her success."

Men in the dictionary examples continued to be active and daring, competitive and combative; but the liberated man could be vulnerable, too. He might be "striving to attain *mastery* over his emotions," but he was not disgraced if "his resolve began to *waver*" or if "tears *welled* up in his eyes." Like the new woman, he had a freer choice of careers than heretofore: "He *teaches* kindergarten" and "he *studies* typing at night."

Ms. was the new word we watched with the greatest degree of interest. Some of us favored adopting it right away, but a problem arose over its pronunciation: it was an abbreviation that anyone could write but that no one could say. Arguments over "miz" or "mis" or "em es" continued through the summer. Then, in October, Bruce Bohle, our usage editor, urged that we enter *Ms.* in the dictionary as an abbreviation whether or not the title could be pronounced with ease. Thus supported, I wrote the definition and Peter Davies provided a note explaining the parallel with *Mr.,* the derivation from *mistress,* and the pronunciation possibilities.

Ms. or *Ms* An abbreviation used as a title of courtesy before a woman's last name or before her given name and last name, whether she is married or not.

At the same time that womanpower in the dictionary was beginning to be felt, consciousness of woman's powerlessness in the language was rising. As a lexicographer and feminist, I had started a notebook on sexism in language, collecting examples of ways in which men and women were classified as human beings by being labeled with male or female words.

One method used in this socializing process is a tactic I called "my-virtue-is-your-vice." Since men and women are supposed to be polar opposites, what is considered admirable in one has to be contemptible in the other. If a woman is commended for the gentle qualities that make her *feminine,* then a man must be condemned for any similar show of softness with the epithet *effeminate.* A man's tears are *womanish;* a woman's uniform *mannish.* The lessons to be learned by both male and female are clear: biology is not only destiny; it is character and personality.

Another trick of socialization is to label what we consider to be the exception to the rule: the *woman* doctor, the *male* nurse, the career *girl* (the phrase *career man* is restricted to government service). The term "feminine logic" illustrates the most negatively sexist use of the modifier tactic since it implies non-logic or lack of logic. Because *logic* unmodified is assumed by men to apply to men, a woman who thinks logically is said to have "a masculine mind" (a supposed compliment that serves as a questionable exception to the my-virtue-is-your-vice rule).

Then there is the "trivializing tactic." This tactic operates through female gender forms, such as *poetess* and *usherette,* and through the put-down process that turns *liberationist* into *libber,* just as it once turned *suffragist* into *suffragette.*

The tendency in the language that I called "praise him/blame her" is still another device. From Eve and Pandora on, the female has been held responsible for evil and assigned to a semantic house of ill fame. Titles of honor illustrate the point particularly well. *Queen, madam, mistress,* and *dame* all acquired degraded meanings, whereas *prince, king, lord,* and *father* are exalted and applied to God—for even God is thought of as a male and is called Him.

Most pervasive of all is the phenomenon I called the "exclusionary tactic." Here the possibility is simply not considered that the person or persons being addressed or discussed might be female. A typical example is the loan application that reads: "Full Name. Wife's First Name and Middle Initial. Your Present Employer. Wife's Employer. Your Monthly Salary. Wife's Income (if any)." But the exclusionary tactic employed most tellingly is the constant, careless overuse of the word *man* in its extended senses. When the speakers refer to "the leading man in the field," to "the man whose book sells half a million copies," or to "the man they would most like to see as President," they effectively rule out the possibility of a female authority, author, or candidate.

To fight these sexist habits of language, the school dictionary had to avoid gender assumptions that other dictionaries imposed more through custom than necessity. *Youth*, one dictionary said, is "the part of life between childhood and manhood." *Youth*, we said, is "the time of life before one is an adult." *Sex*, itself, we defined straightforwardly, with impersonal examples, avoiding a rival dictionary's use of "the fair, gentle, or weaker sex" and "the sterner of stronger sex" dichotomy.

While we were working our way through the alphabet, other word watchers were already speaking out. In Venice, California, Varda One (formerly Varda Murrell) was analyzing and commenting on a phenomenon she called "Manglish." We could not counter her criticism that dictionaries give less space to *woman* than to *man*. This is not the fault of the dictionary makers, but of a language in which the same word denotes both the human species as a whole and those of its members who are male. In English, contradictory propositions are true: a woman is a man; a woman is not a man.

If a woman is swept off a ship into the water, the cry is "Man overboard!" If she is killed by a hit-and-run driver, the charge is "manslaughter." If she is injured on the job, the coverage is "workmen's compensation." But if she arrives at a threshold marked "Men Only," she knows the admonition is not intended to bar animals or plants or inanimate objects. It is meant for her.

In practice, the sexist assumption that man is a species of males becomes the fact. Erich Fromm certainly seemed to think so when he wrote that man's "vital interests" were "life, food, access to females, etc." Loren Eiseley implied it when he wrote of man that "his back aches, he ruptures easily, his women have difficulties in childbirth. ...." If these writers had been using *man* in the sense of human species rather than male, they would have written that man's vital interests are life, food, and access to the opposite sex, and that man suffers backaches, ruptures easily, and has difficulties in giving birth.

At every level of achievement and activity—from primitive man to the man of the hour—woman is not taken into account.

Consider the congressman. He is a man of the people. To prove that he's the best man for the job, he takes his case to the man in the street. He is a champion of the workingman. He speaks up for the little man. He has not forgotten the forgotten man. And he firmly believes: one man, one vote.

Consider the policeman or fireman, the postman or milkman, the clergyman or businessman. Whatever else he may be, he is by title a man, and if his employer feels that he is "our kind of man," he may become "our man in the home office" or "our man in Algiers."

From Wordsworth's line "The Child is father of the Man" to the recent New York subway poster "Give a kid a job and help mold a man," a woman is a possibility everyone tends to forget.

When a culture makes adulthood synonymous with manhood, a girl can never reach adulthood at all. There is a clear demarcation between the words *boy* and *man* that does not exist between *girl* and *woman*. A boy greatly increases his stature when he becomes a man, but a girl loses status and bargaining power when she loses youth. So females are in effect encouraged to cling to girlhood as long as possible. Nor is this reluctance to grow up surprising when one considers the largely negative connotations attached to the word *woman*. To take defeat like a man is to accept it stoically, like a good sport. To take defeat like a woman is usually understood as meaning to weep.

The American Heritage School Dictionary defines sexism as "discrimination by members of one sex against the other, especially by males against females." In order to avoid sexism in language that has come to sound "natural," we devised logical sex-blind substitutes. When referring to the human species, the dictionary employs the term *human beings,* not *man* or *men.*

In our efforts to reduce the superabundance of words referring to the male, we found it was possible to use the word *person* or a more specific substitute instead of *man*. The best man for the job is the best person or candidate; a 12-man jury is a 12-member jury; a real-estate man is a real-estate agent; and machines are used for work formerly done by people or by human beings—not by men.

To avoid unnecessary use of the pronoun *he*, we frequently shifted from the singular to the plural. Instead of saying "insofar as he can, the scientist excludes bias from his thinking," it is easy to change to *they, scientists,* and *their.* Plural pronouns desex themselves. The use of *one* is also convenient. A breadwinner, for example, can be "one who supports a family or household by his or her earnings."

Because of our conscious efforts, the nonsexist dictionary is as free of discrimination against either sex as the reformist editors could make it. But as proud as we are of our lexicographers' revolution, writing a nonsexist school dictionary is only the barest beginning. Most schoolbooks still reflect the assumptions of our sexist society. As writers and teachers and parents, we have an obligation now to weigh our words, to examine them, and to use them with greater care. Children of both sexes deserve equal treatment, in life and in language, and we should not offer them anything less.

Denotation and Connotation

We all know what *woman* means. We all agree that it means or denotes a female human being. We may, however, disagree about additional meanings. Look again at that group of definitions which we began with; some wanted to qualify *woman* with *adult* and others specified an ability to reproduce and yet others insisted on certain psychological attributes. We agree about what *woman* denotes; we disagree about what *woman* connotes.

Every word has a denotative meaning and at least one connotative meaning. Sometimes the meanings coincide. Often they don't and then communication breaks down. When I say *denote*, I mean the naming of what strictly belongs to and characterizes the word I am defining. Most often, dictionary definitions are denotative; for examples, look at that "Webster's" definition for *woman*.

When I say *connote*, I mean the naming of all possible properties and associations which also belong to the word I am defining. The student who wrote that *woman* meant "independent" was giving a connotative definition of what the word meant to her. A connotative meaning suggests or implies more ideas, feelings, characteristics and interpretations than the denotative meaning could describe.

There are two kinds of connotation: personal and general. Personal connotation grows from the unique experiences of an individual. My own reaction to the word *student* and my definition of it comes from all my experiences, memories and feelings about being a student and also working with students. My personal connotation for *student* would include feeling shy in grammar school, working and working again in a chemistry lab, excitement about reading certain books, terror about taking exams and enthusiasm about beginning new semesters. Your personal connotation would be some other network of experiences, memories and feelings. Our definitions of *student* might differ radically.

General connotation grows out of shared personal connotations. Specific responses to words have become substantially the same for each person who hears the word. For example, the word "Nazism" would connote something negative to most people, in addition to denoting an historical political movement. Planners of the Bicentennial celebrations hoped "Bicentennial" would elicit a positive general connotation which would include pride and enthusiasm about America. Think about the words "yellow ribbon"? What do they connote to Americans? Do you think that there is a general connotation for the phrase *college student?* Are there words which you use on your campus which have a general connotation on your campus but which would not hold that connotation at another campus? Do you know of certain terms used by your ethnic group which have a general connotation shared by most members of your group?

Writing task four: Many people experience strong responses to the following list of words. Select three which trigger a sharp response in you. Write a paragraph about each which first cites the denotative meanings and then describes the connotative meanings. Specify whether the connotative meanings are personal or general (or both). Explain why each word affects you the way that it does.

patriotism	inflation	euthanasia	law and order
motherhood	racism	marriage	war
nuclear energy	abortion	revolution	homosexuality

Writing task five: This exercise could also be used as a group activity. You will be playing with denotation and connotation. Five persons should volunteer to role play the person named by these five terms: *girl, chick, lady, broad, woman*. All these terms denote the same thing.

If you decide to use this as a writing exercise, there are three parts to the exercise. First, answer the following series of questions for each person named by *girl, chick, lady, broad, woman*. Then write a two part essay which first compares and contrasts answers and then argues for one positive term to name the adult female human being.

Questions to answer for each person named.

A. What are you called? "I am a girl (chick, etc.)"
   List three adjectives that describe how you feel being a girl (chick, etc.).
   How old are you?
   What is your financial means of support?
   How are you dressed?
   List three verbs that describe you being active.
   Are you married?
   What do you do when you play?
   What do you do when you work?

B. Now compare and contrast the answers, either in class discussion or in writing. What does *girl* connote that is similar and dissimilar from what the other terms connote? Is a broad a lady? Is a chick a woman? Is a woman a girl? Be as specific and thorough as possible in your discussion of personal and general connotations.

C. Finally, choose one term which you would now use to denote an adult female human being and to connote a healthy, independent, loving, imaginative, strong human person. If none of these terms seems adequate or appropriate, invent a term. Persuade your reader to use your term.

Equative Definition

How many of those definitions of *woman* began *woman is?* How many of your definitions begin with phrasing "X is ... "? This pattern of definition we use daily. When I said "language is an open system," I defined through an equation. In algebra it would look like this: $X = Y$. If you consulted the dictionary about *entropy* when you came on that word earlier, you saw one entry that looked like this:

3 : the degradation of the matter and energy in the universe to an ultimate state of inert uniformity.

You read the colon (:) as an equals sign and then translated the entry to the equation *entropy = energy slowing down*.

This pattern of definition might trick you with its seeming simplicity. Using a copula (the verb family of be, is, am) to link two quantities into a whole statement seems to settle any problem of meaning. The definition looks authoritative: X = Y. But what if Y is not detailed enough or not at all familiar? I could give synonyms until a familiar one helped you understand the equation. I could offer several denotations and hope at least one would give enough information. I could also use some other defining paradigms to make the Y of the equation more clear, detailed and familiar. In the essay which follows, you will notice that Jo Goodwin Parker provides several equations for us as she poses and answers the question "What Is Poverty?" She uses the familiar and conventional method of equative defining to stretch our understanding of what poverty is.

Parker frequently repeats the phrasing *Poverty is* and she completes the equation with images and very specific and personal descriptions. She uses this pattern to organize sentences, paragraphs and the entire writing. Originally, she delivered this as a speech. Notice how she adapts her writing to the needs of her audience. Notice the cumulative effect of repeating the equation.

What Is Poverty?

Jo Goodwin Parker

You ask me what is poverty? Listen to me. Here I am, dirty, smelly, and with no "proper" underwear on and with the stench of my rotting teeth near you. I will tell you. Listen to me. Listen without pity. I cannot use your pity. Listen with understanding. Put yourself in my dirty, worn-out, ill-fitting shoes, and hear me.

Poverty is getting up every morning from a dirt- and illness-stained mattress. The sheets have long since been used for diapers. Poverty is living in a smell that never leaves. This is a smell of urine, sour milk, and spoiling food sometimes joined with the strong smell of long-cooked onions. Onions are cheap. If you have smelled this smell, you did not know how it came. It is the smell of the outdoor privy. It is the smell of young children who cannot walk the long dark way in the night. It is the smell of the mattresses where years of "accidents" have happened. It is the smell of the milk which has gone sour because the refrigerator long has not worked, and it costs money to get it fixed. It is the smell of rotting garbage. I could bury it, but where is the shovel? Shovels cost money.

Poverty is being tired. I have always been tired. They told me at the hospital when the last baby came that I had chronic anemia caused from poor diet, a bad case of worms, and that I needed a corrective operation. I listened politely—the poor are always polite. The poor always listen. They don't say that there is no money for iron pills, or better food, or worm medicine. The idea of an operation is frightening and costs so much that, if I had dared, I would have laughed. Who takes care of my children? Recovery from an operation takes a long time. I have three children. When I left them with "Granny" the last time I had a job, I came home to find the baby covered with fly specks, and a diaper that had not been changed since I left. When the dried diaper came off, bits of my baby's flesh came with it. My other child was playing with a sharp bit of broken glass, and my oldest was playing alone at the edge of a lake. I made twenty-two dollars a week, and a good nursery school costs twenty dollars a week for three children. I quit my job.

Poverty is dirt. You can say in your clean clothes coming from your clean house, "Anybody can be clean." Let me explain about housekeeping with no money. For breakfast I give my children grits with no oleo or cornbread without eggs and oleo. This does not use up many dishes. What dishes there are, I wash in cold water and with no soap. Even the cheapest soap has to be saved for the baby's diapers. Look at my hands, so cracked and red. Once I saved for two months to buy a jar of Vaseline for my hands and the baby's diaper rash. When I had saved enough, I went to buy it and the price had gone up two cents. The baby and I suffered on. I have to decide every day if I can bear to put my cracked sore hands into the cold water and strong soap. But you ask, why not hot water? Fuel costs money. If you have a wood fire it costs money. If you burn electricity, it costs money. Hot water is a luxury. I do not have luxuries. I know you will be surprised when I tell you how young I am. I look so much older. My back has been bent over the wash tubs every day for so long, I cannot remember when I ever did anything else. Every night I wash every stitch my school age child has on and just hope her clothes will be dry by morning.

Poverty is staying up all night on cold nights to watch the fire knowing one spark on the newspaper covering the walls means your sleeping child dies in flames. In summer poverty is watching gnats and flies devour your baby's tears when he cries. The screens are torn and you pay so little rent you know they will never be fixed. Poverty means insects in your food, in your nose, in your eyes, and crawling over you when you sleep. Poverty is hoping it never rains because diapers won't dry when it rains and soon you are using newspapers. Poverty is seeing your children forever with runny noses. Paper handkerchiefs cost money and all your rags you need for other things. Even more costly are antihistamines. Poverty is cooking without food and cleaning without soap.

Poverty is asking for help. Have you ever had to ask for help, knowing your children will suffer unless you get it? Think about asking for a loan from a relative, if this is the only way you can imagine asking for help. I will tell you how it feels. You find out where the office is that you are supposed to visit. You circle that block four or five times. Thinking of your children, you go in. Everyone is very busy. Finally, someone comes out and you tell her that you need help. That never is the person you need to see. You go see another person, and after spilling the whole shame of your poverty all over the desk between you, you find that this isn't the right office after all—you must repeat the whole process, and it never is any easier at the next place.

You have asked for help, and after all it has a cost. You are again told to wait. You are told why, but you don't really hear because of the red cloud of shame and the rising cloud of despair.

Poverty is remembering. It is remembering quitting school in junior high because "nice" children had been so cruel about my clothes and my smell. The attendance officer came. My mother told him I was pregnant. I wasn't, but she thought that I could get a job and help out. I had jobs off and on, but never long enough to learn anything. Mostly I remember being married. I was so young then. I am still young. For a time, we had all the things you have. There was a little house in another town, with hot water and everything. Then my husband lost his job. There was unemployment insurance for a while and what few jobs I could get. Soon, all our nice things were repossessed and we moved back here. I was pregnant then. This house didn't look so bad when we first moved in. Every week it gets worse. Nothing is ever fixed. We now had no money. There were a few odd jobs for my husband, but everything went for food then, as it does now. I don't know how we lived through three years and three babies, but we did. I'll tell you something, after the last baby I destroyed my marriage. It had been a good one, but could you keep on bringing children in this dirt? Did you ever think how much it costs for any kind of birth control? I knew my husband was leaving the day he left, but there were no good-bys between us. I hope he has been able to climb out of this mess somewhere. He never could hope with us to drag him down.

That's when I asked for help. When I got it, you know how much it was? It was, and is, seventy-eight dollars a month for the four of us; that is all I ever can get. Now you know why there is no soap, no needles and thread, no hot water, no aspirin, no worm medicine, no hand cream, no shampoo. None of these things forever and ever and ever. So that you can see clearly, I pay twenty dollars a month rent, and most of the rest goes for food. For grits and cornmeal, and rice and milk and beans. I try my best to use only the minimum electricity. If I use more, there is that much less for food.

Poverty is looking into a black future. Your children won't play with my boys. They will turn to other boys who steal to get what they want. I can already see them behind the bars of their prison instead of behind the bars of my poverty. Or they will turn to the freedom of alcohol or drugs, and find themselves enslaved. And my daughter? At best, there is for her a life like mine.

But you say to me, there are schools. Yes, there are schools. My children have no extra books, no magazines, no extra pencils, or crayons, or paper and the most important of all, they do not have health. They have worms, they have infections, they have pink-eye all summer. They do not sleep well on the floor, or with me in my one bed. They do not suffer from hunger, my seventy-eight dollars keeps us alive, but they do suffer from malnutrition. Oh yes, I do remember what I was taught about health in school. It doesn't do much good. In some places there is a surplus commodities program. Not here. The county said it cost too much. There is a school lunch program. But I have two children who will already be damaged by the time they get to school.

But, you say to me, there are health clinics. Yes, there are health clinics and they are in the towns. I live out here eight miles from town. I can walk that far (even if it is sixteen miles both ways), but can my little children? My neighbor will take me when he goes; but he expects to get paid, *one way or another*. I bet you know my neighbor. He is that large man who spends his time at the gas station, the barbershop, and the corner store complaining about the government spending money on the immoral mothers of illegitimate children.

Poverty is an acid that drips on pride until all pride is worn away. Poverty is a chisel that chips on honor until honor is worn away. Some of you say that you would do *something* in my situation, and maybe you would, for the first week or the first month, but for year after year after year?

Even the poor can dream. A dream of a time when there is money. Money for the right kinds of food, for worm medicine, for iron pills, for toothbrushes, for hand cream, for a hammer and nails and a bit of screening, for a shovel, for a bit of paint, for some sheeting, for needles and thread. Money to pay *in money* for a trip to town. And, oh, money for hot water and money for soap. A dream of when asking for help does not eat away the last bit of pride. When the office you visit is as nice as the offices of other governmental agencies, when there are enough workers to help you quickly, when workers do not quit in defeat and despair. When you have to tell your story to only one person, and that person can send you for other help and you don't have to prove your poverty over and over and over again.

I have come out of my despair to tell you this. Remember I did not come from another place or another time. Others like me are all around you. Look at us with an angry heart, anger that will help you help me. Anger that will let you tell of me. The poor are always silent. Can you be silent too?

Aristotelian Definition

You'll quickly recognize what we call the **Aristotelian** or the **inclusion-exclusion definition.** This definition is patterned on equative definition but differs from other equative definitions like stipulative or metaphorical because it explains X (the term to be defined) by first classifying it within some category and then carefully differentiating X from other members of that category. The learner who wrote that "Woman is the member of the human race who bears children" used the Aristotelian paradigm. That writer first included *woman* within the category of human race and then excluded or differentiated her from the other members of the category human race by specifying "who bears children."

When I define *quilt* as "a bed cover of two layers of cloth filled with down, cotton, wool or polyester fiber and held together by stitched designs," I include quilt in the category of bedcovers. I would differentiate it from muslin sheets, wool blankets, woven coverlets, chenille bedspreads and crocheted afghans. Using this method of definition permits me to make precise distinctions. I can carefully analyze just what there is about a quilt that places it in the hierarchy I have designed.

I could have chosen to include *quilt* in some other category. I might have placed it in the category of woman's art or in the class of wall hangings or the groupings of needlecrafts or the classification of folk art. I chose the specific category of bed cover because, in the paragraph which this definition structured, I talked about the functional nature of quilts. Had I chosen to put it in the category of folk art and to talk about function and form, I would have been required to differentiate quilts from wooden decoys, primitive paintings, weathervanes, and scrimshaw swifts.

Your initial choice of category will determine what directions your thinking can follow. For example, taxonomists rarely describe dogs and wolves in the same category even though they are all of the canine family. If you were to define wolves as the adults and dogs as the juveniles of the canine family, choosing that category might lead to new ideas. You might be able to describe how behaviors of both kinds of canines are related. You could even pursue a new idea like the possibilities of learning through *neoteny.* That topic would never have been available had you chosen a smaller category, which excluded wolves, when you were asked to write a definition for dogs.

If you are studying entomology, zoology or botany, you have already practiced this method of defining. When you must identify the order, class and phylum for a scorpion or when you list the species, genus and family for the kinkajou, you make inclusion-exclusion distinctions basic to an Aristotelian definition. Botanists who use a taxonomy or system of classifying plants according to their presumed natural relationships are following the example of Aristotle who devised systems for classifying objects and ideas. His *Poetics* and *Rhetoric* are book-length definitions organized on the model of inclusion-exclusion. When he described Greek drama, he used the paradigm to make distinctions between comedy and tragedy and to make distinctions within the genre of tragedy about kinds of tragic action, tragic characters and tragic heroism.

This form of definition emphasizes the linear and hierarchic relationship of ideas. Categories are distinguished from sub-categories. It is a very logical approach to a topic. It describes an orderly system in which categories fit smoothly in a large ordained pattern and which we can use our reason to figure out. In this definition, the sequence is always from least to largest or from most complex to least complex or from cause to effect or higher order to lower. This definition makes you sound very authoritative and suggests that relationships between categories are fixed and never change.

Writing task six: Write a one sentence inclusion-exclusion definition for any object you see in your room. First, decide what category the object fits in. Then decide on what makes that object unlike all other objects which fit in that category. Then write one sentence in which you define the object by inclusion and exclusion.

Writing task seven: Write a one sentence definition of *prejudice*. Then write a paragraph which extends the definition and which would also serve as a topic paragraph for an essay about prejudice.

Writing task eight: Write an essay about the subject of your choice or about *sexism* using the Aristotelian paradigm not only to inquire into the meaning of the word but also to organize the entire essay. In the prewriting stage of your work, you might ask questions like these to identify the basic structure of the essay: Within what major category does *sexism* fall? Is it an attitude, a philosophy, an emotion, a behavior? How much time do I need to spend identifying the major category? How will I catch the attention of the readers and make them want to read this essay? How do I show that other members of this category should be excluded? If, for example, sexism is a behavior and a form of prejudice, what makes it different from racism or anti-Semitism? Is it an acquired or an innate behavior? What examples or illustrations would best prove my statements? What should I do in the concluding part of the essay? Once you have written the essay, go back and see if you can abstract an Aristotelian definition

"X = a kind of Y but differs from all other kinds of Y in these ways" as the organizing structure.

Writing task nine: Help others in your community of practicing writers by peer editing. Take the essay assigned you by the instructor or given you by a colleague and read it carefully. On a separate sheet of paper, list your reactions to the essay and specify three things that the writer could do to improve the essay. Write a one-sentence definition for the essay; if you can not abstract an Aristotelian definition from the essay, it may be that the writer has not yet succeeded in using that pattern. Tell the writer what you see as a major category and whether that is the best category to choose for what the writer wants to say in the essay. Tell the writer what you see as "exclusion" statements and whether those are clear, accurate and significant. List any additional excluding characteristics which you think might be important to demonstrate what the writer is saying in the essay. Finally, comment specifically on any problems of punctuation, grammar, spelling or word choice which have impeded you in reading the essay.

Writing task ten: Take any definition or series of definitions for poverty from Jo Goodwin Parker's writing and rewrite them using the Aristotelian method for defining. What changes when you use this pattern of definition rather than Parker's original pattern? Do you learn anything new about poverty as a soul-killing way of life when you think about it in terms of an inclusion-exclusion definition?

Metaphorical Definition

While answering the question "What Is Poverty?," Jo Goodwin Parker used two metaphorical equative definitions. She replied that "Poverty is an acid that drips on pride until all pride is worn away. Poverty is a chisel that chips on honor until all honor is worn away." Why would she shift her pattern of detailing grim images of poverty to these comparisons?

We were jolted into a new idea by these comparisons. Parker wanted to show us that poverty not only physically harms and emotionally cripples but also could corrode our very sense of who we are. We had to look at a comparison of two unlike objects and see in a new way. Because metaphors complicate our responses, they make our definitions memorable.

By *metaphor*, I mean thinking and naming one thing in terms of another. I mean comparing like with unlike. Although not all metaphors take the grammatical form of X = not-X, all metaphors can be described with that equation. When Virginia Woolf stated that "words do not live in dictionaries; they live in the mind" and that laws were useless for "such irreclaimable vagabonds," she compared words with human beings and she used verbs and nouns describing human activity to talk about a species of human action. This kind of metaphor is called *personification*. When Adrienne Rich spoke about "a difficult and dangerous walking on the ice, as we try to find language and images for a consciousness we are just coming into," she compares a physical activity with an intellectual and emotional activity. You could call this kind of metaphor *direct metaphor;* it's the same kind Parker used in those metaphors of poverty as acid and chisel. When you describe the task of writing in this manner— "trying to catch the idea on paper is like chasing a rainbow!"—you are using a kind of metaphor called *simile* which always draws attention to the fact that a comparison is being made, by using the signal-words *like* or *as*. There are other kinds of metaphor *(metonymy, synecdoche* and *allegory)* which you have heard and which you have made, even though you might not have thought "Oh, that's a simile!" Making metaphor is basic to naming your world.

Metaphorical definition organizes our perceptions by stating that one thing is another thing which, in literal fact, it is not. Metaphors lie. But they also speak truth by showing us some area, previously unnoticed, where both these things are the same and share life. Usually in a metaphor the areas of dissimilarity are much larger than the area of fused similarity. The novelty of putting mostly dissimilar things together catches our attention. We know that being poor is ninety-nine percent different from being the stone a sculptor chisels but Parker's emphasis on the shared states of being acted upon, being shaped and formed by something outside us, catches our imaginations and makes us see the effects of poverty in a new, startling way.

Making metaphors may be the basic language activity that makes all other combinings and recombinings of words, sentences and ideas possible. Most of our language is figurative but most often we forget that fact. Did you notice that even the word *figurative* must have originally been a metaphor? We make metaphors so frequently when we speak and write that we would have to struggle hard not to make them.

Writing task eleven: Choose a paragraph at random from your own writing or from your reading. Study all the words carefully. Make a list of all the metaphors which you recognize. Then check each term in a dictionary to see whether you might have overlooked metaphors; the OED would be the final authority in any questions about whether a word is, or used to be, metaphorical. Even words like *therefore, spirit* and *moreover* will require a second glance. After listing the metaphors on a sheet of paper, rewrite the paragraph without using metaphor. What happens to the writing when you do this?

Dead metaphors bound through our language. Did that sentence sound strange to you? It should. I mixed metaphors in it to show what can happen when we forget that we have all those metaphors interred in our language. Of course a metaphor can't be both dead and bounding at the same time. As writers, we need to recognize the metaphoric conventions which shape our language and thought, including all those metaphors whose original references we have forgotten. Otherwise we might hear ourselves saying silly or imprecise or illogical things.

What are we to do then with these skeletons? First, we need to recognize them. You could give them a proper burial by editing them out of your writing when you revise. If you find yourself using a metaphor which you see often and hear often, it's probably either on its death-bed or already a corpse. It is certainly overused.

You could also bring the metaphor back to life by shifting the comparison to an allied but new reference area. A form of movement connected with death is *"rigor mortis."* You could use that reference area and make the same point about dead metaphor being frequent in our language. For example: "Dead metaphors create a curious sort of rigor mortis in writing; no one expected the word-corpse to move but there it is, eerily and awkwardly jumping in the sentence."

You could also rejuvenate worn-out metaphors by playing with and extending the terms of the metaphor. When the historian Edward Hallett Carr wanted to compare the way two generations of historians used historical facts, he chose an old metaphor, the cliche "a kettle of fish." First, Carr described the way nineteenth-century historians used facts. I've underlined all the terms which play with the basic metaphor of fish:

> The nineteenth century was a great age for facts. "What I want," said Mr. Gradgrind in *Hard Times,"* is Facts. ... Facts alone are wanted in life." Nineteenth-century historians on the whole agree with him ... The facts are available to the historian in documents, inscriptions, and so on, *like the fish on the fishmonger's slab.* The historian *collects them, takes them home, and cooks and serves them in whatever style appeals* to him. Acton, whose *culinary tastes* were *austere,* wanted them served plain. . . .

Did you notice how Carr played with the metaphor about fishing for facts in such a way that he could introduce metaphors about eating and about taste (see the play of meaning there) in order to make a statement on both the thinking and the writing style of nineteenth-century historians? You might remember a metaphor using these reference areas that was made by Francis Bacon in his essay "Of Studies": "Some books are to be tasted, others to be swallowed, and some few to be chewed and digested."

Later in his comparison of nineteenth and twentieth-century theories about history, Carr hauls in the fish metaphor again. He argues that facts are not objective and advises his readers to consider both the facts and the person who arranged the facts—in this case, the historian as "fisherman":

> Study the historian before you begin to study the facts. That is, after all, not very abstruse. It is what is already done by the intelligent undergraduate who, when recommended to read a work by that great scholar Jones of St. Jude's, goes round to a friend at St. Jude's to ask what sort of chap Jones is and what bees he has in his bonnet. When you read a work of history, always listen out for the buzzing. If you can detect none, either you are tone deaf or your historian is a dull dog. *The facts are really not at all like fish on the fishmonger's slab. They are like fish swimming about in a vast and sometimes inaccessible ocean; and what the historian catches will depend partly on chance, but mainly on what part of the ocean he chooses to fish in, and what tackle he chooses to use—these two factors being, of course, determined by the kind of fish he wants to catch...*

Here, Carr plays again with the metaphor and reverses the simile. Did you also notice him take the cliche "bees in the bonnet" and play with it? Neither of the metaphors he uses are new yet he finds a way to make them new. You can also do this when you find yourself using dead or worn-out metaphors.

Writing task twelve: Look over your previous writing and select a metaphor which you used only once. For five minutes, make yourself list all the words that come to mind when you think of the term. Then take several of the terms and rewrite the paragraph in which your metaphor appeared. Extend the metaphor by using these new words. What changes when you play with metaphor in this way?

As writers, we need to know when and why and how often we are using and borrowing metaphors. We also need to learn to make new metaphors. When Adrienne Rich extended the metaphors of sleep, death, waking, and sight to define writing as "re-vision," she was borrowing old metaphors, giving them new life and making some new metaphors. Her use of metaphor tells us that making and remaking metaphors are basic writing and thinking skills and necessary for growth into consciousness. Combining one subject with a new reference area makes new ways of seeing and gives us new ways of defining.

Writing task thirteen: Practice making metaphors by writing one-sentence definitions for one of the subjects listed below in each of the reference areas listed below. Take a subject like "oppression," which is shown in the examples, and combine that subject with each reference area. The examples were written by Sharon Hanrahan, a learner in an introductory writing course like yours.

Subject Areas: Education. Anger. Community. Glamour. Apartheid. Loneliness. Parenting. Strength. Menstruation. Language. Test-tube babies.

Reference Areas: Sensations (touching, hearing, smelling, tasting, seeing). Sports or games. Economics. Popular Culture. Politics. Art. Nature. Science or medicine. Religion or philosophy. Technology.

Examples: Sensations: Oppression sandbags my spirits and weighs me down.
Sports or games: Oppression is a canoe ride down a swollen river when someone has lost the paddle and rapids are coming up.
Economics: Oppression is cultural bankruptcy.
Popular Culture: Oppression is a black light poster that illuminates only the free and rich parts of life.
Politics: Oppression is a constitution without amendments.
Art: Oppression is the tyrannical sculptor who chisels away individual rights.
Nature: Oppression is a dark forest with no sun or breeze penetrating the tangled growth or the clutter of dead trees.
Science: Oppression, like the neuron bomb, leaves buildings standing but destroys all life. Oppression blasts the soul.
Religion or Philosophy: The seven sacraments of oppression are baptism in bigotry, a first communion of hating spirits, penance by innocent children, confirmation of racist assumptions, holy orders of the Ku Klux Klan, marriage of partners in prejudice, and the final rites of genocide.
Technology: Oppression is the calculating machine that adds loneliness, subtracts happiness, multiplies burdens, divides communities, and erases blessings.

Each of the metaphorical definitions which you have made could be extended so that it organizes a paragraph or an essay. You could also organize a writing by a cluster of metaphors which are all connected; each of the metaphors could use a unique reference yet be a metaphor which underlines the negative and destructive aspects of your topic. Then, each of the new metaphors would reinforce your statements. There is the danger with this second way of defining metaphorically that you might produce too mixed a medley. You can ask yourself in revisions of the paragraph or the essay whether the metaphors work well together.

Notice how the following writer took the basic metaphor "my life is a puzzle" and extended it to one paragraph of self-description:

I am a plain cardboard box containing some pieces of various jigsaw puzzles. At times I gather what pieces I have of a single puzzle, and work with them. At other times, all my pieces lay scattered, not fitting together. I have been jolted and dropped over the years, allowing a few pieces to fall out.

Some I've retrieved with a little help; others are probably lost forever, but I won't quit searching. — Barbara Quigley

Writing task fourteen: Select one metaphor you have written which you consider to be successful and imaginative. Use it to organize an entire paragraph. Then develop the topic of the paragraph into a short essay. Use that metaphor or a cluster of like metaphors to provide the structure for the essay. In your prewriting, draw up a list of words, phrases and ideas associated with the metaphor. If, for example, racism is a cancer in America, who diagnosed it as such? How was a biopsy performed? What treatments were prescribed? Are there painful side-effects of the cure or treatment? Could surgeons excise the cancerous growth? After you have brainstormed a list of metaphorical associations and after you have decided upon your topic, go ahead to use metaphor as the way of defining your idea, experience or feeling.

You may have already noticed how often writers who have organized their work through metaphorical definition will use that metaphor as a title for the work and a lure for the reader. The book and the movie *Jaws* used a one-word title which readers responded to as a metaphor for terror and random, perhaps malicious, violence. In fact, this metaphor became a strong symbol which political cartoonists also picked up.

When Maya Angelou described her first sixteen years of growing up black and female in America, she chose a metaphor to title the autobiography. That metaphoric definition piques our curiosity and describes a pattern of organization. If you have read or should read *I Know Why the Caged Bird Sings*, ask yourself who is the caged bird, how it sings, when it sings, where it sings and why it sings. In this first vignette from the book, notice her skillful use of metaphoric definition.

from I Know Why the Caged Bird Sings

Maya Angelou

"What you looking at me for?
I didn't come to stay..."
I hadn't so much forgot as I couldn't bring myself to remember. Other things were more important.

"What you looking at me for?
I didn't come to stay..."

Whether I could remember the rest of the poem or not was immaterial. The truth of the statement was like a wadded-up handkerchief, sopping wet in my fists, and the sooner they accepted it the quicker I could let my hands open and the air would cool my palms.

"What you looking at me for...?"

The children's section of the Colored Methodist Episcopal Church was wiggling and giggling over my well-known forgetfulness.

The dress I wore was lavender taffeta, and each time I breathed it rustled, and now that I was sucking in air to breathe out shame it sounded like crepe paper on the back of hearses.

As I'd watched Momma put ruffles on the hem and cute little tucks around the waist, I knew that once I put it on I'd look like a movie star. (It was silk and that made up for the awful color.) I was going to look like one of the sweet little white girls who were everybody's dream of what was right with the world. Hanging softly over the black Singer sewing machine, it looked like magic, and when people saw me wearing it they were going to run up to me and say, "Marguerite [sometimes it was 'dear Marguerite'], forgive us, please, we didn't know who you were," and I would answer generously, "No, you couldn't have known. Of course I forgive you."

Just thinking about it made me go around with angel's dust sprinkled over my face for days. But Easter's early morning sun had shown the dress to be a plain ugly cut-down from a white woman's once-was-purple throwaway. It was old-lady-long too, but it didn't hide my skinny legs, which had been greased with Blue Seal Vaseline and powdered with the Arkansas red clay. The age-faded color made my skin look dirty like mud, and everyone in church was looking at my skinny legs.

Wouldn't they be surprised when one day I woke out of my black ugly dream, and my real hair, which was long and blond, would take the place of the kinky mass that Momma wouldn't let me straighten? My light-blue eyes were going to hypnotize them, after all the things they said about "my daddy must of been a Chinaman" (I thought they meant made out of china, like a cup) because my eyes were so small and squinty. Then they would understand why I had never picked up a Southern accent, or spoke the common slang, and why I had to be forced to eat pigs' tails and snouts. Because I was really white and because a cruel fairy stepmother, who was understandably jealous of my beauty, had turned me into a too-big Negro girl, with nappy black hair, broad feet and a space between her teeth that would hold a number-two pencil.

"What you looking..." The minister's wife leaned toward me, her long yellow face full of sorry. She whispered, "I just come to tell you, it's Easter Day." I repeated, jamming the words together, "Ijustcometotellyouit'sEasterDay," as low as possible. The giggles hung in the air like melting clouds that were waiting to rain on me. I held up two fingers, close to my chest, which meant that I had to go to the toilet, and tiptoed toward the rear of the church. Dimly, somewhere over my head, I heard ladies saying, "Lord bless the child," and "Praise God." My head was up and my eyes were open, but I didn't see anything. Halfway down the aisle, the church exploded with "Were you there when they crucified my Lord?" and I tripped over a foot stuck out from the children's pew. I stumbled and started to say something, or maybe to scream, but a green persimmon, or it could have been a lemon, caught me between the legs and squeezed. I tasted the sour on my tongue and felt it in the back of my mouth. Then before I reached the door, the sting was burning down my legs and into my Sunday socks. I tried to hold, to squeeze it back, to keep it from speeding, but when I reached the church porch I knew I'd have to let it go, or it would probably run right back up to my head and my poor head would burst like a dropped watermelon, and all the brains and spit and tongue and eyes would roll all over the place. So I ran down into the yard and let it go. I ran, peeing and crying, not toward the toilet out back but to our house. I'd get a whipping for it, to be sure, and the nasty children would have something new to tease me about. I laughed anyway, partially for the sweet release; still, the greater joy came not only from being liberated from the silly church but from the knowledge that I wouldn't die from a busted head.

If growing up is painful for the Southern Black girl, being aware of her displacement is the rust on the razor that threatens the throat.

It is an unnecessary insult.

Suggested Group Writing and Discussing Activities

1. Underline all the metaphors which Maya Angelou uses and then list them under categories of kinds and reference areas used. What patterns of metaphor are most frequent? Why do you suppose she chose those patterns? Invent five additional metaphors which would work with those you found.

2. Angelou has several similies in this passage; later in the autobiography there are more direct metaphors. Why do you think she would have that pattern? In your group, take several of her similies and take some from group members and practice rewriting them as direct metaphor or as synecdoche. If your metaphors fall into the pattern of "X is not-X," revise them by substituting some verb that extends the metaphor for the copulative verb. What changes can you make on the original metaphors? Discuss the quality of the new or revised metaphors.

3. What does *displacement* mean? How does the writer show us displacement in this narrative? Discuss the theme and write a one-paragraph description of some experience you have had of displacement. In the final sentence, write a metaphoric definition which sums up the feeling of displacement.

4. Do you find any similarities between this autobiographic statement and that of

Jo Goodwin Parker? Your answers to this question might range from listing similarities of writing strategies to discussing attitudes toward the world which they share. Are these two writers at any point naming the same world?

Operational Definition

How would you define *intelligent?* If your definition includes a statement like "a high IQ" or "an IQ over 125," then you are using an **operational definition.** When you define with an operational definition, you do not analyze the constituents of the term nor do you describe them by comparing them to something else. You define by describing the process by which you measure what the term names. You measure the term's operation or functions.

With an operational definition you describe *hardness* by measuring the amount of material that the object which is hard can withstand. You could use a Brinell test to measure. After pressing a steel plate for 30 seconds with a load of 3 tons, measure the depth of indentation on the plate: the deeper the dent, the harder the ball. You could also define *hardness* by measuring the density of atoms in the hard object, by measuring the chemical bondings of the atoms, and by measuring the permanence of the bondings. In each instance, you define operationally.

Writing task fifteen: Write an operational definition for class participation. Decide what characteristics of the classroom are significant in demonstrating "class participation" and then show how that could be measured.

We use the convention of operational definition daily. We define *time* by citing a number of seconds (60 = one minute), of minutes (60 = one hour), of hours (24 = one day), of days (7 = one week, an average of 30 = month, 365 = one year). Without clocks or calendars, to help us measure, we would feel less certain about defining time.

We are learning in the United States to redefine distance, speed, and volume because of a change in the way we measure these quantities. We are discarding yardsticks and 30 mph roadsigns and quart measuring cups because we are switching to a metric system of measure.

Clearly, operational definitions are very efficient ways to define physical characteristics. Are they useful to us in other ways? This pattern of defining has been used frequently since 1938 when the philosopher of science Percy Bridgman used the term to define what Einstein was doing; Bridgman explained *spontaneity* by describing simple operations his readers could duplicate and measure. Writers in the natural and social sciences frequently use operational definitions to organize both their research and their writing about that research. They can use this way of defining to reach a new perspective on ideas or feelings or experiences which we might have described only from our "feelings" before.

For example, one professional and married couple—an anthropologist and a psychologist—defined a quality of human life when they measured the "pace of living." To do so, they measured how fast people walk in big cities and in small towns. They measured the walking speed of solitary and unencumbered pedestrians who strolled, shuffled, ambled, paced, and tripped along a fifty-foot section of the main commercial street. They measured fifteen communities in six countries; they learned that the pace of life in big cities is 2.8 feet per second faster than that in small towns.

They speculated that pedestrians in cities walk faster because they are overloaded by environmental stimuli. Walking faster lets the pedestrian blank out some of the stimuli and alleviates some of the psychological tension that overcrowding triggers. How would an operational definition like this help city planners and architects? How would this operational definition help to redefine the *quality of life?*

Operational definitions are particularly helpful because they are clear and can always be checked for accuracy. If the measuring process is repeated and the same measurements are obtained, then we know that the term has been accurately classified; we have some kind of objectivity about a term. This kind of measuring can be useful to us. The possibility of making clear and precise definitions would help us work with many of the ethical and legal issues which besiege us.

An operational definition of death would be useful. Because respirators, artificial kidneys and other machines can keep a patient functioning despite damage to the brain and vital organs, a person could live indefinitely in a vegetative state. This case was dramatized for us by Karen Anne Quinlan in the 1970s. Medical authorities have dispensed with the formerly legal definition of death as the time when the heart stops beating and the lungs stop breathing. Now authorities refer to *brain death,* the nonfunctioning of the brain as demonstrated by an electroencephalogram. When the EEG measures a flat wave pattern for a certain period of time, the pattern should indicate that the brain has stopped functioning. Because brain tissue cannot be repaired or regenerated, the brain, unlike the heart and other organs, cannot be made to function again. By defining death as brain death, medical authorities hope to differentiate between an appropriate medical practice of withdrawing artificial life support from a patient who is *dead* and the malpractice of murder.

In like manner, an operational definition which could define *life* by measuring specific functions of viability is needed to help in legal, social, and moral struggles. The trial of Dr. Kenneth Edelin in Massachusetts in

1975 for manslaughter, because he performed an abortion, was made more complex because experts disagreed about a definition of *life*. At what point does a fetus exhibit such an amount of "life signs" that it is said to live? What are the functions of living that must be measured? An operational definition might help us in our thinking about these issues.

Women who bear children after the age of forty are termed "high risk pregnancies" because of statistically greater incidence of abnormalities in the fetus. For example, the incidence of Downs Syndrome (often misnamed mongoloidism) increases in dramatic and direct proportion to the age of the mother. The tragedy of the thalidomide children—babies born with stunted and missing limbs because of the drug thalidomide prescribed for use during pregnancy—and the fears about long-range effects of polyvinyl chloride particles on the babies born to women who have been contaminated by living near PVC-producing plants are other instances of possible tragic human mutations.

Many fetal abnormalities can be discovered by a test called amniocentesis which can be used as early as the first trimester. An obstetrician can analyze a sample of the fluid in which the fetus floats. The chromosomal makeup of the fetus can be analyzed and both the sex of the fetus and the possibility of abnormalities determined. The decision to abort an abnormal fetus, however, is complicated by the lack of any operational definition for *life*.

Operational definitions are being used increasingly to define important concepts and to prompt new thinking. The use of operational definition to define certain school systems as *de jure* segregated has provoked confrontation, violence, and change in some cities. The use of the operational definition called *apartheid,* which measures the absence of "black blood," perpetuates mass oppression in South Africa. This method of defining can be used in many ways.

If you choose to use this defining paradigm, you need to understand its advantages and disadvantages. The process of measuring can mislead us. Many critics of intelligence tests and achievement tests argue that the tests use a process of measuring which reflects a white, middle-class culture. They argue that an operational definition is limited by its measures and cannot be expected to measure all that is significant to a concept like intelligence or achievement.

Too often, an operational definition overlooks qualities which cannot easily be quantified. They might measure the least important qualities of the term to be defined. If you joke about being #6265547 in a student body of 22,000, you might be indicating that some other definition would give a more accurate and complete description of you. In a recent Frederick Wiseman documentary about welfare, one man cried when the clerk refused his application for general assistance without a social security number and six months of rent receipts to prove his identity. The computer card which was used to determine "eligibility" had no category for "hungry, cold and frightened." Operational definitions may be the most efficient way to help people; they may also further injure people. You need to be aware of the advantages and disadvantages of the defining paradigm.

Writing task sixteen: A "B.E.M. Sex Roles Inventory" was devised to define operationally three types of behavior: masculinity, femininity and androgyny. Respondents were to rank themselves on a scale of 1 to 7 (from "never true" through "occasionally true" to "almost always true") for a series of characteristics like "self-reliant," "assertive," "analytical," "childlike," etc. They then scored their responses to see what type of behavior they most often practiced. How would you measure and define concepts like *masculine, feminine* and *androgynous?* Describe in an essay the process you would use to measure those characteristics. Explain how you decided to measure in the way and with the measurements which you have chosen. Because this will be a new definition, you must be sure to describe each step of the process carefully to your readers.

Contextual Definition

Contextual definition is a process that you use so often you may not have thought to give it a name. When I asked which was the correct definition and you answered "that all depends," you were indicating that often how to define depends on the context or the environment or the frame of reference from which you define. We shift our frame of reference when we try to solve problems; we have to define terms or problems from each frame of reference.

Contextual definition is a series of equative definitions which specify that in one named context X = Y, in another named context X = Z, and in yet another named context, X = W. You could make an equation like this: *woman* in a discussion of primates (X_1) means the female *homo sapiens* (Y). In a discussion of sex roles, *woman* (X_2) means the human who bears young (Z). *Woman* in a discussion of epistemology (X_3) means a human person who reflects upon the activity of knowing something (W). A complete contextual equation for *woman* would be: $X_1 = Y$; $X_2 = Z$; $X_3 = W$. In a paragraph, that would look like this:

> When anthropologists discuss *woman,* they classify her as the female of the species *homo sapiens.* If they decided to specify sex roles, they'll explain her as the human who reproduces. I would add to their definitions by borrowing the philosopher's distinction about the human being as the only animal who reflects on its act of reflecting.

You use contextual definition whenever you make distinctions for your audience about the "person I was then" and "who I am now." When we differentiated denotation from connotation, we described the several things a word could connote depending on context: the context of where the word is used, the context of who uses it, the context of who hears it, and contexts of what words are like it. Remember that the OED entry for *girl* lists meanings and cites contexts which show how the word functions in specific verbal environments.

I talked about holograph earlier as a word which in 1677 meant something entirely different from what it means today after the invention of the laser beam. That is an example of *external contextual definition:* the word means two different things in two cited contexts because of changes in the world outside. There is also *internal contextual definition:* the word means two different things in two cited contexts because of changes within the world the word inhabits. Your definition of you here and now and your definition of you then and there would be *internal contextual definition.*

Writing task seventeen: Write a contextual definition of *beauty* by defining what the word meant when you were ten (both in the world outside you and inside you), what it meant when you were fifteen, and what it means to you at your present age. Be very specific about describing each frame of reference.

When we define contextually, we show that the meaning of a word is relative to the context which frames the word. We show that meaning is not fixed; it changes depending on context. However, we don't mean that the meaning is completely relative. The word still denotes some basic idea. For example, when opponents of the Equal Rights Amendment define *freedom,* they define from their own frame of reference. Although their definition might not be shared entirely by proponents of the ERA, both groups would agree on some continuous and conventional meaning of freedom. When you use the paradigm of contextual definition, you'll want to show not only the several meanings of a term but also the meaning of the term which is basic to understanding the word. What, for example, would be the basic and continuing abstract idea in the word *beauty?*

Contextual definition offers a convenient structure for organizing paragraphs and essays. It can also help you to think in an interdisciplinary manner; in fact, what we call "cross-cultural studies" rely on contextual definition as a means of thinking and writing. Contextual definition can help you to make clear comparisons and contrasts and also to analyze a whole into its parts. It can be particularly helpful in the introduction to a research paper when you show that you understand the complexity of the issues and the variety of contexts from which they can be studied but have chosen to focus on one or two contexts for research and for writing.

You could also use contextual definition to keep you reader's attention by citing a variety of meanings for one word. In the essay which follows, Una Stannard uses contextual definition to pull us into her writing. She defines from the contexts of historical period, geography, and cultures. She uses contextual definition to demonstrate that the concept of beauty, an enduring concern of humans, is defined by each epoch and culture. After she demonstrates this, she turns her attention to an analysis of the meaning of all those contextual definitions of beauty. Eventually she stipulates her own definition of *beauty*. Notice at what point in the essay the writer stops using contextual definition. After she has demonstated the relativity of *beauty*, what does she describe as the continuous, basic meaning of beauty in all those contextual definitions?

The Mask of Beauty

Una Stannard

Women are the beautiful sex. Who doubts it? Among birds the male may have the pretty plumage, but among human beings it is the female who wears the peacock feathers.

Whatever else is denied women, no one denies that they are better looking than men. Little boys are made of frogs and snails, but little girls are made of sugar and spice, that is, potential cheesecake. When the first baby born in the New Year is a girl, the newspaper predicts that in twenty years she will be Miss America, for just as all men are created equal, all women are created beautiful. Of course, occasionally an unfortunate woman may be an exception, but isn't she the exception that proves the rule? Or rather, just as all men have different I.Q.s, so all women have different Beauty Quotients; although all women are beautiful, some women are more beautiful than others.

When a mother unwraps the pink blanket from her tiny bundle, we say, "My, isn't she pretty." And as the little girl grows up and looks about her, she sees models of female beauty everywhere. As she sits in front of the television set, every deodorant and soap powder is in the hand of a fair lady. The actresses on TV and in the movies are always beautiful, or at least the young ones who get the men are. When the little girls travels on an airplane, the stewardess who gives her a balloon is lovely, and when she peeks over her father's shoulders as he reads a magazine, she sees the beautiful paper dolls in *Playboy*. When she walks beside her mother in the supermarket, her eyes are level with the beautiful women on the covers of the magazines and with the beautiful half-naked women on the covers of the paperback books. When she rides in the family car, her eyes rise to the gigantic beautiful girls papered on billboards; when she is taken to a museum, she sees mostly women in stone and paint, their naked beauty displayed for all to see and admire. Perhaps on the coffee table at home is a heavy book with glossy photographs of beautiful women. On TV every year, she can watch dozens of beauty contests—Miss Peaches, Miss Salt Lake City, Miss Rodeo, Miss Tall San Francisco, Miss Junior Miss, Miss Teen-Age America. From Alabama to Wyoming, every year without fail a new Miss Prettiest in the state is selected, from which crop of beauties Miss U.S.A. is chosen, who may then honor all American womanhood by being selected as Miss Universe, The Most Beautiful Woman in the World.

Little girls not only look endlessly at beautiful women, they hear and read about them too. In the newspapers women are almost always described as the beautiful Miss ——, or the pretty coed, or the attractive Mrs. ——, and, of course, all the brides on the society page are beautiful. All the songs are about beautiful girls too; in stories the fairy princess and later, all the heroines, always overwhelm men with the power of their beauty; the poets too, every last one of them, are forever exclaiming, "O fair is she," "so divinely fair," "the fairest of creation."

Then the little girl looks in the mirror. But she has read the story of the ugly duckling who turns into a swan, and when she visits her relatives they all smile at her and say, "What a sweet face!" and her father is always telling her what a knockout she is going to be when she grows up. She decides that beauty, like menstruation, is something that happens to girls at adolescence. She will wait. When she becomes a woman, she again looks at herself in the mirror—long and hard.

She then begins woman's frantic pursuit of beauty, for she has read in innumerable ads that "every woman has the right to be beautiful. Make-up is magic! It can transform you, create the illusion of perfect feminine loveliness that every woman longs for." In every new jar of face cream, box of powder, tube of lipstick, mascara, eyeliner, she expects to find the magic formula that will transform her into a beauty. Every change of hairdo, every padded bra, every girdle, every pair of high heels or sandals, every mini skirt or midi skirt, every tight sweater or sack dress will somehow make her glamorous, captivating. She never gives up. Her blue hair waved, circles of rouge on her wrinkled cheeks, lipstick etching the lines around her mouth, still moisturizing her skin nightly, still corseted, she dies.

For centuries, in the pursuit of beauty, Chinese women used to bind their feet, trying to compress them to the ideal three inches. To achieve this ideal beauty, no suffering was too great. At about the age of four, a girl's feet were bandaged; the toes were pulled backward so tightly that blood and pus later oozed from the bandages, a toe or two might fall off, and death from gangrene was possible. If the girl survived, she would never be able to walk freely again without a cane or the support of attendants. But the excruciating pain and the loss of freedom were worth it, for the tinier her feet, the richer the husband she might get. She might also win first prize in one of the many tiny-foot beauty contests. All ladies had bound feet; it was fashionable; natural feet were ugly; only tiny feet were beautiful.

Not long ago when narrow-toed shoes were fashionable, many women had their little toes amputated so their feet would more comfortably fit the shoes. These women were like Cinderella's sisters, one of whom cut off her big toe and the other the back of her heel in order to fit the glass slipper. These are extremes, perhaps, but few women alive today have not subjected themselves to the discomfort of high heels, which produce such deformities as calluses, corns, bunions, clawed toes, unduly high arches, and secondary shortening of the calf muscles, deformities different only in degree from those of the bound foot.

In China it used to be said that a girl had to suffer twice—she had to have her ears pierced and her feet bound. But today a girl in her first pair of high heels will rarely admit that her feet hurt; almost every girl begs to have her ears pierced and does not think of it as suffering or mutilation. Apparently, the pursuit of beauty is a great anesthetic. Older women used to wince bravely as they plucked their eyebrows, and who can doubt that if it became fashionable many women would pluck out every eyebrow hair, as Japanese women did not long ago. As it is, women merely razor off the "unfeminine" hair on their legs and under their arms. The women unlucky enough to have "masculine" facial hair endure the pain of electrolysis; millions of women undergo surgery to have their freckles burnt off, their skin peeled, their faces lifted, their noses reshaped, their breasts filled with silicone. Millions of women wear tight girdles, live for weeks on celery and beef broth, or sweat in gyms, or if rich, subject themselves to the luxurious rigors of a beauty farm, just to keep thin. It is now fashionable to be thin, but if it were fashionable to be fat, women would force-feed themselves like geese, just as girls in primitive societies used to stuff themselves because the fattest girl was the most beautiful. If the eighteen-inch waist should ever become fashionable again, women would suffer the tortures of tight lacing, convinced that though one dislocated one's kidneys, crushed one's liver, and turned green, beauty was worth it all.

When Rudi Gernreich predicted that women in the future would shave their heads and wear wigs, everyone laughed, but in ancient Egypt women did precisely that. And though at present women increase the size of their breasts with internal or external falsies, if it became fashionable to be flat-chested women would, as in the 1920s, flatten their breasts with bandages, or, if rich, have a plastic surgeon transform their breasts into the fashionable size. Is it too much to predict that if the ideal became long pendulous breasts, women would, as Nigerian women used to, spend hours pulling at their breasts to make them droop? Black teeth were once considered beautiful in Japan, so all fashionable women blackened their teeth, just as actresses and models now have their teeth filed down to points and capped with shining white porcelain. Because America is the world's most powerful nation, rich Oriental women have their eyelids straightened; if China should become the great world power, American women would have their eyelids lifted.

In the past men pursued beauty as avidly as women; in fact in most primitive societies (just as among animals) the male sex is believed to be the fair sex; only the men wear beads, feathers, flowers, perfumes, and bright colors. In an East African tribe the men wear huge cone-shaped headdresses; when a woman marries she traditionally shaves off her hair and gives it to her husband to pad out his headdress. Among the Tchambuli in New Guinea, women also shave their heads and do not adorn themselves; the men are graceful and charming, curl their hair, and wear bird of paradise headdresses. Similarly, in ancient Greece, men were considered the beautiful sex. Originally, nude statues were all male; even as late as the fifth century B.C., the great period of Greek art, nude statues of women were extremely rare. It was not until a century later that nude statues of women became common, but they did not predominate. We can explain the Greek preference for the male nude by the bisexuality of Greek culture, yet in Italy and other heterosexual Western European countries during the Renaissance, female beauty was not more celebrated than male beauty in painting and sculpture. It was only with Raphael that the female nude began to predominate, and it took 200 years before it was a *fait accompli*. It was not until the nineteenth century that "the nude" in art almost always meant a female nude. ,

The exclusive identification of women with beauty occurred at the same time that men stopped being sex objects. Around the end of the 1830s men gave up wearing bright colors, silks, laces, earrings, and perfumes and stopped setting their hair. Men no longer showed off their legs; instead they wore trousers so loose that a man's sex can only be assumed from the presumptive evidence of the fly; they also covered their chests with loose jackets. Men became modest; they now conceal everything and signify their maleness only by a symbol—the necktie.

Since the Victorian period men have projected all sexuality onto women, whose dress has obediently conformed to whatever aroused men. One hundred years ago the Victorian woman tried to look like Miss Innocent: she wore no make-up except for a touch of rice powder, fluttered her lowered eyelids, and floated about in crinolines as if she lacked legs to walk on. She looked angelic because men were sexually aroused by innocence. Victorian brothels always kept a fresh supply of virgins, who were often extremely young—until 1885 the age of consent was twelve. Adult prostitutes tried to look like children, "You find the women dress like children, and it pays better. Children used to dress like women in the streets and now women dress like children," said an English clergyman testifying before a committee investigating child prostitution.

Men, having tired of innocence, now require women to look sexy. As Caitlin Thomas, wife of Dylan Thomas, once said, the woman who wants to keep a man must continually emphasize "bust, bum, legs, lips." Clare Booth Luce, in a speech given in 1969, advised women who wanted husbands to turn their bodies into a "man-trap" by wearing mini skirts and plunging necklines. Even after marriage, the good woman is supposed to continue to look sexy. Columns in the women's pages instruct them in the art of dressing and undressing sexily; not long ago a New York disc jockey suggested that the really good wife would greet her husband at the door dressed only in Saran wrap, and at least one good woman followed his advice.

Woman's present state of undress, therefore, is not an indication of her own sexiness; it is merely the current way of arousing men, who now like women to look sexually aggressive. But only to look it. A woman must still be innocent of active sexual aggressiveness. The woman in a mini-skirt and plunging neckline must never ask a man to bed, and in bed she must surrender, not assert her sexuality. The modern woman's liberty to expose her legs and most of her body does not signify women's sexual liberation but only her obsessive desire to please men. Women are "free" to start wearing padded bras at the age of nine and to spend forty-eight million dollars annually on eye make-up alone. Women are free to be Playboy bunnies or to be topless and bottomless waitresses. Women are not free *not* to be sexy.

Women are not free to stop playing the beauty game, because the woman who stops would be afraid of exposing herself for what she is—not the fair sex. And yet the woman who does play the beauty game proves the same thing. Every day, in every way, the billion-dollar beauty business tells women they are monsters in disguise. Every ad for bras tells a woman that her breasts need lifting, every ad for padded bras that what she's got isn't big enough, every ad for girdles that her belly sags and her hips are too wide, every ad for high heels that her legs need propping, every ad for cosmetics that her skin is too dry, too oily, too pale, or too ruddy, or her lips are not bright enough, or her lashes not long enough, every ad for deodorants and perfumes that her natural odors all need disguising, every ad for hair dye, curlers, and permanents that the hair she was born with is the wrong color or too straight or too curly, and lately ads for wigs tell her that she would be better off covering up nature's mistake completely. In this culture women are told they are the fair sex, but at the same time that their "beauty" needs lifting, shaping, dyeing, painting, curling, padding. Women are really being told that "the beauty" is a beast.

In the eighteenth century Swift described a "fair nymph" preparing for bed by taking off her artificial hair, false eyebrows, false teeth, the rags she used to "prop her flabby dugs," her corset, and her hip bolsters. How different is she from the twentieth-century woman who at bedtime takes off her wig, peels off her false eyelashes, creams off her eyeliner, eyebrow pencil, and lipstick, and removes her girdle and padded bra? If women were indeed the fair sex, why would they need all these improvements? Why couldn't they simply be as nature made them?

Women's beauty is largely a sham, and women know it. That is why they obediently conform every time the fashion masters crack the whip. A woman conforms to all the whims of the cosmetic and fashion industries so that she will not be singled out from the mass of women, so that she will look like every other woman and thus manage to pass as one of the fair sex. Clothing and cosmetics are the means by which society tries to prove that all women are beautiful, but it is one of our great cultural lies.

Women are the false peacocks of the species. The average woman—and that means a good 95 percent of them—is not beautiful in the way the culture pretends. Look at women and try to see them without their symbols of beauty. How many beautiful women are there then? Then picture men fully adorned—in bright colors, with their hair curled and with eye make-up. How unsettlingly attractive most of them become.

Beauty is rare in either sex. In most species in the animal kingdom, one sex *is* more colorful or attractive than the other; more often than not it is the male. But in the human species neither sex, *au naturel*, is more attractive than the other. But a strong case could be made for considering women the less attractive sex, at least if we maintain our present standards of beauty. Schopenhauer described women as "that undersized, narrow-shouldered, broad-hipped and short legged race." If he had added that their waists are usually large and their bosoms small or, if full, tend to droop, he would have described the average woman's body fairly well. The average woman does not resemble at all the naked women in *Playboy*. And even those beauties were not meant merely for male contemplation but for impregnation, and the pregnant woman is not beautiful. During pregnancy a woman's face may be radiant (and that belief is by large a myth too), but what of her body?—the breasts swollen, the nipples brown, the belly distended and shiny with stretch marks, the belly button protruding. Are women beautiful then? And after pregnancy the breasts of millions of women collapse, the stretch marks remain, the belly sags, and the nipples stay brown.

However beautiful one may think women are, their beauty leads to the nonbeauty of pregnancy. Woman's body is functional. Since the man does not have to carry a child within him, he is better fitted to keep whatever looks he was born with. There are, of course, some people who would insist that the pregnant woman is beautiful because whatever is natural is beautiful. Certainly prehistoric men admired natural women, as their squat, hippy, swollen-bellied, swollen-breasted figurines testify.

But the modern cult of women's beauty has nothing to do with what women naturally look like, which is why *Playboy* doesn't run pictures of pregnant women or average women, and heavily airbrushes its carefully selected beauties. For even the small percentage of women who fulfill the modern ideal of beauty are not allowed to be natural. They too are creatures of artifice. The women who compete in the Miss U.S.A. contest are required to wear false eyelashes, and, like all the other beauties who dazzle us in the media, must be well-groomed, carefully curried like expensive horses, with full make-up, elaborate hair-dos, and the latest fashionable attire. Their beauty is kept at the highest level of artificial polish because they are performing an essential service in our society.

Glittering and smiling in the media, looked at by millions, envied and ogled, these ideal beauties teach women their role in society. They teach them that women are articles of conspicuous consumption in the male market; in other words, that women are made to be looked at, and that females achieve success in the world by being looked at. "My face is my fortune," said the pretty maid in the nursery rhyme, by which she meant that her pretty face would enable her to get a husband—the prettier the face, the richer the husband. The prettiest faces in our society angle for the biggest fortunes. Why else is the office beauty the front office secretary? Why else are airline stewardesses, models and actresses chosen solely for their looks? Why, if not to put them in the most visible places in the market so that the richest men can see and buy them? Men have so structured our society that the most beautiful women, like all other valuable property, càn go to the highest bidder.

In the eighteenth century Swift said that a rich man was able to buy "the finest clothing, the noblest houses, the most costly meats and drinks and have his choice of the most beautiful females." The world has always served up its most beautiful girls to its richest men. In Edwardian days an exceedingly rich man decided to test the claim of Maxim's of Paris that it would serve a customer any dish he desired, no matter how exotic. The rich gentleman ordered a naked girl covered with cherry sauce. He got her, silver platter and all, in one of Maxim's private dining rooms.

What the rich gentlemen obtained in private is now procured for rich men by society, and in public, for we live in a democracy. Therefore, there is no silver platter and the girls are usually only partially naked, but they are on display everywhere—on TV, in movies, ads, and planes—waiting to satisfy the rich man's palate.

Although only the rich can afford these ideal beauties, the not-so-rich man can ogle them and daydream, and the average woman can imitate them. Since the ideal beauties are obviously not quite as nature made them, the average woman is encouraged to artificially aspire. So she pads herself and copies their make-up, hair styles, and clothes, and walks with her breasts and ass jiggling, dangling herself before every man in the street. In our twentieth-century democracy men do not have to be rich to be polygamists. A man may only be able to marry one woman at a time, but every woman bedizens herself and constantly entices him. Every woman in our society, like the few beautiful ones in the media, is a flesh peddler in the harem of this man's world.

The ideal beauties teach women that their looks are a commodity to be bartered in exchange for a man, not only for food, clothing, and shelter, but for love. Women learn early that if you are unlovely, you are unloved. The homely girl prepares to be an old maid, because beauty is what makes a man fall in love. "As fair thou art, my bonnie lass, So deep in love am I," wrote Robert Burns. A man's love is beauty deep. Beauty is man's only and sufficient reason for lusting, loving, and marrying a woman. Doesn't a man always say you're beautiful before he says I love you? Don't we all think it strange when a man marries a girl who isn't pretty and not at all strange when he marries a dumb beauty? Is it therefore surprising that even the great beauty fears a man's love will not survive her looks, and the average woman is convinced that no man can really love her? How can he love her when she lacks what is needed to produce love? That is why she so desperately keeps up her looks and feels that although all the kids have the measles, she ought to greet her husband with her beauty mask on. In France there are beautymobils that dash to the bedside of a newly delivered mother lest papa see her when she isn't beautiful. To keep their men in love, women spend billions on creams and moisturizers so their skin will continue to look youthfully beautiful. To keep their men in love, women read book after book telling them *How To Be Thirty for Forty Years, The Art of Staying Young, Beauty Is Not an Age,* and take the love potions prescribed by modern witchdoctors who devise special hormone therapies to help women stay "feminine forever," which means, of course, beautiful forever.

However, the ideal beauties in the media do remain young forever. They are always there to keep women permanently insecure about their looks, and that includes the great beauties as well. Indeed, the more beautiful a woman, the more she dreads time and younger beauties; for generally the beautiful woman's opinion of herself has depended almost solely on her looks. Elizabeth of Austria, who in the nineteenth century was regarded as the most beautiful woman in Europe, said when she was approaching forty: "Nothing could be more terrible than to feel the hand of time on one's body, to watch the skin wrinkling, to wake and fear the morning light and know that one is no longer desirable. Life without beauty would be worthless to me." In the 1960s when Grace Kelly, Princess of Monaco, turned forty, she said that though forty was a marvelous age for a man, it was torture for a woman because it meant "the end."

Certainly it means the end if a woman's value depends upon her looks and her looks succumb—as they must—to age. The only road to glory this culture offers women is one that cannot last, one that must perish long before they do. The culture discourages women from achieving the kind of glory that does last, the glory that results from using one's mind. The little boy is asked what he's *going to become* when he grows up; the little girl is told she *is* — pretty. A girl's potential is only physical. Like an animal, she is expected to create only with her body, not her mind. The quickest and easiest way for a woman to get ahead (besides hitching her body to a man's star) is by displaying her body, like an animal in a zoo, as a topless waitress, a belly dancer, a model, an airline stewardess, a Miss U.S.A., or that ultimate glory, a Raquel Welch, who at present embodies the height of woman's attainments.

Women are supposed to be bodies, not differentiated complex minds. Who would think of talking to the virtually indistinguishable, vacuous faces in *Playboy?* Women are supposed to be a man's sexual outlets, not his work colleagues, not his intellectual companions. The girl who tries to show off her mind instead of her body is penalized. On a date the girl who stops listening and starts talking is considered rude and aggressive; the girl who presumes to argue, disprove, and refute is not asked out again. In the eighteenth century Mary Wortley Montagu advised her daughter to hide her learning "like a physical defect." No one minded Jayne Mansfield's 160 I.Q. because she kept it hidden well behind her bosom. Men want their women dumb, their beautiful lips sealed. "No dress or garment is less becoming to a woman than a show of intelligence," decreed Martin Luther.

Men feel threatened unless they are with a woman who is less intelligent than they are. Accordingly, men, in order to keep their egos inflated (at least in the presence of the fair sex), for centuries excluded women from schools and colleges, and then sneeringly discoursed on woman's stupidity: "A woman has the form of an angel ... and the mind of an ass" (German proverb). "No woman is a genius; women are a decorative sex" (Oscar Wilde). Max Beerbohm felt that a woman couldn't be charming who had a "masculine-styled brain," which is male for "a powerful intellect."

The woman who, in spite of cultural disapproval and the difficulties of acquiring an education, pursues learning is regarded by men as a sexual freak. Nietzsche said that "when a woman inclines to learning there is usually something wrong with her sex apparatus." Women seem to feel the same way, for when they do use their brains they tend to fear that they have unsexed themselves. In 1787 when Dorothea von Schlözer took her doctorate of philosophy at Göttingen, she dressed herself in white, with a veil on her head and roses and pearls in her hair; that is, she dressed like a bride to reassure herself that she was a woman. Today even female professors, doctors, and lawyers dress sexily and still modestly pretend to know less than they do; they act like dumb blondes and enjoy being mistaken for them.

It is protective covering, for the intelligent woman is disliked, and if she cannot pass as at least "attractive," she has to endure constant adverse comments about her appearance. It took the press about twenty years to stop joking about Eleanor Roosevelt's looks. A journalist recently explained the phenomenon of Bernadette Devlin, M.P., as a compensation for her lack of beauty, the implication being that if Miss Devlin had been prettier she would not have had to be an M.P. but would long ago have happily become Mrs. SomeMan. George Eliot, who was among the two or three greatest novelists of the nineteenth century, was forced by society to agonize about her looks. Even so serious a journal as the *London Times Literary Supplement* recently captioned a review of her latest biography, "Magnificently Ugly," and devoted almost half the review to a discussion of the problem of her looks. But George Eliot was no worse looking than Emerson or Dante; she was ugly only in terms of the beauty ideal artificially set up for women. Critics still like to talk so much about her looks because they do not want to think of her as a mind, but rather as a woman.

In 1966 when a woman was appointed vice president of a corporation, journalists were impressed not by her competence with financial statistics but by her own statistics—34-24-36—which they published so all the world could marvel at the anomaly: a brainy woman who was built too. What they were in reality doing was reducing the vice-president of a corporation to a beautiful body. Similarly, when a woman is appointed a judge, we sometimes see the exclamation, "She's pretty too!" When a good-looking man is appointed a judge, the press rarely exclaims, "He's handsome too!" Men are astonished by the combination of beauty and brains in a woman because they really cannot understand why a good-looking woman should have brains. What does she need them for? In 1837 Alexander Walker, in his discourse on *Beauty; Illustrated Chiefly by an Analysis and Classification of Beauty in Woman,* concluded that the ideal beauty's head ought to be small "because the mental system in the female ought to be subordinate to the vital ... sensibility should exceed reasoning power." Or as a twentieth century song put it, "Why does a beautiful girl need an I.Q. to say I do?" On the same either/or principle is a watch ad in which the woman's watch is described as beautiful, the man's as accurate.

Society has so overvalued beauty that most women, given the choice between unusual intelligence and great beauty, would choose beauty. Charlotte Brontë was so angry at fate for not making her pretty that her publisher believed she would have given "all her genius and all her fame to have been beautiful." How many girls given the choice between Raquel Welch or Maria Goeppert-Mayer, the woman who won a Nobel prize for physics in 1963, would choose to be the physicist?

At present men seem to object somewhat less to the woman who uses her brains. Occasionally one does find an article in the Sunday supplement that tells young girls that it is okay to use their brains. But, why? Because husbands would have no objections to having both an attractive and intelligent wife for entertaining their business friends or a shrewd silent partner with whom they could discuss business strategy. Husbands also do not mind if their wives entertain them in the evening by telling them about something interesting they have been reading. So long as a woman's brains are used in the service of a male, men will permit her to display them. But her brains must be kept subordinate. Even the most enlightened men and women suspect the manliness of a man married to a doctor or a professor. It somehow does not seem right. Men are supposed to marry their intellectual inferiors; if by some unlucky chance, the wife is the husband's intellectual superior, she is always advised to play down her brains and play up her sex appeal if she wants her marriage to last.

Whether a woman has an I.Q. of 60 or 160, whether she is young or old, her first duty is to keep herself attractive. Men have taught women to regard themselves exactly the way men do — as sex objects. A woman's body, accordingly, becomes her lifelong sex object, the physical object she cherishes most. All babies begin by loving their physical selves, but the male baby is encouraged to stop loving just himself and to transfer some of his self-love to the outside world. Girls, on the other hand, are encouraged to continue obtaining gratification the way a baby does—from reveling in and showing off their bodies. A baby's pride is centered in its physical being, not in its accomplishments, and so it is with women. They are never supposed to grow up, but to remain fixated in infantile narcissism. And most women do continue to overvalue their physical selves; this is why all evidence to the contrary notwithstanding, every woman is pleased and secretly believes a man when he tells her she is beautiful. Because women are infant narcissists, they like to be treated like queens, for whom doors are opened and cigarettes lighted, and toward whom the whole male world moves as toward a magnet. These attentions make women feel good about themselves, because they are repetitions of infancy, when one's helplessness forces the whole world to wait upon one.

As narcissists women are incapable of loving anyone but themselves. When a beautiful woman falls in love, it generally only means that she has found a man who overvalues her physical self as much as she does. For the average woman the process of falling in love is more complicated. Since every baby thinks of itself as the greatest thing ever created, the average-looking woman at first overvalues herself the way everyone else does. When she discovers that the ideal image she has of herself is not what society finds ideal, she does not give it up; it remains her secret ideal image, which society encourages her to maintain by the deceptions of clothes and cosmetics. Her real self, which she can't love and which she consequently feels no one else can love, is abandoned, and she typically falls in love by self-abnegation, by unselfishly devoting herself to a man whom she regards as her superior and then living through him, making his life her life. She wants no life of her own because she has no real self. But the superior being she worships is not a real man, but an embodiment of her own self-worship transferred onto him.

Narcissus was so enraptured by his own image reflected on the surface of a lake that he tried to embrace himself. Women, too, are in love with their own body image, are therefore unconscious homosexuals. It would be surprising if they were not, since they grow up in a world in which only the female body is glorified, and in which they are bombarded in all the media with millions of images of beautiful women described as love objects. Far from conditioning women to be heterosexual by holding up for their admiration images of handsome men, the culture keeps women looking constantly at other women. The culture, however, likes to think that women don't look at women in the same way that men do. Psychology textbooks are fond of presenting statistics that prove that men are sexually aroused by looking, but that women are not. The trouble probably is that in their tests psychologists show women only pictures of men. It is pictures of *women* that women are nutured on, and women do look, and look, and look. Women look at other women with a more intense and discriminating eye than any man does. The culture likes to think that a woman's glance is only critical, to see if the other woman is better looking or better dressed than she is, or that women look because they want to identify with the ideal beauties. But envy is looking at what one desires, and identification is one of the most potent forms of love; one wants to merge, with what one identifies with, become one with the beloved. The almost inevitable rivalry between women, the seeming impossibility of women being friends, may well be an overreaction to an overattraction.

What holds women back from widespread homosexuality? Although the female body is glorified, females are regarded as the inferior sex, and women share this male-created attitude. The very cause of women's glorification— her presumptive beauty—is at the same time the stigma of her inferiority. No matter how much a woman is unconsciously attracted to another woman, she also despises the other woman as she despises herself, because she is of the inferior sex. In this culture a woman can lose her sense of inferiority only when she is loved by a member of the superior sex. To be loved by a woman would mean to be loved by someone as inferior as oneself. So women, though intensely in love with the female body image, recoil from women.

Perhaps the only women in the culture who do not despise themselves because they are women, are the active lesbians—at least those who don't imitate men—the many lesbians who look and act intensely feminine. They have wholly identified with the beauty ideal, so much so that they despise men because men are not women and because men really don't admire women, not the way they wish to be totally admired. They want to continue to live in the one-sexed world of infancy, in the cocoon of their mother's or their own unconditional love. Lesbians are merely more unadulterated narcissists than heterosexual women.

Because women are narcissists, they are also exhibitionists, whose exhibitionism, like their narcissism, is approved by the culture. The male exhibitionist who thrusts his penis at a female is put in jail, but the female who thrusts her bosom, behind, and legs at a male is admired. Female exhibitionism is socially approved because the culture wants to keep woman infantile, to keep her identity focused on her physical person, not on her accomplishments. The culture therefore compels a woman to show off her body, makes her feel unfeminine unless she does so, and makes the woman who accomplishes something feel unsexed. The accomplished woman feels unsexed because she has achieved identity the way a man is supposed to — indirectly, through the active use of his abilities. The male exhibitionist is put in jail, for trying to achieve his identity the way women and infants do, directly, by sheer physicality. He wants to prove his masculinity simply by exposing his penis; he does not want to have to prove it indirectly through accomplishments.

The normal man proves his physical maleness indirectly — compelling woman to expose herself as unlike him. The woman with the most exaggerated secondary sexual characteristics is considered the most beautiful because she makes a man feel more like a man, that is, unlike a woman. Men force women to constantly and blatantly expose themselves as women so that men can constantly assure themselves they are men. They need that reassurance, because their masculine identity is weak, because all men have an unconscious desire to be female, to return to the infancy in which they identified with mother, were not yet differentiated into boys. That is why man both desires and despises woman, why he both glorifies her as beautiful and regards her as a temptress, a *femme fatale*. Woman is beautiful to man, because she is the image of his rejected unconscious desire, a desire that he can allow himself to experience only indirectly, through a woman. In sex men unconsciously can take what they desire, become one with their lost female selves, much in the same way that primitive men ritually partake of their forbidden totem animal, their "ancestor" whose characteristics they wish to acquire. That is why men must "take," agressively, powerfully, dominantly, in order to keep unconscious the kind of power they envy—the effortless power of the woman, who, like the infant, is loved simply for her adorable self.

Young childlike women are preferred in this culture because they embody most clearly men's projected desires. "Pretty women always seem to appeal to us as more dependent and childlike," admitted William Dean Howells. Children are pretty and dependent, and man wants woman to remain a pretty, dependent child, so that through woman he can reunite himself with his lost childhood when he was still identified with woman and was allowed to be soft, tender, helpless, narcissistic, exhibitionistic, a cuddly, sweet-smelling naked bunny rather than a developed character and mind, a hard-working, responsible, assertive man.

The cult of beauty in women, which we smile at as though it were one of the culture's harmless follies, is, in fact, an insanity, for it is posited on a false view of reality. Women are not more beautiful than men. The obligation to be beautiful is an artificial burden, imposed by men on women, that keeps both sexes clinging to childhood, the woman forced to remain a charming, dependent child, the man driven by his unconscious desire to be—like an infant—loved and taken care of simply for his beautiful self. Woman's mask of beauty is the face of the child, a revelation of the tragic sexual immaturity of both sexes in our culture.

What is your reaction to this essay? I expect that it may have made you want to talk back to the writer, to question some of her assumptions, to ask for more proofs of her conclusions. I am always surprised when I reread it and notice the many perceptions and unexamined assumptions which are crowded into the second half of the essay. We will talk more specifically about some of those ideas and definitions when we talk about stipulative definition and when we discuss assumptions which organize our thinking and writing.

Writing task eighteen: Write two paragraphs which would update Stannard's description of the pursuit of beauty by women. Use the contexts of your home ' town, television and radio, and conversations with friends to provide proofs.

Suggested Group Writing and Discussing Activities

1. This essay was written more than ten years ago. Are the writer's generaliza- tions, about women believing that their identity lies in being or becoming beautiful and about men valuing women only for their beauty, valid today? List several contexts in which beauty would still be defined the way Stannard finds

it. Then define *male beauty* from as many contexts as you can discover.

2. How valid is Stannard's interpretation of man's behavior toward women? What psychological theories underpin her explanations of behavior? Discuss in a group.

3. Do you agree with the writer's assertion that most of the behavior in pursuit of beauty is the behavior of a child? Do you agree with her stipulation that this pursuit reveals the "tragic sexual immaturity of both sexes in our culture"? Discuss these ideas in a group and then analyze them further in an essay which talks back to the writer.

4. How would men who have attained sexual maturity act? How would women act? Does the writer suggest any alternatives? Have you seen any alternatives? List some alternative behaviors.

5. Select any paragraph from the section of the essay where Stannard analyzes the pursuit of beauty as tragic. Decide whether the writer has given sufficient explanation and illustrations of her interpretations. If you decide that you need more, rewrite the paragraph as you think Stannard would have written it. Then rewrite the paragraph by addressing it to an audience of young women who have just entered junior high.

6. Compare your contextual definitions of beauty with those of others in your discussion group. Are there any shared definitions which you might define as common to American culture? If so, write a short essay which uses contextual definition to arrange your proofs. In the final paragraphs of the essay, interpret the significance of the definitions of beauty you have given.

Lexical Definition

Lexical definition is a kind of contextual definition which describes the ways that one word has changed meaning, shape or function. If you wrote a lexical definition you would ask not only "How is *woman* defined?" but also "How has the word been defined? When did the word change meaning? What do these shifts in meaning tell me about the society which changed what the words meant?" A lexical definition records both the past and the current significant meanings for the word to be defined. You watched Muriel Schulz use lexical definition in the previous chapter when she described a history of changed meanings for the word *woman* and for its synonyms. If you were to write a lexical definition for the term, you would have an equation like this: In time$_1$, X = 'd Y; in time$_2$, X = 'd Y + Z; today, X = Y + Z + A.

Watch how you would use the paradigm of lexical defintion to define *nice*:

> *Nice* meant foolish, stupid and senseless when it was first used in the fourteenth and fifteenth centuries; by 1563 *nice* denoted wanton, loose-mannered and lascivious. In 1598 it denoted slothful, lazy, indulgent, and also

effeminate or unmanly. Eighteenth-century writers used *nice* to mean fastidious, refined, or difficult to please. Two meanings appear in the nineteenth century: punctilious, scrupulous, sensitive, or precise in matters of behavior and reputation; and difficult to decide on settlements. However, beginning in 1837 and continuing to the present, there are records of the word meaning delightful, giving pleasure or satisfaction, and pleasant. All the meanings today are "nice."

Does this give you a complete and accurate record for the word? Do you know of or use any other meanings for *nice?* Have you seen any in print? Have you heard any? A lexical definition cannot record all the meanings for a term because language changes so quickly. However, it offers us more meanings for a word than we might have known the word had. These definitions, like operational definitions, can be tested and verified. Written evidence like a poem by William Cowper shows us that *nice* did once mean fastidious. An early homily demonstrates that it meant foolish. You can check on the statements in this lexical definition by going to the original manuscripts or by using the OED. You can prove that the word has another meaning today by citing some piece of writing which uses the word in that contemporary way; a review in the *Rolling Stone* which uses the word to mean "not misbehaving" proves that some speakers of American English have yet another meaning for the word.

Writing task nineteen: Write as completely as possible the history of a word which you have seen change in your lifetime. Choose a meaning which holds not only personal connotations but also general connotations. In your concluding sentence, speculate about what the word change tells you about changes in your society. Some examples of changed words include *spaced, dope, gay, feedback, rolfing,* and *bad.*

Your desk dictionary might seem to offer lexical definitions; in fact, it only offers you the origin or etymology of the word and a stipulated contemporary meaning. To research the word completely, you must consult an unabridged dictionary or specialized dictionaries. The best tool to use would be the OED which lists entries for roughly half the words in our language. Other dictionaries, like Partridge's *A Dictionary of Slang and Uncommon Words* will give you additional entries. By researching how and when words changed, you can often spot changes in social attitudes and behaviors. Mutations of shape, function and meaning can help you understand the way cultures have adapted through language to new ideas, new environments, and new technologies.

There are several types of word change. Through *generalization,* a word's meaning is broadened. *Aisle* no longer describes only the passageway between church pews; *meal* means more than ground or milled grain; *ordeal* refers to more than a legal trial by physical tests like walking on hot coals. Through *specialization*, a word's meaning narrows. *Wretch* once described an exile; *deer* formerly meant any animal; *meat* and *liquor* described any food and any fluid.

Words change by shifting from the abstract to the *concrete*. *Complexion* originally meant temperament or disposition; *engine* once denoted native intelligence or ingenuity. Words also shift meanings from the concrete to the *abstract*. *Slapstick* was an instrument which made a loud noise when it simulated heavy blows in a farce; *libel* meant a published derogatory pamphlet.

Muriel Schulz showed a process of *pejoration*, of words being degraded in meaning. *Vulgar* came from a Latin word meaning common people; it was degraded to mean common and inferior and unacceptable. Through *amelioration*, meanings are elevated. *Praise* developed from *appraise* meaning to set a value on and became a word which means to value and to describe value highly. *Luxury* changed from lust to sumptuousness. *Fame* was originally any report and rumor but became a good report, celebrity and renown. An interesting word is the German *knabe* meaning young man. The word pejorated into *knave* and ameliorated into *knight*.

Social and moral judgments often make words change. You can see this in the examples we have been talking about. Another process of "amelioration" is a direct response to feelings some speakers might have that some words are or should be taboo. We substitute a less offensive word for the taboo term; this is *euphemism*. The word *die* never appears in Old English written literature. We substitute phrases like *go on a journey, pass away* and *gone to sleep*. The dead we describe as *deceased, dearly departed* and *loved ones*; Victorians called them *the silent majority*.

Victorians also called legs *limbs* so that they wouldn't offend by making an anatomical reference. We call the room that houses the toilet *restroom, lavatory, powder room,* and *comfort station*. Ironically, some of our attempts to mask reality by substituting less offensive terms lead to additional taboo terms in our language. All of the words which follow were originally nonoffensive; each was used as a euphemism for *body odor* (another euphemism) or an unpleasant olfactory sensation (euphemism often uses multi-syllabled words to hide the offense); *aroma, odor, perfume, scent, smell, stench, stink*. Which of these words do you think is the oldest? What word do you think was substituted as an euphemism for it until it in turn became taboo? You could use the OED to check for the earliest recorded date for each being used as an "acceptable" word then consult the OED to see when it became taboo.

Changes in point of view and major beliefs, in social values, and in technology appear in changed meanings. In *Keywords,* Raymond Williams writes a history of ideas by researching semantic mutations which mark large changes of political and social consciousness. He demonstrates that we can define "modern world" by looking at a series of words which either were not used before the nineteenth century or were not used in the ways they were used during the nineteenth century and are still used today. He cites these key words: alienation, bourgeois, capitalism, democracy, equality, family, genetic, history, ideology, labor, masses, nature, organic, positivists, radical, society, therapy, unemployment, violence, and work. If you were to write your own history of American culture for the last two decades, what words would you select to define as words which signal a major change in values and beliefs?

New ideas and new technologies bring new words into the language. How many words which you use daily are in fact words invented or changed in meaning after 1950? Often we make metaphors to define new realities and those words become accepted as words without our thinking of them as being metaphors originally. Research *skyjack* in the OED to find its origin in metaphor. Often we turn proper nouns like Xerox and Coke into common and generalized nouns. Research *bloomers, boycott, chauvinism, leotard, pasteurize, sideburns, tawdry* and *watt* in the OED to learn who originally carried those names.

You can write lexical definitions as a way of investigating the assumptions which shaped our thinking. You can use them to study the interconnections of language and culture. The paragraph which follows was written by one of the students in that same class that gave us all those definitions of woman. She researched two words which developed from the word *shrewd* and found a connection between the histories of the words and some persistent myths about women.

Women who have been called shrewish, step forward. Let your voices drum quietly, ceaselessly, on those men who stay out all night drinking and carousing, who take your hours of work in the home for granted, who eat your food without thanks or compliment, who fill you with babies and leave you with the responsibility of raising them, who work you into old age and demand that you be young, who push you and prod you to the point of anger and then call you "Shrew!"

Women were not always shrews. Not until the middle of the sixteenth century was the word shrew ascribed specifically to women. Originally, and as early as the mid-thirteenth century, any evil person, one who stole or was a trickster was considered a shrew. How easily the slipping has been, from shrewd-evil in the thirteenth century to shrewd-clever by the eighteenth century, a forked definition to the benefit of man.

The man, the trickster, now is considered clever, insightful and therefore admirable; he is shrewd. But the woman who is sharp with her mind and therefore her words is not admirable. She is a shrew. She has forgotten her place. She must be reconditioned, or she will be a weight the man does not deserve, an embarrassment he must suffer. I tell you, the word shrewd has come forward in time to be woman's punishment and man's reward. It is time for the next definition. —Sasha Tranquili

Do you still hear the word shrew applied only to women and the word shrewd applied mostly to men? The OED records this pattern of usage. Do you know other words which are applied only to one sex or the other? Check them in the OED to see when they became sex-typed.

Writing task twenty: In the *Oxford English Dictionary* investigate the semantic history for one or two of the terms listed. Summarize and report the significant changes for the word; cite the date or historical context for each change. If you can, identify the process of word change involved. Then speculate about why the word changed. What does this research help you understand about your own society and culture?

buxom	churl	genteel	siege	cunning	virtue
doom	henchman	magazine	guy	varlet	silly
moral	disparage	fret	diaper	harlot	family
humor	shimmy	coroner	talent	wife	enthusiasm
mistress	zealot	frank	strange	bonfire	phony

Lexical definitions are particularly helpful in examining how language works and in questioning how to best use words. You can use the lexical paradigm to organize many writings. Combine them with contextual definitions when you write essays which describe the origin and development of ideas, theories and behaviors. You could also use them to argue for linguistic or social change. Whether you say "It is time for the next definition" or stipulate a new use for an old word, you must first know the history and current meaning of the word.

In a letter to the editors of the New York *Times,* Barbara Lawrence argued that some obscenities were bound by their semantic histories to certain meanings—meanings which even changes in our attitudes toward sexuality have not altered. The letter was printed in *Redbook* with the title "Dirty Words Can Hurt You" and has been anthologized with the title "Four-Letter Words Can Hurt You." Notice how the writer has used lexical definition to prove her thesis that some words are obscene.

Four-Letter Words Can Hurt You

Barbara Lawrence

Why should any words be called obscene? Don't they all describe natural human functions? Am I trying to tell them, my students demand, that the "strong, earthy, gut-honest" —or, if they are fans of Norman Mailer, the "rich, liberating, existential" —language they use to describe sexual activity isn't preferable to "phony-sounding, middle-class words like 'intercourse' and 'copulate'?" "Cop You Late!" they say with fancy inflections and gagging grimaces. "Now, what is *that* supposed to mean?"

Well, what is it supposed to mean? And why indeed should one group of words describing human functions and human organs be acceptable in ordinary conversation and another, describing presumably the same organs and functions, be tabooed—so much so, in fact, that some of these words still cannot appear in print in many parts of the English-speaking world?

The argument that these taboos exist only because of "sexual hangups" (middle-class, middle-age, feminist), or even that they are a result of class oppression (the contempt of the Norman conquerors for the language of their Anglo-Saxon serfs), ignores a much more likely explanation, it seems to me, and that is the sources and functions of the words themselves.

The best known of the tabooed sexual verbs, for example, comes from the German *ficken,* meaning "to strike"; combined, according to Partridge's etymological dictionary *Origins,* with the Latin sexual verb *futuere;* associated in turn with the Latin *fustis,* "a staff or cudgel"; the Celtic *buc,* "a point, hence to pierce"; the Irish *bot,* "the male member"; the Latin *battuere,* "to beat"; the Gaelic *batair,* "a cudgeller"; the Early Irish *bualaim,* "I strike"; and so forth. It is one of what etymologists sometimes call "the sadistic group of words for the man's part in copulation."

The brutality of this word, then, and its equivalents ("screw," "bang," etc.), is not an illusion of the middle class or a crotchet of Women's Liberation. In their origins and imagery these words carry undeniably painful, if not sadistic, implications, the object of which is almost always female. Consider, for example, what a "screw" actually does to the wood it penetrates; what a painful, even mutilating, activity this kind of analogy suggests. "Screw" is particularly interesting in this context, since the noun, according to Partridge, comes from words meaning "groove," "nut," "ditch," "breeding sow," "scrofula" and "swelling," while the verb, besides its explicit imagery, has antecedent associations to "write on," "scratch," "scarify," and so forth —a revealing fusion of a mechanical or painful action with an obviously denigrated object.

Not all obscene words, of course, are as implicitly sadistic or denigrating to women as these, but all that I know seem to serve a similar purpose: to reduce the human organism (especially the female organism) and human functions (especially sexual and procreative) to their least organic, most mechanical dimension; to substitute a trivializing or deforming resemblance for the complex human reality of what is being described.

Tabooed male descriptives, when they are not openly denigrating to women, often serve to divorce a male organ or function from any significant interaction with the female. Take the words "testes," for example, suggesting "witnesses" (from the Latin *testis*) to the sexual and procreative strengths of the male organ; and the obscene counterpart of this word, which suggests little more than a mechanical shape. Or compare almost any of the "rich," "liberating" sexual verbs, so fashionable today among male writers, with that much-derided Latin word "copulate" ("to bind or join together") or even that anglo-Saxon phrase (which seems to have had no trouble surviving the Norman Conquest) "make love."

How arrogantly self-involved the tabooed words seem in comparison to either of the other terms, and how contemptuous of the female partner. Understandably so, of course, if she is only a "skirt," a "broad," a "chick," a "pussycat" or a "piece." If she is, in other words, no more than her skirt, or what her skirt conceals; no more than a breeder, or the broadest part of her; no more than a piece of a human being or a "piece of tail."

The most severely tabooed of all the female descriptives, incidentally, are those like a "piece of tail," which suggest (either explicitly or through antecedents) that there is no significant difference between the female channel through which we are all conceived and born and the anal outlet common to both sexes — a distinction that pornographers have always enjoyed obscuring.

This effort to deny women their biological identity, their individuality, their humanness, is such an important aspect of obscene language that one can only marvel at how seldom, in an era preoccupied with definitions of obscenity, this fact is brought to our attention. One problem, of course, is that many of the people in the best position to do this (critics, teachers, writers) are so reluctant today to admit that they are angered or shocked by obscenity. Bored, maybe, unimpressed, aesthetically displeased, but — no matter how brutal or denigrating the material — never angered, never shocked.

Any yet how eloquently angered, how piously shocked many of these same people become if denigrating language is used about any minority group other than women; if the obscenities are racial or ethnic, that is, rather than sexual. Words like "coon," "kike," "spic," "wop," after all, deform identity, deny individuality and humanness in almost exactly the same way that sexual vulgarisms and obscenities do.

No one that I know, least of all my students, would fail to question the values of a society whose literature and entertainment rested heavily on racial or ethnic pejoratives. Are the values of a society whose literature and entertainment rest as heavily as ours on sexual pejoratives any less questionable?

Writing task twenty-one: Use lexical definition to argue some issue which you feel strongly about. Write a letter that you could send to a newspaper or a congressperson or some relative whom you want to persuade to understand the issue the way that you do. You could model your own argument on the pattern provided by Lawrence.

Stipulative Definition

When you decide that "it's time for a new definition," you can write stipulative definitions and legislate what the word must mean. Lexical definitions describe the past life of words; stipulative definitions shape a future biography. Many of those definitions for *woman* which begin this chapter are stipulative definitions. They define woman in ways that may not have been used in the past but which may be the most important ways to use in the future. When you stipulate, you invent for your readers a new pattern of naming to replace the old convention. For example, the people who hear *black power*—a stipulative definition made in the 1960s—are to make the equations "black equals beautiful...proud...dignified...active ...assertive." Listeners should forget any previous negative connotations they might have held or heard for *black*.

You can stipulate definitions in several ways. You could choose from among the catch of current and past meanings the one meaning that you want to make the meaning people should use. If I wanted to use *science* to mean more than only the natural science we so often assume it to be, I would dust off the original definition of science as knowledge and carefully explain that both the sciences and the humanities pursue *science*.

You could also assign a new meaning to an old word. When you do this, you will be two steps ahead of other writers if you have already used lexical definition to survey all the possible meanings that could compete with your new meaning. When Humpty Dumpty stipulated that glory meant "a nice knockdown argument," Alice demurred because she knew other, more conventional, meanings. Humpty Dumpty bullied Alice into accepting *his* stipulation. As a writer, you will have to work harder than he did to persuade others to use your definitions and to erase others from their memory banks. How successful was Adrienne Rich in stipulating that "writing is re-vision"? How many words did Una Stannard stipulate definitions for in her essay? Did she persuade you to use her definitions?

When you stipulate new meanings for old words, you question conventions of meaning and you can expect some anger from people who are comfortable with words as they are. You might find it easier to stipulate new meanings for infrequently used words than for those we use often. You might even find it easier to invent new words. However you decide to write stipulative definitions, you need to persuade your readers that it is in their interest too that they accept your definitions. Your new meanings should be novel enough or significant enough that they easily replace old meanings.

For example, how do you define *chauvinism?* If you researched this word in the OED, you learned that the meaning of excessive or blind patriotism came about when Nicolas Chauvin, a common French soldier, spent all his time praising his general Napoleon. During the 1960s a new meaning was stipulated. If your definition of the term specifies excessive and unthinking behavior which asserts the superiority of one sex over another, then you have already been persuaded to accept and use a stipulative definition. When the women's liberation movement (notice that this phrase constitutes a stipulative definition) stipulated a new meaning for an old term, it wanted the word to always signify oppressive behavior by one sex against another.

What about *pig?* How do you define it? During the political unrest of 1968, a group who called themselves Yippies (another stipulative definition) provoked Chicago police by calling them pigs and sending squealing animals out to meet the police who approached them. In their press releases, the Yippies stipulated that *pig* meant police and that all the connotations of stench, laziness, meanness and ugliness were intended. They had borrowed this insult from other angry people who perceived police forces as repressive. The Yippies stipulated that from 1968 on *pig* meant police.

In response, several police groups stipulated that in fact police *are* pigs but that *pig* was an acronym for "pride, integrity and guts." They pointed out that pigs are among the most intelligent animals. They put up billboards and paid for summer league baseball uniforms which stipulated that police were proud to be pigs: pride, integrity, guts, and service. These stipulations were to counterbalance those of the Yippies. Who won? Why?

Writing task twenty-two: Select three terms from those listed below and stipulate a definition for each. Then stipulate for each a meaning that would be accepted by a group which distrusts the idea of "women's liberation." Now stipulate a meaning that would be accepted by a group which stipulates that women's liberation is the major revolution of the twentieth century. You will have three sentences or paragraphs for each term.

reproductive freedom	patriarchy	androgyny	affirmative action
fascinating womanhood	children's rights	sexism	consciousness raising
parenting	contract marriage	mothering	lesbianism

When you write a stipulative definition, you assume that a term is ambiguous until you assign one certain meaning for it. The preceding assignment included many terms which are ambiguous and could provoke disagreement until they are carefully stipulated. Once you have stipulated a definition, your reader is free to agree, to disagree, to accept your definition, to reject it or to adapt it to their own needs. Because key terms have now been defined, the communication process can continue.

Propagandists know that stipulative definition is effective in persuading people to think in certain ways. You can easily spot stipulative definitions in campaign statements, on bumper stickers and billboards, and in radio and TV ads.

Stipulative definition is such a useful tool for molding public opinion that it has been used to heinous effect. At the site of the concentration camp near Dachau in Germany, the government has organized an exhibit of the propaganda which stipulated that some people — whether Jewish tailors or Polish students or German Lutheran ministers — were not to be defined as humans deserving basic rights of decency, freedom, and life. Street posters, newspapers, children's primers, and adult fiction are riddled with stipulative definitions which encouraged prejudice. Definitions of Jews as traitors, swine, exploiters of the working poor, child-murderers, and devils were devised which made the Jews the scapegoats for all the anger, disillusionment and despair experienced by the Germans during the twentieth century up through the collapse of the Weimar republic.

In *Mein Kampf* Adolf Hitler had defined the German state as a group of people united not by geography nor a common language nor a shared legal tradition but by "blood." He stipulated that the pure blood of the "Aryan race" was superior to that of "the subjected people" or "mongrels." His definitions, although irrational and without basis in fact, were accepted by a large audience. That audience accepted a stipulative definition which described with the abstract terms "final solution" the torture and murder of six million people. Thus racist stipulations by a demagogue led to genocide.

Stipulative definition, then, can be used skillfully in any thinking and writing. You can use it to organize essays in which you argue some new idea or research papers in which you suggest some new interpretation of data. When Marcia Seligson decided to write a book about the American wedding, she used stipulative definition to introduce her theory that the

American wedding is primarily an economic event. Watch her introduce stipulative definitions for *marriage:*

> Every culture, in every time throughout history, has commemorated the transition of a human being from one state in life to another. Birth, the emergence into manhood, graduation from school at various levels, birthdays, marriage, death—each of these outstanding steps is acknowledged by a ceremony of some sort, always public, the guests in effect becoming witnesses to the statement of life's ongoingness, of the natural order of history. To insure the special significance of the rite of passage, its apartness from any other event of the day, these rituals usually require pageantry, costumed adornment, and are accompanied by gift-bearing and feasting. We wear black to funerals, bring presents to christenings and birthday parties, get loaded at wakes, eat ourselves sick at bar mitzvahs. Birth, marriage and death, to be sure, are the most elemental and major steps, and as there is only one of those ritual commemorations for which we are *actually,* fully present, the wedding becomes, for mankind, its most vital rite of passage. And for this reason it is anchored at the very core of civilization.
>
> For the rites of passage the ceremony itself is organic to the society for which the individual is being groomed, in his journey from one state to the next. In African hunting societies, for example, a boy at puberty is thrown naked into the jungle and required to kill a lion. His value as a man will be judged by how successful he can be in meeting the demands of his culture. In America, newlyweds are being prepared for their roles in a consumer society, so it is surely appropriate that all of the dynamics of wedding hoo-hah testify to these commercial, mercantile terms. Gifts are purchased not only by the "witnesses' but by bride for groom, groom for bride, bride for attendants, attendants for bride. Prenuptial parties, bachelor dinners, showers. The ever-mushrooming splash and flash circusness of the wedding itself. The American wedding is a ritual event of ferocious, gluttonous consuming, a debauch of intensified buying, never again to be repeated in the life of an American couple.

Writing task twenty-three:
Describe some rite of passage you have experienced and use stipulative definition to define what the event meant to you.

One of the quickest ways of seeing an assumption which influences our behavior is to redefine that belief through stipulative definition. The assumption that "men think, women feel" could be changed by new definitions for all the terms of the statement. What would be stipulations for *think* and *feel* which would show that the behaviors are not independent of each other?

You may have noticed that when a group defines itself as new—NOW or Common Cause or La Raza or the Moral Majority or the Grey Panthers—it invents a glossary of stipulative definitions to describe unequivocably the new ways the group will see their world and the new ways it expects to be described. For example, *Chicano* is a stipulative definition for Spanish-American which like *black* or *Afro-American* now means a person proud of his or her origin, strong in identity, and active in a community.

As a writer, you will find stipulative definition helpful when you are asked to write a position paper or a statement of your beliefs and values. This kind of definition can be easily blended with other definitions. An extended stipulative definition could organize any writing in which you are asked not to equivocate.

Writing task twenty-four: Take one of the stipulative definitions which you wrote and develop it into an essay in which you state and explain your beliefs. During the stage of prewriting, take five minutes to brainstorm words and phrases which will extend your stipulative statement. Decide on what audience you want to address and organize your statements so they will make your beliefs clear.

Writing task twenty-five: Adrienne Rich stated that "the word *love* is itself in need of re-vision." In a short essay, stipulate a new definition for the word love which would resolve the conflict Rich described between love and work.

Of course, there are many more ways to define than we have practiced in this chapter. However, if you can use these paradigms skillfully, you will be able to combine them with other definitions to provide your readers with definitions that say more than Webster's says. Because writing is a process of defining the self, you will find that you often use these definitions in your writing for this class, in your journal, for other classes, on the job, in extracurricular activities, and on other occasions when you feel impelled to or are requested to write.

In the essay which follows, Tillie Olsen defines a silence which she stipulates as unnatural. It is the silence which keeps writers from being creative. She describes and analyzes forces which are the "unnatural thwarting of what struggles to come into being, but cannot." She examines the silences in literary history and the silence in her life. Olsen began a novel in the 1930s which she could not finish because work, family, and personal conflicts interrupted the creative process. In the 1970s she found the manuscript which she thought had been lost during family moves. She worked from drafts to shape what might have been the final draft but could not complete the novel because the naming had been interrupted and she no longer knew how it should be completed. She published *Yonnondio* as a demonstration of the personal and social losses which result when the writing dies within the writer.

Tillie Olsen also published a volume of short stories titled *Tell Me a Riddle*. In the following essay she describes how she felt when she was able again — with time and support — to write what quickened in her. Remember Adrienne Rich referring to the women whose "gifts were buried or aborted"? Tillie Olsen is an example of such a woman.

This essay was first written in the 1960s for a magazine. In 1978, Olsen published *Silences*, a book which includes the essay here, an essay on the same topic written after some fifteen years and some other writings. In the footnotes to this essay and in some changes which she made to the essay, Tillie Olsen has amplified her thesis. She has also shown her readers how an idea takes shape and becomes translated into writing and how, after the essay is finished, a writer might go back and reperceive and revise.

When you read the essay, you will notice that Tillie Olsen understands the sadness of people being unnaturally silenced. Watch how she used definitions to organize her inquiry into what creativity needs in order to function fully. What are the several characteristics of *silences* which Olsen stipulates? How are these silences unlike other silences in literature? in writing?

Silences in Literature

Tillie Olsen

Literary history and the present are dark with silences: some the silences for years by our acknowledged great; some silences hidden; some the ceasing to publish after one work appears; some the never coming to book form at all.

What is it that happens with the creator, to the creative process, in that time? What *are* creation's needs for full functioning? Without intention of or pretension to literary scholarship, I have had special need to learn all I could of this over the years, myself so nearly remaining mute and having to let writing die over and over again in me.

These are not *natural* silences—what Keats called *agonie ennuyeuse* (the tedious agony)—that necessary time for renewal, lying fallow, gestation, in the natural cycle of creation. The silences I speak of here are unnatural: the unnatural thwarting of what struggles to come into being, but cannot. In the old, the obvious parallels: when the seed strikes stone; the soil will not sustain; the spring is false; the time is drought or blight or infestation; the frost comes premature.

The great in achievement have known such silences — Thomas Hardy, Melville, Rimbaud, Gerard Manley Hopkins. They tell us little as to why or how the creative working atrophied and died in them — if ever it did.

"Less and less shrink the visions then vast in me," writes Thomas Hardy in his thirty-year ceasing from novels after the Victorian vileness to his *Jude the Obscure*. ("So ended his prose contributions to literature, his experiences having killed all his interest in this form"—the official explanation.) But the great poetry he wrote to the end of his life was not sufficient to hold, to develop the vast visions which for twenty-five years had had expression in novel after novel. People, situations, interrelationships, landscape—they cry for this larger life in poem after poem.

It was not visions shrinking with Hopkins, but a different torment. For seven years he kept his religious vow to refrain from writing poetry, but the poet's eye he could not shut, nor win "elected silence to beat upon [his] whorled ear." "I had long had haunting my ear the echo of a poem which now I realised on paper," he writes of the first poem permitted to end the seven years' silence. But poetry ("to hoard unheard; be heard, unheeded") could be only the least and last of his heavy priestly responsibilities. Nineteen poems were all he could produce in his last nine years—fullness to us, but torment pitched past grief to him, who felt himself "time's eunuch, never to beget."

Silence surrounds Rimbaud's silence. Was there torment of the unwritten; haunting of rhythm, of visions; anguish at dying powers, the seventeen years after he abandoned the unendurable literary world? We know only that the need to write continued into his first years of vagabondage; that he wrote:

Had I not once a youth pleasant, heroic, fabulous enough to write on leaves of gold: too much luck. Through what crime, what error, have I earned my present weakness? You who maintain that some animals sob sorrowfully, that the dead have dreams, try to tell the story of my downfall and my slumber. I no longer know how to speak.[1]

That on his deathbed, he spoke again like a poet-visionary.

Melville's stages to his thirty-year prose silence are clearest. The presage is in his famous letter to Hawthorne, as he had to hurry *Moby Dick* to an end:

I am so pulled hither and thither by circumstances. The calm, the coolness, the silent grass-growing mood in which a man ought always to compose,—that, I fear, can seldom be mine. Dollars damn me.... What I feel most moved to write, that is banned,—it will not pay. Yet, altogether, write the *other* way I cannot. So the product is a final hash...

Reiterated in *Pierre*, writing "that book whose unfathomable cravings drink his blood... when at last the idea obtruded that the wiser and profounder he should grow, the more and the more he lessened his chances for bread."

To be possessed; to have to try final hash; to have one's work met by "drear ignoring"; to be damned by dollars into a Customs House job; to have only weary evenings and Sundays left for writing—

> How bitterly did unreplying Pierre feel in his heart that to most of the great works of humanity, their authors had given not weeks and months, not years and years, but their wholly surrendered and dedicated lives.

Is it not understandable why Melville began to burn work, then ceased to write it, "immolating [it] ... sealing in a fate subdued"? And turned to occasional poetry, manageable in a time sense, "to nurse through night the ethereal spark." A thirty-year night. He was nearly seventy before he could quit the customs dock and again have full time for writing, start back to prose. "Age, dull tranquilizer," and devastation of "arid years that filed before" to work through. Three years of tryings before he felt capable of beginning *Billy Budd* (the kernel waiting half a century); three years more to his last days (he who had been so fluent), the slow, painful, never satisfied writing and re-writing of it.[2]

Kin to these years-long silences are the *hidden* silences; work aborted, deferred, denied—hidden by the work which does come to fruition. Hopkins rightfully belongs here; almost certainly William Blake; Jane Austen, Olive Schreiner, Theodore Dreiser, Willa Cather, Franz Kafka; Katherine Anne Porter, many other contemporary writers.

Censorship silences. Deletions, omissions, abandonment of the medium (as with Hardy); paralyzing of capacity (as Dreiser's ten-year stasis on *Jennie Gerhardt* after the storm against *Sister Carrie*). Publishers' censorship, refusing subject matter or treatment as "not suitable" or "no market for." Self-censorship. Religious, political censorship—sometimes spurring inventiveness—most often (read Dostoyevsky's letters) a wearing attrition.

The extreme of this: those writers physically silenced by governments. Isaac Babel, the years of imprisonment, what took place in him with what wanted to be written? Or in Oscar Wilde, who was not permitted even a pencil until the last months of his imprisonment?

Other silences. The truly memorable poem, story, or book, then the writer ceasing to be published.[3] Was one work all the writers had in them (life too thin for pressure of material, renewal) and the respect for literature too great to repeat themselves? Was it "the knife of the perfectionist attitude in art and life" at their throat? Were the conditions not present for establishing the habits of creativity (a young Colette who lacked a Willy to lock her in her room each day)? or — as instanced over and over — other claims, other responsibilities so writing could not be first? (The writer of a class, sex, color still marginal in literature, and whose coming to written voice at all against complex odds is exhausting achievement.) It is an eloquent commentary that this one-book silence has been true of most black writers; only eleven in the hundred years since 1850 have published novels more than twice.[4]

There is a prevalent silence I pass by quickly, the absence of creativity where it once had been; the ceasing to create literature, though the books may keep coming out year after year. That suicide of the creative process Hemingway describes so accurately in "The Snows of Kilimanjaro":

> He had destroyed his talent himself—by not using it, by betrayals of himself and what he believed in, by drinking so much that he blunted the edge of his perceptions, by laziness, by sloth, by snobbery, by hook and by crook; selling vitality, trading it for security, for comfort.

No, not Scott Fitzgerald. His not a death of creativity, not silence, but what happens when (his words) there is "the sacrifice of talent, in pieces, to preserve its essential value."

Almost unnoted are the foreground silences, *before* the achievement. (Remember when Emerson hailed Whitman's genius, he guessed correctly: "which yet must have had a long *foreground* for such a start.") George Eliot, Joseph Conrad, Isak Dinesen, Sherwood Anderson, Dorothy Richardson, Elizabeth Madox Roberts, A. E. Coppard, Angus Wilson, Joyce Cary — all close to, or in their forties before they became published writers; Lampedusa, Maria Dermout *(The Ten Thousand Things)*, Laura Ingalls Wilder, the "children's writer," in their sixties.[5] Their capacities evident early in the "being one on whom nothing is lost"; in other writers' qualities. Not all struggling and anguished, like Anderson, the foreground years; some needing the immobilization of long illness or loss, or the sudden lifting of responsibility to make writing necessary, make writing possible; others waiting circumstances and encouragement (George Eliot, her Henry Lewes; Laura Wilder, a writer-daughter's insistence that she transmute her storytelling gift onto paper).

Very close to this last grouping are the silences where the lives never came to writing. Among these, the mute inglorious Miltons: those whose waking hours are all struggle for existence; the barely educated; the illiterate; women. Their silence the silence of centuries as to how life was, is, for most of humanity. Traces of their making, of course, in folk song, lullaby, tales, language itself, jokes, maxims, superstitions—but we know nothing of the creators or how it was with them. In the fantasy of Shakespeare born in deepest Africa (as at least one Shakespeare must have been), was the ritual, the oral storytelling a fulfillment? Or was there restlessness, indefinable yearning, a sense of restriction? Was it, Virginia Woolf in *A Room of One's Own* guesses—about women?

> Genius of a sort must have existed among then, as it existed among the working classes,[6] but certainly it never got itself onto paper. When, however, one reads of a woman possessed by the devils, of a wise woman selling herbs, or even a remarkable man who had a remarkable mother, then I think we are on the track of a lost novelist, a suppressed poet, or some Emily Brontë who dashed her brains out on the moor, crazed with the torture her gift had put her to.

Rebecca Harding Davis whose work sleeps in the forgotten (herself as a woman of a century ago so close to remaining mute), also guessed about the silent in that time of the twelve-hour-a-day, six-day work week. She writes of the illiterate ironworker in *Life in the Iron Mills* who sculptured great shapes in the slag: "his fierce thirst for beauty, to know it, to create it, to *be* something other than he is—a passion of pain"; Margret Howth in the textile mill:

> There were things in the world, that like herself, were marred, did not understand, were hungry to know. . . . Her eyes quicker to see than ours, delicate or grand lines in the homeliest things. . . . Everything she saw or touched, nearer, more human than to you or me. These sights and sounds did not come to her common; she never got used to living as other people do.

She never got used to living as other people do. Was that one of the ways it was?

So some of the silences, incomplete listing of the incomplete, where the need and capacity to create were of a high order.

Now, what *is* the work of creation and the circumstances it demands for full functioning—as told in the journals, letters, notes, of the practitioners themselves: Henry James, Katherine Mansfield, André Gide, Virginia Woolf; the letters of Flaubert, Rilke, Joseph Conrad; Thomas Wolfe's *Story of a Novel*, Valéry's *Course in Poetics*. What do they explain of the silences?

"Constant toil is the law of art, as it is of life," says (and demonstrated) Balzac:

> To pass from conception to execution, to produce, to bring the idea to birth, to raise the child laboriously from infancy, to put it nightly to sleep surfeited, to kiss it in the mornings with the hungry heart of a mother, to clean it, to clothe it fifty times over in new garments which it tears and casts away, and yet not revolt against the trials of this agitated life—this unwearying maternal love, this habit of creation—this is execution and its toils.

"Without duties, almost without external communication," Rilke specifies, "unconfined solitude which takes every day like a life, a spaciousness which puts no limit to vision and in the midst of which infinities surround."

Unconfined solitude as Joseph Conrad experienced it:

> For twenty months I wrestled with the Lord for my creation. . . mind and will and conscience engaged to the full, hour after hour, day after day. . . a lonely struggle in a great isolation from the world. I suppose I slept and ate the food put before me and talked connectedly on suitable occasions, but I was never aware of the even flow of daily life, made easy and noiseless for me by a silent, watchful, tireless affection.

So there is a homely underpinning for it all, the even flow of daily life made easy and noiseless.

"The terrible law of the artist"—says Henry James—"the law of fructification, of fertilization. The old, old lesson of the art of meditation. To woo combinations and inspirations into being by a depth and continuity of attention and meditation."

"That load, that weight, that gnawing conscience," writes Thomas Mann—

That sea which to drink up, that frightful task ... the will, the discipline and self-control to shape a sentence or follow out a hard train of thought. From the first rhythmical urge of the inward creative force towards the material, towards casting in shape and form, from that to the thought, the image, the word, the line, what a struggle, what Gethsemane.

Does it become very clear what Melville's Pierre so bitterly remarked on, and what literary history bears out—why most of the great works of humanity have come from lives (able to be) wholly surrendered and dedicated? How else sustain the constant toil, the frightful task, the terrible law, the continuity? Full self: this means full time as and when needed for the work. (That time for which Emily Dickinson withdrew from the world.)

But what if there is not that fullness of time, let alone totality of self? What if the writers, as in some of these silences, must work regularly at something besides their own work—as do nearly all in the arts in the United States today.

I know the theory (kin to "starving in the garret makes great art") that it is this very circumstance which feeds creativity. I know, too, that for the beginning young, for some who have such need, the job can be valuable access to life they would not otherwise know. A few (I think of the doctors, the incomparables: Chekhov and William Carlos Williams) for special reasons sometimes manage both. But the actuality testifies: substantial creative work demands time, and with rare exceptions only full-time workers have achieved it. Where the claims of creation cannot be primary, the results are atrophy; unfinished work; minor effort and accomplishment; silences. (Desperation which accounts for the mountains of applications to the foundations for grants—undivided time—in the strange bread-line system we have worked out for our artists.)

Twenty years went by on the writing of *Ship of Fools*, while Katherine Anne Porter, who needed only two, was "trying to get to that table, to that typewriter, away from my jobs of teaching and trooping this country and of keeping house." "Your subconscious needed that time to grow the layers of pearl," she was told. Perhaps, perhaps, but I doubt it. Subterranean forces can make you wait, but they are very finicky about the kind of waiting it has to be. Before they will feed the creator back, they must be fed, passionately fed, what needs to be worked on. "We hold up our desire as one places a magnet over a composite dust from which the particle of iron will suddenly jump up," says Paul Valéry. A receptive waiting, that means, not demands which prevent "an undistracted center of being." And when the response comes, availability to work must be immediate. If not used at once, all may vanish as a dream; worse, future creation be endangered — for only the removal and development of the material frees the forces for further work.

There is a life in which all this is documented: Franz Kafka's. For every one entry from his diaries here, there are fifty others that testify as unbearably to the driven stratagems for time, the work lost (to us), the damage to the creative powers (and the body) of having to deny, interrupt, postpone, put aside, let work die.

"I cannot devote myself completely to my writing," Kafka explains (in 1911). "I could not live by literature if only, to begin with, because of the slow maturing of my work and its special character." So he worked as an official in a state insurance agency, and wrote when he could.

These two can never be reconciled.... If I have written something one evening, I am afire the next day in the office and can bring nothing to completion. Outwardly I fulfill my office duties satisfactorily, not my inner duties however, and every fulfilled inner duty becomes a misfortune that never leaves. What strength it will necessarily drain me of.

1911

No matter how little the time or how badly I write, I feel approaching the imminent possibility of great moments which could make me capable of anything. But my being does not have sufficient strength to hold this to the next writing time. During the day the visible world helps me; during the night it cuts me to pieces unhindered.... In the evening and in the morning, my consciousness of the creative abilities in me then I can encompass. I feel shaken to the core of my being. Calling forth such powers which are then not permitted to function.

...which are then not permitted to function...

1911

I finish nothing, because I have no time, and it presses so within me.

1912

When I begin to write after such a long interval, I draw the words as if out of the empty air. If I capture one, then I have just this one alone, and all the toil must begin anew.

1914

Yesterday for the first time in months, an indisputable ability to do good work. And yet wrote only the first page. Again I realize that everything written down bit by bit rather than all at once in the course of the larger part is inferior, and that the circumstances of my life condemn me to this inferiority.

1915

My constant attempt by sleeping before dinner to make it possible to continue working [writing] late into the night, senseless. Then at one o'clock can no longer fall asleep at all, the next day at work insupportable, and so I destroy myself.

1917

Distractedness, weak memory, stupidity. Days passed in futility, powers wasted away in waiting. ... Always this one principal anguish—if I had gone away in 1911 in full possession of all my powers. Not eaten by the strain of keeping down living forces.

Eaten into tuberculosis. By the time he won through to himself and time for writing, his body could live no more. He was forty-one.

I think of Rilke who said, "If I have any responsibility, I mean and desire it to be responsibility for the deepest and innermost essence of the loved reality [writing] to which I am inseparably bound"; and who also said, "Anything alive that makes demands, arouses in me an infinite capacity to give it its due, the consequences of which completely use me up." These were true with Kafka, too, yet how different their lives. When Rilke wrote that about responsibility, he is explaining why he will not take a job to support his wife and baby, nor live with them (years later will not come to his daughter's wedding nor permit a two-hour honeymoon visit lest it break his solitude where he awaits poetry). The "infinite capacity" is his explanation as to why he cannot even bear to have a dog. Extreme—and justified. He protected his creative powers.

Kafka's, Rilke's "infinite capacity," and all else that has been said here of the needs of creation, illuminate women's silence of centuries. I will not repeat what is in Virginia Woolf's A Room of One's Own, but talk of this last century and a half in which women have begun to have voice in literature. (It has been less than that time in Eastern Europe, and not yet, in many parts of the world.)

In the last century, of the women whose achievements endure for us in one way or another,[7] nearly all never married. (Jane Austen, Emily Brontë, Christina Rossetti, Emily Dickinson, Louisa May Alcott, Sarah Orne Jewett) or married late in their thirties (George Eliot, Elizabeth Barrett Browning, Charlotte Brontë, Olive Schreiner). I can think of only four (George Sand, Harriet Beecher Stowe, Helen Hunt Jackson, and Elizabeth Gaskell) who married and had children as young women.[8] All had servants.

In our century, until very recently, it has not been so different. Most did not marry (Selma Lagerlof, Willa Cather, Ellen Glasgow, Gertrude Stein, Gabriela Mistral, Elizabeth Madox Roberts, Charlotte Mew, Eudora Welty, Marianne Moore) or, if married, have been childless (Edith Wharton, Virginia Woolf, Katherine Mansfield, Dorothy Richardson, H. H. Richardson, Elizabeth Bowen, Isak Dinesen, Katherine Anne Porter, Lillian Hellman, Dorothy Parker). Colette had one child (when she was forty). If I include Sigrid Undset, Kay Boyle, Pearl Buck, Dorothy Canfield Fisher, that will make a small group who had more than one child. All had household help or other special circumstances.

Am I resaying the moldy theory that women have no need, some say no capacity, to create art, because they can "create" babies? And the additional proof is precisely that the few women who created it are nearly all childless? No.

The power and the need to create, over and beyond reproduction, is native in both women and men. Where the gifted among women *(and men)* have remained mute, or have never attained full capacity, it is because of circumstances, inner or outer, which oppose the needs of creation.

Wholly surrendered and dedicated lives; time as needed for the work; totality of self. But women are traditionally trained to place others' needs first, to feel these needs as their own (the "infinite capacity"); their sphere, their satisfaction to be in making it possible for others to use their abilities. This is what Virginia Woolf meant when, already a writer of achievement, she wrote in her diary:

> Father's birthday. He would have been 96, 96, yes, today; and could have been 96, like other people one has known; but mercifully was not. His life would have entirely ended mine. What would have happened? No writing, no books; — inconceivable.

It took family deaths to free more than one woman writer into her own development.[9] Emily Dickinson freed herself, denying all the duties expected of a woman of her social position except the closet family ones, and she was fortunate to have a sister, and servants, to share those. How much is revealed of the differing circumstances and fate of their own as-great capacities, in the diaries (and lives) of those female bloodkin of great writers: Dorothy Wordsworth, Alice James, Aunt Mary Moody Emerson.

And where there is no servant or relation to assume the responsibilities of daily living? Listen to Katherine Mansfield in the early days of her relationship with John Middleton Murry, when they both dreamed of becoming great writers:[10]

> The house seems to take up so much time. . . . I mean when I have to clean up twice over or wash up extra unnecessary things, I get frightfully impatient and want to be working [writing]. So often this week you and Gordon have been talking while I washed dishes. Well someone's got to wash dishes and get food. Otherwise "there's nothing in the house but eggs to eat." And after you have gone I walk about with a mind full of ghosts of saucepans and primus stoves and "will there be enough to go around?" And you calling, whatever I am doing, writing, "Tig, isn't there going to be tea? It's five o'clock."
> I loathe myself today. This woman who superintends you and rushes about slamming doors and slopping water and shouts "You might at least empty the pail and wash out the tea leaves." . . . O Jack, I wish that you would take me in your arms and kiss my hands and my face and every bit of me and say, "It's all right, you darling thing, I understand."

A long way from Conrad's favorable circumstances for creation: the flow of daily life made easy and noiseless.

And, if in addition to the infinite capacity, to the daily responsibilities, there are children?

Balzac, you remember, described creation in terms of motherhood. Yes, in intelligent passionate motherhood there are similarities, and in more than the toil and patience. The calling upon total capacities; the reliving and new using of the past; the comprehensions; the fascination, absorption, intensity. All almost certain death to creation —(so far).

Not because the capacities to create no longer exist, or the need (though for a while, as in any fullness of life, the need may be obscured), but because the circumstances for sustained creation have been almost impossible. The need cannot be first. It can have at best, only part self, part time. (Unless someone else does the nuturing. Read Dorothy Fisher's "Babushka Farnham" in *Fables for Parents*.) More than in any other human relationship, overwhelmingly more, motherhood means being instantly interruptable, responsive, responsible. Children need one *now* (and remember, in our society, the family must often try to be the center for love and health the outside world is not). The very fact that these are real needs, that one feels them as one's own (love, not duty); *that there is no one else responsible for these needs*, gives them primacy. It is distraction, not meditation, that becomes habitual; interruption, not continuity; spasmodic, not constant toil. The rest has been said here. Work interrupted, deferred, relinquished, makes blockage — at best, lesser accomplishment. Unused capacities atrophy, cease to be.

When H. H. Richardson, who wrote the Australian classic *Ultima Thule*, was asked why she—whose children, like all her people, were so profoundly written—did not herself have children, she answered: "There are enough women to do the childbearing and childrearing. I know of none who can write my books." I remember thinking rebelliously, yes, and I know of none who can bear and rear my children either. But literary history is on her side. Almost no mothers—as almost no part-time, part-self persons—have created enduring literature ... so far.

If I talk now quickly of my own silences—almost presumptuous after what has been told here—it is that the individual experience may add.

In the twenty years I bore and reared my children, usually had to work on a paid job as well, the simplest circumstances for creation did not exist. Nevertheless writing, the hope of it, was "the air I breathed, so long as I shall breathe at all." In that hope, there was conscious storing, snatched reading, beginnings of writing, and always "the secret rootlets of reconnaissance."

When the youngest of our four was in school, the beginnings struggled toward endings. This was a time, in Kafka's words, "like a squirrel in a cage: bliss of movement, desperation about constriction, craziness of endurance."

Bliss of movement. A full extended family life; the world of my job (transcriber in a dairy-equipment company); and the writing, which I was somehow able to carry around within me through work, through home. Time on the bus, even when I had to stand, was enough; the stolen moments at work, enough; the deep night hours for as long as I could stay awake, after the kids were in bed, after the household tasks were done, sometimes during. It is no accident that the first work I considered publishable began: "I stand here ironing, and what you asked me moves tormented back and forth with the iron."

In such snatches of time I wrote what I did in those years, but there came a time when this triple life was no longer possible. The fifteen hours of daily realities became too much distraction for the writing. I lost craziness of endurance. What might have been, I don't know: but I applied for, and was given, eight months' writing time. There was still full family life, all the household responsibilities, but I did not have to hold an eight-hour job. I had continuity, three full days, sometimes more—and it was in those months I made the mysterious turn and became a writing writer.

Then had to return to the world of work, someone else's work, nine hours, five days a week.

This was the time of festering and congestion. For a few months I was able to shield the writing with which I was so full, against the demands of jobs on which I had to be competent, through the joys and responsibilities and trials of family. For a few months. Always roused by the writing, always denied. "I could not go to write it down. It convulsed and died in me. I will pay."

My work died. What demanded to be written, did not. It seethed, bubbled, clamored, peopled me. At last moved into the hours meant for sleeping. I worked now full time on temporary jobs, a Kelly, a Western Agency girl (girl!), wandering from office to office, always hoping to manage two, three writing months ahead. Eventually there was time.

I had said: always roused by the writing, always denied. Now, like a woman made frigid, I had to learn response, to trust this possibility for fruition that had not been before. Any interruption dazed and silenced me. It took a long while of surrendering to what I was trying to write, of invoking Henry James's "passion, piety, patience," before I was able to re-establish work.

When again I had to leave the writing, I lost consciousness. A time of anesthesia. There was still an automatic noting that did not stop, but it was as if writing had never been. No fever, no congestion, no festering. I ceased being peopled, slept well and dreamlessly, took a "permanent" job. The few pieces that had been published seemd to have vanished like the not-yet-written. I wrote someone, unsent: "So long they fed each other—my life, the writing—;—the writing or hope of it, my life—; but not they begin to destroy." I knew, but did not feel the destruction.

A Ford grant in literature, awarded me on nomination by others, came almost too late. Time granted does not necessarily coincide with time that can be most fully used, as the congested time of fullness would have been. Still, it was two years.

Drowning is not so pitiful as the attempt to rise, says Emily Dickinson. I do not agree, but I know whereof she speaks. For a long time I was that emaciated survivor trembling on the beach, unable to rise and walk. Said differently, I could manage only the feeblest, shallowest growth on that devastated soil. Weeds, to be burned like weeds, or used as compost. When the habits of creation were at last rewon, one book went to the publisher, and I dared to begin my present work. It became my center, engraved on it: "Evil is whatever distracts." (By now had begun a cost to our family life, to my own participation in life as a human being.) I shall not tell the "rest, residue, and remainder" of what I was "leased, demised, and let unto" when once again I had to leave work at the flood to return to the Time-Master, to business-ese and legalese. This most harmful of all my silences has ended, but I am not yet recovered; may still be a one-book silence.

However that will be, we are in a time of more and more hidden and foreground silences, women and men. Denied full writing life, more may try to "nurse through night" (that part-time, part-self night) "the ethereal spark," but it seems to me there would almost have had to be "flame on flame" first; and time as needed, afterwards; and enough of the self, the capacities, undamaged for the rebeginnings on the frightful task. I would like to believe this for what has not yet been written into literature. But it cannot reconcile for what is lost by unnatural silences.

Notes

[1]*A Season in Hell.*

[2]"Entering my eighth decade [I come] into possession of unobstructed leisure...just as, in the course of nature, my vigor sensibly declines. What little of it is left, I husband for certain matters as yet incomplete and which indeed may never be completed." *Billy Budd* never was completed; it was edited from drafts found after Melville's death.

[3]As Jean Toomer *(Cane);* Henry Roth *(Call It sleep);* Edith Summers Kelley *(Weeds).*

[4]Robert Bone. *The Negro Novel in America, 1958.*

[5]Some other foreground silences: Elizabeth (Mrs.) Gaskell, Kate Chopin, Cora Sandel, Cyrus Colter, Hortense Calisher.

[6]Half of the working classes *are* women.

[7]"One Out of Twelve" has a more extensive roll of women writers of achievement.

[8]I would now add a fifth—Kate Chopin—also a foreground silence.

[9]Among them: George Eliot, Helen Hunt Jackson, Mrs. Gskell, Kate Chopin, Lady Gregory, Isak Dinesen. Ivy Compton-Burnett finds this the grim reason for the emergence of British women novelists after World War I: "...The men were dead, you see, and the women didn't marry so much because there was no one for them to marry, and so they had leisure, and, I think, in a good many cases they had money because their brothers were dead, and all that would tend to writing, wouldn't it, being single, and having some money, and having the time—having no men, you see."

[10]Already in that changed time when servants were not necessarily a part of the furnishings of almost anyone well educated enough to be making literature.

Writing task twenty-six: In two or three paragraphs, describe your reaction to this essay. Use at least two of the writing paradigms we have studied to organize your paragraphs.

Writing task twenty-seven: Select one of the topics you have found in this chapter and write a series of definitions for it. Write an Aristotelian, metaphorical, operational, divisional, contextual, lexical and stipulative definition.

Writing task twenty-eight: Use three of the definitions you have just written to develop your topic into an essay which explains or illustrates.

Suggested Group Writing and Discussing Activities

1. List all the definitions which Tillie Olsen uses in the essay. Identify the kind of definition used. Decide if there is a pattern of definition used most often and speculate about why it was chosen rather than some other pattern of organization.

2. Write a one-paragraph description of the silences which thwart creativity in students.

3. Tillie Olsen frequently uses sentences which are "fragments." Why does she choose to do so? Take four of those sentences and rewrite them as complete sentences. Compare them to the original. What is gained and what is lost by using incomplete sentences in this essay?

4. Many of the writers whom Olsen cites may be new to you. Choose one writer and research that writer in the library. Write a brief report you could present to the class.

5. Turn back to the sampler of student definitions of *woman*. Identify the kinds of definition used. Revise any which you think are incomplete or incorrectly written.

CHAPTER FOUR

Naming Assumptions

Adrienne Rich defined the task: "Until we can understand the assumptions in which we are drenched, we cannot know ourselves." In this chapter, in our earlier definitions, and in all the writing and discussing which follows, we are identifying and describing the assumptions which saturate our very hearts and minds. We will now formally name, carefully evaluate and imaginatively rename and change the assumptions which restrict our thinking and feeling. We will come to understand the assumptions which structure the ways we see ourselves and our worlds and examine the assumptive scaffolding of our writing and thinking. We will uncover and discover and name and reclaim and analyze and criticize and name and rename assumptions so that we can more wholly and more articulately define our senses of self.

By *assumption* I mean any named or unnamed, known or unknown, belief which helps determine our behavior. Many of these assumptions are so habitual that we rarely stop to notice them and never bother to name them. When you arrange to meet several friends at a rock concert next Saturday night, you assume that several things will be true on the date specified. You assume linearity in your world and that time will move from today to tomorrow to next Saturday. Do you ever question this basic belief?

You assume that the rock concert will happen at that time you specified. You might be wary about this assumption, and you may have either talked about a raindate or decided on other fun should the concert be cancelled. Your past experience or present geography might remind you of the possibility of stormy weather, faulty sound systems, and the delays caused by blowouts or blowups cancelling the concert.

You assume that you will meet your friends at the concert. You know that freak accidents and sudden random deaths might overtake any of the party. But how often do you question your assumption of immunity to death?

All these assumptions—stated and unstated, consciously examined, or unconsciously articulated—coordinate when you jot down the concert date on a calendar. Obviously, if you were to stop and examine all the implicit and explicit assumptions of your actions, you would be unable to act because of pessimism or fear or despair. To help us structure chaos and chance and flux into patterns which give comfort and sustain us, we rely on sets of beliefs about probable realities. The same ability to structure and shape our social lives through shared beliefs we use to structure and shape our other behaviors.

When we use *assumptions* in our speaking and writing, we will mean statements which we accept as truth without questioning or demanding proof. By assumptions, we will mean those conventions of perceiving and naming reality which are accepted by so many people within one milieu that the conventions seem *true* and are often described and defended as truths. We will be most concerned with discovering and naming those conventions which govern our thinking in reading and writing. We will evaluate whether we should continue to share those conventions.

In each of the short sentences which follow, you will recognize a belief about women shared by many people when the sentences were first formed. Are these assumptions still appropriate to the world we inhabit? Do you hear contemporary versions of them? Do you yourself subscribe to these beliefs? Have you seen them in any advertisements or heard them in any stand-up comedy routines?

> The glory of man is knowledge, but the glory of woman is to renounce knowledge.
> —Chinese proverb

> Women are sisters nowhere.
> —West African proverb

> Do not trust a good woman and keep away from a bad one.
> —Portuguese proverb

> Whenever a woman dies there is one less quarrel on earth.
> —German proverb

> In childhood a woman must be subject to her father; in youth, to her husband; when her husband is dead, to her sons. A woman must never be free of subjugation.
> —The Hindu Code of Mandu, V

> How can he be clean that is born of woman?
> —*Job*, 4:4

Whether they define woman as contentious, unclean, or untrustworthy, all the quotations demonstrate assumptions that woman is less good than man. When these assumptions are accepted without questioning and handed down from generation to generation through a folk tradition, through ritual, and through literature as uncontested truths, they take on the authority of truth and begin to legislate our mental and emotional behavior. We forget that these assumptions are only conventions of thinking and descriptions which we might no longer share. However, we are free to make new assumptions.

Writing task one: Compile a list of assumptions which you make or see others make about the inferiority of one sex and the superiority of another. We will use these lists in a later exercise.

Writing task two: Find an advertisement which explicitly or implicitly makes assumptions which define women as inferior. In a few paragraphs, describe the advertisement and identify the assumption. Is this a new assumption about women or a traditional assumption, a stereotype?

Often we describe our shared beliefs as truths. In the *Declaration of Independence*, Thomas Jefferson cites certain "self-evident truths" when describing the causes which impelled American colonists to separate from Britain.

We hold these truths to be self-evident, that all men are created equal, that they are endowed by their Creator with certain unalienable rights, that among these are life, liberty and the pursuit of happiness.

By describing these assertions as self-evident truths, Jefferson indicates that the set of beliefs with follow are shared by so many enlightened thinkers that no one would contest them as proper ways of describing the essential qualities of human life. Jefferson was, in fact, describing certain ways of understanding the world, ways that were shared by many but not by all people. Some of the truths which Jefferson lists have been dominant assumptions longer than others. Certainly, the belief that human beings were given certain uniquely human rights by a "Creator" is basic to all Western theologies. A more recent assumption scaffolds the Declaration: the belief that people deprived of human rights have the God-given right to resort to revolution dates back only to the Puritan revolution of 1649 when the "divinely ordained" king was removed from power and murdered.

An assumption implied by the reference to the "Creator" predates other assumptions in the passage. A belief in a creator which many people would describe as truth, others would describe as one way of viewing the world. To posit the existence of a creating power provides us with a way of explaining how we stand in the world. Most people share a belief in some creating power. Some people called atheists choose not to share this belief. Other people called agnostics choose not to share the belief that the existence of a creating power can be *proved* with certitude. Because they do not accept the convention of the Creator, they devise some other ways, other assumptions, for understanding and describing the order and existence of the universe.

Each of these assumptions provides us with a model of reality which structures chaos and flux and the unknown into units we can name and know. Because they are models, we are free to accept the models readily available or to reject them. We are also free to modify the models or to invent new models whenever some event or newly discovered idea presents data that can't be defined by the set of shared assumptions or the model which we hold.

What model do you hold for democracy? Do you and Thomas Jefferson share the same assumptions when you say that "all men are created equal"? This statement seems to say that *all* human beings have the same rights to life, liberty and the pursuit of happiness. We know, however, that delegates to the congress which drafted this statement quarreled over the issue of slavery. We know that in 1776 the "self-evident" truth of all men being created equal was a shared belief that many men were created equal but that some human beings were less equal than others.

Every assumption when enacted will have consequences of *implications* which can be anticipated by those who make the assumption. In the nineteenth century, people decided that if the assumption that all men are created equal were valid, then an *implication* of this belief must be the fact that *all* men meant all persons and included the slave who had previously been legally defined as property and as only a fraction of a person. You could read much of our history since the 1850s as a testing of what that initial assumption about being created equal *implies*.

Another implication of the assumption that "all men are created equal" is the idea that all persons, because they are created equal, have the same rights to life, liberty and the pursuit of happiness. Have you noticed how many Americans have agreed that equality means everyone's having the same rights to vote, to work, to live where we choose, and to attend school? How many people do you think agree that equal opportunity is the inevitable implication of the assumption that "all men are created equal"? Do our actions prove this? Civil rights legislation has been an enacting of the implications of the assumption that all men are created equal.

Do you share the assumption that "all men are created equal"? What implications can you predict for this assumption? What do you think and say that results from this assumption? What behaviors have you noticed which contradict this assumption? What would be the counter assumption behind these behaviors? What are the implications of this counter assumption? What do we think and do now which provoked the twentieth-century satirist George Orwell to describe the egalitarianism of the society described in *Animal Farm* as false because one ruling assumption for governance stated that all are equal but "some are more equal than others"?

Writing task three: Identify by listing all the assumptions which stand under the assertion of self-evident truths in the paragraph quoted from the Declaration of Independence. Take one assumption and predict its implications. What does that assumption mean when applied to twentieth-century American society?

Writing task four: The Equal Rights Amendment to the Constitution of the United States is one of the shortest Constitutional amendments proposed; it states:
Section 1. Equality of rights under the law shall not be denied or abridged by the United States or by any State on account of sex.
Section 2. The Congress shall have the power to enforce, by appropriate legislation, the provisions of this article.
Section 3. This amendment shall take effect two years after the date of ratification.
Write a short essay which argues the thesis that the Equal Rights Amendment is an inevitable consequence of an assumption of equality within a society.

When we habitually use only one set of assumptions which we treat as truth, we become blind to alternative ways of seeing and being in the world. For example, you might recognize this famous instance of blindness to new assumptions about how to see our universe: In the second century A.D., a Greek astronomer named Claudius Ptolemy assumed that, because he saw the moon revolve around the earth, the sun and the planets also revolved around the earth. The Ptolemaic model for the heavens become a convention of perception which was accepted as an article of faith by both Arabs and Christians for fourteen hundred years. People believed that all the stars were fixed on spheres and that these spheres made music when they turned. The "music of the spheres" became a metaphor for the idea of a natural order which embraced all aspects of life.

Within the embrace of natural order, human beings lived in a small world which was a miniature of the larger system. The father at the center of the family was assumed to be a microcosm of the larger world of the king at the center of the kingdom. That king/kingdom relationship was in turn a microcosm of the earth/heavens macrocosm. If any cycle or epicycle were somehow thrown out of smooth operation, disharmony would occur in every sphere of the system and the melody of order would be disrupted. Accordingly, any disorders in nature—such as the sudden appearance of a comet or an outbreak of pestilence or a destructive earthquake—were interpreted as both the consequences and the reflections of such disorders in human events as individual disbelief in truth, family quarreling, and civil rebellion. You can watch this assumption of disjunctive human behavior causing civil disorder and unnatural events on earth and in the heavens in the play *King Lear* by Shakespeare. There you will see how the convention of belief in the universe as an earth-centered revolution is mirrored in Lear's tempestuous behavior and mental anguish which send him raging into a bad storm on a heath.

In 1543 Nicholas Copernicus, a churchman and Polish humanist, stated that the sun and not the earth (and, by implication, not man) stood at the center of the heavens. Copernicus discarded the convention of an earth-centered universe by looking again at the movement of the planets from some vantage point other than the earth. He entered the old text about the ordering of the heavens from a new critical direction, namely, a vantage point on the sun. He saw and named a single celestial system which moved around the sun. He hypothesized that the earth with its satellite moon was but one of the planets which revolved around the sun. Copernicus explained his new set of assumptions in *De Revolutionibus Orbium Coelestium* or *The Revolution of Heavenly Orbs*. The collision of his model for the heavens with the Ptolemaic model gave a new meaning to the word "revolution." The term no longer denoted only astronomical movement; since Copernicus, *revolution* connotes a rapid, radical and complete change from one set of assumptions to another set of assumptions.

When Galileo designed a telescope which could be trained on the heavens to see that the Ptolemaic model was inoperable, he found himself in direct conflict with a Church which legislated which temporal and spiritual beliefs could be held. In the confrontation between the authority of established assumptions and the evidence of new assumptions, intelligent people were coerced into rejecting new insights. Galileo himself, after trial by the Inquisition, recanted. In this example, the habit of holding one set of assumptions as absolute truth blinded an entire holy establishment and intellectual community to new visions and new perceptions about the relationships of people to their universe.

When we maintain our habit of using only that set of assumptions which we have been naming truth, and when we refuse to inquire after alternative models, we restrict our growth as individuals and as persons in society. Because we are drenched in sets of shared assumptions, we are often unable to see both the ways that these conventions shape our thinking and writing and the other ways that we might choose from among conventions to organize our thinking and writing. Our task of understanding the assumptions in which we are drenched, although necessary, is difficult. We have acquired our beliefs slowly and often unconsciously from our past, from our parents, from our peers, from our private reading, and from our participation in media. Abstracting assumptions which govern the thinking and writing of our milieu will be at first a slow process. Once we become more skilled at abstracting assumptions from what we read and what we write, we become free to more completely understand and to more clearly express our ideas and feelings.

What assumptions can you abstract from each of the following statements?

1. I can't write; English was always my worst subject.
2. This course will be a "gut"; there are five hundred kids in the lecture hall and all the exams are multiple choice.
3. I didn't read that essay because it was boring.
4. That teacher doesn't know the material very well. He's always asking us to discuss things and hardly ever tells us what the answers are to his questions.
5. But why did I only get a B on the paper if you said that the ideas were interesting and new?
6. I'm here for the credit.
7. Will there be a final exam?
8. I'm in engineering; I don't need rhetoric.
9. My handwriting is not good and my spelling is worse; I hate to write for these reasons.
10. What do you want me to say in the term paper?

When you become more skilled at abstracting assumptions, you will be able to write for any lengthy reading a *precis* which summarizes in a compact form the major assumptions which organize the writing. Can you see that, when you take notes in a class, it would be more beneficial to abstract the assumptions of the argument or lecture than to try and scribble down every fact cited? Can you see that an outline for a paper would actually be most helpful if it identified assumptions and listed possible implications? The more you practice abstracting the major assumptions from your thinking and writing, the more certain you will feel about your grasp of ideas and the more comfortable you will be when you are confronted with alternative assumptions. You won't be worried that those other ways of stating how a thing is perceived will rob you of your own power to name your world.

Writing task five: Read over again the essay "The Mask of Beauty." Begin with the paragraph which states "Whether a woman has an I.Q. of 60 or 160, whether she is young or old, her first duty is to keep herself attractive." Here the writer turns from illustrating her thesis that women wear masks of beauty to interpreting why women persist in this behavior. List all the implicit and explicit assumptions which organize the writer's argument that the mask of beauty is a tragic choice of behavior.

Writing task six: Select one of the assumptions which you have abstracted from the Stannard essay and predict all the consequences you can imagine if the assumption is accepted as a truth.

Writing task seven: What are the implications of Stannard's assumption that "Lesbians are merely more unadulterated narcissists than heterosexual women"? What are Stannard's assumptions about lesbianism? Are these assumptions shared by modern society? Are these your assumptions? What are alternative assumptions about lesbianism? This assignment asks questions that will take more time for response than any of the previous writing tasks. You might, in fact, write a long essay or even a research paper in response. When you set about extrapolating from this assumption, you may find it necessary to define terms using several of the paradigms you have studied.

Writing the Thesis–Development Essay

I assume that for much of your college writing, you use the writing pattern called the expository essay. You may already be skilled at writing exposition. You might know it by some other name like the thesis-development essay or the formal essay. Because you do and will use this structure frequently, we will briefly describe its conventions and practice it.

This type of essay is structured by the assumption that informative writing should be unified by one controlling idea. Unity becomes one criterion by which the essay is judged successful. Unity in an expository essay means a singleness of purpose and a tight connection of all materials with that purpose.

The Latin parent *ex ponere*, "to set out," tells us that all expositions— whether the Montreal Expo of '67 or your writing for chemical engineer- ing—will "expose" materials to the view of an audience for some defined purpose. An arts and crafts exposition sets before fairgoers examples of the possible expressions of an aesthetic experience; its purpose is both communication and entertainment. *Your* purpose in an expository essay might be to explain or to entertain or to teach or to present information or a combination of these purposes.

In the expository essay, you arrange and classify your illustrations, examples, definitions, descriptions, and proofs so that they serve the controlling purpose. You organize those materials into a unified whole that you set out before an audience which agrees to look with you at the materials exposed to view. You inform your audience through an essay composed of three parts: the introduction or statement of a thesis, the middle or the development of the thesis, and the conclusion or restatement of the developed thesis. One name for this essay pattern is the "thesis-development essay."

In section one—the introduction—you tell your audience what you will show them and perhaps why. You state a thesis. In section two — the development of the thesis—you show clearly and tell with sufficient detail. In section three — the conclusion — you summarize and comment upon your process of "show and tell."

1. Introduction

You already know the first rule: you choose a controlling assumption about your topic. The thesis statement is your assumption about the subject, your statement about your relationship to it. Usually, you state that assumption or thesis in one sentence. The more complicated the controlling assumption, the more complex will be your thesis statement.

These thesis statements are culled from previous writings in the textbook. Did you recognize them as thesis statements when you first read them?

> The American wedding is a ritual event of ferocious, gluttonous consuming, a debauch of intensified buying, never again to be repeated in the life of an American couple.

> What is poverty?

> Again and again in the history of the language, one finds that a perfectly innocent term designating a girl or woman may begin with totally neutral or even positive connotations, but that gradually it acquires negative implications, at first perhaps only slightly disparaging, but after a period of time becoming abusive and ending as a sexual slur.

Did you notice that not all these thesis statements were the first sentences of the introductory paragraphs and that some of them were not even introduced in the first paragraph? Sometimes writers delay a thesis statement until they have enticed the audience into hearing their controlling assumptions. A writer might use an anecdote or a "then and now" comparison or a provocative epigram to pique the reader. A writer might also sketch a backdrop to the thesis and earn the reader's trust by first demonstrating through statistics or historical background that what is about to be postulated is worth hearing.

Each of these thesis statements could be rewritten as declarative statements which begin paragraphs. For example, Marcia Seligson could have said "The American wedding is the major ritual for a consumer society," to begin her book on the topic. She wrote an introduction of several paragraphs before she stated her thesis. As a writer, you must decide in what way you can most effectively introduce the major assumption you wish to set to view.

If you write an effective and well-organized introduction, you have written half your essay. You have demonstrated to your reader that you have something important to say, and you have alerted your reader to your method of expression. When you write an introduction to a thesis-development essay, it would be most effective if you included these elements: a promise of action on the thesis; a lure to catch the reader's attention; a background to dramatize the action; a hint about how you will develop the thesis.

Writing task eight: Practice writing thesis statements for (1) an essay describing an assumption you have identified as discriminating and (2) an essay which exposes to the reader some personal belief and (3) an essay which sets before the reader's view a problem men face when they perform roles that used to be called "woman's work."

Writing task nine: Write an introductory paragraph using one of the thesis statements you practiced and incorporating background and audience lure. Rewrite this introductory paragraph by playing with the arrangement, statement of thesis, background, and audience lure. Change one of these items and notice how the purpose for the essay might change.

2. Development of Thesis

Whatever promises you made in the introduction, you must keep in the middle section of the paper. Ideally the middle should be more substantial than either the introduction or the ending; some proportion like 1 to 3 or 4 or 5 to 1 would be an appropriate proportion for most thesis-development essays. Obviously, what you promised to do will determine the girth of the "body" of the essay.

In the middle section of the essay, you develop, unfold gradually, the thesis. You explore the implications of your controlling assumptions. You might describe the range of implications. You might rank the implications according to some specified criterion. You might explore the possible consequences of the assumption by frequent use of examples. You might detail the characteristics of each division. You might show the aptness of the assumption by listing proofs. Often, you will do all these things.

If you have promised your reader three displays in the introduction, you will want to check your writing to see that you have arranged three displays. If one display is gaudier than another, you will want to be sure that you intend it to impress the reader more than the other displays. Listing in the introduction the way you will proceed gives you a convenient trail to follow when you develop the thesis. You won't get lost among the crowd if you have already marked out a path of displays.

Writing task ten: First, take an introductory paragraph and extend the thesis by writing the middle section of the essay. Be sure that you keep all the promises you made. Then, rewrite the middle section of the essay by choosing methods which you did not use on the first writing. How does your thinking change when you play with alternative structures?

3. Conclusion

Once you feel that you have adequately set forth your materials, you will want to draw your reader's attention to the fact that you have finished your task. Frequently, writers end their exposition too peremptorily with something like "That's all, folks." You don't want to shortchange an excellent development of a significant thesis by a careless, choppy closure. The reader feels cheated and you seem less an artisan than an amateur.

The concluding paragraph should function the same way that the last sentence of each paragraph functions. It should signal to the reader that a whole unit has been rounded off. The conclusion closes off exposition by summing up major ideas or by restating the controlling assumption or by pointing out the changes in the assumption which happened during the exposition or by stating the importance of the assumption to unexamined but related assumptions or by drawing an induction from evidence presented throughout. The conclusion should make a lasting impression and send the reader away approving the completeness of the essay.

You can impress the reader in many ways. You can invent slogans to give the readers a catchy abstract of the thesis. You might repeat some skillful phrasing from the essay. You might repeat the introduction in the conclusion and glue the essay together. If you do this, you will want to play with the phrasing so that you don't bore the reader by saying the same thing even after a detailed development. You won't want to introduce any idea that is so new and provocative that it makes the reader hunger for more exposition. You will want to avoid phrasing like "it would seem" or "apparently." You might want to end with a quotation, but it had best be a lively and memorable one. Whatever ending you devise, be sure that all is well because it ends well.

Writing task eleven: Conclude the essay you have been writing. Now, practice alternative endings. Which do you like best?

Writing task twelve: Chop off the final paragraph from any essay in this textbook and rewrite the paragraph in a way that effectively concludes that writer's essay.

Now that we have looked at the elements of an expository essay and practiced some of its conventions, you will want to practice your skills of analyzing an expository essay written by another writer and of writing your own essay. The short essay which follows sets to our view the concept of self-respect. Joan Didion, a contemporary essayist and novelist, explains self-respect through an extended definition which tells us what it is by telling us again and again what it is *not*. While you read, notice the writer's frequent use of parallelism and watch how she extends a metaphor throughout an entire paragraph so that the paragraph becomes a tight, imaginative unit.

On Self-Respect

Joan Didion

Once, in a dry season, I wrote in large letters across two pages of a notebook that innocence ends when one is stripped of the delusion that one likes oneself. Although now, some years later, I marvel that a mind on the outs with itself should have nonetheless made painstaking record of its every tremor, I recall with embarrassing clarity the flavor of those particular ashes. It was a matter of misplaced self-respect.

I had not been elected to Phi Beta Kappa. This failure could scarcely have been more predictable or less ambiguous (I simply did not have the grades), but I was unnerved by it; I had somehow thought myself a kind of academic Raskolnikov, curiously exempt from the cause-effect relationships which hampered others. Although even the humorless nineteen-year-old that I was must have recognized that the situation lacked real tragic stature, the day that I did not make Phi Beta Kappa nonetheless marked the end of something, and innocence may well be the word for it. I lost the conviction that lights would always turn green for me, the pleasant certainty that those rather passive virtues which had won me approval as a child automatically guaranteed me not only Phi Beta Kappa keys but happiness, honor, and the love of a good man; lost a certain touching faith in the totem power of good manners, clean hair, and proven competence on the Stanford-Binet scale. To such doubtful amulets had my self-respect been pinned, and I faced myself that day with the nonplussed apprehension of someone who has come across a vampire and has no crucifix at hand.

Although to be driven back upon oneself is an uneasy affair at best, rather like trying to cross a border with borrowed credentials, it seems to me now the one condition necessary to the beginnings of real self-respect. Most of our platitudes notwithstanding, self-deception remains the most difficult deception. The tricks that work on others count for nothing in that very well-lit back alley where one keeps assignations with oneself: no winning smiles will do here, no prettily drawn lists of good intentions. One shuffles flashily but in vain through one's marked cards—the kindness done for the wrong reason, the apparent triumph which involved no real effort, the seemingly heroic act into which one had been shamed. The dismal fact is that self-respect has nothing to do with the approval of others—who are, after all, deceived easily enough; has nothing to do with reputation, which, as Rhett Butler told Scarlett O'Hara, is something people with courage can do without.

To do without self-respect, on the other hand, is to be an unwilling audience of one to an interminable documentary that details one's failings, both real and imagined, with fresh footage spliced in for every screening. *There's the glass you broke in anger, there's the hurt on X's face; watch now, this next scene, the night Y came back from Houston, see how you muff this one.* To live without self-respect is to lie awake some night, beyond the reach of warm milk, phenobarbital, and the sleeping hand on the coverlet, counting up the sins of commission and omission, the trusts betrayed, the promises subtly broken, the gifts irrevocably wasted through sloth or cowardice or carelessness. However long we postpone it, we eventually lie down alone in that notoriously uncomfortable bed, the one we make ourselves. Whether or not we sleep in it depends, of course, on whether or not we respect ourselves.

To protest that some fairly improbable people, some people who *could not possibly respect themselves,* seem to sleep easily enough is to miss the point entirely, as surely as those people miss it who think that self-respect has necessarily to do with not having safety pins in one's underwear. There is a common superstition that "self-respect" is a kind of charm against snakes, something that keeps those who have it locked in some unblighted Eden, out of strange beds, ambivalent conversations, and trouble in general. It does not at all. It has nothing to do with the face of things, but concerns instead a separate peace, a private reconciliation. Although the careless, suicidal Julian English in *Appointment in Samarra* and the careless, incurably dishonest Jordan Baker in *The Great Gatsby* seem equally improbable candidates for self-respect, Jordan Baker had it, Julian English did not. With that genius for accommodation more often seen in women than in men, Jordan took her own measure, made her own peace, avoided threats to that peace: "I hate careless people," she told Nick Carraway. "It takes two to make an accident."

Like Jordan Baker, people with self-respect have the courage of their mistakes. They know the price of things. If they choose to commit adultery, they do not then go running, in an excess of bad conscience, to receive absolution from the wronged parties; nor do they complain unduly of the unfairness, the undeserved embarrassment, of being named co-respondent. In brief, people with self-respect exhibit a certain toughness, a kind of moral nerve; they display what was once called *character*, a quality which, although approved in the abstract, sometimes loses ground to other, more instantly negotiable virtues. The measure of its slipping prestige is that one tends to think of it only in connection with homely children and United States senators who have been defeated, preferably in the primary, for reelection. Nonetheless, character—the willingness to accept responsibility for one's own life—is the source from which self-respect springs.

Self-respect is something that our grandparents, whether or not they had it, knew all about. They had instilled in them, young, a certain discipline, the sense that one lives by doing things one does not particularly want to do, by putting fears and doubts to one side, by weighing immediate comforts against the possibility of larger, even intangible, comforts. It seemed to the nineteenth century admirable, but not remarkable, that Chinese Gordon put on a clean white suit and held Khartoum against the Mahdi; it did not seem unjust that the way to free land in California involved death and difficulty and dirt. In a diary kept during the winter of 1846, an emigrating twelve-year-old named Narcissa Cornwall noted coolly: "Father was busy reading and did not notice that the house was being filled with strange Indians until Mother spoke about it." Even lacking any clue as to what Mother said, one can scarcely fail to be impressed by the entire incident: the father reading, the Indians filing in, the mother choosing the words that would not alarm, the child duly recording the event and noting further that those particular Indians were not, "fortunately for us," hostile. Indians were simply part of the *donnée*.

In one guise or another, Indians always are. Again, it is a question of recognizing that anything worth having has its price. People who respect themselves are willing to accept the risk that the Indians will be hostile, that the venture will go bankrupt, that the liaison may not turn out to be one in which *every day is a holiday because you're married to me*. They are willing to invest something of themselves; they may not play at all, but when they do play, they know the odds.

That kind of self-respect is a discipline, a habit of mind that can never be faked but can be developed, trained, coaxed forth. It was once suggested to me that, as an antidote to crying, I put my head in a paper bag. As it happens, there is a sound physiological reason, something to do with oxygen, for doing exactly that, but the psychological effect alone is incalculable: it is difficult in the extreme to continue fancying oneself Cathy in *Wuthering Heights* with one's head in a Food Fair bag. There is a similar case for all the small disciplines, unimportant in themselves; imagine maintaining any kind of swoon, commiserative or carnal, in a cold shower.

But those small disciplines are valuable only insofar as they represent larger ones. To say that Waterloo was won on the playing fields of Eton is not to say that Napoleon might have been saved by a crash program in cricket; to give formal dinners in the rain forest would be pointless did not the candlelight flickering on the liana call forth deeper, stronger, disciplines, values instilled long before. It is a kind of ritual, helping us to remember who and what we are. In order to remember it, one must have known it.

To have that sense of one's intrinsic worth which constitutes self-respect is potentially to have everything: the ability to discriminate, to love and to remain indifferent. To lack it is to be locked within oneself, paradoxically incapable of either love or indifference. If we do not respect ourselves, we are on the one hand forced to despise those who have so few resources as to consort with us, so little perception as to remain blind to our fatal weaknesses. On the other, we are peculiarly in thrall to everyone we see, curiously determined to live out — since our self-image is untenable — their false notions of us. We flatter ourselves by thinking this compulsion to please others an attractive trait: a gist for imaginative empathy, evidence of our willingness to give. Of course I will play Francesca to your Paolo, Helen Keller to anyone's Annie Sullivan: no expectation is too misplaced, no role too ludicrous. At the mercy of those we cannot but hold in contempt, we play roles doomed to failure before they are begun, each defeat generating fresh despair at the urgency of divining and meeting the next demand made upon us.

It is the phenomenon sometimes called "alienation from self." In its advanced stages, we no longer answer the telephone, because someone might want something; that we could say *no* without drowning in self-reproach is an idea alien to this game. Every encounter demands too much, tears the nerves, drains the will, and the specter of something as small as an unanswered letter arouses such disproportionate guilt that answering it becomes out of the question. To assign unanswered letters their proper weight, to free us from the expectations of others, to give us back to ourselves — there lies the great, the singular power of self-respect. Without it, one eventually discovers the final turn of the screw: one runs away to find oneself, and finds no one at home.

Writing task thirteen: Write a thesis-development essay which uses the pattern described in this chapter to explore the topic "self-contempt."

Often a person can become alienated from himself or herself even when that person has a strong sense of self. The worlds we move into and work in abrade our sense of self and make us look again at what our assumptions are and what we want them to be. In the essay which follows, Kitti Carriker Eastman uses the standard essay form to describe a work experience which forced her into new questions about her identity. Notice that, unlike Didion who abandoned the first person pronoun after the first two paragraphs in favor of the more formal third person, this writer uses the first person pronoun throughout the essay. Notice her use of dialogue in the essay.

Work Break

Kitti Carriker Eastman

After being a student for five years, I had many adjustments to make when I started my first "full-time, permanent" job. The day after I had finished my B.A. in English, I began an M.A. in the same subject. When the last paper for the last course was turned in, I was thoroughly fatigued yet overjoyed that five wonderful years of reading, writing and intellectual growth were ended. I could not face the prospect of more graduate study. So, I decided to rest and refresh myself by working while my husband went on for another degree.

Even today, I cannot say if I was prepared for what I found. I psyched myself for job-hunting: "You can read, write and think." I had met many people who could not do these things and I had read all the articles in *Time* and *Newsweek* lamenting the lack in every field of just such applicants. I set out believing myself armed with precious abilities.

I know women with accomplishments and qualifications comparable to mine who have found, after extensive searching or through a stroke of luck, jobs which fulfill and satisfy, positions worthy of them. But I was not one of these women.

For me there were self-imposed drawbacks. I did not search the job listings nor go to career fairs. I was "geographically limited." I had decided to live with my husband and move with him to the school of his choice.

In a college town it is not just a temptation of having extra time at Christmas break to earn extra income; it is often a necessity to try the university employment office. The English department didn't need me; telling myself "You can read, write and think," I asked about other staff openings. Of the few available, one seemed to suit my style. Although reading, writing and thinking weren't listed in the job description, the supervisors of a position listed with the admissions office were elated that I could do those things. Of course, I wouldn't receive compensation for those skills and, because typing wasn't in the job description either, of course I would earn even less than a secretary. Despite all this, I took the job. First interview, first day in town—what more could I ask?

I joined the ranks of the oppressed class which keeps the universities of this country running smoothly. These centers which free minds for development and expansion depend for their organization on many women and a few men who, for various reasons, are willing to work for less than their efforts are worth. I came to know this system.

On the first day I met the director of a neighboring office who said, "Nice to meet you but don't expect me to remember your name. I've got more important things on my mind."

"Is that so?" I seethed to myself while smiling politely, "Well, so do I."

And so I was introduced to the men who scurry about, all-important, while scores of women, whose names don't even bear remembering, complete the repetitive, necessarily important daily tasks which make meaningful the positions held by those men.

"Now you understand what a hierarchy is," observed my husband. I talked about my job all the time. I was "experiencing" it. I explained to him how each woman is given dominion over a particular duty: "So they believe they have power. But they don't!"

He responded, "You've just described a classic pattern of oppression."

What I found really unfortunate was that these women do hold responsible positions and they do important work but they are not recognized as doing, nor paid as if they did, something of major importance. They are not compensated for thinking. I learned the degradation of working all day, every day, and still earning hardly enough to make a living. I felt the insulting assumption that the women who fill these positions depend on someone else for their livelihood and, therefore, don't need to earn a living.

I began to know the women I worked with, and I began to understand, at least in some small ways, how they escaped feeling outrage and why the frustration which was engulfing me did not touch them. "How long is your husband going to make you work?" one co-worker asked me. I considered this question, amazed to finally realize her concept of why I was working. She saw it as my husband's choice. I explained that I was working to repay a loan I took to finance a little jaunt to England, that I wanted to earn a little money of my own, that I was saving for a trip to Boston with a close friend. This evoked a strong response but not quite the one I expected. My co-worker was incredulous that I planned to take a trip with a friend. "And leave your husband behind? You'd go without him?" I began to grasp that in her eyes I had turned the control of my life over to my husband and was therefore dependent on him.

The women I worked with cast me as wife, first and foremost. Regardless how I acted or expressed myself, I could not replace nor modify the erroneous assumptions they made about me simply because I had chosen to be married. On one occasion, they laughed and suggested that I must be working on my P.H.T.—the old "putting hubby through" degree. I suppressed my anger. I tried to take the remark as a joke and formulate a rebuttal at the same time. "I plan to get my own Ph.D. and my husband makes as much money as I do, so how can I be putting him through school? He puts himself through school." I had hoped to emphasize the ludicrousness of the fact that I earned, at a full-time job, no more than my husband, a part-time graduate teaching assistant. My attempt fell flat. I felt I had not even been heard.

They insisted, "You work. Your husband goes to school. You're putting him through school."

What amazed me most was the number of people who seemed to see a logical progression in a young woman earning two degrees and then settling down—as a file clerk. All around me were people, many with families, who did not and could not see this job as a work break. They saw it as a terminal position, something I might do for the rest of my life—or until my husband lets me quit! I complained to him, "When you stopped to work, no one believed that you had changed your original plans. Everyone around you realized it was just for a while, that you had an ultimate goal to reach. How can anyone believe it's natural and right for me to settle down in a job that holds no rewards? Do they think I've made all this progress to no end?" To his credit, he had a compassionate and realistic grasp on my situation: "You have additional injustices to deal with because you're a woman."

So I came to see my job as a lab experience, a first-hand confrontation with a system which I had heretofore only heard about. Sure, I suffered injustices as a student. But through my job I became submerged in an economic system based on the oppression of women. I could no longer pretend to be strong and separate, even though in my mind I was. With the others, I sacrificed my integrity and my identity to a system which didn't respect me as a human being. "At least I'm aware," I tried to soothe myself. But sometimes that made me feel the worst of all. I laughed and told my friends, "I like to think of my job as a vacation." In a sense it was. It gave me the change of pace I needed to prepare myself for the final round of my formal education. I became fueled and motivated. It wasn't difficult to extricate my self, but the oppressed are still oppressed. They allow themselves to be oppressed because they do not realize that they are oppressed. After years of social conditioning, many will never realize. There may never be sweeping liberation. Each individual is left to take the injustices personally and to extricate herself.

But we can help each other. Perhaps in my submersion, I touched another. Perhaps during my work break, I helped her realize that her intrinsic worth is overwhelming and that she deserves to be called by her name.

Writing task fourteen: Look at the first sentence (the thesis statement). It is a generalization which gives us few clues about what the essay exposes to your view. Why would the writer choose this approach? Now that you've read the essay, rewrite the thesis statement. Invent three thesis statements which could be used and in a paragraph explain which of the four (yours and the writer's) would be the best choice.

Writing task fifteen: Does the situation which Kitti Carriker Eastman describes exist on your campus? Have you had any work experiences which were similar? Write a thesis-development essay about the topic "women and work."

Suggested Group Writing and Discussing Activities

1. In small group discussions, look at advertisements which group members bring and abstract the assumptions from each. You will want to list both verbal and visual assumptions.
2. Select several advertisements which cluster as materials demonstrating one particular assumption. As a group, select a thesis statement, organize the advertisements so that they develop the thesis, and write a concluding statement. Arrange all these materials in a sentence outline with the three divisions of introduction, body, and conclusion.
3. In group discussion, answer the questions: Who owns the "sleeping hand on the cradle?" What does Didion mean by "Indians always are." Write thesis statements that would organize a paragraph of response.
4. List the assumptions behind the physical environment or "classroom" you are using during this course. Choose the assumption which the group agrees is the most important to "success" and write a thesis statement for an essay that would explain this importance.

Recommended Reading

Joan Didion. *Slouching Towards Bethlehem.* New York: Farrar, Strauss and Giroux, 1968.
——. *The White Album.* New York: Simon and Schuster, 1978.

CHAPTER FIVE

Questioning and Renaming Assumptions

We will begin our work in this chapter by borrowing again from the essay by Adrienne Rich. When she describes the process of writing, she emphasizes the need to question the conventions which we recognize:

> Moreover if the imagination is to transcend and transform experience, it has to question, to challenge, to conceive of alternatives, perhaps to the very life you are living at that moment. You have to be free to play around with the notation that day might be night; love might be hate; nothing can be too sacred for the imagination to turn into its opposite or to call experimentally by another name. For writing is renaming.

"Calling something experimentally" is making assumptions. "Calling something experimentally by another name" is questioning whether the assumptions at hand foster growth and renaming assumptions so that they do foster growth.

In this chapter, in our future studies, in our subsequent writings, we will be shaping and defining ourselves both through a recognition and naming of the assumptions at hand *and* through a questioning and renaming of assumptions. Centuries back, Socrates remarked that the unexamined life was not worth living. I suggest that this criterion should still guide our thinking and, of course, must guide our writing.

We need to question assumptions so that we have mastery over the definitions which determine much of how we live. We need to question assumptions to learn whether these conventions of perceiving and responding are, in fact, the beliefs which we want to affirm in our lives. We need to question assumptions so we can conceive alternatives to any beliefs we choose not to affirm. We need to question assumptions so that we can grow in a world which changes quickly. We need to question assumptions to set ourselves free of any conventions which oppress us rather than support our independence.

How are we to question assumptions? Do we need to say anything more than "Do you mean that?" or "Are they putting me on?" Are we expected

147

by our institutions to question assumptions? Will we find it hard to do so? All these questions we will carry with us through our work. We will shape answers through the very process of questioning and requestioning assumptions. We will respond to those questions through our praxis of thinking and writing because—and this is an assumption I hope we share— we transcend and transform our world through the activity of reflecting upon it and writing about it.

Once you can abstract an assumption from a unit of speech or writing, and once you can predict the possible consequences of an assumption, you are ready to play with the assumption. You are ready to judge whether the assumption is one you can use and one you choose to hold. Some early questions might be: "Is that so?" or "What do I think about this?" or "How can I use this belief?" After these questions you might ask yourself: "Does this belief connect with things I see happening?" or "Does this assumption determine any aspects of culture?" or "If this doesn't fit the way I see things, then whose perceptions does it organize?" Further questions might be: "Should I keep this belief?" or "What behaviors does this assumption determine if I keep it?" or "What do I do and how do I treat other people when I keep this assumption?" After that inquiry, you might question how to make the belief clearly your own belief—how to affirm it or how to restate it or how to stipulate its meaning or how to qualify it or how to change it so that it works best for what you want to do and to be.

What happens if you examine some of your assumptions with that list of questions? What might be other questions you might use to pry into the meaning and the implications of your assumptions?

The Brazilian educator Paolo Freire has posited a theory for education which is based on his belief that every person can look critically at the world through a dialogue with other persons who also are looking critically at that world. Freire believes that every human being can learn to see his or her personal and social reality and can learn to name and rename and change that reality. Although Freire worked most intensively with the impoverished people of Brazil who could neither read nor write and were locked into oppression, he also believes that all people who are made objects of structures can learn to be the subjects or the agents of changing the oppressive structures.

Paolo Freire describes a "banking" concept of education as an instrument which continues oppression. He lists several behaviors as implications of an assumption that education is a bank transaction where teachers make the deposits which students receive, file, and store. In such a concept of education, he says:

(a) the teacher teaches and the students are taught;

(b) the teacher knows everything and the students know nothing;

(c) the teacher thinks and the students are thought about;

(d) the teacher talks and the students listen—meekly;

(e) the teacher disciplines and the students are disciplined;

(f) the teacher chooses and enforces his choice, and the students comply;

(g) the teacher acts and the students have the illusion of acting through the action of the teacher;

(h) the teacher chooses the program content, and the students (who were not consulted) adapt to it;

(i) the teacher confuses the authority of knowledge with his own professional authority, which he sets in opposition to the freedom of the students;

(j) the teacher is the subject of the learning process, while the pupils are mere objects.

Do you recognize any assumption that education is "banking" in the classrooms where you learn? Do you witness any of these "learning behaviors" which are implied by a banking concept of education? If you agree that the banking concept of education organizes your experiences in college, have you thought about questioning whether the deposit system of education should be the model followed? What would classrooms and courses and faculties and student bodies look like if you changed the banking concept of education?

Did you notice that Freire lists classroom behaviors in a series of parallel phrases in which *teachers* always precedes *students?* Did you also notice that *teachers* is always followed by a verb in the active voice while *students* is always followed either by a verb in the passive voice or a copulative verb which shows a state of being but not a state of acting? Whenever you use the passive voice, you indicate that the subject of the verb does not perform the action which the verb cites. "I was defined" says that I had no say about the definition. However, when you use a verb in the active voice, you indicate that the subject of the verb does perform the action which the verb cites. Thus, *"I define."*

Freire has deliberately chosen these two patterns to show by the form what he says in the content. Through these patterns, he demonstrates that education is a system where one group which defines itself as knowledgeable and primary acts *upon* another passive group which has been defined (by their society, by their teachers, and by themselves) as ignorant and secondary.

What would sentences look like when students decide to define their own roles in the classroom? If you wanted to question this assumption about education as a banking system, you would choose verbs and patterns of word order that do not reflect a pattern of depositors and depositories. You might even avoid using the words *teacher* and *students* because of their long histories of meaning the one who does to and the ones who are done to. What happens if you play with *learn* and avoid *teach*? What assumption was being questioned by that introductory description of this course as a "community of practicing writers?" What assumption about education determines this phrasing by Freire: "learners and master-learners." What assumptions lie behind the following statement?

Learners and master-learners in a composition course pose problems which they coinvestigate through dialogue and name through individual and group writings.

Writing task one: Beginning with the question "What do I think about this?" and continuing through to the question "What do I do and how do I treat other people when I keep this assumption?", organize an essay in which you question the banking concept of education. When you have finished this exercise, you may find that you have, in fact, written your own philosophy of education.

Writing task two: Select any behavior described above by Freire as an implication of the assumption that education is a banking system. From your own experience, describe some situation which shows a depositor/depository behavior. After your carefully detailed narrative, list all the negative and positive learning experiences which were involved in the transaction between the depositor and depositories. Finally, evaluate whether this experience of education as banking provides *you* with a valuable model for learning.

Writing task three: Devise a new model for education by questioning the terms and implications of the education = banking assumption. After you carefully describe the model, list all the behaviors for teachers, for students and for administrators which are implied by your assumption. This writing exercise could become a term project for you; it could also be described in an essay of three or four pages. You will have to decide how specific or how general you want your focus to be.

What did you think about those beliefs about women which we read in the last chapter? Did they coincide with the ways in which you perceive women? Do they connect with any discriminatory behavior you have witnessed? Do those assumptions in any way determine misogynous behaviors? Whose perceptions do those assumptions organize? Should we keep those beliefs? What do we do and how do we treat other people when we keep those assumptions? How can we change those assumptions so they let us be free? Did you question any of those assumptions? Did you think of any questions to ask those people who first uttered those beliefs and to ask those people who repeat them as clichés?

One community of practicing writers broke into work groups to question and to rename those assumptions. Each group had to change the assumption, not by a long response to each, but simply by playing with the grammatical pattern of each statement. One rule governed the group activity: members could substitute words so long as they kept the grammatical pattern of the original assumption. The question "How can he be clean that is born of woman?" had to be phrased as a question with the same word order even after the assumption was changed. When they questioned the assumption of this West African proverb, each group was obliged to write a statement that followed the formula Noun-Verb-Noun-Adverb. All these new sentences follow that formula:

Original Assumption: Women are sisters nowhere. West African proverb
Group Responses: Men are brothers nowhere.
                    Women are sisters everywhere.
                    Women become sisters now.
                    Women were enemies formerly.
                    Women trust women everywhere.
                    Men are sisters nowhere.

What happens to the original assumption about women? Each new sentence questions and responds to that assumption. Each shows a way you could question an assumption, whether it is the implicit or explicit belief that organizes a proverb, the thesis statement of a paragraph, the major concept that structures a lengthy essay, the central set of assumptions in a book, or the set of assumptions which function on a higher level of abstraction and which we might call *criteria of relevance*.

Writing task four: Choose one of these new sentences and analyze how the substitution of one word changed the belief.

Writing task five: Practice changing assumptions by taking any assumption about women listed in Chapter 4 and substituting words. Use the same sentence form but substitute any words you choose.

Often we write because we want to question assumptions. Our essays become ways of changing beliefs and questioning them. In her essay "Psychology Constructs the Female," psychologist Naomi Weisstein indicates that her purpose in writing was to question the "super-assumptions" which the field of psychology makes about what makes people "whole." While you read, notice what assumptions she identifies. Also notice what implications she extrapolates from those assumptions that she judges are not true of the psychic lives of women. What techniques does this writer use for questioning assumptions? How does she make the very questioning of assumptions an organizing structure for the writing? Does the essayist offer any alternative assumptions to those she describes as "male fantasies?"

Psychology Constructs the Female

Naomi Weisstein

It is an implicit assumption that the area of psychology that concerns itself with personality has the onerous but necessary task of describing the limits of human possibility. Thus, when we are about to consider the liberation of women, we naturally look to psychology to tell us what "true" liberation would mean: what would give women the freedom to fulfill their own intrinsic natures?

Psychologists have set about describing the true nature of women with a certainty and a sense of their own infallibility rarely found in the secular world. Bruno Bettelheim tells us that "we must start with the realization that, as much as women want to be good scientists or engineers, they want first and foremost to be womanly companions of men and to be mothers."[1] Erik Erikson, upon noting that young women often ask whether they can "have an identity before they know whom they will marry, and for whom they will make a home," explains somewhat elegiacally that "much of a young woman's identity is already defined in her kind of attractiveness and in the selectivity of her search for the man (or men) by whom she wishes to be sought...." Mature womanly fulfillment, for Erikson, rests on the fact that a woman's "...somatic design harbors an 'inner space' destined to bear the offspring of chosen men, and with it, a biological, psychological, and ethical commitment to take care of human infancy."[2] Some psychiatrists even see the acceptance of woman's role by women as a solution to societal problems. "Woman is nurturance," writes Joseph Rheingold, a psychiatrist at Harvard Medical School, "...anatomy decrees the life of a woman...when women grow up without dread of their biological functions and without subversion by feminist doctrine, and therefore enter upon motherhood with a sense of fulfillment and altruistic sentiment, we shall attain the goal of a good life and a secure world in which to live it."[3]

These views from men who are assumed to be experts reflect, in a surprisingly transparent way, the cultural consensus. They not only assert that a woman is defined by her ability to attract men, but they see no alternative definitions. They think that the definition of a woman in terms of a man is the way it should be; and they back it up with psychosexual incantation and biological ritual curses. A woman has an identity if she is attractive enough to obtain a man, and thus, a home; for this will allow her to set about her life's task of "joyful altruism and nuturance." A woman's *true* nature is that of a happy servant.

Business certainly does not disagree. If views such as Bettelheim's and Erikson's do indeed have something to do with real liberation for women, then seldom in human history has so much money and effort been spent on helping a group of people realize their true potential. Clothing, cosmetics, and home furnishings are multimillion dollar businesses. If you do not like investing in firms that make weaponry and flaming gasoline, then there is a lot of cash in "inner space." Sheet and pillowcase manufacturers are anxious to fill this inner space:

> Mother, for a while this morning, I though I wasn't cut out for married life. Hank was late for work and forgot his apricot juice and walked out without kissing me, and when I was all alone I started crying. But then the postman came with the sheets and towels you sent, that look like big bandana handkerchiefs, and you know what I thought? That those big red and blue handkerchiefs are for girls like me to dry their tears on so they can get busy and do what a housewife has to do. Throw open the windows and start getting the house ready, and the dinner, maybe clean the silver and put new geraniums in the box. *Everything to be ready for him when he walks through that door.*[4]

Of course, it is not only the sheet and pillowcase manufacturers, the cosmetics industry, and the home furnishings salesmen who profit from and make use of the cultural definitions of men and women. The example above is blatantly and overtly pitched to a particular kind of sexist stereotype: the child nymph. But almost all aspects of the media are normative, that is, they have to do with the ways in which beautiful people, or just folks, or ordinary Americans, or extraordinary Americans should live their lives. They define the possible, and the possibilities are usually in terms of what is male and what is female.

It is an interesting but limited exercise to show that psychologists and psychiatrists embrace these sexist norms of our culture, that they do not see beyond the most superficial and stultifying conceptions of female nature, and that their ideas of female nature serve industry and commerce so well. Just because it is good for business does not mean it is wrong. What I will show is that it is wrong; that there is not the tiniest shred of evidence that these fantasies of servitude and childish dependence have anything to do with women's true potential; that the idea of the nature of human possibility which rests on the accidents of individual development of genitalia, on what is possible today because of what happened yesterday, on the fundamentalist myth of sex-organ causality, has strangled and deflected psychology so that it is relatively useless in describing, explaining, or predicting humans and their behavior. It then goes without saving that present psychology is less than worthless in contributing to a vision that could truly liberate—men as well as women.

The central argument of my essay, then, is this. Psychology has nothing to say about what women are really like, what they need and what they want, essentially because psychology does not know. I want to stress that this failure is not limited to women; rather, the kind of psychology that has addressed itself to how people act and who they are has failed to understand in the first place why people act the way they do, and certainly failed to understand what might make them act differently.

These psychologists, whether engaged in academic personality research or in clinical psychology and psychiatry, make the central assumption that human behavior rests on an individual and inner dynamic, perhaps fixed in infancy, perhaps fixed by genitalia, perhaps simply arranged in a rather immovable cognitive network. But this assumption is rapidly losing ground as personality psychologists fail again and again to get consistency in the assumed personalities of their subjects.[5] Meanwhile, the evidence is accumulating that what a person does and who he believes himself to be will in general be a function of what people around him expect him to be, and what the overall situation in which he is acting implies that he is. Compared to the influence of the social context within which a person lives, his or her history and traits, as well as biological make-up, may simply be random variations, noise superimposed on the true signal that can predict behavior.

Some academic personality psychologists are at least looking at the counterevidence and questioning their theories; no such corrective is occurring in clinical psychology and psychiatry. Freudians and neo-Freudians, Adlerians and neo-Adlerians, classicists and swingers, clinicians and psychiatrists simply refuse to look at the evidence against their theory and practice. And they support their theory and their practice with stuff so transparently biased as to have absolutely no standing as empirical evidence.

To summarize: psychology has failed to understand what people are and how they act because (1) psychology has looked for inner traits when it should have been noting social context; and (2) theoreticians of personality have generally been clinicians and psychiatrists, and they have never considered it necessary to offer evidence to support their theories.

THEORY WITHOUT EVIDENCE

Let us turn to the second cause of failure first: the acceptance by psychiatrists and clinical psychologists of theory without evidence. If we inspect the literature of personality, it is immediately obvious that the bulk of it is written by clinicians and psychiatrists whose major support for their theories is "years of intensive clinical experience." This is a tradition started by Freud. His "insights" occurred during the course of his work with his patients. Now there is nothing wrong with such an approach to theory *formulation;* a person is free to make up theories with any inspiration that works: divine revelation, intensive clinical practice, a random numbers table. However, he is not free to claim any validity for his theory until it has been tested and confirmed. But theories are treated in no such tentative way in ordinary clinical practice. Consider Freud. What he thought constituted evidence fell short of the most minimal conditions of scientific rigor. In *The Sexual Enlightenment of Children,* the classic document that is supposed to demonstrate empirically the existence of a castration complex and its connection to a phobia, Freud based his analysis on the reports of the father of the little boy, himself in therapy, and a devotee of Freudian theory.[6] I really do not have to comment further on the contamination in this kind of evidence. It is remarkable that only recently has Freud's classic theory on the sexuality of women —the notion of the double orgasm—been actually tested physiologically and found just plain wrong. Now those who claim that fifty years of psychoanalytic experience constitute evidence enough of the essential truths of Freud's theory should ponder the robust health of the double orgasm. Did women, until Masters and Johnson,[7] believe they were having two different kinds of orgasm? Did their psychiatrists cow them into reporting something that was not true? If so were there other things they reported that were also not true? Did psychiatrists ever observe anything different from what their theories had led them to believe? If clinical experience means anything at all, surely we should have been done with the double-orgasm myth long before the Masters and Johnson studies.

But certainly, you may object, "years of intensive clinical experience" are the only reliable measure in a discipline that rests for its findings on insights, sensitivity, and intuition. The problem with insight, sensitivity, and intuition is that they can confirm for all time the biases that one started out with. People used to be absolutely convinced of their ability to tell which of their number were engaging in witchcraft. All it required was some sensitivity to the workings of the devil.

Years of intensive clinical experience are not the same thing as empirical evidence. The first thing an experimenter learns in any kind of experiment that involves humans is the concept of the double blind. The term is taken from medical experiments, where one group is given a drug which is presumably supposed to change behavior in a certain way, and a control group is given a placebo. If the observers or the subjects know which group took which drug, the result invariably comes out of the positive side for the new drug. Only when it is not known which subject took which pill is validity remotely approximated. In addition, with judgments of human behavior, it is so difficult to precisely tie down just what behavior is going on, let alone what behavior should be expected, that one must test again and again the reliability of judgments. How many judges, blind, will agree in their observations? Can they repeat their own judgments at some later time? When in actual practice these judgment criteria are tested for clinical judgments, then we find that the judges cannot judge reliably, nor can they judge consistently; they do no better than chance in identifying which of a certain set of stories were written by men and which by women; which of a whole battery of clinical test results were the products of homosexuals and which were the products of heterosexuals,[8] and which of a battery of clinical test results and interviews (where questions are asked such as "Do you have delusions?")[9] were products of psychotics, neurotics, psychosomatics, or normals. Let me stress the implications of these findings. The ability of judges, chosen for their clinical expertise, to distinguish male heterosexuals from male homosexuals on the basis of three widely used clinical projective tests—the Rorschach, the TAT, and the MAP—was *no better than chance.* The reason this is such devastating news, of course, is that sexuality is supposed to be of fundamental importance in the deep dynamic of personality; if what is considered gross sexual deviance cannot be recognized, then what are psychologists talking about when they, for example, claim that at the basis of paranoid psychosis is "latent homosexual panic?" They cannot even identify what homosexual anything is, let alone "latent homosexual panic."[10] More frightening, expert clinicians cannot be consistent about what diagnostic category to assign to a person, again on the basis of both tests and interviews; a number of normals in the Little and Schneidman study were described as psychotic, in such categories as schizophrenic with homosexual tendencies or schizoid character with depressive trends. But most disheartening, when the judges were asked to rejudge the test protocols some weeks later, their diagnosis of the same subjects on the basis of the same protocols differed markedly from their initial judgments. It is obvious that even simple descriptive conventions in clinical psychology cannot be consistently applied; that these descriptive conventions have any explanatory significance is therefore, of course, out of the question.

As a graduate student at Harvard some years ago, I was a member of a seminar that was asked to identify which of two piles of a clinical test, the

TAT, had been written by males and which by females. Only four students out of twenty identified the piles correctly; this was after one and a half months of intensively studying the differences between men and women. Since this result is below chance—that is, this result would occur by chance about four out of a thousand times—we may conclude that there *is* finally a consistency here; students are judging knowledgeably within th context of psychological teaching about the differences between men and women; the teachings themselves are simply erroneous.

You may argue that the theory may be scientifically "unsound" but at least it cures people. There is no evidence that it does. In 1952 Eysenck reported the results of what is called an "outcome of therapy" study of neurotics which showed that, of the patients who received psychoanalysis, the improvement rate was 44 percent; of the patients who received psychotherapy, the improvement rate was 64 percent; and of the patients who received no treatment at all, the improvement rate was 72 percent.[11] These findings have never been refuted; subsequently later studies have confirmed the negative results of the Eysenck study.[12] How can clinicians and psychiatrists, then, in all good conscience, continue to practice? Largely by ignoring these results and being careful not to do outcome-of-therapy studies. The attitude is nicely summarized by J. B. Rotter: "Research studies in psychotherapy tend to be concerned more with psychotherapeutic procedure and less with outcome ... to some extent, it reflects an interest in the psychotherapy situation as a kind of personality laboratory."[13] Some laboratory.

THE SOCIAL CONTEXT

Since clinical experience and tools can be shown to be worse than useless when tested for consistency, efficacy, agreement, and reliability, we can safely conclude that theories of a clinical nature advanced about women are also worse than useless. I want to turn now to the second major point in my essay: even when psychological theory is constructed so that it may be tested, and rigorous standards of evidence are used, it has become increasingly clear that in order to understand why people do what they do, and certainly in order to change what people do, psychologists must turn away from the theory of the causal nature of the inner dynamic and look to the social context within which individuals live.

Before examining the relevance of this approach for the question of women, let me first sketch the groundwork for this assertion. In the first place, it is clear that personality tests never yield consistent predictions;[14] a rigid authoritarian on one measure will be an unauthoritarian on the next. But the reason for this inconsistency is only now becoming clear; it seems overwhelmingly to have much more to do with the social situation in which the subject finds himself than with the subject himself.

In a series of brilliant experiments, R. Rosenthal and his coworkers have shown that if one group of experimenters has one hypothesis about what they expect to find, and another group of experimenters has the opposite hypothesis, both groups will obtain results in accord with their hypotheses.[15] The results obtained are not due to mishandling of data by biased experimenters; rather, the bias of the experimenter somehow creates a changed environment in which subjects actually act differently. For instance, in one experiment subjects were to assign numbers to pictures of men's faces, with high numbers representing the subject's judgment that the man in the picture was a successful person, and low numbers representing the subject's judgment that the man in the picture was an unsuccessful person. One group of experimenters was told that the subjects tended to rate the faces high; another group of experimenters was told that the subjects tended to rate the faces low. Each group of experimenters was instructed to follow precisely the same procedure: they were required to read to subjects a set of instructions and to *say nothing else.* For the 375 subjects run, the results showed clearly that those subjects who performed the task with experimenters who expected high ratings gave high ratings, and those subjects who performed the task with experimenters who expected low ratings gave low ratings. How did this happen? The experimenters all used the same words, but something in their conduct made one group of subjects do one thing, and another group of subjects do another thing.

The concreteness of the changed conditions produced by expectation is a fact, a reality: even in two separate studies with animal subjects, those experimenters who were told that rats learning mazes had been especially bred for brightness obtained better learning from their rats than did experimenters believing their rats to have been bred for dullness.[16] In a very recent study Rosenthal and Jacobson extended their analysis to the natural classroom situation.[17] Here, they tested a group of students and reported to the teachers that some among the students tested "showed great promise." Actually, the students so named had been selected on a random basis. Some time later, the experimenters retested the group of students: those students whose teachers had been told that they were "promising" showed real and dramatic increments in their I.Q.'s as compared to the rest of the students. Something in the conduct of the teachers toward those whom the teachers believed to be the "bright" students made those students brighter.

Thus, even in carefully controlled experiments and with no outward or conscious difference in behavior, the hypotheses we start with will influence the behavior of the subject enormously. These studies are extremely important when assessing the validity of psychological studies of women. Since it is beyond doubt that most of us start with notions about the nature of men and women, the validity of a number of observations of sex differences is questionable, even when these observations have been made under carefully controlled conditions. Second, and more important, the Rosenthal experiments point quite clearly to the influence of social expectation. In some extremely important ways, people are what you expect them to be, or at least they behave as you expect them to behave. Thus, if women, according to Bettelheim, want first and foremost to be good wives and mothers, it is extremely likely that this is what Bruno Bettelheim and the rest of society want them to be.

Another series of brilliant social psychological experiments point to the overwhelming effect of social context. These are the obedience experiments of Stanley Milgram in which subjects are asked to obey the orders of unknown experimenters, orders which carry with them the distinct possibility that the subject is killing somebody.[18] In Milgram's experiments a subject is told that he is administering a learning experiment and that he is to deal out shocks each time the other subject (in reality, a confederate of the experimenter) answers incorrectly. The equipment appears to provide graduated shocks ranging upward from 15 volts through 450 volts; for each of four consecutive voltages there are verbal descriptions such as "mild shock," "danger, severe shock," and, finally, for the 435 and 450 volt switches, a red XXX marked over the switches. Each time the stooge answers incorrectly the subject is supposed to increase the voltage. As the voltage increases, the stooge begins to cry in pain; he demands that the experiment stop; finally, he refuses to answer at all. When he stops responding, the experimenter instructs the subject to continue increasing the voltage; for each shock administered the stooge shrieks in agony. Under these conditions about 62.5 percent of the subjects administered shocks that they believed to be possibly lethal.

No tested individual differences between subjects predicted how many would continue to obey and who would break off the experiment. When forty psychiatrists predicted how many of a group of 100 subjects would go on to give the lethal shock, their predictions were orders of magnitude below the actual percentages; most expected only one-tenth of one percent of the subjects to obey to the end.

But even though psychiatrists have no idea how people will behave in this situation, and even though individual differences do not predict which subjects will obey and which will not, it is easy to predict when subjects will be obedient and when they will be defiant. All the experimenter has to do is change the social situation. In a variant of Milgram's experiment, two stooges were present in addition to the "victim"; these worked along with the subject in administering electric shocks. When these two stooges refused to go on with the experiment, only 10 percent of the subjects continued to the maximum voltage. This is critical for personality theory. It says that behavior can only be predicted from the social situation, not from the individual history.

Finally, an ingenious experiment by S. Schachter and S. E. Singer showed that subjects injected with adrenalin, which produces a state of physiological arousal in all but minor respects identical to that which occurs when subjects are extremely afraid, became euphoric when they were in a room with a stooge who was acting euphoric, and became extremely angry when they were placed in a room with a stooge who was acting extremely angry.[19]

To summarize: if subjects under quite innocuous and noncoercive social conditions can be made to kill other subjects and under other types of social conditions will positively refuse to do so; if subjects can react to a state of physiological fear by becoming euphoric, because somebody else around is euphoric, or angry, because somebody else around is angry; if students become intelligent because teachers expect them to be intelligent, and rats run mazes better because experimenters are told the rats are bright, then it is obvious that a study of human behavior requires, first and foremost, a study of the social contexts within which people move, of the expectations about how they will behave, and of the authority that tells them who they are and what they are supposed to do.

BIOLOGICALLY BASED THEORIES

Two theories of the nature of women, which come not from psychiatric and clinical tradition, but from biology, can be disposed of now with little difficulty. The first biological theory of sex differences argues that since females and males differ in their sex hormones, and sex hormones enter the brain, there must be innate differences in nature.[20] But this argument only tells us that there are differences in physiological state. The problem is whether these differences are at all relevant to behavior. Recall that Schachter and Singer have shown that a particular physiological state can itself lead to a multiplicity of felt emotional states and outward behavior, depending on the social situation.[21] The second theory is a form of biological reductionism: sex-role behavior in some primate species is described, and it is concluded that this is the natural behavior for humans. Putting aside the not insignificant problem of observer bias (for instance, H. Harlow of the University of Wisconsin, after observing differences between male and female rhesus monkeys, quotes Lawrence Sterne to the effect that women are silly and trivial and concludes that "men and women have differed in the past and they will differ in the future"),[22] there are a number of problems with this approach.

The most general and serious problem is that there are no grounds to assume that anything primates do is necessary, natural, or desirable in humans, for the simple reason that humans are not nonhumans. For instance, it is found that male chimpanzees placed alone with infants will not "mother" them. Jumping from hard data to ideological speculation researchers conclude from this information that *human* females are necessary for the safe growth of human infants. Following this logic, it would be as reasonable to conclude that it is quite useless to teach human infants to speak since it has been tried with chimpanzees and it does not work.

One strategy that has been used is to extrapolate from primate behavior to "innate" human preference by noticing certain trends in primate behavior as one moves phylogenetically closer to humans. But there are great difficulties with this approach. When behaviors from lower primates are directly opposite to those of higher primates, or to those one expects of humans, they can be dismissed on evolutionary grounds — higher primates and/or humans grew out of that kid stuff. On the other hand, if the behavior of higher primates is counter to the behavior considered natural for humans, while the behavior of some lower primate is considered natural for humans, the higher primate behavior can be dismissed also on the grounds that it has diverged from an older, prototypical pattern. So either way, one can select those behaviors one wants to prove an innate for humans. In addition, one does not know whether the sex-role behavior exhibited is dependent on the phylogenetic rank or on the environmental conditions (both physical and social) under which different species live.

Is there then any value at all in prime observations as they relate to human females and males? There is a value but it is limited: its function can be no more than to show some extant examples of diverse sex-role behavior. It must be stressed, however, that this is an extremely limited function. The extant behavior does not begin to suggest all the possibilities, either for nonhuman primates or for humans. Bearing these caveats in mind, it is nonetheless interesting that if one inspects the limited set of existing nonhuman primate sex-role behaviors, one finds, in fact, a much larger range of sex-role behavior than is commonly believed to exist. Biology appears to limit very little; the fact that a female gives birth does not mean, even in nonhumans, that she necessarily cares for the infant (in marmosets, for instance, the male carries the infant at all times except when the infant is feeding).[23] Natural female and male behavior varies all the way from females who are much more aggressive and competitive than males (for example, Tamarins)[24] and male "mothers" (for example, Titi monkeys, night monkeys, and marmosets),[25] to submissive and passive females and male antagonists (for example, rhesus monkeys).[26]

But even for the limited function that primate arguments serve, the evidence has been misused. Invariably, only those primates have been cited that exhibit exactly the kind of behavior that the proponents of the biological basis of human female behavior wish were true for humans. Thus, baboons and rhesus monkeys are generally cited: males in these groups exhibit some of the most irritable and aggressive behavior found in primates, and if one wishes to argue that females are naturally passive and submissive, these groups provide vivid examples. There are abundant counterexamples, such as those mentioned above; in fact, in general a counterexample can be found for every sex-role behavior cited, including, male "mothers." The presence of counterexamples has not stopped florid and overarching theories of the natural or biological basis of male privilege from proliferating. For instance, there have been a number of theories dealing with the innate incapacity of human males for monogamy. Here, as in most of this type of theorizing, baboons are a favorite example, probably because of their fantasy value: the family unit of the hamadryas baboon, for instance, consists of a highly constant pattern of one male and a number of females and their young. And again, the counterexamples, such as the invariably monogamous gibbon, are ignored.

An extreme example of this maiming and selective truncation of the evidence in the service of a plea for the maintenance of male privilege is a recent book, Men in Groups, by a man who calls himself Tiger.[27] The central claim of this book is that females are incapable of honorable collective action because they are incapable of "bonding" as in "male bonding."[28] What is male bonding? Its surface definition is simple: "a particular relationship between two or more males such that they react differently to members of their bonding units as compared to individuals outside of it."[29] If one deletes the word male, the definition, on its face, would seem to include all organisms that have any kind of social organization. But this is not what Tiger means. For instance, Tiger asserts that because females are incapable of bonding, they should be restricted from public life. Why is bonding an exclusively male behavior? Because, says Tiger, it is seen in male primates. All male primates? No, very few male primates. Tiger cites two examples where male bonding is seen: rhesus monkeys and baboons. Surprise, surprise. But not even all baboons: as mentioned above, the hamadryas social organization consists of one-male units; so does that of the Gelada baboon.[30] The great apes do not go in for male bonding much either. The male bond is hardly a serious contribution to scholarship; one reviewer for Science has observed that the book "shows basically more resemblance to a partisan political tract than to a work of objective social science," with male bonding being "some kind of behavioral phlogiston."[31]

In short, primate arguments have generally misused the evidence: primate studies themselves have, in any case, only the very limited function of describing some possible sex-role behavior; and at present, primate observations have been sufficiently limited so that even the range of possible sex-role behavior for nonhuman primates is not known. This range is not known since there is only minimal observation of what happens to behavior if the physical or social environment is changed. In one study different troops of Japanese macaques were observed.[32] Here, there appeared to be cultural differences: males in three out of the eighteen troops observed differed in their aggressiveness and infant-caring behavior. There could be no possibility of differential evolution here; the differences seemed largely transmitted by infant socialization. Thus, the very limited evidence points to some plasticity in the sex-role behavior of nonhuman primates; if we can devise experiments that massively change the social organization of primate groups, it is possible that we may observe great changes in behavior. At present, however, we must conclude that since nonhuman primates are too stupid to change their social conditions by themselves, the innateness and fixedness of their behavior is simply not known. Thus, even if there were some way — which there is not — to settle on the behavior of a particular primate species as being the "natural" way for humans, we would not know whether or not this behavior was simply some function of the present social organization of that species. And finally, once again it must be stressed that even if nonhuman primate behavior turned out to be relatively fixed, this would say little about our behavior. More immediate and relevant evidence, that is, the evidence from social psychology, points to an enormous plasticity in human behavior, not only from one culture to the next, but from one experimental group to the next. One of the most salient features of human social organization is its variety; there are a number of cultures where there is at least a rough equality between men and women.[33] In summary, primate arguments can tell us very little about our innate sex-role behavior; if they tell us anything at all, they tell us that there is no one biologically natural female or male behavior and that sex-role behavior in nonhuman primates is much more varied than has previously been thought.

CONCLUSION

In brief, the uselessness of present psychology with regard to women is simply a special case of the general conclusion: one must understand social expectations about women if one is going to characterize the behavior of women.

How are women characterized in our culture and in psychology? They are inconsistent, emotionally unstable, lacking in a strong conscience or superego, weaker, nurturant rather than productive, intuitive rather than intelligent, and, if they are at all "normal," suited to the home and the family. In short, the list adds up to a typical minority-group stereotype of inferiority:[34] if women know their place, which is in the home, they are really quite lovable, happy, childlike, loving creatures. In a review of the intellectual differences between little boys and little girls, Eleanor Maccoby has shown that there are no intellectual differences until about high school, or, if there are, girls are slightly ahead of boys.[35] In high school girls begin to do worse on a few intellectual tasks, such as arithmetic reasoning, and beyond high school the achievement of women now measured in terms of productivity and accomplishment drops off even more rapidly. There are a number of other, nonintellectual tests which show sex differences; I chose the intellectual differences since it is seen clearly that women start becoming inferior. It is useless to talk about women being different but equal; all of the tests I can think of have a "good" outcome and a "bad" outcome. Women usually end up at the "bad" outcome. In light of social expectations about women, what is surprising is not that women end up where society expects they will; what is surprising is that little girls do not get the message that they are supposed to be stupid until high school; and what is even more remarkable is that some women resist this message even after high school, college, and graduate school.

My essay began with remarks on the task of discovering the limits of human potential. Psychologists must realize that it is they who are limiting discovery of human potential. They refuse to accept evidence if they are clinical psychologists, or, if they are rigorous, they assume that people move in a context-free ether, with only their innate dispositions and their individual traits determining what they will do. Until psychologists begin respecting evidence and until they begin looking at the social contexts within which people move, psychology will have nothing of substance to offer in this task of discovery. I do not know what immutable differences exist between men and women apart from differences in their genitals; perhaps there are some other unchangeable differences; probably there are a number of irrelevant differences. But it is clear that until social expectations for men and women are equal, until we provide equal respect for both men and women, our answers to this question will simply reflect our prejudices.

Notes

[1]B. Bettelheim, "The Commitment Required of a Woman Entering a Scientific Profession in Present-day American Society," in *Woman and the Scientific Professions,* an MIT Symposium on American Women in Science and Engineering (Cambridge, Mass., 1965).

[2]E. Erikson, "Inner and Outer Space: Reflections on Womanhood," *Daedalus* 93 (1964): 582–606.

[3]J. Rheingold, *The Fear of Being a Woman* (New York: Grune & Stratton, 1964), p. 714.

[4]Fieldcrest advertisement in the *New Yorker,* 1965. My italics.

[5]J. Block, "Some Reasons for the Apparent Inconsistency of Personality," *Psychological Bulletin* 70 (1968): 210–212.

[6]S. Freud, *The Sexual Enlightenment of Children* (New York: Collier Books, 1963).

[7]W. H. Masters and V. E. Johnson, *Human Sexual Response* (Boston: Little Brown, 1966).

[8]E. Hooker, "Male Homosexuality in the Rorschach," *Journal of Projective Techniques* 21 (1957): 18–31.

[9]K. B. Little and E. S. Schneidman, "Congruences among Interpretations of Psychological and Anamnestic Data," *Psychological Monographs* 73 (1959): 1–42.

[10]It should be noted that psychologists have been as quick to assert absolute truths about the nature of homosexuality as they have about the nature of women. The arguments presented in this essay apply equally to the nature of homosexuality; psychologists know nothing about it; there is no more evidence for the "naturalness" of heterosexuality than for the "naturalness" of homosexuality. Psychology has functioned as a pseudoscientific buttress for our cultural sex-role notions, that is, as a buttress for patriarchal ideology and patriarchal social organization. Women's liberation and gay liberation fight against a common victimization.

[11]H. J. Eysenck, "The Effects of Psychotherapy: An Evaluation," *Journal of Consulting Psychology* 16 (1952): 319–324.

[12]F. Barron and T. Leary, "Changes in Psychoneurotic Patients with and without Psychotherapy," *Journal of Consulting Psychology* 19 (1955): 239–245; A. E. Bregin, "The Effects of Psychotherapy: Negative Results Revisited," *Journal of Consulting Psychology* 10 (1963): 244–250; R. D. Cartwright and J. L. Vogel, "A Comparison of Changes in Psychoneurotic Patients during Matched Periods of Therapy and No-Therapy," *Journal of Consulting Psychology* 24 (1960): 121–127; E. Powers and H. Witmer, *An Experiment in the Prevention of Delinquency* (New York: Columbia University Press, 1951); C. B. Traux, "Effective Ingredients in Psychotherapy: An Approach to Unraveling the Patient-Therapist Interaction," *Journal of Counseling Psychology* 10 (1963): 256–263.

[13]J. B. Rotter, "Psychotherapy," *Annual Review of Psychology* 11 (1960): 381–414.

[14]Block, *op. cit.*

[15]R. Rosenthal and L. Jacobson, *Pygmalion in the Classroom: Teacher Expectation and Pupil's Intellectual Development* (New York: Holt, Rinehart & Winston, 1968); R. Rosenthal, *Experimenter Effects in Behavioral Research* (New York: Appleton-Century Crofts, 1966).

[16]R. Rosenthal and K. L. Fode, "The Effect of Experimenter Bias on the Performance of the Albino Rat," unpublished manuscript (Cambridge: Harvard University, 1960); R. Rosenthal and R. Lawson, "A Longitudinal Study of the Effects of Experimenter Bias on the Operant Learning of Laboratory Rats," unpublished manuscript (Cambridge: Harvard University, 1961).

[17]Rosenthal and Jacobson, *op cit.*

[18]S. Milgram, "Some Conditions of Obedience and Disobedience to Authority," *Human Relations* 18 (1965): 57–76; S. Milgram, "Liberating Effects of Group Pressure," *Journal of Personality and Social Psychology* 1 (1965): 127–134.

[19]S. Schachter and J. E. Singer, "Cognitive, Social and Physiological Determinants of Emotional State," *Psychological Review* 69 (1962): 379–399.

[20]D. A. Hamburg and D. T. Lunde, "Sex Hormones in the Development of Sex Differences in Human Behavior," in E. Maccoby, ed., *The Development of Sex Differences* (Stanford: Stanford University Press, 1966), pp. 1–24.

[21]Schacter and Singer, *op. cit.*

[22]H. F. Harlow, "The Heterosexual Affectional System in Monkeys," *The American Psychologist* 17 (1962): 1–9.

[23]G. D. Mitchell, "Paternalistic Behavior in Primates," *Psychological Bulletin* 71 (1969): 399–417.

[24]*Ibid.*

[25]*Ibid.*

[26]All these are lower-order primates, which makes their behavior with reference to humans unnatural, or more natural; take your choice.

[27]M. Schwarz-Belkin, "Les Fleurs du Mal," in *Festschrift for Gordon Piltdown* (New York: Ponzi Press, 1914), claims that the name was originally *Mouse*, but this may be a reference to an earlier L. Tiger (putative).

[28]L. Tiger, *Men in Groups* (New York: Random House, 1969).

[29]*Ibid.*, pp. 19–20.

[30]Mitchell, *op cit.*

[31]M. H. Fried, "Mankind Excluding Woman," review of Tiger's *Men in Groups*, *Science* 165 (1969): 884.

[32]J. Itani, "Paternal Care in the Wild Japanese Monkeys, *Macaca fuscata*," in C. H. Southwick, ed., *Primate Social Behavior* (Princeton, N.J.: Van Nostrand, 1963).

[33]M. Mead, *Male and Female: A Study of the Sexes in a Changeing World* (New York: William Morrow, 1949).

[34]H. M. Hacker, "Women as a Minority Group," *Social Forces* 30 (1951); 60–69.

[35]Maccoby, *op. cit.*

Writing task six: Write a thesis development essay which identifies the major argument of Weisstein's essay. List and explain all the writer's supporting evidence in your report about the writer's work. Then write two or three paragraphs suggesting alternative assumptions to those Weisstein lists.

Writing task seven: The author questions prevailing criteria through ironic asides, puns, and witty descriptions. In a short essay identify several uses of humor and speculate about the advantages and disadvantages of questioning assumptions through techniques of humor.

Questioning Assumptions through Dialectic

When you are asked to question and to change an idea or network of ideas, you will find an essay organized by the pattern of thesis-antithesis-synthesis particularly useful. In such an essay you set up a dialectic; you oppose two assumptions and use the resulting tension and conflict between the assumptions to analyze each and to finally synthesize both in some new idea which grows from both assumptions but is larger than either. *Dialectic* is the thinking and writing process of argument or exposition which systematically weighs contradictory facts or ideas with the intention of resolving their real or apparent contradictions.

We frequently use dialectic in our talk and writing. Whenever we talk about a "golden mean" we describe the synthesis of two extremes. Temperance would be the golden mean or the moderation of the opposed behaviors of gluttony and fasting unto death. A person self-described as *middle of the road* has chosen that political response to moderate the extremes he or she may fear in conservatism or liberalism.

When we define *ecology* as the continuous process of interactions between humans and their environment, we have defined dialectically. This synthesis of *ecology* is not so much a balancing on the seesaw between humans and environment as it is the large whole which contains within it contradictory forces. In Chinese dualistic philosophy, two opposed but complementary cosmic principles — yin/yang, the active/passive, sun/moon, masculine/feminine—exist in tension within a whole perception which affirms the two-in-oneness. You've seen this dialectic represented by this symbol: ☯

We use the term *adaptation* to describe the survival techniques which a species uses to respond to a threatening environment. In the struggle to survive, the species learns and adapts some new behavior. The adaptation is a synthesizing of opposed forces of species and environment. What syntheses have you devised for the "opposed" forces of the individual and society, of abstraction and concrete expression, of the sciences and the humanities? Earlier I used a dialectic to organize a chapter explaining the interrelationships of language and culture. You could diagram that dialectic in this manner:

THESIS: Language is conventional and locks us in the past.
ANTITHESIS: Language is creative and adapts to present needs.
SYNTHESIS: The creative and conventional aspects of language can be cross-structured to produce a culture which we can adapt to our future needs.

Another dialectic we could use to represent our discussion in Chapter Two looks like this:

THESIS: Language causes culture.
ANTITHESIS: Culture causes language.
SYNTHESIS: Language and culture interpenetrate each other.

Did you notice that when you use a dialectic, you are in fact combining older assumptions to generate a new assumption?

Many people look to the ideal of androgyny to synthesize and reconcile the sexes. *Androgyny* is a Greek word whose very form —*andro* (male) and *gyn* (female)—describes a union of male and female in a new spirit. Androgyny is a state of mind and range of experience in which individuals are not restricted to the roles and characteristics conventionally assigned by sex. An androgynous person defines the self not as man or woman but as man-in-woman and woman-in-man. You might diagram the dialectic of androgyny in this manner:

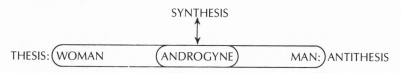

Do you remember the quiz which tested how "androgynous" you were? In that inventory, certain responses were described as "feminine," "masculine" or "androgynous." Do the authors of the inventory define *androgynous* in the same way that the dialectic plotted above defines *androgynous?*

The German philosopher Hegel first systematized dialectic as a new logical mode. Hegel described dialectic as the process of change in which an assumption or thesis set against its opposite or antithesis becomes transformed into the opposite where it is both preserved and fulfilled in an assumption of synthesis which is greater than the two combinants. If you thought about folk rock as such a dialectic, you would say that this new kind of music preserves both the thesis of folk music and the antithesis of rock and roll but that folk rock makes more full each type of music and also exists as an independent category.

When Karl Marx borrowed the Hegelian system of opposing paradoxes to make a new force, he insisted that in the conflict of opposing forces the thesis succumbed to the antithesis. The synthesis which resulted by the antithetical conquest of the first assumption immediately became a thesis and part of another contradiction of forces. Marx insisted that the dialectic is an open system in which the synthesis is never the final statement but always a thesis which can be transformed because it contains within itself contradictions. How might you apply this model of dialectic to the process of education? If "graduation" is the synthesis of a contradiction of forces (perhaps the individual's curiosity as opposed to the cultural criteria of stabilizing and fixing ideas), how would you restate the synthesis as a thesis? What might be an antithesis?

Marxist dialectic or dialectical materialism interprets reality as a continuous process of matter being changed through the constant conflict of the opposites arising from the internal contradictions inherent in matter. This dialectic explains that capitalism was the revolutionary new force which resulted from the conflict of feudalism and individualism. The dialectical materialist predicts that capitalism will be transformed through the opposition which characterizes capitalism: the proletariat and ruling class. What would you predict as the possible "synthesis?"

In this series of statements, you can practice the dialectical model of reasoning. In each set, I will leave one term of the dialectic unstated and you can play with alternative terms which might work in the dialectic:

THESIS: Grades are more punitive than motivating.
ANTITHESIS: Learners need feedback to define tasks and accomplishments.
SYNTHESIS:

THESIS: Groupwork can speed up the process of problem-solving.
ANTITHESIS:
SYNTHESIS: Group participation and individual participation become criteria for grading.

THESIS:
ANTITHESIS: Some men would be uncomfortable in a course focused on the communication of issues important to woman's sense of self.
SYNTHESIS: One agenda for such a course would be dealing with the feelings of all the learners about the course as it happens.

THESIS:
ANTITHESIS:
SYNTHESIS: An "open classroom."

Writing the Thesis–Antithesis–Synthesis Essay

When you write an essay informed by a dialectical structure, you ask your readers to balance in their minds two opposing forces and to trust you to ease the tension. You use a technique of suspense to catch and hold the reader's attention while you set down your view of things. You involve the reader in the tension of a conflict of forces and persuade the reader that the crisis needs solution. Through the process of generating a synthesis, you are often able to invent new ways of approaching and resolving old conflicts.

A dialectical essay has three parts; the length of each depends upon the purpose for which you use the dialectical essay. If resolving the conflict is the purpose of your essay, then the synthesis or third part would be much lengthier than parts one and two—thesis and antithesis. If your purpose is to describe, analyze and perhaps dramatize a conflict, them most of the essay would be parts one and two with part three — the synthesis — functioning as a concluding paragraph. There are two basic ways to write the dialectical essay. In outline form, they would look like this:

I. Thesis—description of some fact, idea, experience, assumption, feeling.
II. Antithesis—description and demonstration that some fact, idea, experience, assumption or feeling exists which directly opposes what has been shown in part I. A conflict between part I and part II is dramatized.
III. Synthesis—a solving of the conflict presented in the essay.

or

I. Thesis in conflict with antithesis
  A. $Thesis_1$–$antithesis_1$
  B. $Thesis_2$–$antithesis_2$
  C. $Thesis_3$–$antithesis_3$
  D. $Thesis_4$–$antithesis_4$
II. Synthesis which resolves all the conflicts demonstrated

Notice that with both of these patterns, the thesis and the antithesis are of equal length and complexity. If one weighed more than the other, then you would lose the tension of opposites which enlivens the essay. You would only be showing a situation where one force dominated over an opposed force. Notice also that you could certainly combine the two patterns into some other structures which would use a dialectic to work toward a synthesis.

In the synthesis you fuse the opposites into some new assumption or idea or reality. The synthesis could be a compromise; it could be a new idea which has aspects of both thesis and antithesis yet is greater than either (do you know *synergy*?); it could be the Marxist synthesis already described in which the thesis is transformed by the antithesis into some new synthesis.

Again, the synthesis can be brief or lengthy. Sometimes, a concise and aphoristically stated synthesis could best dramatize your new ideas. Sometimes, you might have to give the synthesis more rhetorical weight because you want to persuade readers to accept your synthesis.

Both patterns for structuring the thesis-antithesis-synthesis essay give you a tightly controlled essay form which systematically questions assumptions. The first pattern asks the reader to fully understand the thesis before learning about the anti- or opposed thesis. The second pattern of alternation of thesis and antithesis helps the reader because we always remember short units better than long ones. The conflict in this second pattern is always being demonstrated to the reader.

Be sure that your transition from thesis to antithesis is skillful. Otherwise the reader may feel like the ball in a pingpong game. Use transitional terms that point out the conflict by describing opposition. A series of conjunctions signal this opposition: *but, yet, however, nevertheless*. Phrases frequently signal a contrast transition: *and yet, in contrast, in spite of, on the contrary, on the other hand, opposed to, contrary to, despite this, polar to*. You can choose words which either through denotation or through metaphor reinforce the idea of conflict and thus hook thesis to antithesis: *opponents* and *proponents*, *opposed forces, armies, foes, battlelines, debaters, combatants* are helpful nouns. Think about verbs like *contradict, clash, debate, refute, oppose, march (into battle), spar, strike(back), counter*. Some adjectives like *polarized, diametrical, pro* and *con* are useful. What adverbs could be used?

Writing task eight: In a paragraph, state an antithesis to one of the following assumptions and invent an assumption which would be a synthesis.
Capital punishment in a deterrent to crime.
War is inevitable.

Civilization keeps us from being free.
Capital punishment is cruel and unusual punsihment.
A "human life amendment" would guarantee rights for all "persons."
The sexes will always battle.
Anatomy is destiny.

Writing task nine: Take the materials which you just developed and organize two outlines for an essay which would use the dialectical pattern.

Writing task ten: Write a dialectical essay from the materials you have generated.

Writing task eleven: Traditionally, love and work have been named as opposites which create conflicts for men and women. Adrienne Rich described the conflict in her poems and remarked that "The choice still seemed to be between 'love'—womanly, maternal love, altruistic love—a love defined and ruled by the weight of an entire culture—and 'egotis'—a force directed by men into creation, achievement, ambition, often at the expense of others, but justifiably so. For weren't they men, and wasn't that their destiny as womanly, selfless love was ours? I know now that the alternatives are false ones—that the word 'love' is itself in need of re-vision." Write an essay organized by the dialectical pattern which will find some synthesis to permit both men and women to experience both love and work.

Writing task twelve: Exchange essays with a peer and edit the essay, looking for the dialectical structure. In the margin, indicate what you see as thesis and antithesis and where you see the synthesis. Underline all the transitional devices which keep the essay together. In a sentence or two, tell the writer how successfully he or she has used the dialectical structure in the essay. When your essay is returned to you, see whether your peer's editings could help you revise the essay to make it more successful.

Suggested Group Writing and Discussing Activities

1. Prepare a slide show which first identifies and then transforms assumptions and sets of assumptions. Select one specific topic and research it carefully.
2. Practice role playing assumptions. Act out the old assumption. Then act out new assumptions which you have generated to question the old assumption. Topics that might work particularly well here would be dating, courtship, marriage, and family roles.
3. Write a parody of a television or radio program, a current song, or a film. Identify the criteria which organize it and which you will question or change through humor. Remember that for a parody to be successful, your audience needs to know the original. You will burlesque that form by imitating and by exaggerating the discrepancies between the original and the new form.
4. Use the dialectical organization to write a critique of your education and to suggest changes in the system.

Recommended Reading

Phyllis Chesler. *Women and Madness*. New York: Avon books, 1972.
Paolo Freire, *Pedagogy of the Oppressed*. New York; Seabury Press, 1973.

CHAPTER SIX

Writing Outlines

We have been practicing alternative patterns of thinking and writing. The skills which you have acquired or sharpened you can use in any writing situation. Knowing the assumptions which shape us, naming them, reflecting upon them and renaming them are the activities of the liberated thinker. In the chapters which follow, we will continue our practice of writing as "re-vision." We will formally examine several conventions of writing so that we will have a wide range of writing structures to combine and recombine for every writing situation.

You could certainly analyze and practice those conventions as an individual. However, all the writing tasks in the succeeding chapters have been designed so that they could also be completed through group reflection and writing. Through groupwork, we are testing another major assumption which governs most composition classrooms: the writer learns to write through solitary struggle. Let's try an alternative assumption: writers can learn to write through a series of collaborative processes. Some of the complex and difficult tasks become easier and more enjoyable when shared with other practicing writers.

A writing group can dramatize for each individual writer the interplay of thought and feeling which constitute any writing act. Within a group, the variety of skills and perceptions prompts us to see new ideas or new ways of approaching old ideas. What I didn't think to notice in a situation, the person sitting on my left noticed at once. What she didn't think to question, I did. Being too close to a problem sometimes blinds an individual to possible solutions. Having several extra sets of eyes might help him or her to spot a solution.

A group can speed up the prewriting process. When several people brainstorm, ideas come quicker. When they work on defining a thesis and deciding on an organizing strategy and making an outline of that strategy, they can play with more writing possibilities in a short time than a solitary writer might dredge up in a night's labor. Groupwork multiplies all the materials available to a writer. We can move more quickly from recognition to practice to re-cognition to rewriting.

Work that comes from a group is often what Buckminster Fuller calls *synergistic*. The group creates a whole that is more full and more innovative than all the parts summed up. There are many writing tasks where it simply makes good sense to work in a group and reap all the profits of that synergy. One of those tasks is outlining.

Outlining is one of the stages of prewriting. What, you ask, is this prewriting? Every writing process breaks up into at least three stages. During prewriting, you *invent:* you find what you want to write about, you find materials to use, you find patterns to use for writing, you figure out some one pattern for what you think you want to say. I have already asked you in several assignments to work first on these prewriting tasks.

In the stage of composing, you work out your ideas using as much as possible the organizing structure you have chosen. Of course, if you change your mind while you're writing about what you really want to write about, then you'll also change the structure you'll be using to organize and develop your ideas.

In what we call rewriting, you look carefully at your draft and decide how it might be changed, improved, polished, edited, and perhaps reperceived. Now, have you in fact followed these stages on all those occasions when you have written in this course? Yes and no. You might have skipped the prewriting or the rewriting stages and gotten in a jam. Or you might have gone through those stages and not have realized that in fact you were working through a series of complicated thinking tasks. For some writers, prewriting has become so habitual that it merges with the composing into one whole action of selecting, phrasing, questioning, detailing and renaming. For others, it is the hurdle that frustrates them. In this chapter we will practice some of the prewriting techniques you can use any time you write. You will also find some techniques for generating topics in Chapter Ten where we work with the research paper; you might want to read ahead and use those techniques for other essays you write.

Outlines

Every time you abstract assumptions and describe the ways that those assumptions make a scaffolding for thinking and writing, you are already constructing an outline. When you state a controlling thesis or define with the Aristotelian paradigm, you are choosing organizing structures which you can easily diagram in an outline. Outlining begins with your first uncertain selection of a topic and organizing assumptions and is involved in each part of your working with that topic. Without some sense of where to go, you wouldn't be able to write a sentence to follow the one you just wrote. You're not always aware that you do know where you're going.

You also may sometimes have two sets of directions and might be following one path for a while only to switch and set off in the opposite direction. When you make an outline by writing down where you are going, you are bringing to your own attention the method of thinking and organizing that will be best for you to follow and which you've already started to follow.

By diagramming that method, you can generate more ideas about your topic and you can examine the order, relationships, and significance of these ideas. You can use an outline as a diagnostic tool when your writing pulse slows or when you decide to rethink the topic or change the pattern for the writing. Through the x-ray of the outline, you can spot problems of organization or logic or style.

You can also use an outline as a way to look at the writing of others and to see how they have connected ideas. With an outline, you can better understand the topic and the patterns in what you read and you can identify patterns of writing that you might wish to practice. By knowing what patterns have been used by other writers and by diagramming the relationships of parts within the whole through an outline, you help yourself in prewriting, in composing, and in rewriting.

Writing task one: Set up several work groups with five members in each. After rereading the essay "When We Dead Awaken: Writing as Re-vision" by Adrienne Rich, write an outline which lists the main points of the essay. Compare the outlines written by all groups. What looks the same on all outlines? What seem to be the conventions of outlining? Save the group-generated outlines for further revising.

Idea Outline

Your group might have written an idea outline; it might have written a formal outline. Let's look at both kinds. An *idea outline* is often called a scratch outline and it is the first kind of outline we make when we are thinking through what we have read or what we will write. It is simply a list of terms, impressions, examples, definitions, and phrases, jotted down as they occur to the members of the group. I suspect, however, that your group produced a *formal outline* — an ordering which shows the connections between all those terms, impressions, examples, definitions, and phrases. Because Rich's essay was a finished writing, you would have been able to identify and reproduce the major logical units of the essay.

How you outline depends on why you are writing. If you are keeping a record of a chemistry lecture, you need a formal outline to preserve the patterns of subordination which the lecturer used. During a spirited and quick-moving discussion of personal criteria for an interdisciplinary classroom, you might jot down a running outline of suggestions. From that scratch outline, you could later organize the best suggestions into an essay calling for classroom reform.

The idea outline is particularly helpful in the first stages of writing. Through it, you can talk out loud to yourself about a possible subject, about what ideas intersect with your subject, about what words are associated with your topic, about what questions you might need to ask, and about what solutions are possible.

In a group, you could brainstorm and record the work on paper. To brainstorm, set a time limit—perhaps five minutes—and say everything that comes to mind when you think about the topic chosen or assigned. Don't censor any idea as silly or unworkable or inappropriate or irrelevant. Only later, after the group has practiced this "free association," do you read over the list of terms and judge them. Look for connections between all the items on this scratch outline and decide on the pattern of logic or feeling which would best organize them.

When you use this technique of brainstorming, you'll find that you have more ideas than you could use for one essay or even for one research paper. Save those materials for some other writing situation or for rethinking your finished essay.

In the outline which follows, you can see how random yet prolific were the associations of a group which brainstormed the topic "women and music." Do you see some patterns of organization that could be extracted and used for an essay or research paper?

Women *and* music or *in* music? kinds? Clara Schumann, Fanny Mendohlsson — classical music — composers — rediscovered composers — Mrs. Beach—conductors—Sara Caldwell—Antonia Brico—*Antonia*—first women's philharmonic—Judy Collins her student—folk music: Joan Baez, Joni Mitchell, Malvina Reynolds, Jean Redpath, Jean Ritchie, Hazel and Alice—country and folk?—themes: divorce, marriage, stand by your man, love, breaking up — Dolly Parton, Loretta Lynn — comparison of lyrics? — Odetta, Miriam Makeba, Joan Armatradding—jazz: Billy Holiday, Alberta Hunter, women's jazz festival, *Alive*—new women's groups: Lilith, Deadly Nightshade — Olivia Records — Kay Gardner, Meg Christian, Chris Williamson, Holly Near—politics and music—distribution and recording companies—women's music distinct from men's?

From such a list you could identify major themes to develop and new ways to approach the topic "women and music." You could focus on the "unknown women in our musical past" and research the topic further. When you do so, note down data, quotes, questions, and ideas related to the topic. The notes you gather for a researched essay are, in fact, a series of idea outlines which you rearrange into a formal outline and which you develop into an essay.

Writing task two: Brainstorm ideas for a short essay on the topic "new roles for men." Save the idea outline for a later task.

Writing task three: From the idea outline for the topic "women and music," develop three formal outlines.

The idea outline which follows came from a group which brainstormed responses to the cliché that "women are passive." What series of assumptions here would you pick out to develop into a formal outline?

hard to admit, would like to disagree
suppression influenced women's attitude
past beliefs: woman in home not in society; physically incapable, mentally
    incapable
passive — having environment act upon women,
rather than their acting upon the environment. Having no initiative; keeping
    more to themselves; seemingly ambivalent about their situation; meek and
    mild

active — the opposite of passive; out-going; involvement; acting upon the
    environment; enjoys doing things instead of sitting back and doing nothing.

Women's movement brings realization of overcoming fear; movement makes
    women reevaluate, push to change attitudes; make jobs, open more oppor-
    tunities and alternative roles

Contradiction: women are not passive

Why? speaking up for their rights
    more generally active; getting out and doing things
stretching out into the community
    more into sports and politics than ever

alternatives: concentrate on changing men's attitudes
strengthen confidence in things women do that have been put down; reem-
    phasizing the importance of things categorized as women's things and
    inferior
change language, roles

Can you see that the group could write at least six essays by selecting some of these ideas and discarding others? Did you notice that one suggestion included defining terms so the group could most efficiently talk about the assumption? Did you also notice one idea of reversing the assumption by collecting "proofs" and another idea to find alternative behaviors so that women would not be defined as passive? Could you select several of these ideas and combine them with the ideas they provoked in you to write an essay questioning the assumption that women are passive?

Writing task four: From the idea outline for the topic "women are passive," develop two formal outlines.

Writing task five: How does the poem "Planetarium" demonstrate Rich's thesis that writing is "re-vision?" Read over the poem again and then brainstorm responses to this question. Keep the idea outline which you draw up for use in the next writing task.

Formal Outline

This type of outline gives a form to the pattern of assumptions which you have already named in a scratch outline when you brainstormed or when you mulled over a topic. The formal outline evolves from your thinking about a problem and changes when your thinking changes. It is a kind of memo in shorthand about how you plan to organize and develop assumptions. Your outline is always tentative and should never restrict the free play of your thoughts.

When you sit down to write a formal outline, you are asking yourself quite specifically what you will write about and how you will write. You might give yourself the task of solving a problem when you come to this stage of prewriting. You could use the procedure of problem-solving which the educator John Dewey described:

1. Define the problem.
2. Describe and analyze the problem.
3. Suggest possible solutions.
4. Select the best solution.
5. Plan how the solution could be put into effect.

Following this model for problem-solving, you can eliminate ideas from the idea outline and focus on the particular ideas which you want to name. You could also use this model as one formal outline; in step one, you state the thesis and introduce the implications of the thesis. In subsequent steps, you develop the thesis and in step five you conclude by specifying a solution and how to put it into effect. This outline leads you to an argument or persuasive essay.

Often instructors will ask you to append an outline to the essay or the research paper which you have written. That outline would be the final statement about your pattern of organization for the writing. It may look radically unlike the formal outline which you began with; it may be the same; your experience of writing and rewriting the essay determines how it will look. It should provide your reader with an accurate x-ray of the writing; it should show the thesis and the major ideas which advance the thesis. It should show the reader how much of the writing is taken up with each major division and give the reader a good picture of how the divisions are arranged.

You divide the materials into categories and you arrange the materials within each category into a coherent sequence. Most often, you will classify by going from the general to the specific (deduction) or from the specific to the general (induction). Whatever patterns of classification you use, be sure that you are consistent in using the pattern.

Some conventions of sequencing include ordering by time, by space, by cause and effect, by comparison and contrast, by positive and negative arguments, and by an ordering of ideas from the least to the most important (climax). You also know several other ways to sequence: the inclusion-exclusion pattern, the dialectical pattern, and the patterns of the defining paradigms we've studied.

When you write a formal outline, you use a system of outline symbols to show the ranking and paralleling of ideas. One convention used most often follows the sequence: I,A,1,a. In the three outlines which follow you can see these symbols used. Two of the outlines use a chronological pattern. The first outline uses one-word descriptions or short phrases to diagram the design of the paper; it is called a topic outline. The second uses complete sentences and is called a sentence outline. The third combines both types to produce a formal outline which describes major ideas with complete sentences and which uses phrases to describe subordinate ideas or proofs. Whichever pattern you choose, you want to make the outline a clear diagram that will help you develop your ideas in the essay, that will help you diagnose any problems that might occur while you are writing the essay, that will help you to check the finished essay to see that it's unified, and that will help your reader to survey the essay.

The following outlines were developed for essays and research papers about the life and work of Margaret Sanger. Notice that the same research and facts organize all three writing projects.

1. Topic outline

Thesis: Despite great opposition, Margaret Sanger precipitated a twentieth-century social reform: the right to birth control.

I. Early Belief
    A. Parental influence
        1. Father
        2. Mother
II. Birth Control Pioneer
    A. Education
    B. Woman Rebel
        1. Indictment
        2. Defense
        3. Dismissal
    C. Civil Disobedience
        1. First birth control clinic
           a. Arrest
           b. Conviction
        2. Decision of U.S. Court of Appeals
III. Organizer
    A. *Birth Control Review*
    B. American Birth Control League
    C. National and international conferences
    D. National Committee on Federal Legislation for Birth Control
    E. *Journal of Conception*
    F. Birth Control Federation
    G. International Planned Parenthood
IV. Advocate
    A. Nonfiction
    B. Autobiography
V. Influence

You will notice that the sentence outline which follows describes the same subject matter with more detail. Each sentence listed in such an outline functions as the thesis statement for a division of the paper or as the topic sentence for at least one paragraph of exposition.

2. Sentence Outline

Thesis: Despite great odds, Margaret Sanger precipitated a twentieth-century social reform: the right of birth control.

    I. Sanger's conviction about the need for and right to birth control developed early in her career.
        A. Both parents influenced her to see birth control as a woman's right.
           1. Her father advocated women's suffrage, free libraries, books, and education.
           2. Her mother died young after bearing eleven children.
        B. As a young nurse, Sanger saw working-class women, old at thirty-five, die from self-induced abortions.

II. Sanger pioneered in the field of birth control.
   A. In 1912 she renounced nursing for birth control advocacy and traveled abroad to study and observe.
   B. In 1914 she became a "woman rebel" by pressing for birth control clinics and research.
      1. She published in 1914 *Woman Rebel,* the first magazine devoted to the cause of birth control.
         a. Publication defied the Comstock Law which forbade sending any information about obscene materials through the mails and which defined contraceptives as obscene materials.
         b. Sanger was indicted on nine counts and liable to forty-five years sentencing.
         c. When she was denied adequate time to prepare a defense, she left the country and prepared a defense through study abroad.
         d. The case was dismissed in 1916 before coming to trial.
      2. She founded in 1914 the National Birth Control League.
   C. In 1916, Sanger challenged New York state laws forbidding dissemination of contraceptive information.
      1. Sanger, a sister Edith Byrne, and a friend Fania Mindell opened the nation's first birth control clinic in the Brownsville ghetto in Brooklyn.
         a. Police closed the clinic as a "public nuisance" after nine days operation.
         b. Sanger was sent to a workhouse for a thirty-day sentence.
         c. She appealed the conviction.
      2. In 1918 the decision of the U. S. Court of Appeals allowed doctors to give contraceptive advice to women for cure of "disease" broadly defined.
         a. Doctors were previously restricted to giving advice only to males with venereal disease.
         b. The decision was modified to allow doctors to import contraceptives, send them through mails, and use them for a patient's well-being.
III. Sanger later turned from confrontation to organization, education, and new legislation.
   A. In 1917, she founded and published the *Birth Control Review* to encourage research and dissemination of research.
   B. In 1921, she established the American Birth Control League and served as president "to build up public opinion so that women would demand birth control information."
   C. From 1921 on, she organized a series of national and international conferences on the problem of population control.
      1. The first Birth Control Conference met in New York in 1921.
      2. Delegates from seventeen countries attended the International Birth Control Conference in 1925.
      3. Sanger organized the World Population Conference in Geneva in 1927.
      4. At the International Contraceptive Conference in 1930 in Zurich,

delegates discussed the problems of world hunger and overpopulation.

5. The need for birth control information for oppressed peoples was a topic of the American Conference on Birth Control in Washington, D.C., in 1934.

6. New information about contraceptive research was shared with delegates to the Conference on Contraceptive Practice and Clinical Research in New York, 1936.

D. In 1928, Sanger organized the National Committee on Federal Legislation for Birth Control to solicit Congressional support for the cause.

E. She was named in 1939 the honorary chairman when the American Birth Control League and the education branch of the Birth Control Research Bureau merged as the Birth Control Federation which was renamed Planned Parenthood in 1942.

F. Sanger served as the first president of the International Planned Parenthood founded in 1953.

IV. Sanger advocated woman's right to birth control in all her writings.

A. A series of book-length arguments were published which included *The Case for Birth Control* (1917), *Women, Morality and Birth Control* (1922), *Happiness in Marriage* (1926), and *Motherhood in Bondage* (1928).

B. She wrote for her own journals and for other periodicals.

C. She explained the cause and struggle in two autobiographies: *My Fight for Birth Control* (1931) and *Margaret Sanger: An Autobiography* (1938).

V. The effects of Sanger's crusade for birth control are multiple.

A. *Birth control* has entered the English language.

B. Many people now insist that they have the right to learn about and practice birth control.

C. Birth control research has made available the vasectomy, diaphragm, IUD, oral contraceptives, and the Billings method.

D. Research continues to find safe and effective means of birth control.

E. World leaders now view population control as a prerequisite to solving problems of hunger, conflict and war.

F. Because women now have control over their bodies, there are major changes in the ways they define themselves.

Both outlines use the divisions of chronology to organize the writing. Both conclude with a discussion of present and future effects of the social reform Margaret Sanger precipitated. Have you noticed how easily you could write an essay or a research paper from either outline? Have you noticed that you could also take the materials in each outline and rearrange them to serve some thesis other than the one stated?

You could, for example, write a thematic outline. Organizing chronologically is an easier task than organizing thematically and doesn't tax your cognitive muscles much. When you set yourself the task of abstracting assumptions, of identifying them, of tracing the growth of a theme and exploring its various aspects, you can make yourself see a topic in multiple and new perspectives. You not only report data as you would in a chronological organization; you also interpret data and evaluate the reported materials and even reperceive the themes.

You can see in the combination sentence and topic outline which follows how you might use the same research materials cited in the previous outline to identify and question and explore large patterns of thinking and feeling. For example, after citing a history of birth control reforms, you can ask "What does this mean? How is it connected with me today? What themes do I share for discussion and action with Margaret Sanger?" You can learn and name and speculate about the interconnections of one woman rebel with the changed society of the 1980's. You can enter her life from several critical directions—from her effect on your own life, from your assessment of how representative she might be of the idea "liberated woman," from the effects on the mores and morals of your world, from the usefulness of her life as a role model for those who followed her, from an evaluation of the significance of her beliefs, and from an assessment of the effectiveness of civil disobedience. You might argue that Sanger shared the assumptions which today make you more free because you have more options than your parents had and certainly more than your grandparents had. You could argue that her work has complicated the relationships between men and women. Many themes can be identified.

In this outline, watch how the themes introduced in the thesis statement are developed:

3. Combination Sentence and Topic Outline

Thesis: Margaret Sanger provoked a revolution that was personal, so-
      cial, and political by helping women change a definition from "Wom-
      en's Bodies, Men's Selves" to "Our Bodies, Our Selves."

I.   Sanger's crusade was revolutionary activity.
     A. Historically the lack of birth control served the male establishment.
        1. Legislation limited dispersal of contraceptive information to men suf-
           fering from venereal disease.
        2. The Comstock Law limited dispersal of contraceptive information.
     B. Sanger's crusade overthrew establishment dictates.
     C. The present access to birth control serves women and men.
II. The birth control revolution gives every woman personal control over her
     body and her life.
     A. Without birth control, there is a procreative risk from 12 to 50.
     B. Without birth control, options for women are limited.
        1. Marriage or career.
        2. Anxiety about marriage or career choices.

C. With birth control, women can participate in more jobs and more civic, political, social, and religious organizations.
D. With birth control, women exercise their right to sexual gratification.
III. The birth control revolution has changed and will change society.
    A. The most serious problems of the 1980s need Margaret Sangers and not Secretaries of Defense.
        1. Population crisis
           a. world hunger
           b. depletion of resources
           c. war
        2. Environmental crises
    B. Men and women can no longer relate to each other as they did before women controlled their anatomies and destinies.
IV. Reproductive freedom is prerequisite to other social changes.
    A. Women are emancipated and can demand equal rights.
    B. The misery of the working class is somewhat ameliorated.
    C. The idea of the family may be redefined.
    D. Class struggle may intensify when it is no longer true that "the rich get richer and the poor get children."
V. Formerly "Women's Bodies" served "Men's Selves."
    A. Legislation reflected this assumption.
    B. Sanger's crusade questioned and changed this assumption.
        1. Civil disobedience
        2. Research and publication
        3. Education
        4. Legislation
        5. Advocacy in writings
VI. Women today reperceive as Margaret Sanger predicted they would and they stipulate "Our Bodies, Our Selves."
    A. Multiple effects of Sanger's crusade shape our world.
        1. Freedom from procreative risk
        2. Increased options
        3. Birth control assumed a universal right.
        4. Birth control assumed prerequisite to world peace.
        5. Healthy sexuality assumed a universal right.
    B. Shared definitions inform Sanger's life and our lives.
        1. Right to birth control precedes civil and political rights.
        2. Rebellion often precedes the "granting" of equality.
        3. Our bodies, our selves.

Writing task six: Develop the idea outline for the topic "new roles for men" into a formal sentence outline.

Writing task seven: Take the outlines developed for the topics "women in music" and "women are passive" and revise them if necessary so that they use the conventions of the formal outline correctly.

Writing task eight: From the idea outline developed in response to the question "How does the poem 'Planetarium' demonstrate Rich's thesis that writing is re-vision?," construct a formal outline which will be a preliminary guide for a research paper. In Chapter Ten, the writing groups will work on such a research paper.

Suggested Group Writing and Discussing Activities

1. Brainstorm alternatives to the assumption that "women only are responsible for contraception."
2. Write a topic outline that would guide you in writing a long essay about any of the following topics: women in advertising; alternative models for marriage; women and science; househusbands; parenting; aging; surrogate mothers; part-time options for married couples; child abuse; or Title IX and education.

Recommended Reading

The Boston Women's Health Collective. *Our Bodies, Our Selves*. New York: Simon and Schuster, 1976.

——. *Our Selves and Our Children*. New York: Simon and Schuster, 1978.

Both these books grew out of collaborative writing. The writing collective researched and wrote these two health handbooks. Both are easy to read, frequently updated, and can point you to other works about health, women's bodies, parenting, and patients' rights.

Linda Gordon. *Woman's Body, Woman's Right: A Social History of Birth Control in America*. New York: Viking Press, 1976.

CHAPTER SEVEN

Group Writing:
Shaping and Reshaping Sentences

With sentences we make accessible to those who listen to us the thought patterns and the codes which we use to define our worlds. Through a sentence, you can transform your private thought into public statement. From a few sentence kernels, you can combine and recombine structures until you have crafted a new, perhaps previously unwritten, sentence which best embodies your thinking. In this chapter we will look at sentences as individual units, grouped together in introductory and concluding paragraphs, and patterned as comparisons and contrasts in an expository essay. We will identify and analyze the process of making and remaking sentences so that we may continue to define our assumptions, to generate new ideas, and to transform our selves.

You may have heard previous proscriptions which shrilled "Write complete sentences" and "Eliminate sentence fragments." We will be concerned with descriptions about the purpose, the syntax, the shape, and the completeness of thought units named *sentences*. Later you can conciously choose when to write a complete sentence and when to use a sentence fragment in your work.

We build all our sentences from the grammatical and semantic core of a *subject* and a *predicate*. Sometimes we use only the subject like *"You!"* and expect the reader to provide the predicate and any complements like " ... *wrote* this satire!" Sometimes we use only the predicate like "Write!" and expect our readers to supply a subject like *"You"* or *"Y'all"* or *"You guys."* But we always understand that the *two* components are required for a complete thought.

From the core of subject and predicate we have developed four additional sentence patterns which we use as kernel sentences. Each of these sentences we stretch into longer units by compounding and by modifying with words, phrases, and clauses. In each sentence—despite its length or complexity—we can always spot the core structure and classify groupings within the sentence by their relationships to the core structure. These five sentence patterns are basic to the English language.

1. *Subject –* PREDICATE
A *writer* DEFINES.
A very queer, composite, *being* thus EMERGES.
Anonymity RUNS in their blood.
Dogs WILL BARK; *people* WILL INTERRUPT; *money* MUST BE MADE; *health* WILL BREAK DOWN.

The verb in this sentence kernel is called *intransitive* because it does not show an action "going over" (*trans,* across and *ire,* to go) from the subject to an object. A verb which is intransitive in the S-P kernel may become transitive in the S-P-DO kernel.

2. *Subject –* PREDICATE – DIRECT OBJECT
A *writer* DEFINES the WORLD.
History scarcely MENTIONS HER.
She never WRITES her own LIFE and scarcely KEEPS a DIARY.
She DOMINATES the LIVES of kings and conquerors in fiction.

We use this sentence kernel most frequently. The convention may both demonstrate and reinforce over habitual perceptions of our world; you have already noticed the line which runs through this sequence of S-P-DO. The sentence shows some subject acting upon an object. The fact that another culture like the northern Chinese culture infrequently uses this kernel suggests that these speakers may see their world less often as a sequence of someone or something acting upon an object.

3. *Subject –* PREDICATE –*INDIRECT OBJECT –* DIRECT OBJECT
A *writer* GIVES her *AUDIENCE* precise DEFINITIONS of their world.
He WOULD GIVE *HER* a CHAIN of beads or a PETTICOAT, he said.
He also TOLD a *LADY* who applied to him for information THAT CATS DO NOT AS A MATTER OF FACT GO TO HEAVEN.

In this sentence pattern some object intervenes in the action between the subject and the direct object. The indirect object is involved in the transaction but is not the indirect recipient of the action described by the predicate. You can always identify this pattern by adding in the preposition *to* before the indirect object. When you read, you mentally add in the *to*.

4. *Subject –* PREDICATE –OBJECT –*OBJECT COMPLEMENT*
One *writer* CALLS her WORLD a *CAGE* which she escapes through song.
Indeed, if woman had no existence save in the fiction written by man, *one* COULD IMAGINE HER a *PERSON* of the utmost importance.
One KNOWS NOTHING *DETAILED,* NOTHING perfectly *TRUE* and *SUBSTANTIAL* about her.

Sometimes an object complement — either a noun or an adjective — follows the direct object and completes the statement about the direct object.

5. *Subject* – PREDICATE – SUBJECT COMPLEMENT
The writer's *task* is NAMING and RENAMING.
In fact, *she* WAS the SLAVE of any boy whose parents forced a ring upon her finger.
Imaginatively, *she* is OF THE HIGHEST IMPORTANCE; practically *she* is completely INSIGNIFICANT.
It WOULD HAVE BEEN IMPOSSIBLE, completely and entirely, for any woman to have written the plays of Shakespeare in the age of Shakespeare.

In this sentence kernel, a linking verb establishes a relationship between the subject and the word which follows the predicate and completes the statement about the subject. All copulative verbs link the components subject and subject complement; a small number of other verbs function as links. Some of these are *seem, look, appear.* The verbs *grow, become, sound, feel, smell* and *taste* can function as linking verbs whenever they describe the subject.

With the exception of the sentences about "the writer," all the sentences used above to model the basic sentence patterns of English come from the writing of Virginia Woolf in chapter three of *A Room of One's Own.* In this 1929 publication, Virginia Woolf reworked two lectures on "Women and Fiction" which she had earlier delivered at Newnham and Girton, long the only colleges for women at Cambridge University. In the book, Woolf puzzles over the question "Why are there so few literary works by women?" and she describes what is needed for any creative effort by women or men. Woolf demonstrates that in the literature published about women, many emotional responses of the male authors create static which interrupts their "objective analysis." She reminds us that when only men observe and write about women, the resulting view of women will be incomplete and will not encourage women to revise their images of themselves.

Woolf argues that to be creative in any endeavour, a woman requires encouragement, "guineas and locks." The guineas symbolize economic independence which gives the time to work. The locks, or what Woolf names "a room of one's own," symbolize the solitude and autonomy which a writer needs to turn away from the world of family and community in order to turn into the world of the self to think and to write. When you talk today about "needing space" to think through some problems and to work out alternatives, you are referring to the same psychic freedom which Woolf describes through the metaphor of *a room of one's own*.

You should read this writing by Woolf twice: once for undisrupted enjoyment and once for a more critical analysis. When you read it the first time, you will meet a writer of a finely tuned wit who carefully knits up ideas and subtly balances themes. You may find a kinship between this writing and the essays you have read by Adrienne Rich and by Tillie Olsen. All three writers speak about the state of mind essential to "revision." Do you remember also that Tillie Olsen cited Woolf as a model for her own thinking about what happens when people are kept from creating? I think Adrienne Rich also had Woolf's words in mind when she described her own struggle as a woman writer.

When you read the essay a second time, you should read it specifically to identify and analyze the sentence patterns which the writer has chosen. In this selection, you can see Woolf's talent for combining and recombining conventions of sentencing to produce new descriptions. On a separate sheet of paper, you should jot down which sentence core structures each sentence. If you use the shorthand of S-P or S-P-DO and so forth which we cited, this task won't be difficult. You may be surprised to discover the several ways Woolf juggles the elements within the pattern to write sentences that are both conventional and new. When you have completed your survey of kernel sentences within the Woolf selection, you will be asked to work with a group of writers to identify, analyze and evaluate some of the transformations Woolf worked on those kernel sentences.

A Room of One's Own (Chapter Three)

Virginia Woolf

It was disappointing not to have brought back in the evening some important statement, some authentic fact. Women are poorer than men because—this or that. Perhaps now it would be better to give up seeking for the truth, and receiving on one's head an avalanche of opinion hot as lava, discoloured as dish-water. It would be better to draw the curtains; to shut out distractions; to light the lamp; to narrow tne enquiry and to ask the historian, who records not opinions but facts, to describe under what conditions women lived, not throughout the ages, but in England, say in the time of Elizabeth.

For it is a perennial puzzle why no woman wrote a word of that extraordinary literature when every other man, it seemed, was capable of song or sonnet. What were the conditions in which women lived, I asked myself; for fiction, imaginative work that is, is not dropped like a pebble upon the ground, as science may be; fiction is like a spider's web, attached ever so lightly perhaps, but still attached to life at all four corners. Often the attachment is scarcely perceptible; Shakespeare's plays, for instance, seem to hang there complete by themselves. But when the web is pulled askew, hooked up at the edge, torn in the middle, one remembers that these webs are not spun in midair by incorporeal creatures, but are the work of suffering human beings, and are attached to grossly material things, like health and money and the houses we live in.

I went, therefore, to the shelf where the histories stand and took down one of the latest, Professor Trevelyan's *History of England*. Once more I looked up Women, found "position of," and turned to the pages indicated. "Wife-beating," I read, "was a recognised right of man, and was practised without shame by high as well as low. ... Similarly," the historian goes on, "the daughter who refused to marry the gentleman of her parents' choice was liable to be locked up, beaten and flung about the room, without any shock being inflicted on public opinion. Marriage was not an affair of personal affection, but of family avarice, particularly in the 'chivalrous' upper classes. ... Betrothal often took place while one or both of the parties was in the cradle, and marriage when they were scarcely out of the nurses' charge." That was about 1470, soon after Chaucer's time. The next reference to the position of women is some two hundred years later, in the time of the Stuarts. "It was still the exception for women of the upper and middle class to choose their own husbands, and when the husband had been assigned, he was lord and master, so far at least as law and custom could make him. Yet even so," Professor Trevelyan concludes, "neither Shakespeare's women nor those of authentic seventeenth-century memoirs, like the Verneys and the Hutchinsons, seem wanting in personality and character." Certainly, if we consider it, Cleopatra must have had a way with her; Lady Macbeth, one would suppose, had a will of her own; Rosalind, one might conclude, was an attractive girl. Professor Trevelyan is speaking no more than the truth when he remarks that Shakespeare's women do not seem wanting in personality and character. Not being a historian, one might go even further and say that women have burnt like beacons in all the works of all the poets from the beginning of time — Clytemnestra, Antigone, Cleopatra, Lady Macbeth, Phédre, Cressida, Rosalind, Desdemona, the Duchess of Malfi, among the dramatists; then among the prose writers: Millamant, Clarissa, Becky Sharp, Anna Karenina, Emma Bovary, Madame de Guermantes—the names flock to mind, nor do they recall women "lacking in personality and character." Indeed, if woman had no existence save in the fiction written by men, one would imagine her a person of the utmost importance; very various; heroic and mean; splendid and sordid; infinitely beautiful and hideous in the extreme; as great as a man, some think even greater.[1] But this is woman in fiction. In fact, as Professor Trevelyan points out, she was locked up, beaten and flung about the room.

A very queer, composite being thus emerges. Imaginatively she is of the highest importance; practically she is completely insignificant. She pervades poetry from cover to cover; she is all but absent from history. She dominates the lives of kings and conquerors in fiction; in fact she was the slave of any boy whose parents forced a ring upon her finger. Some of the most inspired words, some of the most profound thoughts in literature fall from her lips; in real life she could hardly read, could scarcely spell, and was the property of her husband.

It was certainly an odd monster that one made up by reading the historians first and the poets afterwards—a worm winged like an eagle; the spirit of life and beauty in a kitchen chopping up suet. But these monsters, however amusing to the imagination, have no existence in fact. What one must do to bring her to life was to think poetically and prosaically at one and the same moment, thus keeping in touch with fact — that she is Mrs. Martin, aged thirty-six, dressed in blue, wearing a black hat and brown shoes; but not losing sight of fiction either—that she is a vessel in which all sorts of spirits and forces are coursing and flashing perpetually. The moment, however, that one tries this method with the Elizabethan woman, one branch of illumination fails; one is held up by the scarcity of facts. One knows nothing detailed, nothing perfectly true and substantial about her. History scarcely mentions her. And I turned to Professor Trevelyan again to see what history meant to him. I found by looking at his chapter headings that it meant—

"The Manor Court and the Methods of Open-field Agriculture ... The Cistercians and Sheep-farming ... The Crusades ... The University ... The House of Commons... The Hundred Years' War... The Wars of the Roses... The Renaissance Scholars... The Dissolution of the Monasteries... Agrarian and Religious Strife ... The Origin of English Sea-power... The Armada..." and so on. Occasionally an individual woman is mentioned, an Elizabeth, or a Mary; a queen or a great lady. But by no possible means could middle-class women with nothing but brains and character at their command have taken part in any one of the great movements which, brought together, constitute the historian's view of the past. Nor shall we find her in any collection of anecdotes. Aubrey hardly mentions her. She never writes her own life and scarcely keeps a diary; there are only a handful of her letters in existence. She left no plays or poems by which we can judge her. What one wants, I thought—and why does not some brilliant student at Newnham or Girton supply it?—is a mass of information; at what age did she marry; how many children had she as a rule; what was her house like; had she a room to herself; did she do the cooking; would she be likely to have a servant? All these facts lie somewhere, presumably, in parish registers and account books; the life of the average Elizabethan woman must be scattered about somewhere, could one collect it and make a book of it. It would be ambitious beyond my daring, I thought, looking about the shelves for books that were not there, to suggest to the students of those famous colleges that they should re-write history, though I own that it often seems a little queer as it is, unreal, lop-sided; but why should they not add a supplement to history? calling it, of course, by some inconspicuous name so that women might figure there without impropriety? For one often catches a glimpse of them in the lives of the great, whisking away into the background, concealing, I sometimes think, a wink, a laugh, perhaps a tear. And, after all, we have lives enough of Jane Austen; it scarcely seems necessary to consider again the influence of the tragedies of Joanna Baillie upon the poetry of Edgar Allan Poe; as for myself, I should not mind if the homes and haunts of Mary Russell Mitford were closed to the public for a century at least. But what I find deplorable, I continued, looking about the bookshelves again, is that nothing is known about women before the eighteenth century. I have no model in my mind to turn about this way and that. Here am I asking why women did not write poetry in the Elizabethan age, and I am not sure how they were educated; whether they were taught to write; whether they had sitting-rooms to themselves; how many women had children before they were twenty-one; what, in short, they did from eight in the morning till eight at night. They had no money evidently; according to Professor Trevelyan they were married whether they liked it or not before they were out of the nursery, at fifteen or sixteen very likely. It would have been extremely odd, even upon this showing, had one of them suddenly written the plays of Shakespeare, I concluded, and I thought of that old gentleman, who is dead now, but was a bishop, I think, who declared that it was impossible for any woman, past, present, or to come, to have the genius of Shakespeare. He wrote to the papers about it. He also told a lady who applied to him for information that cats do not as a matter of fact go to heaven, though they have, he added, souls of a sort. How much thinking those old gentlemen used to save one! How the borders of ignorance shrank back at their approach! Cats do not go to heaven. Women cannot write the plays of Shakespeare.

Be that as it may, I could not help thinking, as I looked at the works of Shakespeare on the shelf, that the bishop was right at least in this; it would have been impossible, completely and entirely, for any woman to have written the plays of Shakespeare in the age of Shakespeare. Let me imagine, since facts are so hard to come by, what would have happened had Shakespeare had a wonderfully gifted sister, called Judith, let us say. Shakespeare himself went, very probably—his mother was an heiress—to the grammar school, where he may have learnt Latin—Ovid, Virgil and Horace—and the elements of grammar and logic. He was, it is well known, a wild boy who poached rabbits, perhaps shot a deer, and had, rather sooner than he should have done, to marry a woman in the neighbourhood, who bore him a child rather quicker than was right. That escapade sent him to seek his fortune in London. He had, it seemed, a taste for the theatre; he began by holding horses at the stage door. Very soon he got work in the theatre, became a successful actor, and lived at the hub of the universe, meeting everybody, knowing everybody, practising his art on the boards, exercising his wits in the streets, and even getting access to the palace of the queen. Meanwhile his extraordinarily gifted sister, let us suppose, remained at home. She was as adventurous, as imaginative, as agog to see the world as he was. But she was not sent to school. She had no chance of learning grammar and logic, let alone of reading Horace and Virgil. She picked up a book now and then, one of her brother's perhaps, and read a few pages. But then her parents came in and told her to mend the stockings or mind the stew and not moon about with books and papers. They would have spoken sharply but kindly, for they were substantial people who knew the conditions of life for a woman and loved their daughter—indeed, more likely than not she was the apple of her father's eye. Perhaps she scribbled some pages up in an apple loft on the sly, but was careful to hide them or set fire to them. Soon, however, before she was out of her teens, she was to be betrothed to the son of a neighbouring wool-stapler. She cried out that marriage was hateful to her, and for that she was severely beaten by her father. Then he ceased to scold her. He begged her instead not to hurt him, not to shame him in this matter of her marriage. He would give her a chain of beads or a fine petticoat, he said; and there were tears in his eyes. How could she disobey him? How could she break his heart? The force of her own gift alone drove her to it. She made up a small parcel of her belongings, let herself down by a rope one summer's night and took the road to London. She was not seventeen. The birds that sang in the hedge were not more musical than she was. She had the quickest fancy, a gift like her brother's, for the tune of words. Like him, she had a taste for the theatre. She stood at the stage door; she wanted to act, she said. Men laughed in her face. the manager—a fat, loose-lipped man—guffawed. He bellowed something about poodles dancing and women acting — no woman, he said, could possibly be an actress. He hinted—you can imagine what. She could get no training in her craft. Could she even seek her dinner in a tavern or roam the streets at midnight? Yet her genius was for fiction and lusted to feed abundantly upon the lives of men and women and the study of their ways. At last—for she was very young, oddly like Shakespeare the poet in her face, with the same grey eyes and rounded brows—at last Nick Greene the actor-manager took pity on her; she found herself with child by that gentleman and so—who shall measure the heat and violence of the poet's heart when caught and tangled in a woman's body? — killed herself one winter's night and lies buried at some cross-roads where the omnibuses now stop outside the Elephant and Castle.

That, more or less, is how the story would run, I think, if a woman in Shakespeare's day had had Shakespeare's genius. But for my part, I agree with the deceased bishop, if such he was—it is unthinkable that any woman in Shakespeare's day should have had Shakespeare's genius. For genius like Shakespeare's is not born among labouring, uneducated, servile people. It was not born in England among the Saxons and the Britons. It is not born today among the working classes. How, then, could it have been born among women whose work began, according to Professor Trevelyan, almost before they were out of the nursery, who were forced to it by their parents and held to it by all the power of law and custom? Yet genius of a sort must have existed among women as it must have existed among the working classes. Now and again an Emily Brontë or a Robert Burns blazes out and proves its presence. But certainly it never got itself on to paper. When, however, one reads of a witch being ducked, of a woman possessed by devils, of a wise woman selling herbs, or even of a very remarkable man who had a mother, then I think we are on the track of a lost novelist, a suppressed poet, of some mute and inglorious Jane Austen, some Emily Brontë who dashed her brains out on the moor or mopped and mowed about the highways crazed with the torture that her gift had put her to. Indeed, I would venture to guess that Anon, who wrote so many poems without signing them, was often a woman. It was a woman Edward Fitzgerald, I think, suggested who made the ballads and the folk-songs, crooning them to her children, beguiling her spinning with them, or the length of the winter's night.

This may be true or it may be false—who can say?—but what is true in it, so it seemed to me, reviewing the story of Shakespeare's sister as I had made it, is that any woman born with a great gift in the sixteenth century would certainly have gone crazed, shot herself, or ended her days in some lonely cottage outside the village, half witch, half wizard, feared and mocked at. For it needs little skill in psychology to be sure that a highly gifted girl who had tried to use her gift for poetry would have been so thwarted and hindered by other people, so tortured and pulled asunder by her own contrary instincts, that she must have lost her health and sanity to a certainty. No girl could have walked to London and stood at a stage door and forced her way into the presence of actor-managers without doing herself a violence and suffering an anguish which may have been irrational—for chastity may be a fetish invented by certain societies for unknown reasons—but were none the less inevitable. Chastity had then, it has even now, a religious importance in a woman's life, and has so wrapped itself round with nerves and instincts that to cut it free and bring it to the light of day demands courage of the rarest. To have lived a free life in London in the sixteenth century would have meant for a woman who was poet and playwright a nervous stress and dilemma which might well have killed her. Had she survived, whatever she had written would have been twisted and deformed, issuing from a strained and morbid imagination. And undoubtedly, I thought, looking at the shelf where there are no plays by women, her work would have gone unsigned. That refuge she would have sought certainly. It was the relic of the sense of chastity that dictated anonymity to women even so late as the nineteenth century. Currer Bell, George Eliot, George Sand, all the victims of inner strife as their writings prove, sought ineffectively to veil themselves by using the name of a man. Thus they did homage to the convention, which if not implanted by the other sex was liberally encouraged by them (the chief glory of a woman is not to be talked of, said Pericles, himself a much-talked-of man), that publicity in women is detestable. Anonymity runs in their blood. The desire to be veiled still possesses them. They are not even now as concerned about the health of their fame as men are, and, speaking generally, will pass a tombstone or a signpost without feeling an irresistible desire to cut their names on it, as Alf, Bert or Chas. must do in obedience to their instinct, which murmurs if it sees a fine woman go by, or even a dog, *Ce chien est à moi*. And, of course, it may not be a dog, I thought, remembering Parliament Square, the Sieges Allee and other avenues; it may be a piece of land or a man with curly black hair. It is one of the great advantages of being a woman that one can pass even a very fine negress without wishing to make an Englishwoman of her.

That woman, then, who was born with a gift of poetry in the sixteenth century, was an unhappy woman, a woman at strife against herself. All the conditions of her life, all her own instincts, were hostile to the state of mind which is needed to set free whatever is in the brain. But what is the state of mind that is most propitious to the act of creation, I asked. Can one come by any notion of the state that furthers and makes possible that strange activity? Here I opened the volume containing the Tragedies of Shakespeare. What was Shakespeare's state of mind, for instance, when he wrote *Lear* and *Antony and Cleopatra*? It was certainly the state of mind most favourable to poetry that there has ever existed. But Shakespeare himself said nothing about it. We only know casually and by chance that he "never blotted a line." Nothing indeed was ever said by the artist himself about his state of mind until the eighteenth century perhaps. Rousseau perhaps began it. At any rate, by the nineteenth century self-consciousness had developed so far that it was the habit for men of letters to describe their minds in confessions and autobiographies. Their lives also were written, and their letters were printed after their deaths. Thus, though we do not know what Shakespeare went through when he wrote *Lear,* we do know what Carlyle went through when he wrote the *French Revolution;* what Flaubert went through when he wrote *Madame Bovary;* what Keats was going through when he tried to write poetry against the coming of death and the indifference of the world.

And one gathers from this enormous modern literature of confession and self-analysis that to write a work of genius is almost always a feat of prodigious difficulty. Everything is against the likelihood that it will come from the writer's mind whole and entire. Generally material circumstances are against it. Dogs will bark; people will interrupt; money must be made; health will break down. Further, accentuating all these difficulties and making them harder to bear is the world's notorious indifference. It does not ask people to write poems and novels and histories; it does not need them. It does not care whether Flaubert finds the right word or whether Carlyle scrupulously verifies this or that fact. Naturally, it will not pay for what it does not want. And so the writer, Keats, Flaubert, Carlyle, suffers, especially in the creative years of youth, every form of distraction and discouragement. A curse, a cry of agony, rises from those books of analysis and confession. "Mighty poets in their misery dead" — that is the burden of their song. If anything comes through in spite of all this, it is a miracle, and probably no book is born entire and uncrippled as it was conceived.

But for women, I thought, looking at the empty shelves, these difficulties were infinitely more formidable. In the first place, to have a room of her own, let alone a quiet room or a sound-proof room, was out of the question, unless her parents were exceptionally rich or very noble, even up to the beginning of the nineteenth century. Since her pin money, which depended on the good will of her father, was only enough to keep her clothed, she was debarred from such alleviations as came even to Keats or Tennyson or Carlyle, all poor men, from a walking tour, a little journey to France, from the separate lodging which, even if it were miserable enough sheltered them from the claims and tyrannies of their families. Such material difficulties were formidable; but much worse were the immaterial. The indifference of the world which Keats and Flaubert and other men of genius have found so hard to bear was in her case not indifference but hostility. The world did not say to her as it said to them, Write if you choose; it makes no difference to me. The world said with a guffaw, Write? What's the good of your writing? Here the psychologists of Newnham and Girton might come to our help, I thought, looking again at the blank spaces on the shelves. For surely it is time that the effect of discouragement upon the mind of the artist should be measured, as I have seen a dairy company measure the effect of ordinary milk and Grade A milk upon the body of the rat. They set two rats in cages side by side, and of the two one was furtive, timid and small, and the other was glossy, bold and big. Now what food do we feed women as artists upon?

I asked, remembering, I suppose, that dinner of prunes and custard. To answer that question I had only to open the evening paper and to read that Lord Birkenhead is of opinion—but really I am not going to trouble to copy out Lord Birkenhead's opinion upon the writing of women. What Dean Inge says I will leave in peace. The Harley Street specialist may be allowed to rouse the echoes of Harley Street with his vociferations without raising a hair on my head. I will quote, however, Mr. Oscar Browning, because Mr. Oscar Browning was a great figure in Cambridge at one time, and used to examine the students at Girton and Newnham. Mr. Oscar Browning was wont to declare "that the impression left on his mind, after looking over any set of examination papers, was that, irrespective of the marks he might give, the best woman was intellectually the inferior of the worst man." After saying that Mr. Browning went back to his rooms—and it is this sequel that endears him and makes him a human figure of some bulk and majesty—he went back to his rooms and found a stable-boy lying on the sofa—"a mere skeleton, his cheeks were cavernous and sallow, his teeth were black, and he did not appear to have the full use of his limbs.... 'That's Arthur' [said Mr. Browning]. 'He's a dear boy really and most high-minded.'" The two pictures always seem to me to complete each other. And happily in this age of biography the two pictures often do complete each other, so that we are able to interpret the opinions of great men not only by what they say, but by what they do.

But though this is possible now, such opinions coming from the lips of important people must have been formidable enough even fifty years ago. Let us suppose that a father from the highest motives did not wish his daughter to leave home and become writer, painter, or scholar. "See what Mr. Oscar Browning says," he would say; and there was not only Mr. Oscar Browning; there was the *Saturday Review*; there was Mr. Greg—the "essentials of a woman's being," said Mr. Greg emphatically, "are that *they are supported by, and they minister to, men*"—there was an enormous body of masculine opinion to the effect that nothing could be expected of women intellectually. Even if her father did not read out loud these opinions, any girl could read them for herself; and the reading, even in the nineteenth century, must have lowered her vitality, and told profoundly upon her work. There would always have been that assertion — you cannot do this, you are incapable of doing that — to protest against, to overcome. Probably for a novelist this germ is no longer of much effect; for there have been women novelists of merit. But for painters it must still have some sting in it; and for musicians, I imagine, is even now active and poisonous in the extreme. The woman composer stands where the actress stood in the time of Shakespeare. Nick Greene, I thought, remembering the story I had made about Shakespeare's sister, said that a woman acting put him in mind of a dog dancing. Johnson repeated the phrase two hundred years later of women preaching.

And here, I said, opening a book about music, we have the very words used again in this year of grace, 1928, of women who try to write music. "Of Mlle. Germaine Tailleferre one can only repeat Dr. Johnson's dictum concerning a woman preacher, transposed into terms of music. "Sir, a woman's composing is like a dog's walking on his hind legs. It is not done well, but you are surprised to find it done at all.'"[2] So accurately does history repeat itself.

Thus, I concluded, shutting Mr. Oscar Browning's life and pushing away the rest, it is fairly evident that even in the nineteenth century a woman was not encouraged to be an artist. On the contrary, she was snubbed, slapped, lectured and exhorted. Her mind must have been strained and her vitality lowered by the need of opposing this, of disproving that. For here again we come within range of that very interesting and obscure masculine complex which has had so much influence upon the woman's movement; that deep-seated desire, not so much that *she* shall be inferior as that *he* shall be superior, which plants him wherever one looks, not only in front of the arts, but barring the way to politics too, even when the risk to himself seems infinitesimal and the suppliant humble and devoted. Even Lady Bessborough, I remembered, with all her passion for politics, must humbly bow herself and write to Lord Granville Leveson-Gower: "...notwithstanding all my violence in politics and talking so much on that subject, I perfectly agree with you that no woman has any business to meddle with that or any other serious business, farther than giving her opinion (if she is ask'd)." And so she goes on to spend her enthusiasm where it meets with no obstacle whatsoever upon that immensely important subject, Lord Granville's maiden speech in the House of Commons. The spectacle is certainly a strange one, I thought. The history of men's opposition to women's emancipation is more interesting perhaps than the story of that emancipation itself. An amusing book might be made of it if some young student at Girton or Newnham would collect examples and deduce a theory—but she would need thick gloves on her hands, and bars to protect her of solid gold.

But what is amusing now, I recollected, shutting Lady Bessborough, had to be taken in desperate earnest once. Opinions that one now pastes in a book labelled cock-a-doodle-dum and keeps for reading to select audiences on summer nights once drew tears, I can assure you. Among your grandmothers and great-grandmothers there were many that wept their eyes out. Florence Nightingale shrieked aloud in her agony.[3] Moreover, it is all very well for you, who have got yourselves to college and enjoy sitting-rooms—or is it only bed-sitting-rooms?—of your own to say that genius should disregard such opinions; that genius should be above caring what is said of it. Unfortunately, it is precisely the men or women of genius who mind most what is said of them. Remember Keats. Remember the words he had cut on his tombstone. Think of Tennyson; think—but I need hardly multiply instances of the undeniable, if very unfortunate, fact that it is the nature of the artist to mind excessively what is said about him. Literature is strewn with the wreckage of men who have minded beyond reason the opinions of others.

And this susceptibility of theirs is doubly unfortunate, I thought, returning again to my original enquiry into what state of mind is most propitious for creative work, because the mind of an artist, in order to achieve the prodigious effort of freeing whole and entire the work that is in him, must be incandescent, like Shakespeare's mind, I conjectured, looking at the book which lay open at *Antony and Cleopatra*. There must be no obstacle in it, no foreign matter unconsumed.

For though we say that we know nothing about Shakespeare's state of mind, even as we say that, we are saying something about Shakespeare's state of mind. The reason perhaps why we know so little of Shakespeare — compared with Donne or Ben Jonson or Milton — is that his grudges and spites and antipathies are hidden from us. We are not held up by some "revelation" which reminds us of the writer. All desire to protest, to preach, to proclaim an injury, to pay off a score, to make the world the witness of some hardship or grievance was fired out of him and consumed. Therefore his poetry flows from him free and unimpeded. If ever a human being got his work expressed completely, it was Shakespeare. If ever a mind was incandescent, unimpeded, I thought, turning again to the bookcase, it was Shakespeare's mind.

Notes

[1]"It remains a strange and almost inexplicable fact that in Athena's city, where women were kept in almost Oriental suppression as odalisques or drudges, the stage should yet have produced figures like Clytemnestra and Cassandra, Atossa and Antigone, Phèdre and Medea, and all the other heroines who dominate play after play of the 'misogynist' Euripides. But the paradox of this world where in real life a respectable woman could hardly show her face alone in the street, and yet on the stage woman equals or surpasses man, has never been satisfactorily explained. In modern tragedy the same predominance exists. At all events, a very cursory survey of Shakespeare's work (similarly with Webster, though not with Marlowe or Jonson) suffices to reveal how this dominance, this initiative of women, persists from Rosalind to Lady Macbeth. So too in Racine; six of his tragedies bear their heroines' names; and what male characters of his shall we set against Hermione and Andromaque, Bérénice and Roxane, Phèdre and Athalie? So again with Ibsen; what men shall we match with Solveig and Nora, Hedda and Hilda Wangel and Rebecca West?"—F. L. Lucas, Tragedy, pp. 114–15.

[2]A *Survey of Contemporary Music*, Cecil Gray, p. 246.

[3]See *Cassandra*, by Florence Nightingale, printed in *The Cause*, by R. Strachey.

Writing task one: Compare notes about Woolf's use of sentence patterns and describe which kernels she uses most frequently and which she uses least often. Can you speculate how those writing choices have best served her purposes in the selection? Select four sentences which group members relish and identify in each the core structure. Then for each sentence play with other ways to build a sentence from the core structure. You might see what happens when you switch verb tense or switch from active to passive voice. Try reversing the order of words and phrases. Experiment with changing subordinate clauses to independent clauses and with changing clauses to phrases. Use doublets or triplets to compound subjects, predicates, objects, and complements. Always maintain the sentence core but see how many variations you can work upon that core. While you generate new sentences, watch carefully how sentence structures and thoughts interconnect. Each group should hand in a list of sentence transformations by the end of their discussion.

When you identified the basic sentence pattern behind one Woolf sentence, you might have wondered why — out of the myriad possible combinations — Woolf chose *that* combination which she selected. For example, you might have been puzzled over her shift from a series of declarative sentences which described the family's feelings when Shakespeare's sister refused to marry. Suddenly she writes two short questions: "How could she disobey him? How could she break his heart?"

Who did you hear in those sentences? Perhaps you heard Virginia Woolf the narrator *and* the distraught father *and* Virginia Woolf the lecturer who has posed a set of questions to herself and to her audience. Certainly Woolf cues us as readers to pay attention in a new way when she shifts from declarative to interrogative sentencing. She could have reported the father's remarks as she had been reporting them in a statement of indirect discourse. Why do you think she chose another pattern?

Our responses to this question will be speculative, but they are ways for us to crawl into the vehicles which writers choose for meaning and see why those vehicles work. Woolf might have used the questions simply to build variety into her prose. She knows that readers find it easier to stay with a writer when the writer changes stimuli. She might also have realized that we had been lulled by her pattern of declarative sentences, even though she has used sentences of varying lengths and complexities. It might be that she didn't want us to overlook the real struggle of any artist caught between duty to self and duty to others which is captured in that moment when the daughter runs off.

Woolf clearly believes that the woman's struggle was painful, arduous, and even fatal and that "The force of her own gift alone drove her to it." In this sentence which follows the two questions, Woolf emphasizes the enormity of the action by emphasizing *own* and *alone* and *drove*. Why do you think that she chose *this* combination? She might have written "Her talent drove her to it."

The more we can consciously identify the range of possible sentence combinations (and the range of paragraph structures and the range of essay choices), the more we can freely choose alternatives when we write. The more we can see why one combination is more appropriate to the purpose and the structure than another might be, the more we can use the awareness to rewrite and make our words best embody our thoughts and feelings.

Writing task two: So that we can analyze and appreciate how sentences are clustered into paragraphs, we'll play with restructuring and reordering one of Woolf's paragraphs. Each group should select one short paragraph from the Woolf selection. Look carefully at the ways that Woolf nets the sentences together as one unit. See what happens if you threw out any parts. Then rewrite the paragraph by deliberately changing each sentence by changing the sentence core. Notice how the paragraph is an eco-system. When you change one sentencing element, you change the entire system. The difficult task here will be to try to preserve Woolf's ideas while you change the structures she used to make those ideas accessible.

Classifications of Sentences

Traditionally, we classify sentences by citing purpose, describing syntax, identifying the form, and gauging the completeness. We can find in the Woolf reading, sentences which serve as models for most of these classifications or grammatical conventions. We will name each convention and watch it operate in Woolf's writing.

1. Citing Purpose

Whenever you write a sentence, you have one of four purposes in mind: declaration, interrogation, command, or exclamation. If within one sentence, you mix these moods you are likely to confuse your reader. Because each sentence should show one major assumption or one independent idea, you should rewrite any sentences where you switched purpose midway. When you write a sentence like "My problem wasn't whether to take a composition course, but—well—should I get involved in a discussion of controversial ideas?", you divide your reader's attention between your statement of a problem and your direct question. How would you rewrite that sentence or how would you write two separate sentences so that you can say what you mean?

Most English sentences are declarative in mood and make statements. Most of Woolf's sentences are declarative and focus our attention upon whatever topic she's selected or whatever assumption she wants us to examine. For example, Woolf states:

> For surely it is time that the effect of discouragement upon the mind of the artist should be measured, as I have seen a dairy company measure the effect of ordinary milk and Grade A milk upon the body of the rat.

You can cull other examples of declarative sentences which Woolf crafted.

When you ask questions and write interrogative sentences, you show that you want your reader to be directly involved in thinking through the problem you indicate. Sometimes writers seem to invite their readers to a dialogue when in fact they intend to answer their own questions and have only asked the question to pique the interest of the reader. Such a question is called a rhetorical question. Often this technique helps to draw emphasis to the statement which follows. It also breaks up any monotony caused by hearing only one pattern of sentence.

Throughout her essay, Woolf has been dramatizing for us the very process of questioning an assumption and thinking through responses. Did you notice how often she talked about asking herself questions?

> What were the conditions in which women lived, I asked myself....

> What one wants, I thought — and why does not some brilliant student at Newnham or Girton supply it?—is a mass of information; at what age did she marry; how many children had she as a rule; what was her house like; had she a room to herself; did she do the cooking; would she be likely to have a servant?

> Here I am asking why women did not write the poetry in the Elizabethan age, and I am not sure they were educated...

> But what is the state of mind that is most propitious to the act of creation, I asked? Can one come by any notion of the state that furthers and makes possible that strange activity?

Woolf uses inquiry as a means of both learning about women and fiction and as an organizing structure for this chapter.

She also uses rhetorical questions. We saw her do that earlier when she asked what could make the daughter break the father's heart and then answer that her gift alone impelled Judith Shakespeare to run away. Frequently, she uses questions to create little dramas within the exposition. When contrasting the indifference of the world to men of genius with the hostility of the world to women who would write, Woolf could have reported the drama. Instead she sets up for us another scene of a woman struggling to create within a world which denies that women can create. Do you remember this drama?

The world did not say to her as it said to them, Write if you choose, it makes no difference to me. The world said with a guffaw, Write? What's the good of your writing?

You could use an imperative sentence whenever you want to command: Don't smoke. Don't park here. When you exhort or firmly request — Please stop smoking—you want your audience to respond by performing the task you specify. Woolf uses the imperative sentence infrequently. When she invents Judith Shakespeare, she invites her readers to play along with her fantasy:

Let me imagine, since facts are so hard to come by, what could have happened had Shakespeare had a wonderfully gifted sister, called Judith, let us say.

Woolf insists that genius suffers when it is ignored, derided, or denied. She indicates that the women pained by lack of opportunity to create, lack of a supportive tradition of women creating, and lack of encouragement were no weaker when they wept aloud than men of genius who have been hurt by hostile responses to their work. She exhorts us to "Remember Keats... Think of Tennyson."

Woolf uses the imperative sentence only for these two purposes. What other ways have *you* used an imperative sentence? What would be your purpose in using one? What response do you anticipate from your readers when you use one?

In an essay which recounts a long history of oppression of creative minds, Woolf only uses exclamatory sentences twice. She uses ironic statement and questions most often to make *us* go away from the essay exclaiming and protesting. When she chooses to use exclamation points, she shows us clearly what she thinks about the old man who argued women never had, do not possess and never can have the genius of a Shakespeare. I'm sure you noticed her use of parallel exclamatory sentences:

How much thinking those old gentlemen used to save one!
How the borders of ignorance shrank back at their approach!

You might use an exclamatory sentence when you want to emphasize an attitude or to express a strong feeling. These sentences announce a judgment you've made or a sensation you've felt. Sometimes they let you blow off steam—remember the pattern for an exclamatory sentence you found in the comics? Something like "*!@#!%!*#!*"

Writing task three: Each group should take one sentence I have cited for each mood and rewrite it by changing its purpose. Watch what happens—both to the tone of the writing and to the attitude about the subject — when the group switches from one purpose to another. The group should hand in a list of three changes for each of the four models. For example, watch what happens when I rewrite "How much thinking those old gentlemen used to save one!" as "Those old gentlemen saved us much thinking." Other revisions would be "Didn't those old gentlemen save us from thinking?" or "Old gentlemen, save us from thinking." Is each sentence equally ironic?

2. Describing Syntax

These terms are no doubt familiar to you from your previous experiences with studying grammar: simple, compound, complex and compound-complex. We'll review these terms quickly so that you will have the labels at hand when you want to describe what you see in your writing. If you can describe gramatically, you can evaluate your choice of convention and consciously select another convention which lets you play more. A simple sentence contains only one clause. Its syntax shows only one idea in the subject-predicate unit. Within that clause, the subject, the predicate, and any objects or complements can be compounded and can be modified by words and phrases. For example, the three sentences preceding this one are simple sentences. We can also find many instances of simple sentences in the writing of Virginia Woolf:

Nor shall we find her in any collection of anecdotes.

Cats do not go to heaven. Women cannot write the works of Shakespeare.

For genius like Shakespeare's is not born among labouring, uneducated, servile people.

A compound sentence contains two or more independent clauses, and those clauses both share the same mood. The clauses may be connected by *and, or,* and *nor,* or any coordinating conjunction; they may be linked by the semicolon. Each clause contains a distinct idea; each clause could stand alone; all the clauses connected constitute a logical unit. Have you already noticed that the three preceding sentences are compound sentences? Did you also notice how Virginia Woolf used compound sentences to contrast the woman of fiction with the woman of fact?

Imaginatively, she is of the highest importance; practically she is completely insignificant. She pervades poetry from cover to cover; she is all but absent from history.

When you write a complex sentence, you subordinate one or more dependent clauses to an independent clause. When you shape one idea unit in a clause that cannot stand alone as a complete sentence and when you make that idea unit subordinate to another which can stand alone as a complete sentence, then you show in the structure of the complex sentence the relationship of dependency. The three sentences which you are reading in this paragraph are, of course, complex sentences.

Woolf made complex sentences serve her purposes when she wrote:

> Subordinate clause
> The birds/that sang in the hedge/were not more musical than she

> Subordinate clause
> How, then, could it have been born among women/whose work began, according to Professor Trevelyan, almost before they were out of the nursery,/...who were forced to it by their parents and held to it by all the power of law and custom?/Subordinate clause

Perhaps you have anticipated a definition of compound-complex sentences; perhaps you have combined the definitions of the compound sentence and the complex sentence into a description which says that the compound-complex sentence has two or more independent clauses and at least one dependent clause. You might have invented one already; you might have noticed that the sentence which began this paragraph and that this very sentence both qualify as compound-complex sentences. In the paragraph where she contrasted women of fact with woman of fiction, Woolf began with the simple sentence which stated that from such conflicting views of women "a very queer, composite being thus emerges"; Woolf then contrasted both views by using compound sentences; she concludes the paragraph with two compound-complex sentences:

> She dominates the lives of kings and conquerors in fiction; in fact she was the slave of any boy whose parents forced a ring upon her finger. Some of the most inspired words, some of the most profound thoughts in literature fall from her lips; in real life she could hardly read, could scarcely spell, and was the property of her husband.

Once you can identify what form the sentence you write takes, you might ask yourself why you have selected *that* form. What can you not do in, say, a simple sentence that you can do in a complex sentence? What are the advantages of using a complex sentence? What happens to your thought if you change it from a complex sentence to a compound-complex sentence? Once you have written a first draft of, say, an essay about thermal pollution, you may decide you've fallen into too well-worn a path of sentence structuring. Then you can play with shades of meaning and even discover new relationships between assumptions about thermal pollution by changing a sentence from one form to another.

> **Writing task four:** Use the model beginning "She dominates the lives..." which Woolf uses. Write a paragraph contrasting two views of women which group members have encountered. Build from a simple sentence to a compound sentence to a compound-complex sentence.

3. Identifying the Form

Generally, English sentences assume one of three shapes: periodic, cumulative, and balanced. In a periodic sentence—like this sentence—the core of meaning is only completed when the reader reaches the last word of the sentence. Although these two periodic sentences I have just written follow an order familiar to us, many periodic sentences will have words shifted — perhaps for purposes of emphasis — out of familiar order into some new ordering. A periodic sentence like "There but for a fortunate choice made at age 18 go I" teases the reader's expectations of the Subject-Predicate core and builds suspense into the reading of the sentence. Because the end position of a sentence—or a paragraph or an essay —always commands the most emphasis, you can underscore your ideas by using periodic sentences with inverted word order, with a series of repeated phrases or ideas, and with the placement of the key concept immediately before the period.

You may remember this dramatic use of the periodic sentence in Woolf's imaginative biography of Judith Shakespeare:

> At last—for she was very young, oddly like Shakespeare the poet in her face, with the same grey eyes and rounded brows — at last Nick Greene the actor-manager took pity on her; she found herself with child by that gentleman and so—who shall measure the heat and violence of the poet's heart when caught and tangled in a woman's body—killed herself one winter's night and lies buried at some cross-roads where the omnibuses now stop outside the Elephant and Castle.

The cumulative sentence, often called the loose sentence, differs from the periodic sentence in that the core meaning for the sentence is dropped into place at some point and then the sentence adds on whatever additional details might be needed—somewhat in the manner of this sentence. You don't want to think that cumulative sentences are necessarily unstructured because the core meaning drops into place and succeeding ideas might resemble postscripts, or "fade with a drying fall." Often writers will find useful this pattern of stating the core idea and then qualifying it and amending that qualification, working on until the writer has detailed the idea convincingly. Sometimes this sentence resembles "thinking out loud" and charms readers. We watched Virginia Woolf adding on to her core idea that one important task for scholars would be to research and write the histories of forgotten women:

> It would be ambitious beyond my daring, I thought, looking about the shelves of books that were not there, to suggest to students of those famous colleges that they should re-write history, though I own that it often seems a little queer as it is, unreal, lopsided; but why should they not add a supplement to history? calling it, of course, by some inconspicuous name so that a woman might figure there without impropriety?

Only simple and complex sentences can be described as periodic or cumulative; compound and compound-complex sentences are described as balanced sentences. You have already seen why they are called balanced; you watched ideas and phrases on one side of the connective balance those that were written on the other side:

> She stood at the stage door; she wanted to act, she said.

> Their lives also were written, and their letters were printed after their deaths.

> Certainly, if we consider it, Cleopatra must have had a way with her; Lady Macbeth, one would suppose, had a will of her own; Rosalind, one might conclude, was an attractive girl.

You don't want to confuse balance with parallelism. Sometimes writers will balance ideas without making the structures of the same length or shape. Sometimes one idea will be described with many words; the other will take few words. In this last sentence — "Sometimes one idea ... the other ... you can see a balanced statement; you also see that neither the numbers of words in each clause nor the voices of the verbs in each run parallel.

You watched Virginia Woolf use balanced sentences with parallelism and without parallelism. We can look again at the sentence "Dogs will bark; people will interrupt; money must be made; health will break down." The writer has not made the third clause follow the pattern of subject and predicate in future tense. Because she wanted to emphasize the intrusion of material circumstances into the writer's needed solitude, the writer described money being acquired as yet another outside material happening. What meaning would she have lost had she maintained parallelism? "You must silence the barking dog; you must meet interrupting visitors; you must make sufficient money; you must lose good health."

In the sentences which set the woman of fact off from the woman of fiction, Woolf does not select parallel phrasing. When she states that woman "pervades poetry" but "is all but absent," Woolf wants the reader to know that she hasn't used a verb to parallel "pervades" such as "scarcely haunts history" because the copula better characterizes the woman of fact as someone not acknowledged as acting. In the same manner, she writes that the woman "dominates lives... in fiction but "was the slave" in fact. When you write a paragraph or an essay, you'll want to decide when it would be best to use parallel structure in balanced sentences. You might find that you can emphasize a contrast by using a balanced sentence which describes the first idea in the active voice and then describes the next idea in the passive voice. Remember the balanced statements which Paolo Freire wrote in Chapter Five to show how being a teacher contrasted with being a student in a banking system of education?

4. Gauging Completeness

We will end our discussion of sentences where we began, talking about complete sentences and sentence fragments. A complete sentence is grammatically independent. It either has or, in the instance of an imperative sentence can supply, a subject and predicate upon which other units of the sentence are built.

A sentence fragment does not stand alone. The sentence fragment is a grammatical shard which piques our curiosity about how the complete artifact might look. There are two kinds of sentence fragments: the intentional and the accidental. We'll talk about accidents first because they can be easily remedied when you read over the first draft of your work. Often, you write sentence fragments because you are thinking faster than you hand moves or because you've changed directions in the middle of an idea. Perhaps you started the sentence with a dependent clause and then decided to make the clause independent but you forgot to remove the word which made it subordinate (which, whose, when, while, that, etc.). Perhaps you used a participle rather than a verb. You can eliminate accidental sentence fragments by asking yourself whether the unit can be read by the audience as gramatically independent. If you can say no emphatically, then you can change the sentence fragment into a complete sentence—perhaps by adding in the predicate you omitted or by removing the subordinating element (but, which, that, etc.).

If you waffle and say "Well, it sort of makes a complete thought if...," then you've probably written an intentional sentence fragment. You can also call it an elliptical sentence. You have left out elements which deny the sentence grammatical completion, but you know that your reader can supply the missing elements and can understand the complete idea from the context of the sentence. Elliptical sentences are frequent in our conversation; we chirp "Nice day, Just fine. And you?" in response to a friend's query. We supply any omissions in the sentence by the tones of our voices, by the faces we make, and by the way we move our hands.

In written English, you might choose elliptical sentences to recreate dialogue, to echo a particularly pleasing or apt phrase, to provide directional signals for the reader (Now. Again. Here.) and to make aphorisms (the more, the merrier; our bodies, our selves). Although Virginia Woolf hasn't used any sentence fragments in the selection which we read, she does use elliptical sentences in the full work and she also uses sentence fragments as leitmotifs to structure a book-length exposition about women's rights for education in *Three Guineas*. Look back at Tillie Olsen's use of elliptical sentences. When you write, if you plan for your sentences to be fragmentary for an appropriate reason and if your reader can reconstruct the artifact from the shard, no one will tell you not to use them.

You know, of course, that any sentence you write can fall into each of the classifications discussed. You generate a sentence from one of the five kernel sentences and you decide its purpose, choose its syntactic pattern, select its form and opt whether or not to complete it. You do this without thinking about it. During the rewriting stage, you should think carefully about the sentences you have written. If they don't say what you want them to say, you can change them.

Writing the Comparison-Contrast Essay

In your college writing, you will often be asked to write an exam essay or a term paper in which you contrast or compare. For example, you may be asked to contrast the ideologies of, for example, the New Left and the Right or to compare two scientific paradigms or to compare and contrast Keynesian and neo-classical economic theories. You might want to write out in your personal journal the way today's feeling of euphoria compares and contrasts with earlier highs. In a letter, you might want to tell your friend about how your new job contrasts with your previous job or compares to your dream about the perfect job. Because this pattern of organization is so important to writing in all areas, you will want to practice the comparison-contrast essay.

When you write a comparison-contrast essay, you show on paper a thinking process you go through daily. By comparing two similar but not identical assumptions, operations, feelings, or objects, you are able to evaluate and to judge. By finding a point of similarity between two unlike objects, you see something new and can create a metaphor. By finding the similarities and the dissimilarities in one convention of thinking, you can choose new combinations.

We can quickly identify the differences between two things. We spend energy making distinctions between "them" and "us" which are often unproductive. We find it more difficult to see the similarities between things which have clear dissimilarities.

Seeing similarities is necessary for making new structures. William James, a nineteenth-century psychologist, believed that some people could more readily see and point out similarities than others. He described "the wits, the poets, the inventors, the scientific men, the practical geniuses" as people who were most sensitive to similarities of unlike things. James alluded to Isaac Newton and Charles Darwin when he remarked that

> The flash of similarity between an apple and the moon, between the rivalry for food in nature and the rivalry for man's selection, was too recondite to have occurred to any but exceptional minds.

You can test James's assumption that only a few minds can see similarities by learning how to use the writing skill of making comparisons and contrasts so that you make a habit of thinking always about both the ways some other ideas contrast with your way of seeing and naming and the ways that these other ideas compare with yours. Seeing points where ideas intersect sets you free to combine those ideas in some new way.

When you are asked to compare, you name similarities and demonstrate that one thing is like another in carefully detailed ways. You illustrate your statement about similarity with examples which connect parts to parts and wholes to wholes. When you are asked to contrast, you name differences and you document them by paralleling parts to parts and wholes to wholes. When you are asked to compare and contrast, you name both similarities and dissimilarities; you also decide and explain whether the similarities are greater or lesser than the dissimilarities.

There are two basic patterns for the comparison-contrast essay. In outline form they look like this:

I. Introduction: include a thesis	I. Introduction: include a thesis
II. X,Y	II. X
III. X,Y	1.
IV. X,Y	2.
V. Conclusion	3.
	4.
	III. Y
	1.

2.
3.
4.
IV. Conclusion

You saw Virginia Woolf use the first pattern of alternating X and Y when she compared two images of women. Woolf demonstrated that the woman she found in fiction and the woman she met in history contrasted sharply. It is always easiest—both for you and the reader—to organize comparisons and contrasts in this way. The second pattern—where you treat X as a whole topic before you treat Y as a whole topic—makes the reader do some of the work of comparing and contrasting in his or her head while reading the parts of the essay. You can, of course, take these two patterns and combine them. What is most important in any pattern you devise is that you compare part with part, subpart with subpart. Parallel structure keeps the points you are making before the reader's eyes.

Writing task five: Select a topic which could be developed into an essay and brainstorm points of comparison and contrast. Use the outlines listed here and write an outline for each of two essays. Possible topics: compare roles of men and women in a nonwestern society; contrast an historical role for men with a role for men in the 1980's; compare and contrast your view about what is necessary for creativity with Virginia Woolf's.

Although the sample outlines show a pattern or organization for working in pairs, you can and should also use the comparison-contrast essay to research, analyze and reperceive the similarities and dissimilarities among several processes or ideas which are related in some important way. In the paragraph which follows, a political analyst compares the life of an inmate of a concentration camp with those of three other oppressed persons:

Forced labor as a punishment is limited as to time and intensity. The convict retains his rights over his body; he is not absolutely tortured and he is not absolutely dominated. Banishment banishes only from one part of the world to another part of the world, also inhabited by human beings; it does not exclude from the human world altogether. Throughout history slavery has been an institution within a social order; slaves were not, like concentration camp inmates, withdrawn from the sight and hence the protection of their fellow-men; as instruments of labor they had a definite price and as property a definite value. The concentration camp inmate has no price, because he can always be replaced; nobody knows to whom be belongs, because he is never seen. From the point of view of acute labor shortage, as in Russia and in Germany during the war, he is used for work.

In this paragraph Hannah Arendt suggests by her ordering of comparisons and contrasts that although all these persons are oppressed and acted upon by others, some forms of oppression are more heinous than others. She describes the life of the concentration camp inmate last to emphasize the complete dehumanization of the inmate.

If you adapted her pattern to an essay, you would talk in one or two paragraphs about one of the class of objects or ideas which are similar yet different. In a second section, you would talk about another from that class. You would proceed in this order until you had described each class member. You would always describe last that member of the class of ideas or objects which you think most significant.

In the selection which follows, you can watch the anthropologist Margaret Mead use the rhetorical techniques of comparison and contrast to structure one section of *Sex and Temperament in Primitive Societies*. Although she compares the Arapesh culture on the island of New Guinea in Malaysia with our culture, she describes American culture scantily. Throughout, Mead implies contrasts between the two cultures. She expects her audience to reach into their own knowledge about American culture and to supply examples which contrast with those she cites when she explains Arapesh culture. While you read the essay, make notes about similarities and dissimilarities and jot down examples of contrast which occur to you.

A Co-operative Society

Margaret Mead

Arapesh life is organized about this central plot of the way men and women, physiologically different and possessed of differing potencies, unite in a common adventure that is primarily maternal, cherishing, and oriented away from the self towards the needs of the next generation. It is a culture in which men and women do different things for the same reasons, in which men are not expected to respond to one set of motivations and women to another, in which if men are given more authority it is because authority is a necessary evil that someone, and that one the freer partner, must carry. It is a culture in which if women are excluded from ceremonies, it is for the sake of the women themselves, not as a device to bolster up the pride of the men, who work desperately hard to keep the dangerous secrets that would make their wives ill and deform their unborn children. It is a society where a man conceives responsibility, leadership, public appearance, and the assumption of arrogance as onerous duties that are forced upon him, and from which he is only too glad to escape in middle years, as soon as his eldest child attains puberty. In order to understand a social order that substitutes responsiveness to the concerns of others, and attentiveness to the needs of others, for aggressiveness, initiative, competitiveness, and possessiveness—the familiar motivations upon which our culture depends—it is necessary to discuss in some detail the way in which Arapesh society is organized.

There are no political units. Clusters of villages are grouped into localities, and each locality and its inhabitants have names. These names are sometimes used rhetorically at feasts, or to refer to the region, but the localities themselves have no political organization. Marriages, feasting organizations, and occasional semi-hostile clashes between neighbouring groups take place between hamlets or clusters of hamlets across locality lines. Each hamlet belongs theoretically to one patrilineal family line, which again has a name to distinguish it. The patrilineal families, or small localized clans, also possess hunting and gardening land, and located somewhere on their hunting-land is a water-hole or a quicksand or a steep waterfall that is inhabited by their *marsalai,* a supernatural who appears in the form of a mythical and bizarrely coloured snake or lizard, or occasionally as a larger animal. In the abode of the *marsalai* and along the borders of the ancestral lands live the ghosts of the clan dead, including the wives of the men of the clan, who after death continue to live with their husbands instead of returning to their own clan-lands.

The Arapesh do not conceive of themselves as owning these ancestral lands, but rather as belonging to the lands; in their attitude there is none of the proud possessiveness of the landowner who vigorously defends his rights against all comers. The land itself, the game animals, the timber trees, the sago, and especially the bread-fruit-trees, which are thought of as very old and dear to the ghosts—these all belong to the ghosts. For the feelings and attitudes of the ghosts the *marsalai* is a focusing-point. This being is not exactly an ancestor and not exactly not an ancestor—Arapesh casualness does not attempt to answer the question. The *marsalai* has a special touchiness about a few ritual points; he dislikes menstruating women, pregnant women, and men who come directly from intercourse with their wives. Such trespass he punishes with illness and death to the women or unborn children, unless he is specially placated by a mimic offering of a pig's tusk, an empty betel-sheath, a sago-container, and a taro-leaf, on which one of the ancestor souls will alight as a bird or a butterfly and absorb the spirit of the offering. The ghosts themselves are the residents of the lands, and a man going upon his own inherited land will announce himself, his name and relationship to them, remarking: "It is I, your grandson, of Kanchoibis. I have come to cut some posts for my house. Do not object to my presence, nor to my timber-cutting. As I return pluck back the brambles from my path, and bend back the branches so that I walk easily." This he must do even if he goes alone on the land that he has inherited from his forefathers. More often he has with him someone less directly connected, a relative or a brother-in-law, who is hunting with him or plans to make a garden on his land. Then introductions are in order. "See, my grandfathers, this is my brother-in-law, the husband of my sister. He comes to garden here with me. Treat him as your grandson, do not object to his being here. He is good." If these precautions are neglected, a hurricane will knock down the careless man's house or a landslip destroy his garden. Wind and rain and landslips are sent by the *marsalais*, who employ these means to discipline those who are careless about expressing the proper attitudes towards the land. In all of this there is none of the sense of ownership with which a man bids a stranger welcome to his land or proudly chops down a tree because it is his.

On a neighbouring hill-top, the village of Alipinagle was sadly depleted. In the next generation there would not be enough people to occupy the land. The people of Alitoa sighed: "Alas, poor Alipinagle, after the present people are gone, who will care for the land, who will there be beneath the trees? We must give them some children to adopt, that the land and the trees may have people when we are gone." Such generosity had, of course, the practical consequences of placing a child or so in a more advantageous position, but it was never phrased in this way, nor did the people recognize any formulations based upon possessiveness about land. There was just one family in the locality that was possessive, and its attitude was incomprehensible to everyone else. Gerud, a popular young diviner and the eldest son of this family, once in a *séance* suggested as a motive for an alleged theft of dirt that the accused grudged to the children of a new-comer in the village a future share in the hunting-grounds. The rest of the community regarded his reasoning as little short of mad. Surely, people belonged to the land, not land to the people. As a correlate of this point of view, no one is at all particular as to where he lives, and as often as not members of a clan live not in their ancestral hamlets, but in the hamlets of cousins or brothers-in-law. Without political organization, without any fixed and arbitrary social rules, it is easy enough for people to do this.

As with residence sites, so with gardens. The Arapesh gardening is of two types: taro-gardens and banana-gardens, in which the men do the initial clearing, tree-lopping, and fencing, and the women do the planting, weeding, and harvesting; and yam-gardens, which with the exception of a little help rendered by women in weeding and in carrying the harvest are entirely men's work. Among many New Guinea tribes each married pair clears and fences a patch of land in their own inherited gardening-bush, and cultivates it more or less alone, with the help of their immature children, perhaps calling in other relatives at the harvest. In this way a New Guinea garden becomes a private place, almost as private as a house, and is frequently used for copulation; it is their own place. A man or his wife can go to the garden every day, repair any gaps in the fencing, and so protect the garden from the inroads of bush animals. All the external circumstances of the Arapesh environment would suggest such a gardening method as exceedingly practical. The distances are long and the roads difficult. People often have to sleep in their gardens because they are too far from other shelter, so they build small, badly thatched, uncomfortable huts on the ground, as it is not worth while to build a house on piles for one year's use. The steep slopes make fencing unsatisfactory and the pigs are always breaking in. Food is scarce and poor and it would seem likely that under these conditions of hardship and poverty people would be very possesive of and attentive to their own gardens. Instead the Arapesh have evolved a different and most extraordinary system, expensive in time and human effort, but conducive to the warm co-operation and sociability that they consider to be much more important.

Each man plants not one garden, but several, each one in co-operation with a different group of his relatives. In one of these gardens he is host, in the others he is guest. In each of these gardens three to six men, with one or two wives each, and sometimes a grown daughter or so, work together, fence together, clear together, weed together, harvest together, and while engaged in any large piece of work, sleep together, crowded up in the little inadequate shelter, with the rain dripping down the necks of more than half of the sleepers. These gardening groups are unstable — some individuals are unable to stand the strain of a bad crop; they tend to blame their gardening partners for it, and to seek new alliances the following year. Choice, now of one piece of long-fallow ground, now of another, sometimes makes next year's gardening-plot too far away for some of those who planted together last year. But each year a man's foodstakes lie not in one plot directly under his control, but scattered about, beneath the ghosts and on the land of his relatives, three miles in one direction, five miles in another.

This arrangement of work has several results. No two gardens are planted at the same time and therefore the Arapesh lack the "time hungry" so characteristic of yam-raising peoples where all of the yam-gardens are planted simultaneously. Where several men work together to clear and fence one plot before scattering to co-operate in clearing and fencing other plots, the harvests succeed each other. This method of gardening is not based upon the slightest physical need for co-operative labour. Tall trees are simply ringed, not felled, and the branches are cut off to let in light, so that a garden looks like an army of ghosts, white against the surrounding deep-green of the bush. The fencing is done with saplings that an adolescent boy could cut. But the preference is strong for working in small happy groups in which one man is host and may feast his guest workers with a little meat—if he finds it. And so the people go up and down the mountain sides, from one plot to another, weeding here, staking vines there, harvesting in another spot, called hither and thither by the demands of gardens in different states of maturity.

This same lack of individualism obtains in the planting of coconut-trees. A man plants such trees for his young sons, but not upon his own land. Instead, he will walk four or five miles carrying a sprouting coconut in order to plant it by the door-step of his uncle, or of his brother-in-law. A census of the palm-trees in any village reveals a bewildering number of distantly residing owners and bears no relation to the actual residents. In the same way, men who are friends will plant new sago-palms together, and in the next generation their sons become a working unit.

In hunting, too, a man does not hunt alone, but with a companion, sometimes a brother, as often a cousin or a brother-in-law; the bush, the ghosts, and the *marsalai* belong to one of the pair or trio. The man, be he host or guest, who sees the game first claims it, and the only tact that is necessary here is the tact of not seeing game very much more often than other people do. Men who make a practice of always claiming first sight are left to hunt by themselves, and may develop into far better hunters, with increasingly unsocial characters. Such a man was Sumali, my self-nominated father, who in spite of his skill was little esteemed in co-operative enterprises. It was his son who divined stinginess about hunting-lands as a motive for imputed sorcery; and when Sumali's house burned accidentally to the ground, Sumali attributed the accident to jealousy over land. His traps yielded more than the traps of anyone else in the region, his tracking skill was greatest and his aim most accurate, but he hunted alone, or with his young sons, and presented his game to his relatives almost as formally as he might have presented it to strangers.

It is the same also with house-building. The houses are so small that they actually require very little communal labour. Materials from one house or several dilapidated houses are reassembled into another house; people take their houses down and rebuild them in another orientation; there is no attempt made to cut the rafters the same length or to saw off the ridge-pole if it is too long for the projected house — if it does not fit this house it will undoubtedly fit the next one. But no man, except one who has failed to help with the house-building of others, builds alone. A man announces his intention of building a house, and perhaps makes a small feast for raising the ridge-pole. Then his brothers and his cousins and his uncles, as they go about the bush upon their several errands, bear his partly completed house in mind, and stop to gather a bundle of creeper to bind the roof, or a bunch of sago-leaves for the thatching. These contributions they bring to the new house when they pass that way, and gradually, casually, a little at a time, the house is built, out of the uncounted labour of many.

But this loosely co-operative fashion in which all work, even the routine of everyday gardening and hunting, is organized means that no man is master of his own plans for many hours together. If anything, he is less able to plan and carry through any consecutive activities than are the women, who at least know that meals and firewood and water must be provided each day. The men spend over nine-tenths of their time responding to other people's plans, digging in other people's gardens, going on hunting-parties initiated by others. The whole emphasis of their economic lives is that of participation in activities others have initiated, and only rarely and shyly does anyone tentatively suggest a plan of his own.

This emphasis is one factor in the lack of political organization. Where all are trained to a quick responsiveness to any plan, and mild ostracism is sufficient to prod the laggard into co-operation, leadership presents a different problem from that in a society where each man pits his own aggressiveness against that of another. If there is a weighty matter to be decided, one that may involve the hamlet or a cluster of hamlets in a brawl or accusations of sorcery, then the decision is arrived at in a quiet, roundabout, and wholly characteristic fashion. Suppose for instance that a young man finds that a pig belonging to a distant village has strayed into his garden. The pig is a trespasser, meat is scarce, he would like to kill it. But would it be wise to do so? Judgment must be made in terms of all kinds of relationships with the pig's owners. Is a feast pending? Or is a betrothal still unsettled? Does some member of his own group depend upon the pig's owner for assistance in some ceremonial plan? All these things the young man has not the judgment to decide. He goes to his elder brother. If his elder brother sees no objection to killing the pig, the two will take counsel with other elder male relatives, until finally one of the oldest and most respected men of the community is consulted. Of such men every locality with a population of one hundred and fifty to two hundred has one or two. If the big man gives his approval, the pig is killed and eaten and no censure will fall upon the young man from his elders; everyone will stand together to defend their bit of legal piracy.

Warfare is practically unknown among the Arapesh. There is no head-hunting tradition, no feeling that to be brave or manly one must kill. Indeed, those who have killed men are looked upon with a certain amount of discomfort, as men slightly apart. It is they who must perform the purificatory ceremonies over a new killer. The feeling towards a murderer and that towards a man who kills in battle are not essentially different. There are no insignia of any sort for the brave. There is only a modicum of protective magic which can be used by those who are going into a fight: they may scrape a little dust from their fathers' bones and eat it with areca-nut and magic herbs. But although actual warfare—organized expeditions to plunder, conquer, kill, or attain glory—is absent, brawls and clashes between villages do occur, mainly over women. The marriage system is such that even the most barefaced elopement of a betrothed or married woman must be phrased as an abduction and, since an abduction is an unfriendly act on the part of another group, must be avenged. This feeling for righting the balance, for paying back evil for evil, not in greater measure, but in exact measure, is very strong among the Arapesh. The beginning of hostilities they regard as an unfortunate accident; abductions of women are really the result of marital disagreements and the formation of new personal attachments, and are not unfriendly acts on the part of the next community. So also with pigs, since people attempt to keep their pigs at home. If the pigs stray, it is a bad accident, but if a pig is killed, it should be avenged.

All such clashes between hamlets start in angry conversation, the aggrieved party coming, armed but not committed to fighting, into the village of the offenders. An altercation follows; the offenders may justify or excuse their conduct, disclaim any knowledge of the elopement, or deny having known the ownership of the pig—it had not had its tail cut yet, how could they know it was not a bush pig? and so on. If the aggrieved party is protesting more as a matter of form than from real anger, the meeting may end in a few harsh words. Alternatively, it may progress from reproach to insult, until the most volatile and easily angered person hurls a spear. This is not a signal for a general fracas; instead everyone notes carefully where the spear—which is never thrown to kill—hits, and the next most volatile person of the opposite party throws a spear back at the man who hurled the first one. This in turn is recorded during a moment of attention, and a return spear thrown. Each reprisal is phrased as a matter of definite choice: "Then Yabinigi threw a spear. He hit my cross-cousin in the wrist. I was angry because my cross-cousin was hit and I threw a spear back and hit Yabinigi in the ankle. Then the mother's brother of Yabinigi, enraged that his sister's son had been wounded, drew back his arm and hurled a spear at me which missed," and so on. This serial and carefully recorded exchange of spears in which the aim is to wound lightly, not to kill, goes on until someone is rather badly wounded, when the members of the attacking party immediately take to their heels. Later, peace is made by an interchange of rings, each man giving a ring to the man whom he has wounded.

If, as occasionally happens, someone is killed in one of these clashes, every attempt is made to disavow any intention to kill: the killer's hand slipped; it was because of the sorcery of the Plainsmen. Almost always those on the other side are called by kinship terms, and surely no man would willingly have killed a relative. If the relative killed is a near one, an uncle or a first cousin, the assumption that it was unintentional and due to sorcery is regarded as established, and the killer is commiserated with and permitted to mourn whole-heartedly with the rest. If the relative is more distant, and the possibility of genuine intent more open, the killer may flee to another community. No blood feud will follow, although there may be an attempt to subsidize the sorcery of the Plainsmen against him. But in general sorcery deaths are avenged with sorcery deaths, and all killings within the locality or within avenging distance are regarded as too aberrant, too unexpected and inexplicable, for the community to deal with them. And each man who is wounded in a fight has a further penalty to pay, for he must reimburse his mother's brothers, and his mother's brothers' sons, for his own shed blood. All blood comes to the child from its mother; it is therefore the property of the mother's group. The mother's brother has the right to shed a sister's son's blood; it is he who must open a boil, he who scarifies the adolescent girl. So the man who is injured in any way suffers not only in his person but in his supply of valuables: he must pay for having been in any scene in which he is injured. This sanction is extended to cover injuries in hunting, and involvement in a shameful situation.

The general policy of Arapesh society is to punish those who are indiscreet enough to get involved in any kind of violent or disreputable scene, those who are careless enough to get hurt in hunting, or stupid enough to let themselves become the butt of public vituperation from their wives. In this society unaccustomed to violence, which assumes that all men are mild and co-operative and is always surprised by the individuals who fail to be so, there are no sanctions to deal with the violent man. But it is felt that those who stupidly and carelessly provoke violence can be kept in order. In mild cases of offence, as when a man has been one member of a fighting group, his individual mother's brother calls out for payment. After all, the poor sister's son has already suffered a wound and loss of blood. But if instead he has got himself involved in an undignified public disputation with a wife, or with a young relative who has been overheard by others to insult him, then the whole men's group of the hamlet or cluster of hamlets may act, still instigated by the mother's brothers, who are the official executors of the punishment. The men's group will take the sacred flutes, the voice of the *tamberan* — the supernatural monster who is the patron of the men's cult — amd going by night to the house of the offender, play his wife and himself off the premises, break into his house, litter his house-floor with leaves and rubbish, cut down an areca-palm or so, and depart. If the man has been steadily falling in the esteem of the community, if he has been unco-operative, given to sorcery, bad-tempered, they may take up his fire-place and dump it out, which is practically equivalent to saying that they can dispense with his presence—for a month at least. The victim, deeply shamed by this procedure, flees to distant relatives and does not return until he has obtained a pig with which to feast the community, and so wipe out his offence.

But against the really violent man the community has no redress. Such men fill their fellows with a kind of amazed awe; if crossed they threaten to burn down their own houses, break all their pots and rings, and leave that part of the country for ever. Their relatives and neighbours, aghast at the prospect of being deserted in this way, beseech the violent man not to leave them, not to desert them, not to destroy his own property, and placate him by giving him what he wishes. It is only because the whole education of the Arapesh tends to minimize violence and confuse the motivations of the violent that the society is able to operate by disciplining those who provoke and suffer from violence rather than those who actually perpetrate it.

With work a matter of amiable co-operation, and the slight warfare so slenderly organized, the only other need that the community has for leadership is for carrying out large-scale ceremonial operations. Without any leadership whatsoever, with no rewards beyond the daily pleasure of eating a little food and singing a few songs with one's fellows, the society could get along very comfortably, but there would be no ceremonial occasions. And the problem of social engineering is conceived by the Arapesh not as the need to limit aggression and curb acquisitiveness, but as the need to force a few of the more capable and gifted men into taking, against their will, enough responsibility and leadership so that occasionally, every three or four years or at even rarer intervals, a really exciting ceremonial may be organized. No one, it is assumed, really wants to be a leader, a "big man." "Big men" have to plan, have to initiate exchanges, have to strut and swagger and talk in loud voices, have to boast of what they have done in the past and are going to do in the future. All of this the Arapesh regard as most uncongenial, difficult behaviour, the kind of behaviour in which no normal man would indulge if he could possibly avoid it. It is a rôle that the society forces upon a few men in certain recognized ways.

While boys are in their early teens, their elders tend to classify their potentialities to become "big men." Native capacity is roughly divided into three categories: "those whose ears are open and whose throats are open," who are the most gifted, the men who understand the culture and are able to make their understanding articulate: "those whose ears are open and whose throats are shut," useful quiet men who are wise but shy and inarticulate: and a group of the two least useful kinds of people, "those whose ears are closed but whose throats are open" and "those whose ears and throats are both shut." A boy of the first class is specially trained by being assigned in early adolescence a *buanyin,* or exchange partner, from among the young males of a clan in which one of his elder male relatives has a *buanyin.* This *buanyin* relationship is a reciprocal feast-giving relationship between pairs of males, members of different clans, and preferably of opposite dual organization membership—which is loosely hereditary. It is a social institution that develops aggressiveness and encourages the rare competitive spirit. It is the duty of *buanyins* to insult each other whenever they meet, to inquire sneeringly whether the other *buanyin* ever means to make anything of his life — has he no pigs, no yams, has he no luck in hunting, has he no trade-friends and no relatives, that he never gives feasts or organizes a ceremony? Was he born head first like a normal human being, or perhaps he came feet first from his mother's womb? The *buanyin* relationship is also a training-ground in the kind of hardness that a big man must have, which in an ordinary Arapesh is regarded as undesirable.

The functioning of this *buanyin* relationship must be understood against Arapesh attitudes about the exchange of food. To a people who disguise all their trading as voluntary and casual gift-giving, any rigid accounting is uncongenial. As with trading from village to village, so it is in all exchange between relatives. The ideal distribution of food is for each person to eat food grown by another, eat game killed by another, eat pork from pigs that not only are not his own but have been fed by people at such a distance that their very names are unknown. Under the guidance of this ideal, an Arapesh man hunts only to send most of his kill to his mother's brother, his cousin, or his father-in-law. The lowest man in the community, the man who is believed to be so far outside the moral pale that there is no use reasoning with him, is the man who eats his own kill—even though that kill be a tiny bird, hardly a mouthful in all.

There is no encouragement given to any individual to build up a surplus of yams, the strong reliable crop that can be stored and the increase of which depends upon the conservation of seed. Anyone whose yam crop is conspicuously larger than his neighbour's is graciously permitted to give an *abūllū*, a special feast at which, having painted his yams in bright colours and having laid them out on a ratan measuring-tape, which he may keep as a trophy, all of his yams are given away for seed. His relatives and neighbours come bringing a return gift of their own selection, and carry away a bag of seed. Of this seed he may never eat; even when it has multiplied in the fourth or fifth generation, a careful record is kept. In this way, the good luck or the better gardening of one man does not redound to his personal gain, but is socialized, and the store of seed-yams of the entire community is increased.

From all of this socialized treatment of food and property, this non-competitive, unaccounted, easy give and take, the *buanyin* partnership stands out. Within it are definitely encouraged all the virtues of a competitive, cost-accounting system. A *buanyin* does not wait for the stimulus of an insult given in anger; he insults his *buanyin* as a matter of course. He does not merely share with him of his abundance, but he definitely raises pigs or hunts game in order to give it publicly and ostentatiously to his *buanyin*, accompanied by a few well-chosen insults as to his *buanyin's* inability to repay the gift. Careful accounting is kept of every piece of pig or haunch of kangaroo, and a bundle of coconut-leaf rib is used to denote these in the public altercation during which *buanyins* dun each other. Most astonishing of all is the definite convention of stinginess between *buanyins*. A generous *buanyin* will set aside a special basket of choice entrails and his wife will give it secretly to his *buanyin's* wife, after a feast. For this there need be no return. But while good behaviour is expected everywhere else in social life, people are reconciled to their *buanyins'* neglecting to make this generous gesture.

Thus in a society where the norm for men is to be gentle, unacquisitive, and co-operative, where no man reckons up the debts that another owes him, and each man hunts that others may eat, there is a definite training for the special contrasting behaviour that "big men" must display. The young men on the way to become big men suffer continual pressure from their elders, as well as from their *buanyins*. They are urged to assume the responsibility of organizing the preliminary feasts that will finally culminate in a big initiation ceremony or the purchase of a new dance-complex from the beach. And a few of them yield to all this pressure, learn to stamp their feet and count their pigs, to plant special gardens and organize hunting-parties, and to maintain the long-time planning over several years that is necessary in order to give a ceremony which last no longer than a day or so. But when his eldest child reaches puberty, the big man can retire; he need no longer stamp and shout, he need no longer go about to feasts looking for opportunities to insult his *buanyin*; he can stay quietly at home, guiding and educating his children, gardening, and arranging his children's marriages. He can retire from the active competitive life that his society assumes, usually correctly, to be eminently uncongenial and distasteful to him.

Writing task six: Compare the notes you took on the Mead essay with the notes taken by other members of your group. What contrasting descriptions of American culture did you infer from her description of Arapesh culture? Write down several of the examples which contrast American and Arapesh culture. Use the same form of sentence which Mead has used. Imitate her pattern but bring to it your own idea. For example, you could imitate the pattern of "Warfare is practically unknown among the Arapesh people" and describe American culture by saying "Warfare is not unknown among the American people." In the next sentence, you'd talk about the War between the States, the Indian Wars, gang wars, and other kinds of warfare among Americans.

Writing task seven: The statement that "woman is the new black" has been furiously debated. Discuss this analogy in the group with the task of writing three paragraphs after your discussion. In the first, compare the oppression of women with the oppression of blacks. In the second, contrast the oppression of women with the oppression of blacks. In the third, compare and contrast and decide whether there are more similarities or differences between the treatment of women and that of blacks. How effective do you think this analogy will be when you want to persuade an opponent that women have been enslaved and must break free?

Writing task eight: Brainstorm all the points of comparison and contrast you can generate when you think about the essays you have read in this book by Adrienne Rich, Tillie Olsen, and Virginia Woolf. Arrange these comparisons and contrasts in an outline which would result in an essay.

Writing task nine: Write a comparison-contrast essay which treats the essays by Rich, Olsen and Woolf as relatives. This writing task will take you more time than many of the previous tasks.

Suggested Group Writing and Discussing Activities

1. Take the list of learning behaviors described by Freire as the implications of a banking concept of education and change each assumption by changing the sentence which embodies the belief.
2. Take a paragraph from an individual's essay or from some previous group writing and play with the sentence structures chosen. Practice writing the essay with only compound sentences and see what new tones and what new ideas are generated by the revision.

Recommended Reading

Margaret Mead. *Male and Female: A Study of the Sexes In a Changing World.* New York: Morrow, 1949.

Virginia Woolf. *A Room of One's Own.* New York: Harcourt, Brace and World, 1957.

——. *A Writer's Diary.* New York: Harcourt, Brace and World, 1954.

CHAPTER EIGHT

Writing the Persuasive Essay

Although Humpty Dumpty insisted that a nice, knock-down argument means glory, we will use the term "argument" in this chapter to mean a kind of reasoned discourse which intends to persuade a reader to believe or to act in a new way. You've already noticed that many of the essays we are reading present arguments which ask us to see and to believe and to act in new, nonsexist ways. Through the persuasive essay, we invite our readers to share the definitions, beliefs, and recommendations which we have firmly expressed. We present our perspectives in so convincing a manner that the readers accept the way we see and name as the way they will see and name.

Persuasion differs from exposition because of the avowed purpose of changing beliefs and responses. When you write an expository essay you might use rhetorical techniques of persuasion but as a writer you only hope that your audience will listen to your ideas and will observe and evaluate how effectively you have displayed your ideas. When you write a persuasive essay you might use rhetorical techniques of exposition but you intend that your audience enter your space, observe and evaluate how aptly you've filled that space, and accept your definitions of that space as their definitions. In exposition, you identify and name an old or existing order; in persuasion, you identify and recommend a new order.

When you argue or when you persuade, your first task is deciding what issue you strongly believe in that you could present to an audience for consideration. In an essay, you specify who comprises your audience. If, for example, you wanted to argue in favor of a woman's right to elective abortion, you must imagine who will sit in your audience. A persuasive essay addressed to the world at large has no force. A persuasive essay addressed to a group of older mothers who never had the option of birth control, let alone abortion, would make you work hard to convince the audience of your proposal. You would have to carefully question your own assumptions as well as those of your audience to know how to begin your essay. You would learn to see several sides to an issue, to extrapolate several implications from an assumption.

Once you have specified your audience, you "psyche it out." You analyze what might be the responses of your audience to your thesis. You can assume that your audience does not share those beliefs and criteria for belief which you will recommend that they accept. In fact, you can often assume that the audience may be hostile to your assumptions. The more innovative your idea, the more likely it is that the audience will be fearful and unfriendly.

The sensitive writer will respect the fact that the audience holds to and may continue to cling to beliefs opposed to the writer's. That writer will not characterize the audience as ignorant or malicious for doing so but will understand how difficult it can be for people to learn to see in new ways. Skillful arguers will place themselves in their readers' skins and try to see the problem with their readers' eyes. Such an identification with your reader helps you to lead readers from their present belief toward those new beliefs you want them to accept.

Once you identify with your audience, you can more easily decide what focus you need to direct their thinking about your topic. You can sort out what interests you share with the audience which you can later cite to convince the audience that your proposal best serves them. Through audience analysis and identification, you can demonstrate that what you are arguing is important to you and to your audience. Then you should provide enough proof for your argument so that the audience will believe your idea is sound and the best idea to use.

You can watch how a writer has analyzed her audience and adapted her introductory remarks and statement of thesis to her audience in the Introduction to *A Vindication of the Rights of Woman* by Mary Wollstonecraft. Mary Wollstonecraft, an Englishwoman whose political and social beliefs were shaped by Enlightenment assumptions about the people's use of reason to make life good, wrote a pamphlet vindicating the "rights of man" in response to the *Reflections on the Revolution in France* of the conservative Whig politician Edmund Burke. Wollstonecraft objected to what seemed to be an acceptance of social injustice and an enthusiasm for the spirit of religion and chivalry in the old French government. Mary Wollstonecraft subscribed to the principles of "liberté, égalité, fraternité" of the French Revolution and insisted that the "rights of man" was both a reasonable and a humane concept. Public response to her pamphlet gave her the self-confidence and the "guineas and locks" she needed to write *A Vindication of the Rights of Woman*.

The argument of this essay is as important to understanding the women's revolution as the *Declaration of Independence* is to understanding the American revolution. In the book the author argues that education was both the cause of and the solution to the problem of the inequality of women. Wollstonecraft believed that ignorance, prejudice, poverty, and sin all resulted from lack of knowledge and would be solved by the dissemination of learning. She did not believe that any racial, sexual or social class differences between men and women were innate; she thought all these differences grew out of the environment and could be erased once the environment was changed by the democratizing process of education.

A pamphlet by Talleyrand which described his proposals for national education under the new French government provoked Wollstonecraft's argument. She was also responding to the contention by Rousseau that woman's education should be relative to man's and should only make her better able to nurture and support man. Both Talleyrand and Rousseau recommended that girls receive minimal formal training and that their learning center on the interests and activities of the home. Wollstonecraft objected to educational reforms which espoused naturalistic child rearing but ignored the rights of women to develop into rational, healthy persons prepared for the strains of motherhood or whatever other activities they might choose.

In her introductory chapter, Wollstonecraft needs to persuade women —whose self-image might not focus on their reason and their strength of body and mind—and to persuade men—who might fear change—that the education of women is a critical need for a healthy society. How success-fully has she analyzed her audience and stated her thesis in the following statements?

"Introduction" to A Vindication of the Rights of Woman

Mary Wollstonecraft

After considering the historic page, and viewing the living world with anxious solicitude, the most melancholy emotions of sorrowful indignation have depressed my spirits, and I have sighed when obliged to confess, that either nature has made a great difference between man and man, or that the civilization which has hitherto taken place in the world has been very partial. I have turned over various books written on the subject of education, and patiently observed the conduct of parents and the management of schools; but what has been the result? — a profound conviction that the neglected education of my fellow-creatures is the grand source of the misery I deplore; and that women, in particular, are rendered weak and wretched by a variety of concurring causes, originating from one hasty conclusion. The conduct and manners of women, in fact, evidently prove that their minds are not in a healthy state; for, like the flowers which are planted in too rich a soil, strength and usefulness are sacrificed to beauty; and the flaunting leaves, after having pleased a fastidious eye, fade, disregarded on the stalk, long before the season when they ought to have arrived at maturity.—One cause of this barren blooming I attribute to a false system of education, gathered from the books written on this subject by men who, considering females rather as women than human creatures, have been more anxious to make them alluring mistresses than affectionate wives and rational mothers; and the understanding of the sex has been so bubbled by this specious homage, that the civilized women of the present century, with a few exceptions, are only anxious to inspire love, when they ought to cherish a nobler ambition, and by their abilities and virtues exact respect.

In a treatise, therefore, on female rights and manners, the works which have been particularly written for their improvement must not be overlooked; especially when it is asserted, in direct terms, that the minds of women are enfeebled by false refinement; that the books of instruction, written by men of genius, have had the same tendency as more frivolous productions; and that, in the true style of Mahometanism, they are treated as a kind of subordinate beings, and not as a part of the human species, when improveable reason is allowed to be the dignified distinction which raises men above the brute creation, and puts a natural sceptre in a feeble hand.

Yet, because I am a woman, I would not lead my readers to suppose that I mean violently to agitate the contested question respecting the equality or inferiority of the sex; but as the subject lies in my way, and I cannot pass it over without subjecting the main tendency of my reasoning to misconstruction, I shall stop a moment to deliver, in a few words, my opinion.—In the government of the physical world it is observable that the female in point of strength is, in general, inferior to the male. This is the law of nature; and it does not appear to be suspended or abrogated in favour of woman. A degree of physical superiority cannot, therefore, be denied — and it is a noble prerogative. But not content with this natural pre-eminence, men endeavour to sink us still lower, merely to render us alluring objects for a moment; and women, intoxicated by the adoration which men, under the influence of their senses, pay them, do not seek to obtain a durable interest in their hearts, or to become the friends of the fellow creatures who find amusement in their society.

I am aware of an obvious inference: —from every quarter have I heard exclamations against masculine women; but where are they to be found? If by this appellation men mean to inveigh against their ardour in hunting, shooting, and gaming, I shall most cordially join in the cry; but if it be against the imitation of manly virtues, or, more properly speaking, the attainment of those talents and virtues, the exercise of which ennobles the human character, and which raise females in the scale of animal being, when they are comprehensively termed mankind;—all those who view them with a philosophic eye must, I should think, wish with me, that they may every day grow more and more masculine.

This discussion naturally divides the subject. I shall first consider women in the grand light of human creatures, who, in common with men, are placed on this earth to unfold their faculties; and afterwards I shall more particularly point out their peculiar designation.

I wish also to steer clear of an error which many respectable writers have fallen into; for the instruction which has hitherto been addressed to women, has rather been applicable to *ladies*, if the little indirect advice, that is scattered through Sandford and Merton be excepted; but, addressing my sex in a firmer tone, I pay particular attention to those in the middle class, because they appear to be in the most natural state. Perhaps the seeds of false-refinement, immorality, and vanity, have ever been shed by the great. Weak, artificial beings, raised above the common wants and affections of their race, in a premature unnatural manner, undermine the very foundation of virtue, and spread corruption through the whole mass of society! As a class of mankind they have the strongest claim to pity; the education of the rich tends to render them vain and helpless, and the unfolding mind is not strengthened by the practice of those duties which dignify the human character.—They only live to amuse themselves, and by the same law which in nature invariably produces certain effects, they soon only afford barren amusement.

But as I purpose taking a separate view of the different ranks of society, and of the moral character of women, in each, this hint is, for the present, sufficient; and I have only alluded to the subject, because it appears to me to be the very essence of an introduction to give a cursory account of the contents of the work it introduces.

My own sex, I hope, will excuse me, if I treat them like rational creatures, instead of flattering their *fascinating* graces, and viewing them as if they were in a state of perpetual childhood, unable to stand alone. I earnestly wish to point out in what true dignity and human happiness consists—I wish to persuade women to endeavour to acquire strength, both of mind and body, and to convince them that the soft phrases, susceptibility of heart, delicacy of sentiment, and refinement of taste, are almost synonymous with epithets of weakness, and that those beings who are only the objects of pity and that kind of love, which has been termed its sister, will soon become objects of contempt.

Dismissing then those pretty feminine phrases, which the men condescendingly use to soften our slavish dependence, and despising that weak elegancy of mind, exquisite sensibility, and sweet docility of manners, supposed to be the sexual characteristics of the weaker vessel, I wish to shew that elegance is inferior to virtue, that the first object of laudable ambition is to obtain a character as a human being, regardless of the distinction of sex; and that secondary views should be brought to this simple touchstone.

This is a rough sketch of my plan; and should I express my conviction with the energetic emotions that I feel whenever I think of the subject, the dictates of experience and reflection will be felt by some of my readers. Animated by this important object, I shall disdain to cull my phrases or polish my style;—I aim at being useful, and sincerity will render me unaffected; for, wishing rather to persuade by the force of my arguments, than dazzle by the elegance of my language, I shall not waste my time in rounding periods, or in fabricating the turgid bombast of artificial feelings, which, coming from the head, never reach the heart.—I shall be employed about things, not words!—and, anxious to render my sex more respectable members of society, I shall try to avoid that flowery diction which has slided from essays into novels, and from novels into familiar letters and conversation.

These pretty superlatives, dropping glibly from the tongue, vitiate the taste, and create a kind of sickly delicacy that turns away from simple unadorned truth; and a deluge of false sentiments and overstretched feelings, stifling the natural emotions of the heart, render the domestic pleasures insipid, that ought to sweeten the exercise of those severe duties, which educate a rational and immortal being for a nobler field of action.

The education of women has, of late, been more attended to than formerly; yet they are still reckoned a frivolous sex, and ridiculed or pitied by the writers who endeavour by satire or instruction to improve them. It is acknowledged that they spend many of the first years of their lives in acquiring a smattering of accomplishments; meanwhile strength of body and mind are sacrificed to libertine notions of beauty, to the desire of establishing themselves,—the only way women can rise in the world,—by marriage. And this desire making mere animals of them, when they marry they act as such children may be expected to act:—they dress; they paint, and nickname God's creatures.—Surely these weak beings are only fit for a seraglio!—Can they be expected to govern a family with judgment, or take care of the poor babes whom they bring into the world?

If then it can be fairly deduced from the present conduct of the sex, from the prevalent fondness for pleasure which takes place of ambition and those nobler passions that open and enlarge the soul; that the instruction which women have hitherto received has only tended, with the constitution of civil society, to render them insignificant objects of desire—mere propagators of fools! — if it can be proved that in aiming to accomplish them, without cultivating their understandings, they are taken out of their sphere of duties, and made ridiculous and useless when the short-lived bloom of beauty is over, I presume that rational men will excuse me for endeavouring to persuade them to become more masculine and respectable.

Indeed the word masculine is only a bugbear: there is little reason to fear that women will acquire too much courage or fortitude; for their apparent inferiority with respect to bodily strength, must render them, in some degree, dependent on men in the various relations of life; but why should it be increased by prejudices that give a sex to virtue, and confound simple truths with sensual reveries?

Women are, in fact, so much degraded by mistaken notions of female excellence, that I do not mean to add a paradox when I assert, that this artificial weakness produces a propensity to tyrannize, and gives birth to cunning, the natural opponent of strength, which leads them to play off those contemptible infantine airs that undermine esteem even whilst they excite desire. Let men become more chaste and modest, and if women do not grow wiser in the same ratio, it will be clear that they have weaker understandings. It seems scarcely necessary to say, that I now speak of the sex in general. Many individuals have more sense than their male relatives; and, as nothing preponderates where there is a constant struggle for an equilibrium, without it has naturally more gravity, some women govern their husbands without degrading themselves, because intellect will always govern.

In *A Vindication of the Rights of Woman*, Mary Wollstonecraft organizes her book-length argument along the lines of a traditional argument. She follows a pattern of argument which you can use any time you are asked to argue an issue. It looks like this:

I. Statement or description of the problem
II. Formal statement of the solution
III. Explanation of the solution
IV. Disqualification of all other solutions
V. Recommendation of the solution

Although you might rearrange the order of these parts, all five of these activities are important to an effective argument. In the first part—what would be the introduction—you demonstrate that there is a problem which needs solving. You use whatever techniques are appropriate to demonstrating the problem—definition, narrative, anecdote, quote, description, rhetorical question, statistics. Catch the attention of the reader and show that the problem needs to be solved or that the belief which is important to you does need to be examined and eventually adopted by the reader.

Part II of the argument is also part of the introduction. This part is rarely more than a paragraph in length. Here you clearly state what you believe is the best solution or what belief you want the reader to adopt. Make sure that the terms of the thesis are clearly specified.

In part III, you explain all aspects of the solution which the reader must consider. You might define terms, predict the outcome, estimate the expenses, argue from some set of clearly defined criteria, discuss advantages and disadvantages or quote authorities and cite statistics. In short, you define and illustrate the solution by marshaling all the evidence you need in order to convince the reader that your solution is the best solution.

After you have stated your position clearly, you turn to the arguments of your opponents (part IV). You want to acknowledge and discuss the possible arguments of your "worthy opponents" for two reasons. One, you can steal your opponents' thunder and leave them speechless. Because the "opponents" could often be readers hostile to or skeptical about your belief or proposal, you may change their minds by anticipating their opposition and by showing them why your ideas are stronger and better than their objections. Two, you convince your readers that you care enough about this belief to have studied it carefully and to have even thought through what possible objections might be raised. This willingness to meet opposition and deal with it openly and critically makes the audience trust you and your ideas. It enhances your "ethos."

After refuting the assumptions of your opponents, you will want to restate your recommendation and emphasize its significance (part V). This is the conclusion and it must be dramatic. You want to be sure that this last section sends your readers out convinced they should act or feel or believe the way you have argued.

You can use this basic pattern for all persuasive writing. There are additional patterns of organization that you can choose to cross-structure with the basic pattern. You may use logic to reinforce your solution. You may reach the reader through an emotional appeal. You may persuade through an ethical appeal. Certainly, the techniques you use must be consistent with your ethos. What is this ethos? *Ethos* means the character or personality which you create for yourself and which gives you the authority to argue for a solution or belief. Ethos is built in many ways. You might demonstrate that the reader should accept your view of things because you have personal experience which makes you an accurate reporter. You could show that you have researched the issue carefully and have statistics which substantiate your claim and authorities who think like you do. You might present yourself as a person who is calm and reasonable or you could show that you are just "a good old Joe."

The ethical appeal asks readers to change the way they think or act because the writer is considered so trustworthy, fair and knowledgeable that his or her proposals should be accepted on face value. The reader trusts the writer either because of the reputation of the writer or because of the way the writer has argued. You've seen this argument reduced to an imperative sentence on billboards urging you to "Trust Reagan." This sentence is shorthand for a longer process of reasoning that says because Mr. Reagan has a certain ethos, he is a person whom we can trust.

Although ethical appeals are not effective for all persuasive tasks, you can use some elements of the ethical appeal to organize an argument. You must establish your authority in the introduction. Prove that you are completely informed about your topic all the way through the essay.

When you use information that you have researched, persuade the reader of the acuity of your sources by identifying your sources, either in the text or in footnotes. You show that you have done careful research by citing primary rather than secondary sources. If you decide that you have no choice but to use a secondary source, you should indicate its reliability by using terms more specific than "sources close to Simone de Beauvoir" or "the highest levels of the White House." Your reader will also judge your reliability and knowledge by gauging the authority of your secondary sources. Eleanor Flexner, who wrote a major critical biography about Mary Wollstonecraft, would be a more authoritative secondary source than someone who heard that Wollstonecraft "was one of those hothead libbers."

Readers will trust you as a persuader when they see you acting fair and talking honestly. They will not trust you if they see you distort the views of your opponents. They hear you argue that your opponent favors the ERA because it eliminates alimony. They know that the ERA would extend the rights of alimony to men so that men economically dependent on their wives could receive support just as women economically dependent on their husbands can receive support. They recognize that you have distorted facts. Your distortion of facts will cost you your readers' trust. In writing and in discussion, it's a good idea to repeat fully what your opponent said before you refute it. You won't then be accused of distortion.

You can also lose a reader's trust by quoting out of context. When readers see you selecting certain facts which support your generalization and suppressing others which do not support it, they become suspicious about your trustworthiness. If you base a generalization about feminists being men-haters on comments you have taken out of chapters of Ingrid Bengis's book *Combat in the Erogenous Zone*, you should also describe the context for each comment. If you reported that Ingrid Bengis was a feminist but did not report the series of insults, sexual assaults, and abuse which built into anger and hatred at one time in her life, you have violated both the contract you make with a writer to read honestly and the contract you have made with your readers to write honestly.

You can also destroy your credibility as an intelligent and trustworthy persuader by calling your opponent names. Although emotional language can often be used effectively to advance your meaning, overuse might make the reader reject your argument, because it no longer seems to be based on reason. You can show your readers how your opponent might be mistaken and might argue ideas not in the readers' best interests without describing the opponent as a *male chauvinist pig, a crypto-fascist* or *a bleeding heart liberal.*

In the speech which follows, you can watch Sojourner Truth make an ethical appeal. She argues that she knows more fully and can describe more aptly what women can do than can the ministers who have spoken against women's rights. Sojourner Truth refutes her opponent's arguments by citing the "facts" of her own experience as a black woman with a strength of body and mind equal to that of any other person. She spoke about the rights of women—over the objections of racists in the audience —at a Women's Rights Convention in Akron, Ohio, in 1851. She spoke after several opponents of women's rights argued that women lacked the strength, the intellect and the morality (daughters of Eve that they are) to be equal to men. She spoke when no other woman in the assembly dared:

Wall, chilern, whar dar is so much racket dar must be somethin' out o' kilter. I tink dat 'twixt de niggers of de Souf and de women at de Norf, all talkin' 'bout rights, de white men will be in a fix pretty soon. But what's all dis here talkin' 'bout?

Dat man ober dar says dat women needs to be helped into carriages, and liften ober ditches, and to hab de best place everywhar. Nobody eber helps me into carriages, or ober mud-puddles, or gibs me any best place! And a'n't I a woman?

Look at me! Look at my arm! I have ploughed and planted, and gathered into barns, and no man could head me! And a'n't I a woman? I could work as much and eat as much as a man—when I could get it—and bear de lash as well! And a'n't I a woman? I have borne thirteen chilern and seen 'em mos' all sold off to slavery, and when I cried out with my mother's grief, none but Jesus heard me! And a'n't I a woman?

Den dey talks 'bout dis ting in de head; what dis dey call it? Intelligence. Dat's it, honey. What's dat got to do wid women's rights or nigger's rights? If my cup won't hold but a pint and yourn holds a quart, wouldn't you be mean not to let me have my half-measure full?

Den dat little man in black dar, he say women can't have as much rights as men, 'cause Christ wan't a woman! Whar did your Christ come from? Whar did your Christ come from? From God and a woman! Man had nothin' to do wid Him.

If the first woman God ever made was strong enough to turn de world upside down all alone, dese women togedder ought to be able to turn it back, and get it right side up again! And now dey is asking to do it, de men better let 'em.

'Bleeged to ye for hearin' on me, and now old Sojourner han't got nothin' more to say.

Writing task one: Work as a group to brainstorm and evaluate grading alternatives and ethical appeals. Select the best combination and write, either as a group or individually, two introductory paragraphs which argue for a grading situation alternative to that used on your campus. Carefully establish your *ethos* and make it clear why an audience should trust you and should agree to your proposed grading system.

Emotional Appeal

To completely persuade readers to accept and act on your assumptions, you will want to involve them emotionally and intellectually in your process of arguing. Often we shy away from emotional appeals because some writers have abused this technique of tugging at our hearts while speaking to our minds. For example, I recently received a letter from advocates of gun control legislation. The letter began with a grisly narrative about a disturbed young mother who purchased a gun and killed each member of her family beginning with her husband and ending with her three-year-old son and two-month-old daughter. The lobbyist wanted to persuade me that gun control legislation was necessary by triggering in me responses of shock, horror, grief, and outrage.

Because you can drastically affect a reader's emotions, you will want to be sure that the problem you argue for is so grave that you need to jolt your audience into consciousness through emotional appeals. Once readers have been convinced emotionally that they must act on a problem, you can more easily persuade them through a logical argument how you think they should act.

Effective appeals to the emotions can dramatize a problem through examples and illustration. In the periodic sentence which follows, the satirist Jonathan Swift appeals to our moral sense when he demonstrates that a grave social problem exists in Ireland:

It is a melancholy object to those who walk through this great town, or travel in the country, when they see the streets, the roads and cabin-doors crowded with beggars of the female sex, followed by three, four or six children, all in rags and importuning every passenger for an alms.

In *A Modest Proposal*, Swift wrote an argument in favor of just and humane treatment of colonized Ireland by Great Britain and in favor of responsible actions by the Irish to ameliorate those inequities they could correct. Swift argued these issues ironically by having a citizen propose yet another solution to the problems of overpopulation and unemployment. That citizen describes himself as a humble but public-spirited citizen who is horrified by the sights he sees. When you read the argument, make a list of all the ethical and emotional appeals you find.

The citizen also prides himself on his use of logic and reason to solve the problems which he describes. Ask yourself about the effectiveness of his logically sound proposal.

A Modest Proposal

Jonathan Swift

FOR PREVENTING THE CHILDREN OF POOR PEOPLE IN IRELAND
FROM BEING A BURDEN TO THEIR PARENTS OR COUNTRY,
AND FOR MAKING THEM BENEFICIAL TO THE PUBLIC

It is a melancholy object to those who walk through this great town or travel in the country, when they see the streets, the roads, and cabin doors, crowded with beggars of the female-sex, followed by three, four, or six children, all in rags and importuning every passenger for an alms. These mothers, instead of being able to work for their honest livelihood, are forced to employ all their time in strolling to beg sustenance for their helpless infants, who, as they grow up, either turn thieves for want of work, or leave their dear native country to fight for the Pretender in Spain, or sell themselves to the Barbadoes.

I think it is agreed by all parties that this prodigious number of children in the arms, or on the backs, or at the heels of their mothers, and frequently of their fathers, is in the present deplorable state of the kingdom a very great additional grievance; and therefore whoever could find out a fair, cheap, and easy method of making these children sound, useful members of the commonwealth would deserve so well of the public as to have his statue set up for a preserver of the nation.

But my intention is very far from being confined to provide only for the children of professed beggars; it is of a much greater extent, and shall take in the whole number of infants at a certain age who are born of parents in effect as little able to support them as those who demand our charity in the streets.

As to my own part, having turned my thoughts for many years upon this important subject, and maturely weighed the several schemes of other projectors, I have always found them grossly mistaken in their computation. It is true, a child just dropped from its dam may be supported by her milk for a solar year, with little other nourishment; at most not above the value of two shillings, which the mother may certainly get, or the value in scraps, by her lawful occupation of begging; and it is exactly at one year old that I propose to provide for them in such a manner as instead of being a charge upon their parents or the parish, or wanting food and raiment for the rest of their lives, they shall on the contrary contribute to the feeding, and partly to the clothing, of many thousands.

There is likewise another great advantage in my scheme, that it will prevent those voluntary abortions, and that horrid practice of women murdering their bastard children, alas, too frequent among us, sacrificing the poor innocent babes, I doubt, more to avoid the expense than the shame, which would move tears and pity in the most savage and inhuman breast.

The number of souls in this kingdom being usually reckoned one million and a half, of these I calculate there may be about two hundred thousand couples whose wives are breeders; from which number I subtract thirty thousand couples who are able to maintain their own children, although I apprehend there cannot be so many under the present distresses of the kingdom; but this being granted, there will remain an hundred and seventy thousand breeders. I again subtract fifty thousand for those women who miscarry, or whose children die by accident or disease within the year. There only remain an hundred and twenty thousand children of poor parents annually born. The question therefore is, how this number shall be reared and provided for, which, as I have already said, under the present situation of affairs, is utterly impossible by all the methods hitherto proposed. For we can neither employ them in handicraft or agriculture; we neither build houses (I mean in the country) nor cultivate land. They can very seldom pick up a livelihood by stealing till they arrive at six years old, except where they are of towardly parts; although I confess they learn the rudiments much earlier, during which time they can however be looked upon only as probationers, as I have been informed by a principal gentleman in the county of Cavan, who protested to me that he never knew above one or two instances under the age of six, even in a part of the kingdom so renowned for the quickest proficiency in that art.

I am assured by our merchants that a boy or a girl before twelve years old is no salable commodity; and even when they come to this age they will not yield above three pounds, or three pounds and half a crown at most on the Exchange; which cannot turn to account either to the parents or the kingdom, the charge of nutriment and rags having been at least four times that value.

I shall now therefore humbly propose my own thoughts, which I hope will not be liable to the least objection.

I have been assured by a very knowing American of my acquaintance in London, that a young healthy child well nursed is at a year old a most delicious, nourishing, and wholesome food, whether stewed, roasted, baked, or boiled; and I make no doubt that it will equally serve in a fricassee or a ragout.

I do therefore humbly offer it to public consideration that of the hundred and twenty thousand children, already computed, twenty thousand may be reserved for breed, whereof only one fourth part to be males, which is more than we allow to sheep, black cattle, or swine; and my reason is that these children are seldom the fruits of marriage, a circumstance not much regarded by our savages, therefore one male will be sufficient to serve four females. That the remaining hundred thousand may at a year old be offered in sale to the persons of quality and fortune through the kingdom, always advising the mother to let them suck plentifully in the last month, so as to render them plump and fat for a good table. A child will make two dishes at an entertainment for friends; and when the family dines alone, the fore or hind quarter will make a reasonable dish, and seasoned with a little pepper or salt will be very good boiled on the fourth day, especially in winter.

I have reckoned upon a medium that a child just born will weigh twelve pounds, and in a solar year if tolerably nursed increaseth to twenty-eight pounds.

I grant this food will be somewhat dear, and therefore very proper for landlords, who, as they have already devoured most of the parents, seem to have the best title to the children.

Infant's flesh will be in season throughout the year, but more plentiful in March, and a little before and after. For we are told by a grave author, an eminent French physician, that fish being a prolific diet, there are more children born in Roman Catholic countries about nine months after Lent than at any other season; therefore, reckoning a year after Lent, the markets will be more glutted than usual, because the number of popish infants is at least three to one in this kingdom; and therefore it will have one other collateral advantage, by lessening the number of Papists among us.

I have already computed the charge of nursing a beggar's child (in which list I reckon all cottagers, laborers, and four fifths of the farmers) to be about two shillings per annum, rags included; and I believe no gentleman would repine to give ten shillings for the carcass of a good fat child, which, as I have said, will make four dishes of excellent nutritive meat, when he hath only some particular friend or his own family to dine with him. Thus the squire will learn to be a good landlord, and grow popular among the tenants; the mother will have eight shillings net profit, and be fit for work till she produces another child.

Those who are more thrifty (as I must confess the times require) may flay the carcass; the skin of which artificially dressed will make admirable gloves for ladies, and summer boots for fine gentlemen.

As to our city of Dublin, shambles may be appointed for this purpose in the most convenient parts of it, and butchers we may be assured will not be wanting; although I rather recommend buying the children alive, and dressing them hot from the knife as we do roasting pigs.

A very worthy person, a true lover of his country, and whose virtues I highly esteem, was lately pleased in discoursing on this matter to offer a refinement upon my scheme. He said that many gentlemen of this kingdom, having of late destroyed their deer, he conceived that the want of venison might be well supplied by the bodies of young lads and maidens, not exceeding fourteen years of age nor under twelve, so great a number of both sexes in every county being now ready to starve for want of work and service; and these to be disposed of by their parents, if alive, or otherwise by their nearest relations. But with due deference to so excellent a friend and so deserving a patriot, I cannot be altogether in his sentiments; for as to the males, my American acquaintance assured me from frequent experience that their flesh was generally tough and lean, like that of our schoolboys, by continual exercise, and their taste disagreeable; and to fatten them would not answer the charge. Then as to the females, it would, I think with humble submission, be a loss to the public, because they soon would become breeders themselves: and besides, it is not improbable that some scrupulous people might be apt to censure such a practice (although indeed very unjustly) as a little bordering upon cruelty; which, I confess, hath always been with me the strongest objection against any project, how well soever intended.

But in order to justify my friend, he confessed that this expedient was put into his head by the famous Psalmanazar, a native of the island Formosa, who came from thence to London above twenty years ago, and in conversation told my friend that in his country when any young person happened to be put to death, the executioner sold the carcass to persons of quality as a prime dainty; and that in his time the body of a plump girl of fifteen, who was crucified for an attempt to poison the emperor, was sold to his Imperial Majesty's prime minister of state, and other great mandarins of the court, in joints from the gibbet, at four hundred crowns. Neither indeed can I deny that if the same use were made of several plump young girls in this town, who without one single groat to their fortunes cannot stir abroad without a chair, and appear at the playhouse and assemblies in foreign fineries which they never will pay for, the kingdom would not be the worse.

Some persons of a desponding spirit are in great concern about that vast number of poor people who are aged, diseased, or maimed, and I have been desired to employ my thoughts what course may be taken to ease the nation of so grievous an encumbrance. But I am not in the least pain upon that matter, because it is very well known that they are every day dying and rotting by cold and famine, and filth and vermin, as fast as can be reasonably expected. And as to the younger laborers, they are now in almost as hopeful a condition. They cannot get work, and consequently pine away for want of nourishment to a degree that if at any time they are accidentally hired to common labor, they have not strength to perform it; and thus the country and themselves are happily delivered from the evils to come.

I have too long digressed, and therefore shall return to my subject. I think the advantages by the proposal which I have made are obvious and many, as well as of the highest importance.

For first, as I have already observed, it would greatly lessen the number of Papists, with whom we are yearly overrun, being the principal breeders of the nation as well as our most dangerous enemies: and who stay at home on purpose to deliver the kingdom to the Pretender, hoping to take their advantage by the absence of so many good Protestants, who have chosen rather to leave their country than to stay at home and pay tithes against their conscience to an Episcopal curate.

Secondly, the poorer tenants will have something valuable of their own, which by law may be made liable to distress, and help to pay their landlord's rent, their corn and cattle being already seized and money a thing unknown.

Thirdly, whereas the maintenance of an hundred thousand children, from two years old and upwards, cannot be computed at less than ten shillings a piece per annum, the nation's stock will be thereby increased fifty thousand pounds per annum, besides the profit of a new dish introduced to the tables of all gentlemen of fortune in the kingdom who have any refinement in taste. And the money will circulate among ourselves, the goods being entirely of our own growth and manufacture.

Fourthly, the constant breeders, besides the gain of eight shillings sterling per annum by the sale of their children, will be rid of the charge of maintaining them after the first year.

Fifthly, this food would likewise bring great custom to taverns, where the vintners will certainly be so prudent as to procure the best receipts for dressing it to perfection, and consequently have their houses frequented by all the fine gentlemen, who justly value themselves upon their knowledge in good eating; and a skillful cook, who understands how to oblige his guests, will contrive to make it as expensive as they please.

Sixthly, this would be a great inducement to marriage, which all wise nations have either encouraged by rewards or enforced by laws and penalties. It would increase the care and tenderness of mothers toward their children, when they were sure of a settlement for life to the poor babes, provided in some sort by the public, to their annual profit instead of expense. We should see an honest emulation among the married women, which of them could bring the fattest child to the market. Men would become as fond of their wives during the time of their pregnancy as they are now of their mares in foal, their cows in calf, or sows when they are ready to farrow; nor offer to beat or kick them (as is too frequent a practice) for fear of a miscarriage.

Many other advantages might be enumerated. For instance, the addition of some thousand carcasses in our exportation of barreled beef, the propagation of swine's flesh, and improvement in the art of making good bacon, so much wanted among us by the great destruction of pigs, too frequent at our tables, which are no way comparable in taste or magnificence to a well-grown, fat, yearling child, which roasted whole will make a considerable figure at a lord mayor's feast or any other public entertainment. But this and many others I omit, being studious of brevity.

Supposing that one thousand families in this city would be constant customers for infants' flesh, besides others who might have it at merry meetings, particularly weddings and christenings, I compute that Dublin would take off annually about twenty thousand carcasses, and the rest of the kingdom (where probably they will be sold somewhat cheaper) the remaining eighty thousand.

I can think of no one objection that will possibly be raised against this proposal, unless it should be urged that the number of people will be thereby much lessened in the kingdom. This I freely own, and it was indeed one principal design in offering it to the world. I desire the reader will observe, that I calculate my remedy for this one individual kingdom of Ireland and for no other that ever was, is, or I think ever can be upon earth. Therefore let no man talk to me of other expedients: of taxing our absentees at five shillings a pound: of using neither clothes nor household furniture except what is of our own growth and manufacture: of utterly rejecting the materials and instruments that promote foreign luxury: of curing the expensiveness of pride, vanity, idleness, and gaming in our women: of introducing a vein of parsimony, prudence, and temperance: of learning to love our country, in the want of which we differ even from Laplanders and the inhabitants of Topinamboo: of quitting our animosities and factions, nor acting any longer like the Jews, who were murdering one another at the very moment their city was taken: of being a little cautious not to sell our country and conscience for nothing: of teaching landlords to have at least one degree of mercy toward their tenants: lastly, of putting a spirit of honesty, industry, and skill into our shopkeepers; who, if a resolution could now be taken to buy only our native goods, would immediately unite to cheat and exact upon us in the price, the measure, and the goodness, nor could ever yet be brought to make one fair proposal of just dealing, though often and earnestly invited to it.

Therefore I repeat, let no man talk to me of these and the like expedients, till he hath at least some glimpse of hope that there will ever be some hearty and sincere attempt to put them in practice.

But as to myself, having been wearied out for many years with offering vain, idle, visionary thoughts, and at length utterly despairing of success, I fortunately fell upon this proposal, which, as it is wholly new, so it hath something solid and real, of no expense and little trouble, full in our own power, and whereby we can incur no danger in disobliging England. For this kind of commodity will not bear exportation, the flesh being of too tender a consistence to admit a long continuance in salt, although perhaps I could name a country which would be glad to eat up our whole nation without it.

After all, I am not so violently bent upon my own opinion as to reject any offer proposed by wise men, which shall be found equally innocent, cheap, easy, and effectual. But before something of that kind shall be advanced in contradiction to my scheme, and offering a better, I desire the author or authors will be pleased maturely to consider two points. First, as things now stand, how they will be able to find food and raiment for an hundred thousand useless mouths and backs. And secondly, there being a round million of creatures in human figure throughout this kingdom, whose sole subsistence put into a common stock would leave them in debt two millions of pounds sterling, adding those who are beggars by profession to the bulk of farmers, cottagers, and laborers, with their wives and children who are beggars in effect; I desire those politicians who dislike my overture, and may perhaps be so bold to attempt an answer, that they will first ask the parents of these mortals whether they would not at this day think it a great happiness to have been sold for food at a year old in the manner I prescribe, and thereby have avoided such a perpetual scene of misfortunes as they have since gone through by the oppression of landlords, the impossibility of paying rent without money or trade, the want of common sustenance, with neither house nor clothes to cover them from the inclemencies of the weather, and the most inevitable prospect of entailing the like or greater miseries upon their breed forever.

I profess, in the sincerity of my heart, that I have not the least personal interest in endeavoring to promote this necessary work, having no other motive than the public good of my country, by advancing our trade, providing for infants, relieving the poor, and giving some pleasure to the rich. I have no children by which I can propose to get a single penny; the youngest being nine years old, and my wife past childbearing.

1729

Were you persuaded by this argument to adopt his "fair, cheap and easy method of making these children sound and useful members of the commonwealth"? What solution would you offer?

Writing task two: Write an outline that shows how the argument breaks into five parts. After the group decides which paragraphs constitute the demonstration of the problem, where the solution is formally stated, what sections contain the explanation, where other solutions or beliefs are refuted, and what recommendations make up the conclusion, go back and write another outline. This time decide where Swift the satirist demonstrates that there is a problem, what solutions he recommends, where he disqualifies the solution of cannibalism, and how and where he recommends another solution.

Obviously, we are dealing with an ironic argument. There is the carefully worked out proposal by a madman who forgets that we solve human problems with criteria that are moral as well as economic. This is an excellent sample of what Iris Murdoch meant when she said that eloquence is no guarantee of goodness. Again, the skills of writing and thinking have been used effectively but for a purpose that is heinous.

Swift of course does not think that we should eat babies; he thinks that as human beings we should stop preying on each other. He ironically attacks the social and political conditions which spawn poverty, rapacity, and brutality. He satirizes the kind of overly rational thinking indulged in by men like this modest proposer. To do this, he organizes a pattern of implicit emtional appeals which covertly contradict the proposer's overt statement of a logical solution.

Most readers recognize the irony which Swift created by making so large a discrepancy between the emotional and the logical organizations of the argument. Notice, however, that in both the overt argument by the immodest madman and in the more hidden argument by Swift, the satirist has used all the steps of the argument and all the techniques which have been described. This is a very skillful use of writing conventions to provoke new ideas or feelings in an audience which has somehow stopped seeing the things which make Swift indignant.

Always when you write an argument, you have to consider your audience very carefully. You have to choose the best materials to catch their attention and you have to decide on the most appropriate way to present yourself. Let's watch some contemporary writers argue for a new perception. Notice the writing choices that are made.

When you want to make a stated problem concrete and personal to your readers, you might give a face and biography to the abstraction. In an argument from *MS.*, Judy Syfers insists that a wife is such a useful person to live with that even a wife would want one. She has given the abstractions *wife* and *husband* life by referring to her experience; she appeals to the complex of emotions that any person who feels herself to be always serving others might feel. How successfully do you think she has tugged at the emotions of her readers?

I Want a Wife

Judy Syfers

I belong to that classification of people known as wives. I am a Wife. And, not altogether incidentally, I am a mother.

Not too long ago a male friend of mine appeared on the scene fresh from a recent divorce. He had one child, who is, of course, with his ex-wife. He is obviously looking for another wife. As I thought about him while I was ironing one evening, it suddenly occurred to me that I, too, would like to have a wife. Why do I want a wife?

I would like to go back to school so that I can become economically independent, support myself, and, if need be, support those dependent on me. I want a wife who will work and send me to school. And while I am going to school I want a wife to take care of my children. I want a wife to keep track of the children's doctor and dentist appointments. And to keep track of mine, too. I want a wife to make sure that my children eat properly and are kept clean. I want a wife who will wash the children's clothes and keep them mended. I want a wife who is a good nurturant attendant to my children, who arranges for their schooling, makes sure they have an adequate social life with their peers, takes them to the park, the zoo, etc. I want a wife who takes care of the children when they are sick, a wife who arranges to be around when the children need special care, because, of course, I cannot miss classes at school. My wife must arrange to lose time at work and not lose the job. It may mean a small cut in my wife's income from time to time, but I guess I can tolerate that. Needless to say, my wife will arrange and pay for the care of the children while my wife is working.

I want a wife who will take care of *my* physical needs. I want a wife who will keep the house clean. A wife who will pick up after me. I want a wife who will keep my clothes clean, ironed, mended, replaced when need be, and who will see to it that my personal things are kept in their proper place so that I can find what I need the minute I need it. I want a wife who cooks the meals, a wife who is a *good* cook. I want a wife who will plan the menus, do the necessary shopping, prepare the meals, serve them pleasantly, and then do the cleaning up while I do my studying. I want a wife who will care for me when I am sick and sympathize with my pain and loss of time from school. I want a wife to go along when our family takes a vacation so that someone can continue to care for me and my children when I need a rest and change of scene.

I want a wife who will not bother me with rambling complaints about a wife's duties. But I want a wife who will listen to me when I feel the need to explain a rather difficult point I have come across in my course of studies. And I want a wife who will type my papers for me when I have written them.

I want a wife who will take care of the details of my social life. When my wife and I are invited out by my friends, I want a wife who will take care of the babysitting arrangements. When I meet people at school that I like and want to entertain, I want a wife who will have the house clean, prepare a special meal, serve it to me and my friends, and not interrupt when I talk about the things that interest me and my friends. I want a wife who will have arranged that the children are fed and ready for bed before my guests arrive so that the children do not bother us. I want a wife who takes care of the needs of my guests so that they feel comfortable, who makes sure that they have an ashtray, that they are passed the hors d'oeuvres, that they are offered a second helping of the food, that their wine glasses are replenished when necessary, that their coffee is served to them as they like it.

And I want a wife who knows that sometimes I need a night out by myself.

I want a wife who is sensitive to my sexual needs, a wife who makes love passionately and eagerly when I feel like it, a wife who makes sure that I am satisfied. And, of course, I want a wife who will not demand sexual attention when I am not in the mood for it. I want a wife who assumes the complete responsibility for birth control, because I do not want more children. I want a wife who will remain sexually faithful to me so that I do not have to clutter up my intellectual life with jealousies. And I want a wife who understands that *my* sexual needs may entail more than strict adherence to monogamy. I must, after all, be able to relate to people as fully as possible.

If, by chance, I find another person more suitable as a wife than the wife I already have, I want the liberty to replace my present wife with another one. Naturally, I will expect a fresh, new life; my wife will take the children and be solely responsible for them so that I am left free.

When I am through with school and have a job, I want my wife to quit working and remain at home so that my wife can more fully and completely take care of a wife's duties.

My God, who wouldn't want a wife?

Writing task three: Draw on your individual experiences as a student during a group discussion to brainstorm emotional appeals which you can combine with the ethical appeals for an essay arguing for an alternative grading system. After selecting the appeals the group decides would be most effective, write—either as a group or as individuals—an argument for an alternative grading system.

Appeal to Logic

When you use the logic of argument to persuade your readers, you diagram on paper the relationships which you have observed and identified between your perceptions and your assumptions. You trace the process of observing and making inferences or making judgments from your observations. The thought relationship between what you observe and what you conclude, you show in the written structure of the argument. You demonstrate for your readers a way to think through an assumption so that they too conclude what you have concluded.

You can show the reader the reasoning process which you used and want them to share through two methods: you can use the patterns of formal logic or you can use the pattern of premise followed to a conclusion. *Formal logic* is composed of two reasoning processes: induction and deduction. With inductive reasoning, you conclude from having observed a series of particular facts some generalization which describes all the particulars observed. Naomi Weisstein used induction to identify and then question the general assumption about woman's identity which the individual psychological, biological and anthropological theorists shared.

Many of our assumptions result from induction. Whenever you make a conclusion about a general class from your observation of class members, you have made an inductive leap from the particular to the general. So that you don't misstep when you leap, you'll need a sample or evidence which is accurate, as representative as possible, relevant to your generalization, and complete. Two types of evidence are gathered for induction: the evidence of fact which can be verified by a witness or by the common experience of people, and the evidence of judgment or opinion based upon reasoning.

Sometimes when you conclude a general principle from specific evidence, you leap too soon and state a hasty generalization, an assumption based on too scanty a sample or too limited a review of facts or too narrowly focused a survey of evidence to warrant such a large generalization. To avoid making hasty generalizations, you should look carefully at any statements which you've made about all members of a class—whether you have stated *all* as in *all children* or implied it as in *parents are monsters*. Reword your generalization so that it states a conclusion about only that evidence which you studied and only those class members who are *probably* other instances of your generalization.

Did you notice how Mary Woolstonecraft carefully restated her generalization that men always dominated women? If you look at the last sentence in the selection, you will see her reword the generalization so that it is true of most situations but does not deny some situations in which women are equal or are dominant. By showing that her generalizations were not hasty but were stated and revised to fit the survey of humankind, she tells the reader that she will be willing to argue and to change her ideas if persuaded by her opponents. She demonstrates that she knows the limits of the method of thinking she uses and that she will be honest about stating limits.

Science uses induction as a way of thinking about and researching the world. From careful observation of particular phenomena, scientists hypothesize certain generalizations which they can test and then state as general principles which seem to describe and explain the phenomena observed. Darwin studied the geology and zoology of small islands while serving as a naturalist on the *Beagle*. From his observations of species adapting to multiple contingencies, he concluded that some principle of natural selection explained the evolution of a higher species from a lower species. Contemporary scientists can use his assumption of natural selection as a model for defining the process of evolution.

Once they have made an inductive leap from the particular to the general, scientists do not fix that generalization as law. They do not, as we often do, use the general principle to reason to specific truths in a process of deduction. Instead, scientists think about conclusions as working models which may have to be changed once they encounter some anomaly which refutes the universality of the generalization. Scientists look again at all the evidence and notice how the addition of the anomaly changes the ways they had defined relationships among the phenomena. Out of the crisis of contested generalizations, scientists create new models and new assumptions. You can see this happening today as physicists scramble to explain the *psi* particle.

When scientists argue inductively, they remember that their generalizations are only as accurate and as complete as their sample. They know that new evidence may force them to rethink the relationships of phenomena and to make an inductive leap in some other direction. Scientists call their generalizations *models* to keep themselves alerted to the fact that inductive conclusions are always tentative. They persuade their audience and colleagues to accept their model and assumptions for awhile because their way of thinking and acting works best *now*.

Through inductive reasoning, you can often identify cause-effect relationships. You can use causal reasoning to argue your thesis. Identifying what causes the effect you see can be difficult. These questions will help you to sort out primary causes from immediate causes and to organize the pattern of cause and effect you want to argue. Is the connection I see, in fact, causal or is it coincidental? Does this effect always and necessarily follow from this cause? Can this cause produce this effect? Does naming this factor as the cause oversimplify the relationship? Are there other possible causes?

Through inductive reasoning, you can also spot similarities which make you reason by analogy that because these ideas and objects are similar in some respects they will be similar in other respects. You can see at once that reasoning by analogy might make problems. You remember from our discussion of metaphors that the objects compared are often more dissimilar than similar and the charm of the metaphor results from fusing unlikely things together in a novel manner. You can be led astray from the logical pattern when you try to chase a will-o'-the-wisp analogy which is more ephemeral than real and connected to the issue at hand. You've heard children reasoning by analogy and making verbs like *drinked* and *goed*. Although their verbs are sensible, they are not the conventional forms we use and recognize. Your analogy might be imaginative but not connected to the issue at hand. You cannot *prove* by analogy but you can certainly clarify and emphasize and illustrate an idea.

When you reason deductively, you move from general principle to specific fact. You can see this pattern of deduction in the persuasive writing of the *Declaration of Independence*. Usually you plot this movement through a convention of logic called a syllogism. A syllogism contains two premises and an inference which necessarily follows from the premises. For example:

First premise: All generalizations are capable of being false.
Second premise: "Women are passive" is a generalization.
Conclusion: "Women are passive" can be proved false.

What is your response to this syllogism?

First premise: All students are interested only in getting by.
Second premise: You are a student.
Conclusion: You are only interested in getting by.

You object? You say that the first premise is not necessarily true? Then you have differentiated empirical truth from logical validity. A syllogism can be valid but incorrect as a description of fact. If you believe that "all students are interested only in getting by" accurately describes few students and defames many students, then you have questioned the empirical truth of the conclusion about you as a student. Syllogistic reasoning is only as accurate as the premises which it uses. If you choose this method of reasoning, you need to begin with premises which your opponent can't easily refute.

We usually don't talk in syllogisms but we often think with them. Then we omit one or more premises and make statements which are enthymemes or incomplete syllogisms. If you scowl at an overcast sky and mutter about another rainy day, you are stating the conclusion of a syllogism you thought but did not notice as a syllogism because this process of abstraction is so habitual to you. The syllogism would look like this.

First premise: Cloudy days bring rain.
Second premise: Today is cloudy.
Conclusion: Today it will rain.

You might have already noticed that your first premise resulted from another unconscious but experienced process of abstraction. Your experiences have led you to reason that because clouds are present before rain, cloudy days bring rain. You made an inductive leap to determine a cause-effect relationship. The processes of induction and deduction are so much a part of your everyday thinking that you can easily draw attention to them when you look over what you've written and when you revise the first draft of your argument.

You've already noticed that you can make mistakes when you leap from premises to conclusion. Some cloudy days are dry. Some students are eager to learn all they can. Because in argument you use a network of intertwined syllogisms, you can often make logical fallacies. You might even contradict yourself by first stating that "all women are destined to be mothers" and then stating that "the reason women are stereotyped as mothers is that they haven't done anything to be something else." When you look over your first draft, you can use the diagram of the syllogism to catch any points where you have contradicted your own premises or have jumped to a conclusion not warranted by the premises.

If you want to use logic to argue well, you might read a good textbook in logic and learn all the conventions. You can teach yourself to detect fallacies in arguments. When you identified and examined the assumptions and implications of assumptions which organized an essay, you were in fact tracing the reasoning processes which resulted in the stated beliefs. You can make many of those assumptions more visible to yourself by putting them in the form of a syllogism. You can better understand what abstractions your writer made while thinking through an issue and you can see how those unstated abstractions direct actual behaviors.

Writing task four: Turn back to those assumptions listed in Chapter Four which defined women negatively. Select two, and in group discussion, draft three syllogisms for each assumption. First use the assumption as a premise and reason through to a logical conclusion. Then use the assumption as a conclusion and reconstruct the premises which led to that conclusion. Finally write a syllogism which you would use to argue against the logic of the oppressive assumptions.

Informal Logic

The processes of formal induction and formal deduction are often most useful in the prewriting stage when you are thinking out your thoughts on paper. You may find formal deduction, particularly, a bit too stiff for the easy flow of argument you want to present to your readers. Both methods of thinking and writing are abstractions from the world you inhabit and may not be close enough to the particular world you want your readers to inhabit. In the disciplines of philosophy and science, your audience may be more comfortable with such abstractions because they too are expected to abstract in their work. In other disciplines, audiences may expect you to anchor abstractions in concrete statements.

You might find that informal logic—a reasoning process which moves from one premise to any of many possible conclusions—better accommodates the several concrete realities you want to include in an argument. Certainly, you can indicate that an issue has both emotive and cognitive implications. When you argue from a premise to a conclusion, you are still identifying and analyzing the relationships of those assumptions which govern thinking and feeling. In your premise, you state overtly what you perceive as fact. Behind this premise stand unstated but implicit assumptions which made you arrive at your fact. The interaction of the fact and those assumptions produces a belief which you state overtly as a conclusion. In this premise-to-conclusion structure, you may see many unstated but implicit assumptions:

Premise: That woman never speaks in class.
Conclusion: That woman is not a good student.

What do *you* hear? I hear someone—perhaps the instructor, perhaps a classmate—judging the woman's abilities to learn by *their* criteria of class participation and assertiveness. Because someone assumes that good students always speak in class, this woman has been characterized as not a good student. I would speculate that a prior assumption that a person who says nothing thinks nothing resulted in the criterion of speaking to evaluate studenting.

Do you agree with those assumptions? Do you define yourself and the other learners in your courses through an operational definition which measures ability to learn by the frequency of classroom speech? How then do you account for the student who talks all the time and whom you suspect of talking only to impress the teacher?

We have observed that a woman never speaks in class. We probably noticed that behavior because our previous assumptions make us value speaking in class. Isn't it interesting that someone might describe the behavior observed in this way?

Premise: That woman always listens in class.
Conclusion: She must be a good student.

Whom do you hear speaking now? What unstated assumptions do you hear?

If we chose not to assume that the woman's silence meant inability to learn, what other things might we assume about the silence? Why do you speak and why do you not speak in class? Perhaps this woman has not been encouraged to speak in the particular class where she sits. It could happen that the behavior of the instructor and peers has given her negative feedback about her value in the classroom. Perhaps the instructor had indicated, overtly or covertly, that student speaking is not valued. Perhaps the student yawns and glazed expressions and obvious indifference to what other students say persuaded her that her audience would be indifferent or hostile.

Perhaps the woman is shy and feels like she has to pull words out of her gut when she wants to speak. Maybe she needs to sit in the classroom longer until she feels comfortable enough to speak. Do you ever feel timid about speaking out in class?

Perhaps the woman feels more confident about her writing skills than her speaking skills. Often, learners tell me early in the course that "I can write but I can't say what I mean out loud" or "I'm quiet in class but you can see that I'm paying attention by what I write." Do you ever remain quiet in class even though you're involved in what's going on?

Perhaps the woman has had previous bad experiences when she spoke in class. Maybe the instructor misunderstood her ideas or maybe a peer laughed at her expressions when they weren't intended to make peers laugh. If you were ever defined as a less serious student or as the "C/D" student, did you find yourself less willing to express and defend your ideas?

Perhaps the woman has never had a real audience. Many black students tell me that they feel they are talking into space when they talk in class. They feel that the other students do not hear them and do not see them. Many women have heard so often that women's talk is trivial that they may have concluded their audience has already tuned them out. Have you ever felt that your words bubbled up out of a fishbowl and were not heard by those who should be listening?

What other conclusions might you make from the premise "that woman never speaks in class"? Whenever you use the premise-to-conclusion pattern of reasoning, you will want to anticipate the conclusions which your audience might draw from your premises and discuss those conclusions. You will need to demonstrate why *your* conclusion is the most reasonable conclusion and how it best accounts for the complex logico-emotive experience of the audience.

Writing task five: Use some pattern of logic to argue for an alternative grading situation. The writing group should generate patterns of logic and select which pattern best combines this argument with those appeals to ethos and emotion which they already drafted to produce a persuasive essay. Then—as a group or as individuals—they should revise the argument they wrote for Writing Tasks One and Three by developing and emphasizing a pattern of logic.

Writing task six: Develop an argument which has as its thesis the belief that androgyny should be an ideal. Use personal experience as a means of evidence and be sure to define the term carefully. The audience for your essay does not understand the term and may confuse it with issues like bisexuality and homosexuality. Create an ethos that the audience can trust.

Writing task seven: Because you can often learn alternative ways to name and rename by arguing for a belief which you do not hold, play Devil's Advocate. The group should discuss ways to play Devil's Advocate and outline an essay which would persuade the audience that the alternative grading solution for which you argued in Writing Task Five should never be used.

You know of course that you can combine the conventions of argument with any of the defining paradigms or essay patterns which we have previously practiced when you want to write an effective persuasive essay. In the essay which follows, you will notice that Anne Roiphe uses techniques of comparison and contrast in her argument that women who believe women are superior to men are sexists. While you read the essay, notice how she uses empirical evidence from her own life to prove her thesis. Does the writer anticipate and refute the objections of her opponents? What techniques does she use to establish her authority? Does she make any emotional appeals? What patterns of logical argument has she selected?

Confessions of a Female Chauvinist Sow

Anne Roiphe

I once married a man I thought was totally unlike my father and I imagined a whole new world of freedom emerging. Five years later it was clear even to me—floating face down in a wash of despair—that I had simply chosen a replica of my handsome daddy-true. The updated version spoke English like an angel but—good God!—underneath he was my father exactly: wonderful, but not the right man for me.

Most people I know have at one time or another been fouled up by their childhood experiences. Patterns tend to sink into the unconscious only to reappear, disguised, unseen, like marionette strings, pulling us this way or that. Whatever ails people—keeps them up at night, tossing and turning—also ails movements no matter how historically huge or politically important. The women's movement cannot remake consciousness, or reshape the future, without acknowledging and shedding all the unnecessary and ugly baggage of the past. It's easy enough now to see where men have kept us out of clubs, baseball games, graduate schools; it's easy enough to recognize the hidden directions that limit Sis to cake-baking and Junior to bridge-building; it's now possible for even Miss America herself to identify what *they* have done to us, and, of course, *they* have and *they* did and *they* are.... But along the way we also developed our own hidden prejudices, class assumptions and an anti-male humor and collection of expectations that gave us, like all oppressed groups, a secret sense of superiority (co-existing with a poor self-image—it's not news that people can believe two contradictory things at once).

Listen to any group that suffers materially and socially. They have a lexicon with which they tease the enemy: ofay, goy, honky, gringo. "Poor pale devils," said Malcolm X loud enough for us to hear, although blacks had joked about that to each other for years. Behind some of the women's liberation thinking lurk the rumors, the prejudices, the defense systems of generations of oppressed women whispering in the kitchen together, presenting one face to their menfolk and another to their card clubs, their mothers and sisters. All this is natural enough but potentially dangerous in a revolutionary situation in which you hope to create a future that does not mirror the past. The hidden anti-male feelings, a result of the old system, will foul us up if they are allowed to persist.

During my teen years I never left the house on my Saturday night dates without my mother slipping me a few extra dollars—mad money, it was called. I'll explain what it was for the benefit of the new generation in which people just sleep with each other: the fellow was supposed to bring me home, lead me safely through the asphalt jungle, protect me from slithering snakes, rapists and the like. But my mother and I knew young men were apt to drink too much, to slosh down so many rye-and-gingers that some hero might well lead me in front of an oncoming bus, smash his daddy's car into Tiffany's window or, less gallantly, throw up on my new dress. Mad money was for getting home on your own, no matter what form of insanity your date happened to evidence. Mad money was also a wallflower's rope ladder; if the guy you came with suddenly fancied someone else, well, you didn't have to stay there and suffer, you could go home. Boys were fickle and likely to be unkind; my mother and I knew that, as surely as we knew they tried to make you do things in the dark they wouldn't respect you for afterwards, and in fact would spread the word and spoil your rep. Boys liked to be flattered; if you made them feel important they would eat out of your hand. So talk to them about their interests, don't alarm them with displays of intelligence — we all knew that, we groups of girls talking into the wee hours of the night in a kind of easy companionship we thought impossible with boys. Boys were prone to have a good time, get you pregnant, and then pretend they didn't know your name when you came knocking on their door for finances or comfort. In short, we believed boys were less moral than we were. They appeared to be hypocritical, self-seeking, exploitative, untrustworthy and very likely to be showing off their precious masculinity. I never had a girl friend I thought would be unkind or embarrass me in public. I never expected a girl to lie to me about her marks or sports skill or how good she was in bed. Altogether — without anyone's directly coming out and saying so — I gathered that men were sexy, powerful, very interesting, but not very nice, not very moral, humane and tender, like us. Girls played fairly while men, unfortunately, reserved their honor for the battlefield.

Why are there laws insisting on alimony and child support? Well, everyone knows that men don't have an instinct to protect their young and, given half a chance, with the moon in the right phase, they will run off and disappear. Everyone assumes a mother will not let her child starve, yet it is necessary to legislate that a father must not do so. We are taught to accept the idea that men are less than decent; their charms may be manifold but their characters are riddled with faults. To this day I never blink if I hear that a man has gone to find his fortune in South America, having left his pregnant wife, his blind mother and taken the family car. I still gasp in horror when I hear of a woman leaving her asthmatic infant for a rock group in Taos because I can't seem to avoid the assumption that men are naturally heels and women the ordained carriers of what little is moral in our dubious civilization.

My mother never gave me mad money thinking I would ditch a fellow for some other guy or that I would pass out drunk on the floor. She knew I would be considerate of my companion because, after all, I was more mature than the boys that gathered about. Why was I more mature? Women just are people-oriented; they learn to be empathetic at an early age. Most English students (students interested in humanity, not artifacts) are women. Men and boys — so the myth goes — conceal their feelings and lose interest in anybody else's. Everyone knows that even little boys can tell the difference between one kind of a car and another — proof that their souls are mechanical, their attention directed to the non-human.

I remember shivering in the cold vestibule of a famous men's athletic club.

Women and girls are not permitted inside the club's door. What are they doing in there, I asked? They're naked, said my mother, they're sweating, jumping up and down a lot, telling each other dirty jokes and bragging about their stock market exploits. Why can't we go in? I asked. Well, my mother told me, they're afraid we'd laugh at them.

The prejudices of childhood are hard to outgrow. I confess that every time my business takes me past that club, I shudder. Images of large bellies resting on massage tables and flaccid penises rising and falling with the Dow Jones average flash through my head. There it is, chauvinism waving its cancerous tentacles from the depths of my psyche.

Minorities automatically feel superior to the oppressor because, after all, they are not hurting anybody. In fact, they feel they are morally better. The old canard that women need love, men need sex—believed for too long by both sexes—attributes moral and spiritual superiority to women and makes of men beasts whose urges send them prowling into the night. This false division of good and bad, placing deforming pressures on everyone, doesn't have to contaminate the future. We know that the assumptions we make about each other become a part of the cultural air we breathe and, in fact, become social truths. Women who want equality must be prepared to give it and to believe in it, and in order to do that it is not enough to state that you are as good as any man, but also it must be stated that he is as good as you and both will be humans together. If we want men to share in the care of the family in a new way, we must assume them as capable of consistent loving tenderness as we.

I rummage about and find in my thinking all kinds of anti-male prejudices. Some are just jokes and others I will have a hard time abandoning. First, I share an emotional conviction with many sisters that women given power would not create wars. Intellectually I know that's ridiculous; great queens have waged war before; the likes of Lurleen Wallace, Pat Nixon and Mrs. General Lavelle can be depended upon in the future to guiltlessly condemn to death other people's children in the name of some ideal of their own. Little girls, of course, don't take toy guns out of their hip pockets and say "Pow, pow" to all their neighbors and friends like the average well-adjusted little boy. However, if we gave little girls the six-shooters, we would soon have double the pretend body count.

Aggression is not, as I secretly think, a male-sex-linked characteristic: brutality is masculine only by virtue of opportunity. True, there are 1,000 Jack the Rippers for every Lizzie Borden, but that surely is the result of social forms. Women as a group are indeed more masochistic than men. The practical result of this division is that women seem nicer and kinder, but when the world changes, women will have a fuller opportunity to be just as rotten as men and there will be fewer claims of female moral superiority.

Now that I am entering early middle age, I hear many women complaining of husbands and ex-husbands who are attracted to younger females. This strikes the older woman as unfair, of course. But I remember a time when I thought all boys around my age and grade were creeps and bores. I wanted to go out with an older man: a senior or, miraculously, a college man. I had a certain contempt for my coevals, not realizing that the freshman in college I thought so desirable, was some older girl's creep. Some women never lose that contempt for men of their own age. That isn't fair either and may be one reason why some sensible men of middle years find solace in young women.

I remember coming home from school one day to find my mother's card game dissolved in hysterical laughter. The cards were floating in black rivers of running mascara. What was so funny? A woman named Helen was lying on a couch pretending to be her husband with a cold. She was issuing demands for orange juice, aspirin, suggesting a call to a specialist, complaining of neglect, of fate's cruel finger, of heat, of cold, of sharp pains on the bridge of the nose that might indicate brain involvement. What was so funny? The ladies explained to me that all men behave just like that with colds, they are reduced to temper tantrums by simple nasal congestion, men cannot stand any little physical discomfort—on and on the laughter went.

The point of this vignette is the nature of the laughter—us laughing at them, us feeling superior to them, us ridiculing them behind their backs. If they were doing it to us we'd call it male chauvinist pigness; if we do it to them it is inescapably female chauvinist sowness and, whatever its roots, it leads to the same isolation. Boys are messy, boys are mean, boys are rough, b oys are stupid and have sloppy handwriting. A cacophony of childhood memories rushes through my head, balanced, of course, by all the well-documented feelings of inferiority and envy. But the important thing, the hard thing, is to wipe the slate clean, to start again without the meanness of the past. That's why it's so important that the women's movement not become anti-male and allow its most prejudiced spokesmen total leadership. The much-chewed-over abortion issue illustrates this. The women's-liberation position, insisting on a woman's right to determine her own body's destiny, leads in fanatical extreme to a kind of emotional immaculate conception in which the father is not judged even half-responsible—he has no rights, and no consideration is to be given to his concern for either the woman or the fetus.

Woman, who once was abandoned and disgraced by an unwanted pregnancy, has recently arrived at a new pride of ownership or disposal. She has traveled in a straight line that still excludes her sexual partner from an equal share in the wanted or unwanted pregnancy. A better style of life may develop from an assumption that men are as human as we. Why not ask the child's father if he would like to bring up the child? Why not share decisions, when possible, with the male? If we cut them out, assuming an old-style indifference on their part, we perpetuate the ugly divisiveness that has characterized relations between the sexes so far.

Hard as it is for many of us to believe, women are not really superior to men in intelligence or humanity—they are only equal.

Writing task eight: In groups, discuss how your own assumptions about an *other* influenced you to act as an oppressor and without tolerance, respect, understanding and love. You might describe your preconceptions about the opposite sex, about an older or younger generation, about an ethnic group or social group, about persons of another race or religion, about another occupational group or political group. Select one pattern of "chauvinism" and brainstorm alternative assumptions which would influence you to affirm the humanity and equality of that group which you treated as inferior. List each assumption on a sheet of paper and draft a companion sentence which uses the active voice and present tense for the predicate and which names a behavior implied by the new assumption. Be as specific as possible.

Writing task nine: Write a brief persuasive essay to convince people who shared your previous assumptions that they should now believe and act in the new way which the task group generated.

Suggested Group Writing and Discussing Activities

1. Read over the arguments which individuals wrote in support of the Equal Rights Amendment. Identify the techniques of persuasion used and suggest other techniques which could be used in each essay. Select one essay for revision. Rewrite the essay so that it argues yet more effectively the group belief that the ERA should be ratified.
2. Write an editorial for your college newspaper recommending grading alternatives or some reform of curriculum.
3. Revise the editorial and write a group argument recommending some change in grading policy or in curriculum which will convince the governing body which determines grading policies or curriculum of the validity of your argument.
4. In a persuasive essay, recommend learner and master-learner behaviors needed for a classroom which chooses to function as a community of practicing writers and speakers.
5. Argue for some linguistic change which you think would eradicate some of the negative images of women. Remember that your audience is likely to be hostile to your argument or to at least find it too funny for words.

Recommended Reading

Alice S. Rossi. *The Feminist Papers: From Adams to de Beauvoir.* New York: Columbia University Press, 1973. In this comprehensive anthology of the major feminist writings from the eighteenth century through the 1960s, you will find many skillful essays and speeches written to convince an audience that women have the right to equal opportunity.

Mary Wollstonecraft. *A Vindication of the Rights of Woman*. New York: W. W. Norton, 1975. In this critical edition by Carol A. Poston, you will also find introductory materials acquainting you with eighteenth-century assumptions and treatment of women and footnotes which explain allusions whose context we may not know.

CHAPTER NINE

Revisions and Re-Vision

You receive from your sociology professor the first draft of the research paper on aging which you submitted at the instructor's request. A note scrawled across the top of page one exhorts "REVISE!" You grimace and mull over what you must do to make your ideas more clear, your statements more concrete, and your report more interesting. You sit down and begin again to write your thoughts into new life.

You read a poet's descriptions of the challenge and promise and the danger and difficulty of exploring a new psychic geography and finding language to chart a new consciousness. She pulls an old term out of her lexicon, dusts off its etymology, adds a hyphen to signal a new meaning and exhorts "Re-vise!" You crinkle your brow and puzzle over what you must do for this "act of survival" and this act of "expressing the self into existence." You sit down and begin again to write your thoughts into new life.

Revising and editing the first draft of an essay or the final draft of a research paper are not simply mechanical operations of the writer. They can also be the first conscious actions of the writer who chooses to see again with fresh eyes and to know the self and society by analyzing how that self and society interacted in the artifact of written words that writer crafted yesterday. You should make it a habit to edit and revise for these varied reasons:

1. The writing process is so complex that some operations may be incomplete when the writer first feels "finished." When you revise, when you edit and when you proofread, you can knot up any loose ends of argument, unravel unnecessary stitches of exposition, tat down loose details, seam together unconnected paragraphs, and add the trim which will make the garment distinctive. Once you have carefully edited and revised, your thoughts are ready to wear.

2. By entering your expressed and now familiar thoughts from a new direction—even if the new stance is only the distance of time—you often discover new ways to see the topic, new assumptions that can shape your thinking, new ways to structure and style your namings. You can make a piece of writing which you decided yesterday was "dull and boring" scintillate.

3. By systematically and consistently reading over and questioning your work, you practice thinking skills that you may use more consciously the next time you write. You could become so skilled at re-vision that you would prewrite, write and rewrite simultaneously. Subsequent writing, becomes, it not easier, more enjoyable because you are aware *as you shape* how well you are shaping. This state of heightened consciousness I think is what great poets describe as rapture: the rapt state we can all grow towards.

4. By reviewing and rewriting, you train yourself in the creative skill of reperception which you need especially in a society and technology which changes more rapidly than our structures for coping with it change. By making yourself see your writing as an intellectual artifact separate now from you and that you are capable of reworking, you help yourself discover strengths of feeling and thinking which are not so much defensive as self-supporting. You learn that you can change and name and grow and re-vise and change and grow. You learn that *you* can make yourself whole and your world more healthy by reperceiving.

Had I told you this in Chapter One, you would have been skeptical. After all, didn't "revise" always mean to correct punctuation and to clean up spelling and to make smooth transitions? Yes, but hasn't "revise" also meant to look again and see the work fresh so that you notice and fix unnecessarily unconventional spelling, grammar, and usage and so that you notice and rework ideas which do not yet say what you mean them to say?

Now that you have practiced these skills of reading and "righting" and have, in fact, seen new ways to write the sentences of other writers and seen new ways to write your own work, I'm sure that you realize that you have been seeing in ways you didn't expect to see and thinking in ways that you weren't conscious that you thought. You have written alone, following the conventional definition of writing. You have written in a group and tested conventions about what groups can accomplish.

Let's look at some revisions. The self-description which follows came from an exercise when I asked writers to select a geometrical shape to use as a metaphor for their self-definitions. Then I asked each to extend the metaphor into a longer piece of writing. When you read the first essay, set yourself in the place of an editor and jot down any revisions which you think would improve the writing:

Paper One: September 26

In describing my behavior, I feel that I can tie in the exercise performed in class where we chose a geometrical object to define ourself. I chose the star.

I think that I can best describe my behavior as that of a star following a somewhat set pattern (or line) through the galaxy (of life) with all my interests and experiences shooting off from the star.

What I'm really trying to say is that I see myself and everyone else each as their own star and we're caught up in this big galaxy of ours, revolving and moving along in a basically definite pattern. And from the numerous points found on the star's surface, we shoot off in infinite tangents, each one being representative of some experience that touched us and helped us along the way.

To conclude I would have to say that my behavior is lineal in many respects, but not so well defined that I couldn't change.

Maura Kelley

My reader's response to this writing described the difficulty which I experienced understanding the analogy, the fact that the writer's use of faulty pronoun reference confused me, and a belief I held that if the writer stopped spending energy talking about what would be described ("In describing... ," "I think that...." "What I'm really trying to say... ," "To conclude... ") and just *described,* the essay would be much tighter and more interesting. What would be your reader's response?

The writer decided to revise and in the process of revision described a less linear life. When you read this essay, set it against the original and judge when the revisions are effective and when they are not:

Paper Two: A revision, October 1

Life's Lodestar

Our life becomes much the same as that of a star; a celestial body of the heavens, a scintillating diamond in animated suspension hung in a black satin sky.

Visualize the beginnings of a star as a light glowing in the distant dark, amassing knowledge and force as it rushes towards its destiny. It knows not where it's going, only that it's going there, wherever there may be.

Following a spherical orbit through the galaxy, a glittering conglomerate with kaleidoscopic visions of that which it has seen, a path ever-changing with infinite minute deviations; all experiences stellated, piercing rays of a shining light in the web of a dark unknown.

Each event adds another facet, another side to this shining prism of life, glorifying it in all its splendor, outshining all other glittering gems by its sheer magnificence.

Sure of itself, reflecting the past, viewing all in retrospect; a twinkling lodestar, slowly disintegrating until — in a burst of flames it falls from the heavens.

Cycle ended.

Maura Kelley

What is your reader's response to this essay? Do you understand the comparison the writer has described? Has the writer avoided vague pronoun reference? Do you see anything tentative about the way this is written? What questions would you ask this writer to help her?

Writing task one: In a group discuss anything you find new in the second essay. If you find parts of the essay problematic, revise them.

Have you revised any of the definitions you made for yourself when you first began this course? How do you define *woman* now? What do you mean by *liberation?* What definitions do you make about your activity as a writer?

Writing task two: Define yourself as a writer now. Take thirty minutes and tell the instructor anything which she or he needs to know to work with you as a writer. Identify if you can your particular strengths and weaknesses as a writer.

How *do* you define yourself now as a writer? If you set the definition you just wrote next to the definition you wrote when first I asked you to write, do you see anything changed in what you have said and how you have said it? Are you using the same voice you used the first time you wrote? Do you describe the same confidence, the same strengths, the same weaknesses? Have you used the same sentence patterns and sentence clusters (paragraphs)? Have you used any paradigms for defining that you did not choose and use before? Do you hold the same view of yourself as a writer? Now that you have been thinking and writing and thinking again with new patterns, have you also redefined yourself as a writer?

We'll practice another kind of revision. Often you must finish incomplete thoughts or sentences; often you must find the precise word that best completes a phrase. Words have been purposely omitted from the following poem by Sylvia Plath so that you can play with this process of searching for the "right" word to complete a phrase, to establish a tone (the attitude of the writer towards the reader), to create a persona (the voice the writer chooses to write in) and to define the attitude of the writer towards the subject. In this exercise, you "finish" the poem twice. First you fill in the blanks with a word you deem appropriate for what the poem seems to say. Once you have written your revision, work with a group to "finish" the poem. Notice the several ways of understanding and naming which group members will demonstrate when each reads his or her version.

Morning Song

Sylvia Plath

Love set you going like a fat _____ watch.
The _____ slapped your footsoles, and your _____ cry
Took its place among the elements.

Our voices echo, _____ your arrival. New _____
In a drafty _____, your nakedness
Shadows our safety. We stand round blankly as _____.

I'm no more your mother
Than the cloud that distils a mirror to reflect its own slow
Effacement at the wind's hand.

All night your _____-breath
Flickers among the _____ pink _____. I wake to listen:
A far sea moves in my ear.

One cry, and I _____ from bed, _____ and floral
In my _____ nightgown.
Your mouth opens _____ as a _____'s. The window square

Whitens and _____ its dull stars. And now you try
Your handful of notes;
The clear vowels rise like _____.

What *is* Plath's attitude about mothering? How is it unlike your attitude? How is it similar? What is your response to Plath's poem? When
you compare the several group poems with the poem which Sylvia Plath
wrote, what do you learn? How many class members share her attitudes
about mothering?

Previous learners have compared their poems with Plath's and discovered that they saw mothering and childbirth in ways very unlike Plath's.
They remarked that the metaphors they would have chosen to describe
the birth of a child reflected another set of assumptions than those which
structured Plath's poem. Some learners — always mothers themselves —
delighted in finding a poet who described things the way they sometimes
experienced them but never saw them described.

I assume that you entered into Plath's poem in a way that you may never
have before. Any time you set yourself the task of not only carefully
analyzing what patterns a writer has chosen but also trying to complete

that writer's idea in patterns that the writer *might* have chosen, you have made yourself reperceive the poem, your role as a reader, your relationship with the writer and the writer's struggle to shape. You can use this procedure on another piece of writing to help yourself sort out alternatives.

Writing task three: Take an essay which was written earlier or which you read earlier and practice "cloze procedure" (the process of revision you used with the Plath poem) on it. Delete several phrases. Then edit and rewrite the essay so that you have made it coherent and unified.

In the following paragraphs written during the first class session in a composition course, students introduce themselves. Each writer has selected the first person singular to define the self as a writer. After you read the introductions, we will talk specifically about persona and tone, two elements of style which you can play with and change most readily and most profitably when you turn again to your first draft. Although we can't divorce what we say from how we say it, we can in a revision check for consistency and unity and flow in the *how* or in the form. It follows that the *what* or the content will become more consistent, unified, and fluid. In these passages what voice do you hear the writer use? What adjectives would you use to describe the voice? What seems to be the writer's attitude toward the audience?

1. Hi! I'm Marybeth and I *hate* to write. I know that this skill is necessary for succeeding in college. I will try very hard to improve what little skill I have. I know that if this were a conversation, you would be asking "Why do you hate to write?" I'd answer "Because I can't." I know that I understand people and their emotions better when I hear the dialogue. I speak better than I write and I prefer to speak—so ... Maybe one reason I write so little is because I never can record my thoughts fast enough. My mind goes 10X faster than my Flair. Right now, my mind is off this page and about three pages ahead. I'll bring it back so I can finish. I have always wanted to be a lawyer—and all the people suggesting that I think instead about being a court stenographer or a legal secretary make me more sure of law.

   Marybeth Joyce

2. Well, first of all, I hate the name Florence even though it is my first name. Call me Kim. I am born under the sign of Scorpio. If you know anything about the stars, you know a little about me. I don't talk much. I like to listen and to learn as much as I can. I would like to talk more but I guess I can't really express myself the way I really want to. This communicating in words and in writing I hope you can help me with in this course.

   Kim Hill

3. I would define myself as one of many nonplussed freshmen at a large university and one of many nonpowerful women in an American society. Both parts of me seek a place to fit and power to make me free. Although I have many ideas, I often find it difficult to set them down in an interesting manner. My writing might indicate a strong writing background but I feel very weak as a writer. I have many interests, particularly sports, music and art. My mind is open to many things. I would rate my reading ability as poor at this stage but it will improve after a few college assignments. I have enjoyed high school although I think that in many ways I am not as prepared as I should be. I believe in truth and justice. I am easygoing and get along with all types of people. I have come to college to learn as much as possible and to prepare myself for whatever lies ahead.

Debbie Picciato

Each writer has chosen to present a character to us through a certain way of speaking. The writer's voice is but one of many ways of speaking and writing which each writer has available as alternatives. You choose that voice or that persona—which means *mask,* like the masks of Greek drama which represented individual emotions—to suit the purpose of your writing.

We don't call this voice a persona or mask to say that we are using a voice not true to our beliefs or that we are camouflaging our ideas. In fiction, of course, you might create such personae. But when I use persona here I mean the way you've decided to modulate your pitch and select your words out of deference to your audience and to your own purpose of sharing. Although you might speak with a different persona— more cautious or less friendly—to someone whom you've just met than you would speak to someone whom you love, you are not being dishonest in the first instance. You are only selecting how much of your person you want to share when you state your beliefs. It's like talking in a whisper or talking louder; you decide what voice best suits your purpose *here* and *now.* When you change volume later, you don't become another person; you only assert yourself in another way.

For example, the first writer wants to emphasize the fact that she thinks she talks better than she writes so she has used a persona of the conversationalist. Did you notice that her paragraph sounds more like talk—like a monologue—than have many of the formal essays you have read? When writer one uses exclamations, underlines words and lets a sentence trail off into points of ellipsis (...), she is trying to emphasize written words the way she would emphasize them when she talks. Did you notice how many of her sentences were simple sentences and how many contractions ("I'm," "can't") she uses? These conventions are typical of speaking and less typical of formal writing.

The second writer mixes speaking and writing conventions. What would you label the persona she's used? Did you notice the variety of sentence patterns which she has selected? She writes short simple sentences and longer complex sentences. She too uses phrases more common to speaking ("Well, first of all ... ," "I guess") but she also uses phrases more common to writing ("I am born" rather than "I was born" or "I am a Scorpio"). In her last sentence she inverts word order and begins the sentence with the object of the adverbial preposition. How often do you hear such a pattern in conversation?

The third writer uses few speaking patterns and many conventions of formal writing. Did you notice the parallel structures in sentences one, two, and the last? Did you notice that most of the sentences are lengthy and either complex or compound-complex? Although people can of course phrase their ideas these ways when they converse, these patterns are more typical of the essay or the formal speech. It seems that this writer uses the persona of the essayist in this definition.

We can also describe the tone which controls the words in each paragraph. When you say that "Marybeth sounds friendly like she's sitting right here and grinning at me," you describe her tone or the attitude which she has towards her reader. Another way to describe the close relationship of writer and reader here might be *informal*. You might say *personal* except that all three writers are being personal when they use the *I*. *Informal* or *friendly* make clear distinctions just as the adjective *reserved* might make the best description for the third writer. Does the writer of the third paragraph sound as "easygoing" as she states that she is? Do writers one and two seem more friendly than writer three because they both name themselves? What other writing choices determine the tones of the paragraphs?

All three writers share an attitude about the subject of writing; each writer defines herself as less able a writer than she might hope to be. I find the definitions particularly interesting because I see each writer establishing a clear voice and tone and stating rather well how "weak" their writing skills are. Each writer describes herself as a worse writer than her writing would indicate. It would seem that each lacks the confidence she should have.

In any writing situation you can identify and analyze voice, tone, and subject matter. Aristotle first described these three components of voice, audience, and subject as the interacting elements of any speech or writing act in his treatise called *Rhetoric*. If you were to change any part of this triad, the other components would be affected. If you changed your persona, for example, from that of non-hierarchic collaborator to that of authoritarian judge, the way you perceive the subject matter and the way you feel and act towards your audience would also change. You would be likely to see the subject in terms of individualism and elitism and you would more likely be writing a lecture than a dialogue. If you change the persona consciously, you'll always want to ask: "Even if this is a new way of seeing for me, have I made the words mine? Do I say them the way I feel them?"

In similar manner, should $\acute{y}$ou write for a different audience than the one you specified when you first wrote, you would change the persona you use and the ways that you focus and present subject matter. Do you recall the writing choices you made when you played "Devil's Advocate"? You deliberately chose a voice that differed from the one you used when you argued the value of listening in the classroom. You also changed your attitude about the value of listening.

You could diagram the interrelationships of voice, audience and subject. Then when you revise any of the triad, you could plot for yourself the ways the entire triad was transformed. You can use a diagram like this:

If you were to diagram the triad for the first paragraph, you might have something that looks like this.

Paragraph three might look like this.

In the following two paragraphs, what are the persona, tone and attitude of the writer towards the subject? Diagram the relationships of these three elements of any rhetorical act:

I am a writer. I make this statement not so much as fact, but rather, as opinion. I view myself as a writer, an observer recording human nature. I will not argue about the worth of my writing. I leave that for the critics or, in this case, for the teacher to determine. Ultimately, of course, only the readers (my peers in class) can judge the value put on my work and the ideas contained in it. As a writer, sharing my experiences, I hope that, by developing a sense of recognition in my audience, they might learn more about themselves as human beings while entertaining them as well.

Riley D. Ellerbusch

You don't know me, then again I'm not sure I know myself. I'm the student who comes to class late, sits in the back of the room and observes the teacher and the classes every move. Why do I do this? I'm trying to give everyone a false impression. I want people to think I don't know anything about English or a writing class. Eventually that opportunity will come and then I do my thing! I show through my questioning and answering how I really shine when it comes to writing. I don't care if others resent me, when you've got it, you've got it.

Kathleen Lindsey

Remember that these writers did not have the opportunity to revise for correctness. There are in these paragraphs, which I think are good examples of effective writing, some problems of syntax, punctuation and spelling. Identify those problems and think about how important they might be. What conventions should the writers follow when they revise these paragraphs so that the writings show exactly the persons whom both describe themselves to be?

Writing task four: Look again at the definitions you wrote earlier about yourself as a writer. Identify the voice, audience and subject of each. Choose one from among those which the group examines and play with it by writing several revisions in which you adopt various personae, tones and attitudes. Make final corrections of any inappropriate punctuation, grammar, syntax, usage, and diction.

One September afternoon, I asked a group of students to look at several paragraphs of introduction written by their peers and to identify and analyze the persona, tone and writer's attitude towards the subject.

"Okay," I said, "let's read this first paragraph and talk about the voice we hear. What voice do you hear? What do you speculate about the writer when you look at this writing? What do you know about the writer through the writing?"

One student described the voice: "One thing for sure—some girl wrote this!"

The male football player who had written the paragraph argued heatedly that there was nothing "girlish" about his use of adjectives, exclamation points, dashes and the pronoun I. Other class members argued—as heatedly—that even though he had written the paragraph, it still "sounded like a girl wrote it." They insisted that men and women write in ways that can be identified as by a man or woman writ.

Well, do they?

Do you think that there are distinctions that we can make between the way men write and the way women write? Is there such a thing as women's rhetoric which is somehow unlike men's rhetoric? Are the ways that women and men perceive the world so dissimilar and gender-linked that there would, in fact, be separate languages for each sex? Many people have been asking these questions recently. We'll try to formulate some answers through the revisions which follow.

Writing task five: Describe some object in your bedroom using what you assume or what you might imagine to be the perspective, the voice, the tone and the attitude of a *man*. Then describe the same object using what you assume or what you might imagine to be that of a *woman*. In group discussion, discuss, debate, discover, deliberate, and detail what group members categorize as male and as female writing patterns.

What writing patterns do you characterize as male? as female? Or do you make any distinctions at all? What are the criteria which you used to make your evaluations? What are the assumptions which you held or have now formulated about men's rhetoric and women's rhetoric? To spur your discussion, I am including several uncredited passages from works published by men and women writers. I ask you to read each paragraph and then make an educated guess about who—man or woman—wrote the paragraph. If you would also like to guess who wrote the passage—if you recognize the style from your reading or have a hunch that this would be how Lillian Hellman wrote the paragraph if she wrote it—then please guess. When you decide on an author, list the reasons why you chose whom you chose. Thus we can compile even more data for our discussion of men's and women's and people's languages.

First you will read four passages of description and choose an author. Then you will read three passages of autobiographic narrative and description and choose an author. Who wrote what?

1. Looking down at himself, as he crouched in the grass, he saw his legs and body splotched with dark objects. My God, they were all over him, large, horny, beetle insects, clumsily waving their feelers and moving up over him. He let out a yell of fear and brushed them off with frantic hands.

The insects clung and when they fell off, fell heavily into the grass and lay waving their legs—like some kind of monster—he thought wildly, every particle of his flesh crawling with loathing. Five, six, ten—while he lay there, on the soil, they had been crawling on to him, and had even started to make their noise, as if he had not been there at all. Now as he stood, half crouched, his eyes moving warily about him, he saw them everywhere in the grass and half a dozen paces away, they were still clicking and singing as if he didn't exist. But they were everywhere! He let out another yell of pure terror and ran fast off away from the camp into the trees, beating at his legs and body with his hands as if he were on fire and he were beating out the flames.

2. Few things, certainly, could have caused more stir in the house. What had been foreseen as a day of formality became one of fierce exertion; housemaids began making a fire, removing covers, unfolding linen; men in aprons, never formally seen, shifted furniture; the estate carpenters were collected to dismantle the bed. It came down the main staircase in pieces, at intervals during the afternoon; huge sections of rococo, velvet covered cornice; the twisted gilt and velvet columns which formed its posts; beams of unpolished wood, made not to be seen, which performed invisible, structural functions below the draperies; plumes of dyed feathers, which sprang from gold-mounted ostrich eggs and crowned the canopy; finally, the mattresses with four toiling men to each. Lord Marchmain seemed to derive comfort from the consequences of his whim; he sat by the fire, watching the bustle, while we stood in a half-circle—Cara, Cordelia, Julia and I—and talked to him.

3. But in the morning all the ordinary currents of conjecture were disturbed by the presence of a strange mourner who had splashed among them as if from the moon. This was the stranger described by Mrs. Cadwallader as frog-faced: a man perhaps two or three and thirty, whose prominent eyes, thin-lipped, downward curved mouth, and hair sleekly brushed away from a forehead that sank suddenly above the ridge of the eyebrows certainly gave his face a batrachian unchangeableness of expression. Here, clearly, was a new legatee; else why had he been bidden as a mourner?

4. Snow fell against the high school all day, wet big-flaked snow that did not accumulate well. Sharpening two pencils, William looked down on a parking lot that was a blackboard in reverse: car tires had cut smooth arcs of black into the white, and wherever a school bus had backed around, it had left an autocratic signature of two V's. The snow, though at moments it whirled opaquely, could not quite bleach those scars away. The temperature must be exactly 32°. The window was open to a crack, and a canted pane of glass lifted air into his face, coating the cedarwood scent of pencil shavings with the transparent odor of the window sill. With each revolution of the handle, his knuckles came within a fraction of an inch of the tilted glass, and the faint chill this proximity breathed on them sharpened his already acute sense of shelter.

5. Now that school was out and there was no one for us to stay with, we

would sit on the porch and rock in the rocking chair most of the day. We were scared to go out and play because of the snakes. Often as we sat on the porch we saw them coming up the hill from the swamp. Sometimes they would just go to the other side of the swamp. But other times they just went under the house and we didn't see them come out. When this happened, we wouldn't eat all day because we were scared to go inside. The snakes often came into the house. Once as I was putting wood in the stove for Mama, I almost put my hands on one curled up under the wood. I never touched the woodpile again.

6. Mama ran in . . . She jumped up and down, screaming like a crazy woman. I began to think about dying. The worst part of dying was thinking about the things and the people that I'd never see again. As I lay there trying to imagine what being dead was like, the policeman who had been trying to control Mama gave up and bent over me. He asked who had shot me. Before I could answer, he was asking me if I could hear him. I told him that I didn't know who had shot me and would be please get Mama to stop jumping up and down. Every time Mama came down on that shabby floor, the bullet lodged in my stomach felt like a hot poker.

7. We are talking now of summer evenings in Knoxville, Tennessee, in the time that I lived there so successfully disguised to myself as a child. It was a little bit mixed sort of block, fairly solidly lower middle class, with one of two juts apiece on either side of that. The houses corresponded: middle-sized gracefully fretted wood houses built in the late nineties and early nineteen hundreds, with small front and side and more spacious back yards, and trees in the yard, and porches. These were soft-wooded trees, poplars, tulip trees, cottonwoods. There were fences around two or three of the houses, but mainly the yards ran into each other with only now and then a low hedge that wasn't doing very well. There were few good friends among the grown people, and they were not poor enough for the other sort of intimate acquaintance, but everyone nodded and spoke, and even might talk short times, trivially, and at the two extremes of the general and the particular, and ordinarily next door neighbors talked quite a bit when they happened to run into each other, and never paid calls. The men were mostly small businessmen, one or two very modestly paid executives, only two worked with their hands, most of them clerical, and most of them between thirty and forty-five.

Writing task six: In a group, compare results and the assumptions stated about men's language and women's language. List any assumptions which recur often for examination and future use.

When learners guess who wrote what, they often guess correctly. Just as often they guess wrong. In fact, we have found no consistency in theories about women's writing and men's writing. Often we work from generalizations about what we expect men to write and women to write;

those generalizations are usually based on past experience and are more descriptive of what men and women have usually written than how they could write. Most often learners base their theories of authorship on the subject matter and their presuppositions about what are the subjects that men and women write about. When learners do describe and defend some writing pattern as female—say, the close attention to detail—their defenses crumble because their woman writer turns out to be a man writer. Were the members of your writing community able to clearly differentiate the male authors from the female authors?

Discussing masculine and feminine style is difficult also because of two opposed theories about style. Some believe that style is totally the series of writing choices made by an individual. Others believe there may be a group style, a pattern of characteristic writing choices which is shared by a group of writers or by writers from a certain time period. Clearly, we've been assuming that perhaps we can describe a group style: the way women write as compared to the way men write.

Often, masculine written language has been described as *terse, logical, strong, rational* and *convincing;* in contrast feminine written language has been labelled *verbose* and *overly complicated, illogical, timid, emotional* and *uncertain.* Other adjectives attached to the style are *flowery, sentimental, silly* and *meaningless.* Notice that all these adjectives are pejorative.

Dr. Mary Hiatt decided to test these assumptions about group style. She selected fifty books of non-fiction written by men and women and fifty books of fiction written by men and women. She selected from each book four passages of prose with a length of 500 words. After keypunching each word on an IBM card, she had a computer scan all the samples and look for characteristics of style like the logical sequencing of ideas, the length and complexity of sentences, the use of adverbs, similes, parenthetical statements, parallel structure, and other rhetorical techniques. She learned through her research that, in her sample, there was a feminine style distinct from a masculine style.

However, the style she found wasn't that which had been conventionally described. She found that men used long sentences more often than women. Thus, women weren't verbose. She found that both men and women used a variety of complex sentences, although some of the men writers had patterns of sentence complexity unique to each man.

When Hiatt examined the use of signals of logic—transition terms which show how one idea connects to another — both groups used signals equally. Men used terms like *for example, that is, for instance, therefore, so* and *thus*; these introduced examples or illustrations or drew attention to the conclusions derived from premises. Women used terms like *how-*

ever, but, yet, because, since and *and* more often. Could the fact that women use terms which further explain or justify an idea have led to the assumption that they are timid in their style? Do you think that using examples and illustrations makes writing more definite and strong than defining and expanding explanations? Certainly both writing choices demonstrate logic in the writing.

People who examine women's speech report that women use more *-ly* adverbs. Hiatt found that in writing this was not true; both groups used the same number and variety of adverbs. However, men used *simply* more often than women; only men used *awfully*; no one used *utterly*.

Hiatt looked at adverbs like *angrily* and *amiably* which might show emotion. In fiction women used twice as many adverbs of emotion as men; in non-fiction there was no difference. Men used twice as many adverbs of pace like *slowly* and *quickly* in fiction; in non-fiction there was no difference. When she considered both types of adverbs together, she found that women fiction writers used about the same number of adverbs of pace and adverbs of emotion in their writing while men fiction writers used about four times as many adverbs of pace as adverbs of emotion. What might account for those writing choices?

One final difference which Hiatt found was the fact that women use *really* two and a half times more often than men in non-fiction and one and a half times more often than men in fiction. She speculated that this happens because women writers feel they will not be taken seriously and so they repeat *really* to persuade their audiences to accept their ideas. Are there any other possible explanations for this?

Do these patterns coincide with any which your group identified? Are there some other characteristics of style that we should examine if we followed Hiatt's example of analysis? Why do you think she used the computer rather than her own observations?

Writing task seven: Compare the two definitions of yourself as a writer in terms of tone, persona, attitude and patterns of writing choices which would constitute a style. Do you see any changes? Were they changes you set out to make? Are there changes which you would like to make to develop your own personal style? Do you have any writing which might be characteristic of some group style?

What about spoken language? Is there a feminine style which contrasts with a masculine style? How many of your assumptions about he-says/she-says are based on your hearing patterns of speech which seem to be particular to one group? Linguistic research indicates that there is a woman's spoken language which differs from a man's spoken language, just as there are spoken languages for one ethnic group using American English which differ markedly from those used by another group. If there is a separate woman's language, is it considered equal to a man's language? Are there ways we might use it to reperceive and to change?

A casual interest in the interrelations of gender and language shows up in literature in the seventeenth century. In 1664 a report described different men's forms and women's forms in the speech of Carib people. Johnson in his dictionary cited certain terms for usage "by females." Speculations about language sex differences are scattered throughout literature. Virginia Woolf talked about a traditional "man's sentence" and stated that women needed to develop a new sentence in her book *A Room of One's Own*. It would be interesting to know what characteristic writing choices she had observed which led her to talk about a "man's sentence." Based on Hiatt's work, what might it look like?

Twentieth-century anthropologists report the use of separate languages by men and women among non-Western groups of people. However, a more organized and formal investigation of sex differentiation in the English language began with the publication of Otto Jesperson's *Language: Its Nature, Development and Origin* in 1922. After labeling as masculine all those elements of English which he admired (terseness, logicality and freedom from pedantry), he characterized as feminine or childish what he disliked (effusiveness, long-windedness, and ebullience). Jesperson insisted that women use euphemisms and hyperbole more often and that men use slang more often and innovate more freely. His study reflects his own biases and assumptions more than it carefully demonstrates real differentiation of men's and women's language. He had no carefully sampled data like that Hiatt gathered. However, his work influenced other linguists to begin to investigate variations by sex in the English language.

From 1900 to 1950, twenty articles about sex difference in language were published. Between 1951 and 1960, twelve appeared. From 1961 to 1970, thirty-four articles reached print. Between 1971 and 1976, eighty-one publications discussed sex differences in language. I hesitate to cite a number for the articles on the subject that have appeared from 1977 to today because another one may be published tomorrow. Why do you suppose there is rapidly increasing interest in this topic? What does it tell us about relationships of language and social change?

In *Language and Sex: Difference and Dominance* edited by Barrie Thorne and Nancy Henley, a series of articles describes research and interpretation of data in the area of language and an extensive bibliography annotates the materials currently available in this area. The bibliography is cross-referenced so that the reader can see how the major ideas or research findings in one article connect with those in other writings.

Who asks these questions? You will find lexicographers, sociologists, educators, folklorists, linguists, novelists, speech physiologists, rhetoricians, feminist editors, literary critics, anthropologists, and teachers and learners in composition courses asking these questions about how language and sex are related. Certainly, this new area of study has vigor and universality. Thinkers from many disciplines perceive that language and social change are interrelated. Their research and writing both reflects social change and hastens social change. These writings raise our consciousness about how language has served oppression and how our use of language can free us.

When Robin Lakoff, a linguist, wanted to posit that a separate women's language exists and that it restricts women because it is not considered equal to the dominant men's language, she first wrote to the general audience which reads *Ms.* magazine. Later, she published a book which described her thesis more carefully and which expanded her interpretation of how women's language restricts women's growth. She reports that women are allowed to make more precise discriminations in naming colors than men are allowed to make; that women use expletives or swear words which are not as harsh as those used by men; that women have adjectives for approbation or admiration for something which men do not use (examples are *adorable, charming, sweet* and *lovely*); and that women use a tag-question ("This topic is interesting, isn't it?) which is neither a statement nor a question. Then she interprets these facts to conclude that this language used by women is perceived as being less desirable than men's language.

In the series of writings which follow, you will see a student respond to the book *Language and Woman's Place* by Robin Lakoff. The essay would be what we could call a *critical essay.* You write this kind of essay whenever you are asked to criticize or to review a book, article, play, movie, concert, song, sports event, or fashion show. The critical essay does not have as carefully defined a structure as some of the essays we have written. It does, however, require a description of what is being reviewed and a judgment about it. It is more than a summary and also more than just a personal response. In it, you apply criteria for relevance; those criteria are either stated directly or implied.

The writer wrote three drafts of the essay which she handed in; she indicated that "it still doesn't seem done." We will look at two of the drafts. Watch the process of revision of a writer by reading through these materials. Notice that the revision ranges from reorganization of ideas to deletion of materials to substitution of one word for another.

Draft A

Karen Olsen

While reading Robin Lakoff's *Language and Woman's Place,* many of her statements and assertions made me wince under the onslaught of remembered events and discussions that fit exactly the situations described. The topic "Ms." —will it be accepted into society?—brought to mind conversations with my mother, who adamantly demands to be known as "Mrs." because only single women use "Ms." and a simple title change would not change her anyway. The implied statement in the conclusion that women may not move socially until they change linguistically seemed sound enough; most of the "girls" I know who are over twenty are usually "women" until someone calls them "girls," at which time they become air-headed, witless puppets.

Though I did agree with many parts of the book, more parts disturbed and distressed me. Why is a man's being a "pig" different from a woman's being one? Why must a woman laugh at Women's Lib jokes or be thought to be poor sports? And why doesn't calling a woman a "lady" reflect just as badly on the speaker as it does on the woman? The most distressing part of the book was one section concerning the inflectional patterns of women. Among the most annoying statements in this section were the following, in which (a) is a man and (b) is a woman.

> There is a peculiar intonation pattern, found in English as far as I know only among women, which has the form of a declarative answer to a question, and is used as such, but has the rising inflection typical of a yes-no question, as well as being especially hesitant. . . .
> (a) When will dinner be ready?
> (b) Oh . . . around six o'clock . . . ?
> It is as though (b) were saying, "Six o'clock, if that's OK with you, if you agree." (a) is put in the position of having to provide confirmation, and (b) sounds unsure.
> . . . One likely consequence is that these sorts of speech patterns . . . play a part in not taking a woman seriously or trusting her with any real responsibilities, since "she can't make up her mind" and "isn't sure of herself." (p. 17)

Neither of these exchanges sounds unnatural or makes (b) sound effeminate. He merely seems to be considerate of (a)'s feelings and opinions. But Lakoff maintains that a normal man would not normally speak in such a manner because "women's speech sounds much more polite than men's" (pp. 17–18).

What led Lakoff to this assertion? Perhaps it was her method of data gathering, mainly by introspection. "I have examined my own speech and that of my acquaintances, and have used my own intuitions in analyzing it" (p. 4), or perhaps it was the friends and the self about whom Lakoff was introspective that led to this bizarre finding. What group of people is composed of exclusively polite women and impolite men? What observer would typify the two sexes in this way?

Using Lakoff's method among my own acquaintances and myself, my findings differ markedly. Granted, I too know some rude men, barking orders at children, dogs, and colleagues without thought, and forcing their opinions on those same children, dogs and colleagues and even some captive audiences like shoppers standing in checkout lines, commuters riding on public transportation, receptionists in dentists' offices, and parakeets in cages, without first considering the possibility of their disagreeing or not caring. And I know some overly polite women, not willing to mention the dead aardvarks in the bathtub or the Second Coming, for fear of offending someone or of being corrected. But I also know rude women of the barking, inflicting variety and timid, shrinking-violet men. For the most part, my associates and I speak politely with one another, no one taking it upon himself to mandate (?) the time to begin any activity involving other people without first consulting them to find out what they think would be best. Is such courtesy the mark of a weak person who "isn't sure of herself" and "can't make up her mind"? Is it even the mark of a her? Is it uncommon?

Though Lakoff points out that neither rude nor polite speech taken to the extreme is always or even usually correct, and that a compromise is in order, her typifying male and female as rude and polite in the first place—though it has doubtlessly been done before—seems completely out of order. In her introduction, she states that "the majority of the claims I make will hold for the majority of speakers of English" (p. 5). How could such a majority, to be determined from the "educated, white, middle-class" in any way resemble my own, if she was planning on covering the majority of English speakers? I feel heartened by the knowledge that Lakoff presented her findings as "less the final word on the subject of sexism in language ... than as a goad to further research" (p. 5).

Call me goaded.

Draft B: A Critical Look at *Language and Woman's Place: or Who Says I'm Polite?*

Karen Olsen

What an "interesting" book!

After hours of deliberation, I feel that that is one of the least gender-distinctive ways to express my feelings about Robin Lakoff's *Language and*

Woman's Place. It is neither too polite and therefore female, nor is it too rude and so male. Though Lakoff deals with other issues in the book, she seems to focus heavily on the difference between men's and women's speech, marked by the degree of politeness found in each.

Some of the other, less perplexing issues discussed include the title "Ms." and whether it will be accepted into society to replace "Miss" and "Mrs.," the sharply different connotations of formerly equivalent terms, such as "bachelor" and "spinster" and the substitution of "lady" for "women" in inappropriate places. The first part of the book is subtitled "Language and Woman's Place" and describes women's use of language and the language used to describe women. Part II is subtitled "Why Women Are Ladies" and analyzes the data presented in the first half of the text. But somehow, everything comes back to the difference between men's and women's speech being politeness.

This is demonstrated in the following passage. In Lakoff's example, (a) is a man and (b) is a woman.

> There is a peculiar sentence intonation pattern, found in English as far as I know only among women, which has the form of a declarative answer to a question, and is used as such, but has the rising inflection typical of a yes-no question, as well as being especially hesitant....
> (a) When will dinner be red? (sic)
> (b) Oh...around six o'clock...?
> It is as though (b) were saying, "Six o'clock, if that's OK with you, if you agree." (a) is put in the position of having to provide confirmation, and (b) sounds unsure....One likely consequence is that these sorts of speech patterns are taken to reflect something real about character and play a part in not taking a woman seriously or trusting her with any real responsibilities, since "she can't make up her mind" and "isn't sure of herself."[1]

The problems with this example and Lakoff's discussion of it are many. First, this intonation pattern does not seem to be exclusive to women. I showed this example to two of my colleagues, one male, one female, seeking their opinions about Lakoff's findings. They had little to say about the passage concerning the research, because they were still trying to decide whether (a) or (b) was supposed to be the woman. Not only does this point out Lakoff's failure to mention just who she intended to be who, but it also shoots an extremely large hole in the idea that (b's) speech pattern occurs only among women. If two (three, including myself) educated intelligent people see nothing distinctly feminine in (b)'s intonation pattern, perhaps

---

[1]Robin Lakoff, *Language and Women's Place* (New York: Harper & Row, 1975). p. 17. All further references to this work appear in the text.

nothing feminine is there. Rather than sounding feminine, (b) merely sounds polite and considerate of (a)'s feelings. This is part of Lakoff's theory, though, that "women's speech sounds much more "polite" then men's (pp. 17–18).

It is difficult to see what led Lakoff to make this assertion. Perhaps it was her method of data gathering, "mainly by introspection: I have examined my own speech and that of my acquaintances, and have used my own intuitions in analyzing it" (p. 4), or perhaps it was the friends and the self about whom Lakoff introspected. I had trouble imagining a group of people made up solely of rude men and polite women. And I could not fathom coming up with such assertions as Lakoff's in regard to an average group of people. So I used her method among my own acquaintances and myself, and my findings differed greatly from hers.

Granted, I, like most everyone else, know some nude men, barking orders at small children, dogs, and colleagues, and forcing their opinions on these same children, dogs, colleagues, and even on shoppers standing in checkout lines, commuters riding on public transportation, receptionists in dentists' offices, and parakeets in cages, without first considering the possibility of their disagreeing or not caring. And I, too, know some overly polite women, unwilling to mention the dead aardvark in the bathtub or the Second Coming, for fear of offending someone or of being corrected. But I also know barking women of the inflicting, rude variety and timid, shrinking-violet men. For the most part, all of my colleagues and I speak politely with one another, no one taking it upon himself or herself to mandate the time to begin any activity involving other people without first consulting them. Such courtesy is not the mark of a weak person who "isn't sure of herself" and "can't make up her mind," nor is it distinctly feminine. It is merely polite. Lack of courtesy is not masculine, merely rude.

If such a research method can produce such varying answers when performed by two different people, maybe the method is not scientifically valid. This may invalidate the entire book. However, one might feel heartened by the knowledge that Lakoff presented her findings "less as the final word on the subject of sexism in language ... than as a goad to further research" (p. 5).

Call me goaded.

How successful is this critical essay? Has the writer described the main ideas of the book in a way that you know what you would find in it? Has the writer made her evaluation clear? Do you know from what criteria of relevance she is judging?

Writing task eight: Write a critical review of a song, book, magazine article, film, TV show, or radio program which deals with some topic of men's and women's identities in contemporary society.

Look carefully at the two drafts of the essay. Notice the revisions which the writer has made and ask yourself why each revision was made. In an intermediate draft the writer had this sentence: "What an annoying book!" In subsequent revisions she changed the adjective from *annoying* to *inaccurate* to *provocative* to *"interesting."* What is the significance of each change? Why did she settle on "interesting" and why is the adjective set off in quotes?

If the writer's first reaction to the book was negative ("What an annoying book!"), how did she show that annoyance without stating it directly in the first sentence? Look carefully at the revisions which establish a tone with the reader and which demonstrate her attitude about the subject. Why does she add (sic) to Draft B? How has she made her feelings about the book clear? Why, for example, does she include that long descriptive passage about the rude, barking man? Why cite the "dead aardvark in the bathtub"?

Writing task nine: The writer was not yet satisfied with Draft B. What changes could be made to make it even better? In a group, discuss any problems you find in the essay. Consider every writing choice, from the title to the last sentence with its playful literary allusion. Then write a paragraph which critiques this critical essay.

Are you persuaded that revision is a necessary step to "re-vision"? This stage in the writing process is often neglected by writers when, in fact, it is the most important stage in practicing the craft of writing. By habitually revising what you write, you give yourself both the opportunity to shape what you have to say into the most satisfactory essay and the opportunity to reperceive. This practice must accompany all the other steps of thinking and writing which you have learned to pace. Most teachers of writing agree that "there is no good writing — only good rewriting." Certainly, rewriting guarantees that the self you are shaping into existence has the shape which is healthiest and most attractive and most true to your self.

Suggested Group Writing and Discussing Activities

1. Rewrite any essay in this textbook so that it would speak to the audience you have stipulated.
2. Write a style sheet for an androgynous language. In the style sheet, describe patterns for organizing thinking and writing. Recommend how and when to use parts of speech. Suggest metaphors that would be particular to androgyny. This assignment requires imagination and careful thinking about language and its functions. You might find some useful models in the novel *The Cook and the Carpenter* by June Arnold or in *The Handbook of Nonsexist Writing: For Writers, Editors and Speakers* by Casey Miller and Kate Swift.

3. Research patterns of speech used by women and men by audiotaping or videotaping conversations or by recording patterns you hear used. This kind of research will provide you with raw data that you will need to interpret. A linguist would observe the data, identify any patterns and try to account for them. If the data cannot be explained by some existing theory, then the linguist would shape an hypothesis and test it by collecting more data, analyzing it and deciding if the hypothesis seems to be valid when tested. Your research into this topic might result in some new information about the topic of separate or androgynous languages for men and women to use.

4. Write a lexicon of terms for naming persons who are active in a community of practicing writers. Invent terms which could lead others to rethink a conventional assumption that "some people can write and others can't."

Recommended Reading

Robin Lakoff. *Language and Woman's Place*. New York: Harper and Row, 1975.

Doris Lessing. *The Golden Notebook*. New York: Simon and Schuster, 1971. This novel by a major contemporary writer explores the themes of woman as artist and the conflict of love and work.

Anne Moody. *Coming of Age in Mississippi*. New York: Harcourt, Brace and Jovanovich, 1975. You'll enjoy this autobiography about being black and female in twentieth-century America. Moody came into her maturity during the 1960s, a period of rapid social change and civil rights activity.

Sylvia Plath. Both a poet and a prose writer, Plath is regarded as a major contemporary poet. Her books of poetry include *The Colossus* (New York: Harper and Row, 1962), *Ariel* (New York: Harper and Row, 1973), *Crossing the Water* (New York: Harper and Row, 1973), and *Winter Trees* (New York: Harper and Row, 1971). A novel, *The Bell Jar,* (New York: Harper and Row, 1973), which many people read as Plath's autobiography, was published after her death.

Mary Ritchie Key. *Male/Female Language*. Metuchen, New Jersey: The Scarecrow Press, 1975).

Barrie Thorne and Nancy Henley, editors. *Language and Sex: Difference and Dominance*. Rowley, Massachusetts: Newbury House, 1975. This anthology of writings about sex and language includes a comprehensive annotated bibliography. The bibliography has also been published separately by Know, Inc., P. O. Box 10197, Pittsburgh, Pennsylvania 15323, under the title *He Said/She Said*.

CHAPTER TEN

Group Writing: Research Projects and Papers

Whether the instructor in Art History requires that you write a research paper on the Fauvists or whether you initiate a research project for your independent study tutorial in cybernetics, you involve yourself in a process of inquiry, analysis, interpretation, naming and renaming. When you move to another city and want to write a lease fair both to you and the landlord (note the assumption), you study and analyze the municipal housing codes. This chapter will describe the conventional process of research writing for your individual use when you write a term paper, for your use as a group member whenever you work in a group research project, and for your use whenever you need to "check the facts." What you do when you work with several people who research and present their research about alternative marriage contracts or about women in theatre, you also do when you write a term paper about women and consumerism for your course in marketing, and when you survey hospitals to select one which respects your patient's rights.

You can pace a research project and a research paper off in these steps:
1. Defining a topic or problem
2. Researching: collecting and evaluating relevant data
3. Making models and hypotheses from the data
4. Organizing the material; outlining the presentation
5. Writing the paper; citing the data

This step-by-step process seems not to acknowledge the spontaneous cross-structure, the eureka! insight, the sometimes leap from observation to critical awareness, the false starts, the serendipity, and the thinking and naming impasses met by groups and individuals. In fact, the "step-by-step" process has been identified and abstracted from the vigorous often confused but creative struggles of questioners to see and name their worlds. You will frequently perform several activities simultaneously, but when you review and revise and prepare your presentation for your audience you can analyze each step of thinking and writing by this pattern to check the congruence of form and content. You should adapt this step-by-step process to your current writing needs. You might use the information, description, and advice in this chapter as a springboard to new topics and ideas and approaches; you might use it as a guide to consult when you momentarily lose direction; you might use it as an agenda for group work; you might use it as a checklist when you revise the first drafts; you might use it to organize your proposal for a day care co-op.

Defining the Topic

You hear: "You must write a fifteen-page research paper about some topic relevant to the course with footnotes and bibliography."

You ask: "What's a good subject? Where do I start? How?"

You hear: "Prepare a group project for class presentation and evaluation."

You ask: "What will we research? When should we start? Where?"

If the instructor has specified a topic, you can begin immediately. If the instructor asks you to choose or to generate a topic, you can use brainstorming techniques to provide yourself and your group with a list of more topics than you could possibly explore. Then you can eliminate topics which are not suitable or practical. You can select topics worth researching by asking a series of questions: First and most important, what is it that *I* need to research? What do I need to say? How can I better shape my self through a research process? What needs doing and saying? What questions shriek for answers? How can we change ideas by re-searching a topic? Then, can we research this topic in the time and with the breadth expected? Is the topic too broad? How might we narrow the topic to a workable focus? Is this a subject that can be researched and supported with facts and the opinions of others? Might it be too subjective a topic as we now phrase it? Will this topic be too controversial for us to successfully sort out contrary reports? Might our prior assumptions hinder us from free inquiry? Is this topic new or unfamiliar enough that it won't bore us or the audience? Will the topic require technical knowledge or some expertise which we lack and couldn't acquire to work on this topic?

When encouraged to collaborate in group research projects, you accept the responsibilities of defining a topic, conducting research, questioning and playing with data, developing theses or hypotheses, planning a mode for presentation of the group's work to the class of learners, and, finally, presenting their ideas. This you do every time you write a research paper or plan a class presentation.

To select a topic for group research, you ask whether suggested issues intersect with how you live, where you live, and who you are. You could decide that every issue could be named and researched and then renamed and seen in a new way as a *woman's* issue. Almost automatically, that choice of focus would lead to new research and new ways of looking at even very old topics. For example, the topic *alcoholism* is an overused and too general topic for a research project. However, looking more carefully at women alcoholics has led to identification of "fetal alcohol syndrome" and other problems. If you want your research project to be somehow *new,* cross-structure already existing topics.

The list which follows reports many of the topics which became available as subjects of research when a group cross-structured *woman* and some other reality. You can use these techniques to generate topics for research. Let's say you believe strongly that science (or socialism or senescence) makes us more free and you want to explore more ways to think about science (or socialism or senescence). You begin by stating the term science and then linking it grammatically with a second term. You can investigate "science and...," "science of...," "science about...," "science for...," "science in...," and "science's...."

Many possible topics are suggested by rearranging terms: women and medicine, women in medicine, women of medicine, women's medicine, medicine for women, medicine by women, and medicine about women. Did you notice how each rephrasing shifts the focus of the topic and suggests issues to research which might not be required by the previous phrasing?

In the list which follows, you can see how multiple topics can be generated for research. You've no doubt already decided to follow up on topics in this course which jolted you into a new level of awareness about who you are, where you are going, why you do what you do. You can also find here ideas you could use or topics you could restate for your own use in future research projects. They are listed alphabetically for convenience: Women and...Art; Business; Communications; Death; Ecology; Folklore; Government; Health; Independence; Justice; *Kinder, Kurche, Kuchen;* Language; Marriage; Nationalism; Obstetrics; Politics; Quilting; Rape; Sports; Television; Utopias; Violence; Work; Xenophobia; Youth; *Zeitgeist.* Another twenty-six possible topics might be women's autobiographies, women's businesses, women's collectives, women's dorms, women's education, women's fantasies, women's groups, women's health, women's independence, women's justice, women's kinship terms, women's liberation, women's magazines, women's newspapers, women's organizations, women's photography, women's quotas, women's rights, women's studies, women's therapy, women's unions, women's votes, women's work, women's X-rated movies, Women's Years, and women's zealotry. Which of these topics has been researched too much? Which of these topics needs further narrowing? Which of these topics needs restatement?

Use *woman* a second way as an adjective and you generate several research subjects: woman athlete, woman power, woman priests. You could talk about images or roles of women by linking *woman, as* and a noun. You can see here twenty-six ways to think about women:

Woman as artist; woman as banker; woman as comedienne; woman as dancer; woman as editor; woman as filmmaker; woman as gaff; woman as hero; woman as inventor; woman as judge; woman as kibbutznik; woman as lawyer; woman as mother; woman as neurophysicist; woman as outsider; woman as poet; woman as quiet radical; woman as rebel; woman as sister; woman as theoretician; woman as usurper; woman as visionary; woman as witch; woman as Xanthippe; woman as youth; woman as Zenobia.

Writing task one: Brainstorm topics which a group could research for class presentation. Select three topics and brainstorm for each possible directions for research. List all questions and statements in an idea outline and then organize an initial research schedule.

The successful research paper and the best group presentations result from questioning and requestioning, from continued effort, from careful and thorough gathering of materials, from critical analysis of data, from writing first drafts or practicing presentations, from evaluation and improvements of first drafts and project run-throughs. You should begin your research project as soon as you learn of it. The questions which you ask yourself should jostle about in your consciousness for a long time while you look for published materials and other resources which might offer answers to your questions and while you examine your own assumptions and those of the sources you find.

When you write a research paper or when you work in a group research project, you'll want to give yourself ample time for collecting and reading and discussing and organizing materials. You'll want to reserve ample space for turning around in your inquiries, for changing directions when some new data demand reperception, for stepping sideways when some associated idea looks enough like a relative to research. For example, if your task group decided to research the images of women in textbooks so that they might describe present conventions and assumptions, extrapolate and predict implications of the assumptions, and create new assumptions, you will need enough time so that all the group members can explore and read and chew over ideas before you convene again to narrow the topic and to select a controlling thesis for the project. If your group decides to create new assumptions by writing a new nonsexist primer with illustrations that will please the audience, group members must arrange to work in such a way that no one has to stay up all night. Organizing a personal schedule for a research project may be a bit difficult at first but it is a prerequisite of fine writing. Once you have clarified the purpose of your research paper, you can articulate a controlling thesis. If your task in the research project is that of *reporting,* then you are obligated to select materials most relevant to the topic, to peruse the materials and to abstract from them the ideas and data that you need and that you consider significant to your thesis, to document what you have borrowed and to carry back (Latin origin of *report*) to your audience a clear, whole picture of the topic. You needn't worry if your report sometimes centers on one source if you are convinced that that source is unique and relevant.

If your task is that of *evaluation,* you must both report and interpret materials according to the criteria which you indicate. You are obligated to thoroughly research the topic, to abstract from the readings ideas and patterns from which you can generalize, to draw conclusions from the research, to demonstrate that your interpretation of the research is apt and supported by various authorities. Your evaluation will use many sources.

When your task is that of *reperception,* you report, evaluate, and then reevaluate. After identifying and analyzing the assumptions and events which shape your subject, you focus on the conventions within your own and others' reports and evaluations and you try to generate new ways of thinking through and researching the subject. You generate alternative solutions and models. Although you may not always be asked to reperceive when you write a research paper or work in a group project, you can always *take* the opportunities of research to discover and to generate and to express original and imaginative ideas.

Researching

Once you've selected a narrow topic for research and presentation, and have mulled over possible divisions and organizations of the topic and have articulated a tentative thesis, you should make up a bibliography. You can compile a preliminary bibliography—sort of a shopping list for the library—by looking into the card catalogues, the printed bibliographies, and the indexes in the reference section of your college library. In a bibliography you list all the readings which you think may be important to your inquiry; often you work on hunches about what should be covered in a book or a magazine article because the title seems pertinent. Sometimes the hunches are wrong but most often you can find materials that are relevant to your topic even though they may not be the exact materials you need.

Those 3 × 5 cards are helpful here. If you write each possible source on a note card, it's best to write "no good" on it and keep it as a reminder that you've looked at that source. You can arrange the useful sources alphabetically for easy reference. On each card you should list all the pertinent data — not only the title and author but where and when the reading appeared. If you are meticulous about writing the original entries, you won't find yourself muttering and pacing at 2 A.M. when you need to type the bibliography and find that you hadn't jotted down an author's first name or a complete title or the volume of the magazine where the source appeared. You save yourself time and energy by being careful when you begin your research.

When you write down a possible source, you might also make a quick note to yourself about the content you expect to find in it and the way you expect to use the source. Then when you find the book in the stacks or on the bookshelves you might also check the books to its left and right to see whether they too might treat your subject. When you scout out an article in a magazine, you could check whether the magazine typically prints articles dealing with the subject you are researching. You can make notes for yourself on the cards which then become a part of your quick recall anytime you need to research. If you get in the habit of thinking consciously about your hunches, you will grow more adept at saying "Well, I don't know that answer but I do know where to look."

Once you track down possible sources through a preliminary bibliography, you can find hints of other trails in the readings, in their footnotes and in their appended bibliographies. A reference by Adrienne Rich to Virginia Woolf might direct you to another essay which supports your ideas but which, for some reason, wasn't mentioned in the reference works you consulted.

A preliminary bibliography will often provide you with more material than you need. You must learn early on whether you can find material for your topic. If you can't find material, you may need assistance from the reference staff of the library or from your instructor. If you learn that there is no material published, then you will want to devise additional research methods — perhaps interviews, surveys or tests — to collect the data you need.

For example, one writing group in a composition course decided to research the attitudes towards women reflected in the captions of the daily comics. This group soon learned that no one had yet published research on language usage and sex-role stereotyping in the comics. The learners were surprised about this lack of research because they knew from their study in a mass communications course that newspaper readers turn first to the comic page. When they found no research to help them in their inquiry, they devised a test somewhat like the exercise in Chapter Nine where you assigned authors to written paragraphs.

In their group presentation, the learners supplied captions and asked the other learners to decide who was speaking. Then they projected the captions with their cartoons onto a screen and showed who had in fact spoken. The group members were able to make correlations between the responses of their audience and the patterns of women's language described by researchers like Robin Lakoff. The group members sampled several audiences and then analyzed the data and drew conclusions about the attitudes towards women reflected in popular culture. In other words, when they could not find materials to answer their questions, they changed their methodology to garner and interpret data.

Another group of learners decided to research women composers and to report who had been and who are women composers. They assumed that their task was one of discovering and making known women who were composers but whom we don't know because of the selectivity of the history we have read. This group learned that materials about women composers are scarce, incompletely indexed, and frequently biased. They also learned that a conventional assumption that women cannot and should not create anything other than babies resulted in some women's being ignored and even ridiculed when they composed. They learned that few contemporary writers and almost no previous writers thought the topic of women composers significant enough to research. Thus, they could be "pioneers" in the field.

When the group ran up against these obstacles in their research, they decided that the purpose of their research should be not only to report about women composers but also to report about the difficulties of researching women composers and to ask the questions which Virginia Woolf asks about the effects of an indifferent and hostile world on the creative process. They expanded their purpose from a report about women composers to an analysis of the obstacles set before these composers and to a reperception of a traditional assumption that "there are and can be no truly great women artists." This group recommended to their audience that they too research the topic "women in music" and learn more about the topic so that more women would become free to be composers. To help their audience, they reported on their research, showed a documentary film, *Antonia,* about a contemporary woman conductor and composer Antonia Brico, and gave the audience an annotated bibliography about women composers which they had compiled and annotated during their research.

You can be as innovative and creative when you write a research paper or work in a group research paper as you are when you write a persuasive essay or a short story or a statement of belief. Once you become confident about tracing sources and knowing how to research a problem, you can intelligently and critically analyze, question, name and rename. The research you practice for a term paper is literally your re-search of your world.

You already know that you can find source materials by looking under subject, author and title headings in the card catalogue. Have you also used *Subject Headings* to spot book titles which might be pertinent? The Library of Congress publishes this index so that you won't have to pull open dozens of drawers to find all the possible titles you might need. You can survey related subject headings and see whether additional titles would be classified under some associated heading. Often you find the exact data you need for your new interpretation under a category which is related to your subject but which didn't jump immediately to mind. For a long time, specific information about women's issues lay buried because the titles were listed under general subject headings and not under the umbrella heading of "woman." With the proliferation of women's studies courses and of writings about women, many new subject headings like *women's movement* appeared in the card catalogues; these headings were not library conventions fifteen years ago.

If you've written reports and research papers before, then you know about the advantages and disadvantages of using encyclopedias. They are most helpful when you are defining a topic and they can often point you to other topics to research. You are no doubt familiar with the *Reader's Guide to Periodical Literature* which indexes some one hundred general magazines, but have you also used the *International Index to Periodicals* and the *Social Sciences Index* and the *Humanities Index* which index more scholarly journals as well? There is an even more comprehensive index called the *Bibliographic Index* which will refer you to books, to collections and to other bibliographies; it's a good starting point. The *Biography Index* helps if your research is focused on people who are well known; the *Essay and General Literature Index* will help you find essays within books that you might not have expected to check. For example, the essay "What Is Poverty?" used in this textbook comes from a textbook used more often in education and sociology courses than in literature courses. I found it through the *Essay and General Literature Index*. Most academic disciplines have specialized reference works which you could consult: some examples would be *Art Index, Chemical Abstracts, Motif-Index of Folk-Literature, Encyclopedia of Social Workers, Legal Studies Index, Dictionary of the History of Ideas, Public Affairs Information Service,* and *Psychological Abstracts.* Some of these texts simply point you to materials published on the subjects listed;

others, like *Dissertation Abstracts,* not only tell you where to find published materials but also provide you with a synopsis or an *abstract* of the work. You can learn what are the major themes of the work, what is the pattern of organization, and what evidence is used or process is reported. You can use these basic reference tools to make the best and most efficient use of your time.

Newspapers often provide the most up-to-date information on your topic. The *New York Times Index* helps both by referring you to materials you can find in the *New York Times* (and that are probably filed on microfilm) and by pinpointing a time and place for news stories which you could use to check back copies of your local paper. If you wanted to check book reviews to learn about a contemporary publication, you could use the *Book Review Digest,* which gives you the main criticisms you would find in each review.

A particularly useful index for any research into education is called ERIC, the *Educational Resources Information Clearing-House Index.* The Department of Health, Education and Welfare organized a series of clearing houses or resource centers in the late 1960s for the fostering of and dissemination of educational research. Each clearing house serves a particular interest in education—perhaps these interests of junior colleges or of older learners or of nontraditional students or of educators who want to revise the curriculum to make it reflect cross-cultural values. You can use both the ERIC index and the ERIC thesaurus which provide synonyms or alternative descriptions of the topic. More and more libraries can help you conduct a computer search using the ERIC holdings. In fact, many libraries have computer technology that can help you locate sources that may not be in your campus holdings but could be borrowed from some other library through an interlibrary loan system. Some campuses even have computer hookups which could bring you photocopies of materials held in other libraries which may be too rare or too specialized to send on loan.

Other reference works help you to research the lives of persons whom you encounter in your studies. I have already mentioned the *Biography Index.* The *Dictionary of American Biography* (used to research the lives of dead people), *Current Biography* (used to research the lives of living people) and *Who's Who* all provide basic biographical data. More specialized works like the dictionary *Liberty's Women* (published by Merriam-Webster) and *Notable American Women: A Biographical Dictionary* (published in several volumes by Harvard University) would help you if you chose a women's studies approach for a research project.

We've already discussed the unabridged dictionaries and the *Oxford English Dictionary on Historical Principles* and the ways you can use them to conduct research. Many other specialized dictionaries are shelved in your library.

Another source would be the "vertical files" where a library stores pamphlets, news clippings, speeches, booklets, and other materials which are not indexed or shelved like other materials. An index to pamphlet material would be the *Vertical File Index: A Subject and Title Index to Selected Pamphlet Material.*

The increased attention to women's and men's selves in a changing society has resulted in several new reference tools. If you research a women's studies issue, you could use them in your work. *Women Studies Abstracts* annotates entries which locate and describe research and writings about women and about issues pertinent to women and men. *Women and Society: A Critical Review of the Literature with Selected Annotated Bibliographies* cites collections of women's studies materials, describes much of the literature about women and indexes other bibliographies of writings about women. You could also use *Bibliography on Women: With Special Emphasis on Their Roles in Science and Society.*

There's the *Index to the Women of the World from Ancient to Modern Times: Biographies and Portraits* which could give you a "crash course" in women who have shaped our world. If you narrowed your focus somewhat, you might want to consult *Black Women in White America* or *The Women's Rights Movements in the United States; 1948–1970: A Bibliography and Sourcebook* or *The Women's Rights Movement in the Seventies: An International English-Language Bibliography.*

Women's Work and Women's Studies, 1973–1974 provides abstracts of books, essays, and research on women's activities. It is published by the Feminist Press in Old Westbury, New York. This press has pioneered many publications about women, has brought many neglected writers back to our view, and has arranged with McGraw Hill to copublish a series of texts *Women's Lives/Women's Work,* which is multiracial and multiethnic. It also publishes the *Women Studies Newsletter,* a source of new ideas and information about women's studies issues.

Womanhood Media: Current Resources about Women looks carefully at the mass media but also includes a bibliography of "basic books" about women and suggests many topics for research papers. Women on Words and Images edits a book called *Dick and Jane as Victims: Sex Stereotyping and Children's Readers.* Two reference works look at women and work: *Women in the American Economy: A Documentary History, 1675–1929* and *Discrimination against Women: Congressional Hearings on Equal Rights in Education and Employment.*

In the bookstore on campus or in town, you might find a series of "how to" books for women. This field bulges with new titles and new writings.

Some examples are the *Women Rights Almanac* which offers information about the social, political and legal status of women. A popular text modeled on the *Whole Earth Catalog* is *The New Woman's Survival Sourcebook*. Many bookstores now routinely list "Women" as a category for books along with "Fiction," "Poetry," and "Psychology." More women are writing than at any time in our history; more women and more men are writing about issues particular to the self and their identities in society than at any time in our history. This new "psychic geography" Adrienne Rich named is being explored by many researchers and writers.

Almost monthly a newsletter or a magazine or a journal focused on issues which you have studied in this textbook begins publication. Although some do not manage to reach and maintain an audience, others take hold and become very useful to our society. I will list some of the magazines and journals which have established themselves; check your library and bookstore shelves to see whether they are ordered. *Ms.* magazine may be the most famous; it has become a symbol of sorts. Despite predictions that it could not succeed, it ended its first year of publication in the black—a difficult feat for any new publication. It has now been published ten years and also publishes books which pull together articles from the magazine and affiliated materials.

Other periodicals and journals include *Signs, Collegiate Woman's Career Magazine, Frontiers, Everywoman, Feminist Studies, Sinister Wisdom, Womanpower, NOW Times, Women's Studies, Women's Rights Law Reporter, Chrysalis, Thirteenth Moon, Women's World, Women: A Journal of Liberation,* and *Women and Literature.* Newsletters for special interest groups like women's music, alternative health care, various professional organizations, and political affiliates can be discovered by searching footnotes, classified ads, and bibliographies in these periodicals and journals.

Writing task two: Sharpen your research skills through this "scavenger hunt." Break into several work groups and either take the entire list or break it into sections. Research each woman or idea listed until you can write one clear and factual paragraph for each. When you return, you receive points for two tasks: for each clear identification, you receive two points and for each clearly defined resource, you receive two points. You want to learn not only who the woman is but also in how many ways you can gather information about her. The card catalog would be one resource, an index a second, and an encyclopedia a third. Don't restrict your search to the reference area of the library; check the audio-visual holdings, special collections areas and oral history sections as well. By the time your group has thoroughly researched each topic on your list, you should be thoroughly comfortable in your campus library. The group that has done the most thorough research would earn the most points and "win." However, no group which identifies each topic on the list and finds at least two resources could lose. Competency in research here could be demonstrated by knowing at least two ways to do research; superior competency is demonstrated by a thorough use of all resources possible—and by even generating new resources.

Hypatia	Lillian Smith	Ntozake Shange
Lisa Alther	Betty Friedan	Indira Gandhi
"fascinating womanhood"	#27	cliteroidectomy
Lucy Strong	Harriet Tubman	Emma Goldman
Anna Aknatova	Etel Adnan	Nelly Sachs
Yosano Akiko	Hien Luong	the Grimke sisters
Dorothea Lange	Kate Chopin	Rosalind Yalow
Rachel Carson	Ruth Benedict	Judith Jamison
Fannie Lou Hammer	Crystal Jordan	Mother Jones
May Sarton	Nora Ephron	Pat Schroeder
Grace Paley	Ellen Craft	Mary Church Terrell
Gloria Fuertes	Olga Broumas	Kaethe Kollwitz
Gaea-Tellus	Rosa Bonheur	Sofonsiba Anguissola
Hannah Hoch	Emmeline Pankhurst	Alice Paul
Rosalind Franklin	Maria of San Ildefonso	Charlotte Perkins Gilman

Writing task three: Write a "profile" or a biographical essay about one of the women whom you have researched. Don't stop at simply reporting the life of the woman. Choose a thesis to organize your writing; examples might be "What made Harriet Tubman risk her life so often?" or "What social forces shaped the thoughts and principles of Mother Jones?" or "How did Rachel Carson define pollution?" In your essay, you want to show a particular view, like the profile we describe in a photograph or painting.

Although you will find many of your materials in books, scholarly journals, and other library holdings, there are other sources which you could use. Order materials listed in the *Vertical File Index* and request materials from corporations, philanthropic associations, museums, and research libraries. Often large corporations underwrite research as public relations projects: how many times have you heard that a certain program on a PBS channel was supported by a grant from Mobil Oil? In the same manner, philanthropic organizations and political caucuses are always eager to send educational materials both about their organizations and also about their philosophies and the issues they fight for. Many museums and research libraries have materials used for education about specific topics; often these have been funded by grants or endowments and are intended for public distribution.

One student decided to research the furor over the "toxic shock syndrome" widely reported by the media in 1980. She questioned whether the outcry was proportionate to the problem. Because she was dealing with a timely topic, she supplemented her newspaper sources with letters written directly to the Center for Disease Control in Atlanta and tele-phoned one of the corporations which manufactured and removed from market a tampon product that might be associated with the illness. She discovered a "hotline" set up to answer questions about the situation. Many national hotlines have been established to inform the public about problems like child abuse, battered spouses, rape and alcoholism. Those hotlines can be a resource because they can direct you to other sources.

Interviews with persons who have expertise or special knowledge in the area which you are researching often provide new materials and new ideas. In recent years, the process of "oral history" has been used extensively by folklorists and historians to catch and preserve some of the information which is passed by word of mouth. "Slave narratives" were collected during the 1930s as part of a government-sponsored work project. Because of these interviews, we have primary sources from former slaves about their lives under slavery. Contemporary oral history projects have recorded the narratives of large numbers of elderly persons who migrated to America during the large immigrations of the 1890s and early 1900s. You can see this technique employed by Studs Terkel in three books: *Hard Times* grew out of interviews he held with survivors of the Depression; *Working* was a project of the late 1960s and early 1970s; *American Dreams* was published in 1980.

If you decide to use the interview technique, you'll want to do some "prewriting" and decide on some key questions beforehand. Research what you can about the person whom you interview. When you request an interview, explain clearly why you think this person would be a valuable resource person and what topics you hope to discuss. If you think that this person would be a major resource, you may need to plan several sessions for an interview.

During the interview, you want to take mental notes of the conversation which you would set to paper afterwards. If the person whom you inter-view does not object, it might be best to tape the interview on a cassette recorder. This process is often the least distracting and it gives you a tape you can listen to over and over. This insures accuracy of quotation; it also allows you to use the unique speaking style of the person whom you interview.

Be sure to ask whether the person whom you interview could refer you to other sources which would aid you in your study. If you have taken notes on your readings, you might restate these and discuss the main ideas with your resource person. Perhaps he or she will help you to rethink your work or can guide you in evaluating your other sources.

Some topics which you select may require that you discover other resources. There are official archives at many institutions but there are also "personal archives." These include relatives and friends of the people who figured prominently in the area you are studying. Again, letters might often uncover materials which have been kept after the death of the subject. One student who researched his grandmother's life found diaries and letters which contained references to her work in the early women's suffrage movement. The materials had been stored in an attic and forgotten; his grandmother had died years before he was born. This research added some new perspectives to his paper for an American history course and also gave him some new and valuable information about his "roots." Remember how Alex Hailey used a combination of research techniques like these to trace his roots back to Kunta Kinte?

Often you can find valuable source materials in the published and unpublished correspondence, diaries, and personal journals of people who are important to your research. The writer Anais Nin believes that the process of journal writing so well illustrates the many problems of self-actualization and so well defines the self in growth that she began publishing her own diaries during her life time. Often we need to look to the personal writings of "forgotten" persons to learn how they lived and what they lived for.

Those slave narratives which were handed down by oral tradition described the process of either escaping to or working for freedom. A few of these narratives were recorded in diaries or journals. They are important resource materials to historians who plan to describe and to interpret the historical reality of slavery.

Clearly, the process of researching a topic can be a process of reperception. You need to allow yourself sufficient time for the project. The materials are available to you but you must go after them in an orderly, well-paced fashion. All the time that you are researching, be sure to take clear and accurate notes.

You should also check the microfilm and microfiche holdings of your college library. Often materials which would be too rare or too difficult to acquire have been photographed and made available. Because the microfilm, microfiche and microcard materials are not always fully described in the card catalog, be sure to ask a reference librarian for assistance.

An important research tool to use for evaluating the data which you have located through a preliminary bibliography would be the series of notes which you take when you read to explore and when you read again to serve your defined writing purpose. During the prewriting stage of research, you are in fact shaping the paper. The notes which you take can be expanded into sections of the paper or into parts of the defined problem. Any fact or opinion which supports your controlling thesis should be noted on a blank card. The first time you take a note, you should write down all the bibliographic data (title, author, source, pages). After that, you can save time by just citing author and pages. These notes you can arrange and rearrange into a formal outline and a first draft.

Besides the tools which you use to help you remember the ideas and arguments of your reading, you will take notes which specifically quote the assumptions, the style, and the statements of other thinkers. You would no doubt choose to use a quotation rather than your own statement of an idea whenever the original naming carries more weight, more significance and more color than your rephrasing. When you note a quotation, you'll want to be very precise in copying the original, both as a fair treatment of your source and to insure accuracy in your research.

When you use quotations which you have written down on note cards, you'll want to take care that you not quote out of context or distort the original environment. If you decide to omit phrases or sentences from a quoted passage, you should indicate the omission by points of ellipsis. If you quote a passage which contains some grammatical or orthographic awkwardness, you can write [*sic*] to tell your readers that you have not misrepresented the original nor failed to proofread carefully.

When you borrow the words and the wisdom of some other writer, you must acknowledge the loan by enclosing the original phrasing in quotation marks or in display quotations and by describing the sources of the borrowed material in footnotes. Even should you paraphrase, you will want to give credit for the ideas and statements to the person who first named them. You should always document carefully lest a reader suspect you of intentional or unintentional plagiarism.

Sometimes you might want to digress a bit from the pattern of report and analysis which you are using and to chat with your audience about some related but not essential idea or event. In a "chatty footnote" you can digress and tell the readers those extra things you think enliven the reading and learning experience but which distract from the main purpose or pattern of the research paper.

Writing task four: Each group should draw up a list of references, unfamiliar words and new ideas which Adrienne Rich includes in the essay "When We Dead Awaken: Writing as Re-vision." Group members should research in standard reference works any allusions, words, facts, or persons mentioned by Rich and which seem important to know to understand the entire essay.

Writing task five: Groups should divide into two research teams. One team should report back about the life of Caroline Herschel; the other should report back about the life of Adrienne Rich.

Making Hypotheses

After you have carefully gathered and read research materials and after you have identified a pattern of assumptions which seems to structure or to account for the data, you should describe that thesis or controlling assumption. You should write that thesis clearly and thoroughly so that you can later predict its implications or consequences. You make a model for thinking about the topic and you describe the model to your reader. You describe both the components of the model and the methodology; you tell the reader what you intend to study or to demonstrate or to question or to analyze and how you will do so. You are describing a hypothesis for a longer paper; because you have already practiced writing thesis statements, you will not find it hard to make a hypothesis. Once you have drawn a conclusion from your research, you have in fact decided upon the purpose and the inevitable structure for the research paper.

In this introduction to a twelve-page research paper for a psychology course, you can watch a learner state the hypothesis created from the analysis and questioning of research:

> Is there any place where sexism does not exist? Perhaps, people report, in a person's mind. However, sexist assumptions certainly prevail in the science which explores the person and her mind — the science of psychoanalysis. Phyllis Chesler, author of *Women and Madness* has concluded that:
>
> > Clinicians, most of whom are men, all too often treat their patients, most of whom are women, as "wives" and "daughters" rather than as people: treat them as if female misery, by biological definition, exists outside the realm of what is considered human or adult. A double standard of mental health — and humanity — one for women, another for men, seems to good-naturedly and unscientifically dominate most theories — and treatments — of women and men.
>
> In this paper I will report some of the consequences which the sexist relationship between a therapist and his female patient produces. I will report and examine the effects of such a relationship on any woman who seeks assurance and help from psychoanalysis. Finally, I will discuss how the prevalence of sexist assumptions in psychoanalysis solidifies our oppression.
>
> Kathy San Antonio

The writer predicts that the prevalence of sexist assumptions in psychoanalysis will perpetuate behaviors and attitudes which have been identified in a survey of past psychoanalytic theory and practice. She tells the reader that she will describe how sexism affects therapy and the person who seeks help. Notice that she is reporting, analyzing and evaluating in the essay.

It sometimes happens that the hypothesis which you frame to organize your paper proves unworkable or insufficient or less exciting than one which you generate even as you are writing out the original hypothesis. You might suddenly see another way to think about the topic or an alternative explanation for research results. When this happens, you can be flexible in your writing because you have been thorough in your research. You wouldn't be starting from scratch should you begin again with a new hypothesis because you have the research materials which you can rearrange and reinterpret. Because a new hypothesis or a new question or a new assumption can be generated through the very process of writing the paper, you'll want to be sure to give yourself more than enough time for starting over, for outlining and studying the new draft, and for revising.

If you can write the research paper in one sitting, you should. Once you have formulated and stated the controlling thesis, you should arrange your data and write out your report and analysis connecting all descriptions and definitions to the hypothesis you believe they create. When you can write the research paper in a single sitting, you can be more alert to the internal organization which you've designed and you can be more aware of how you are playing and might play with language. You can consciously craft later sections from the introductory themes and motifs. You might even imagine yourself composing some musical form like the sonata in which you sound a melody in the early sections of the piece and later amplify, echo, complicate and work variations on the melody. You can compose the paper in ways that use principles of crescendo and diminution.

When you can't write the paper in one sitting, you should try to write each division at one time. When you read over the first draft, you should be sure to ask whether the separate divisions of the paper work in harmony. You will want to watch that you have maintained a consistent tone, that you have used rhythms which syncopate, that you have balanced motifs, and that you have used the same system of notation throughout.

Writing task six: Use a reference tool in the natural sciences to research the specialized astronomical terms and concepts Adrienne Rich uses in the poem "Planetarium" within her essay. After discussing whether Rich uses scientific metaphor effectively, formulate a hypothesis which accounts for Rich's choice of these metaphors to describe her sense of self as a woman writer.

Writing task seven: Group members should share the results of all research generated by the Adrienne Rich essay. Each group should formulate a hypothesis based on the research and on shared group discussion which responds to the question "How is the poem 'Planetarium' an instance of writing as re-vision?" Each group should write an introduction to a research paper which states the hypothesis formulated by the group.

Outlining the Presentation

When you write a research paper, you should construct a formal outline to use as a scaffolding and as a map. When you organize a group presentation of research results, you will also need an outline both to shape the classroom event and to insure unity and wholeness for the event. The mode of presentation which you have chosen will determine what kind of outline you will use. If your group decided to parody a television program which reflects and perpetuates attitudes and behaviors you find restricting, then you should work from an outline called a script. If your group decided to use some techniques from gestalt art therapy to encourage dyads or groups of two to communicate ideas and feelings nonverbally, your outline will be the schedule you plan and will include introductory remarks and explanation, time for the projects and for classroom discussion of results, and concluding remarks. Too often, imaginative group projects end with less force than they deserve. To avoid this, when you formulate your hypothesis, you could set down in outline form the responses and events you think predictable and you can practice several endings so that your spontaneous wrap-up is also as thoughtful and incisive as your project.

Often instructors will request that you hand in the formal outline with your research paper. You'll want to be sure that your final formal outline—which may differ from your preliminary formal outline—accurately diagrams the research paper. Thus, you can use an outline to provoke yourself to write, to support yourself while you write, to evaluate what you have written, and to provide your audience with an abstract of your research.

Writing task eight: Group members should look again at the preliminary formal outline they wrote for Chapter Six. If the hypothesis your group just articulated for Writing Task Six necessitates a new outline, revise the formal outline in any ways dictated by the hypothesis newly formulated. After writing an outline, group members should decide how to write the research paper about Rich's use of "Planetarium" as naming and renaming. Perhaps a different individual will take responsibility for each section and the group will make the paper unified and smooth in a revision. Perhaps the group will labor collectively to perform all the tasks. This group writing project will take continued effort and frequent collaboration. The finished research paper will undoubtedly run over ten pages.

Writing and Citing

Because a research paper is a cross-structure of data and individual interpretation, you want to tell your audience which structures were originally yours and which you have culled from other writings. The reader will assume that anything which you do not specifically identify as borrowed has been your work. You want to document the origins of the ideas both to be an honest writer and to teach your readers how they might also cross-structure materials and arrive at new ideas.

In a research paper, you document sources in two ways: in footnotes and in a bibliography. When you revise the first draft, you can check that you have skillfully incorporated all borrowed material into the paper either through quotations marked off by quotation marks or through longer quotations displayed in block form. You can also check whether you have cited sources whenever you have quoted directly or borrowed phrasings or perceptions which are neither common knowledge nor original to you. You cite the immediate source of a borrowing in a footnote; you cite the general influence of a source in the bibliography.

You have watched this process of citation in the essays of this textbook. Many writers have used both footnotes and bibliography. You might remember that Adrienne Rich used a convention of documentation which allows the writer to place author, title, place of publication, date and pages cited in a note either at the bottom of the text or after the conclusion of the essay. She uses the forms recommended by the Modern Language Association and described by the *MLA Style Sheet*. This pattern of documentation is used for writings in the humanities and is frequent in general literature. Look back at the documentation used in the several essays in this textbook.

Another pattern of documentation—that of the sciences—is becoming more frequent in general literature and is used extensively in scientific and technical writing. Muriel Schulz used one variation of the science style when she cited the author of a study and the year of publication in parentheses immediately after a reference. She could have also used a number system which refers the reader to the sources listed in the bibliography after the writing. Although internal citation is most common to writings in the natural and social sciences, you will also find writers like Schulz using explanatory footnotes at the foot of the page. These are the scientific equivalent to those "chatty footnotes" I mentioned earlier.

You will want to use the form of documentation most appropriate to the academic field for which you are writing. When you are writing an inter-disciplinary research paper, you'll have to choose the documentation you think most of your readers will know. You will want to check with your instructor about what conventions of documentation are appropriate and expected. Perhaps the most important proscription about citing sources would be that you be consistent and accurate.

In the final bibliography, you list everything you have read which has influenced your thinking and writing. You list all the materials which you cited in footnotes for the text and any other materials which figured in your research — even if you have not borrowed directly from them. Sometimes you might need to divide the list into primary sources—say the poems of Adrienne Rich — and secondary sources — like critical essays about Rich's poetry. You list all the readings alphabetically and with all the details about the reading which your audience needs to locate the materials. You can consult the style sheets recommended by your instructor for proscriptions about capitalization, abbreviation, identation, and description.

Writing task nine: Document the research paper you wrote about Adrienne Rich.

The research paper which you submit and the research project which you present to a community of practicing writers should be as holistic, as well-considered, as eloquent, and as reperceptive as any other definitions you have crafted during your participation in this course. You can use the conventions of the formal research paper to create a new piece of writing and a new statement of the way you see. You can report, analyze, name, interpret, understand and rename through the research and writing process. You can use your art of speaking and writing — your rhetoric — to shape and to change your self and your world.

Suggested Activities for Group Research and Presentation

This list of activities—provocative but not exhaustive—may help groups to cluster around themes for reflection and action. The list may facilitate some of the group processes of generating themes for dialogue, of deciding upon research methodologies, and of creating thinking-feeling presentations of topics which intersect with how we live and who we are. Group research projects should make a praxis of the assumption that an education of liberation should be a dialectical process which transforms the world. These projects should make use of the dialogue of all practicing writers about their reflection, research and action upon their world. These projects should show "worlds changed" through their first naming of their world, their redefinition, and their renaming. The primary objective of a group research project should be reperception — what you might call consciousness raising. The rhetoric we make to express thought into being and to act as human persons through making symbols should — I think I want to say *must*—be reperceptive.

Prepare a slide presentation of advertisements which argue for a new assumption about the identity of woman.

Parody some aspect of pop culture which restricts men and women by the assumptions it reflects. Think about comic strips, movies, radio programs, concerts, billboards, television, citizen's band radios, song lyrics.

Prepare a radio script which gives women equal time.

Write a TV pilot which will provide pictures of men and women in roles other than those portrayed daily on TV.

Make a happening — poetry, music, dance, communication games, handcrafts, mixed media—about the new woman.

Research the assumptions of children about male and female identities. Recommend educational projects to help children stay or become androgynous in their thinking.

Improvise scenes from a marriage, old and reperceived.

Role play any of the writers we have read and set up a dialogue with the community of practicing writers.

Fabricate an alternative magazine for women and men.

Write a new soap opera.

Analyze any general interest magazine and evaluate its complicity in oppressing people. Recommend changes.

Share some sports activity and discuss perceptions about the statement "our bodies, our selves."

Organize a panel of persons who see or experience life in ways that are less sexist than those you are most familiar with. Possible topics: reversed roles, androgyny, homosexuality, communal living, new family models.

Organize a symposium on rape.

Write a history unit which redefines what is valued so that the silent minorities receive a voice.

Produce a one-act play by, for, about, with, women.

Interview a family in which new roles have been defined and one which you believe is the traditional family. How do they compare with reference to shared household responsibilities, child care, leisure activities, division of income? What problems do you see and what solutions do you propose?

Research the image of the American Indian woman presented in curricular materials, films, TV programs, fiction and nonfiction.

Study the affirmative action program used on your campus. Evaluate its effectiveness.

Write a science fiction short story which shows us an androgynous world.

Prepare an annotated bibliography for any area of women's studies which needs research and rediscovery.

Plan and produce a documentary film about some "lost woman."

Construct a curriculum for any level of education which has as a primary objective the changing of sexist values.

Prepare an anthology of learners' repreceptive rhetoric.

Present a slide presentation of works by women artists whom you have rediscovered.

Prepare a handbook of information needed by women. Possible models include *Our Bodies, Our Selves; The Legal Rights of Women in Fifty States;* rape handbooks; directories of services for women; bibliography of writings by/for women.

Rewrite song lyrics which perpetuate old assumptions about men and women.

Compose a new rock opera about new identities of women and men.

Write book reviews of important or new works by women for publication in your hometown newspapers.

Dramatize nonsexist fairy tales in children's classrooms.

Organize a people's rights convention on your campus.

Design courses to raise the consciousness of students about a pedagogy of oppression.

Sponsor a women's health fair.

Start a women's center if your campus lacks one.

Organize men's consciousness-raising groups.

Research daycare facilities and legislation in your community. Recommend new facilities and projects.

Plan a careers day focused on nontraditional careers for women and men.

Recommended Reading

Here are more recommended readings. The list contains some "basic books" about women and men in a changing world, some autobiographies and several anthologies of writings by and about women. More entries in the bibliography are focused on women than on men because the new writings about men as they experience themselves in a changing world are scarce. What will be exciting will be the discovery of new writers writing about the liberation of men and women.

I have not listed individual publications of fiction, drama and poetry by women because these are carefully annotated in the bibliography *Women in Literature*. More women are defining themselves as writers now than ever before; more men and more women are talking and writing about the issues we've been discussing. We live in invigorating times now that we define our selves new. Good reading and good writing!

Basic Books

Judith Bardwick. *In Transition: How Feminism, Sexual Liberation and the Search for Self Fulfillment Have Altered Our lives.* New York: Holt, Rinehart and Winston, 1979.
——. *Psychology of Women: A Study of Bio-Cultural Conflicts.* New York: Harper and Row, 1978.
Ingrid Bengis. *Combat in the Erogenous Zone.* New York: Alfred Knopf, 1972.
Caroline Bird. *Born Female: The High Cost of Keeping Women Down.* New York: McKay, 1970.
Simone de Beauvoir. *The Second Sex.* New York: Alfred Knopf, 1953.
Susan Brownmiller. *Against Our Will: Men, Women and Rape.* New York: Simon and Schuster, 1975.
Phyllis Chesler. *Women, Money and Power.* New York: Morrow, 1976.
Ann Douglas. *The Feminization of American Culture.* New York: Knopf, 1977.
Mary Daly. *Beyond God the Father: Toward a Philosophy of Women's Liberation.* Boston: Beacon, 1973.
——. *Gyn-Ecology.* Boston: Beacon, 1975.
Shulamith Firestone. *The Dialectic of Sex: The Case for Feminist Revolution.* New York: Morrow, 1970.

Nancy Friday. *My Mother, My Self.* New York: Delacorte, 1977.

Betty Friedan. *The Feminine Mystique.* New York: Norton, 1974.

Germaine Greer. *The Female Eunuch.* New York: McGraw-Hill, 1971.

——. *The Obstacle Race: The Fortunes of Women Painters and Their Work.* New York: Farrar, Strauss and Giroux, 1979.

Elizabeth Hardwick. *Seduction and Betrayal: Women and Literature.* New York: Random House, 1974.

Carolyn Heilbrun. *Toward a Recognition of Androgyny.* New York: Knopf, 1973.

——. *Reinventing Womanhood.* New York: Norton, 1980.

Ruth Herschberger. *Adam's Rib.* New York: Pellegrini and Cudahy, 1948.

Elizabeth Janeway. *Between Myth and Morning: Women Awakening.* New York: Morrow, 1974.

——. *Man's World; Woman's Place: A Study in Social Mythology.* New York: Morrow, 1974.

Margaret Mead. *Male and Female: A Study of the Sexes in a Changing World.* New York: Morrow, 1967.

Casey Miller and Kate Swift. *The Handbook of Non-Sexist Writings for Writers, Editors and Speakers.* New York: Lippincott and Crowell, 1980.

Kate Millet. *Sexual Politics.* Garden City: Doubleday, 1970.

Sheila Rowbotham. *Woman's Consciousness, Man's World.* Baltimore: Penguin Press, 1974.

Rosemary Ruether. *Religion and Sexism: Images of Women in Jewish and Christian Tradition.* Simon and Schuster, 1974.

Mary Jane Sherfy. *The Nature and Evolution of Female Sexuality.* New York: Random House, 1972.

Autobiographies

Simone de Beauvoir. *Memoirs of a Dutiful Daughter.* Cleveland: World, 1959.

——. *The Prime of Life.* Cleveland: World, 1962.

Co-operative Working Women. *Life as We Have Known It: Jobs, Families and Political Conditions of Early Twentieth Century Britain.* Edited by Margaret Llewelyn Davies. New York: Norton, 1975.

Bernadette Devlin. *The Price of My Soul.* London: Deutsch, 1961.

Nikki Giovanni. *Gemini.* Indianapolis: Bobbs-Merrill, 1972.

Carolina Maria de Jesus. *Child of the Dark.* Translated from the Portuguese. New York: Dutton, 1961.

Margaret Mead. *Blackberry Winter: My Earlier Years.* New York: Morrow, 1972.

Eve Merriam, editor. *Growing Up Female in America: Ten Lives.* New York: Doubleday, 1971.

Anais Nin. *Diaries.* 7 vols. New York: Harcourt, Brace and World, 1980.

Margaret Sanger. *My Fight for Birth Control.* New York: Farrar, Rinehart, 1931.

May Sarton. *Plant Dreaming Deep.* New York: Norton, 1954.

Mary Jane Moffat and Charlotte Painter, eds. *Revelations: Diaries of Women.* New York: Random House, 1975.

Anthologies

Elsie Adams and Mary Lou Briscoe. *Up Against the Wall, Mother* ... Beverly Hills, California, 1973.

Louise Bernikow. *The World Split Open: Four Centuries of Women Poets in England and America.* New York: Random House, 1974.

Toni Cade. *The Black Woman: An Anthology.* New York: New American Library, 1970.

Lee R. Edwards and Arlyn Diamond. *American Voices, American Women.* New York: Avon, 1973.

Vivian Gornick and Barbara K. Moran. *Woman in Sexist Society: Studies in Power and Powerlessness.* New York: Basic Books, 1971.

Joan Goulianos. *by a Woman writt: Literature from Six Centuries By and About Women.* New York: Anchor Press, 1973.

Nancy Hoffman and Florence Howe. *Women Working: An Anthology of Stories and Poems.* New York: Feminist Press and McGraw-Hill, 1979.

Joan Huber. *Changing Women in a Changing Society.* Chicago: University of Chicago Press, 1973.

Linda Heinlein Kirschner and Marcia McClintock Folsom. *By Women: An Anthology of Literature.* Boston: Houghton Mifflin, 1976.

Robin Morgan. *Sisterhood Is Powerful.* New York: Random House, 1970.

Gail Parker. *Ovenbirds: American Women on Womanhood. 1820–1920.* Garden City, N.Y.: Anchor Press, 1972.

Betty Roszak and Theodore Roszak. *Male/Female: Readings in Sexual Mythology and the Liberation of Women.* New York: Harper Colophon, 1969.

John Snodgrass, Editor. *For Men against Sexism.* New York: Times Change, 1977.

Leslie Tanner. *Voices from Women's Liberation.* New York: New American Library, 1970.

Mary Ann Washington. *Black-Eyed Susans: Classic Stories by and about Black Women.* New York: Doubleday, 1975.

Jeannette Webber and Joan Grunman. *Woman as Writer.* Boston: Houghton Mifflin, 1978.

Histories

Rosemary Agonito. *History of Ideas on Women: A Source Book.* New York: Putnam, 1977.

William H. Chafe. *The American Woman: Her Changing Sociological, Economic, and Political Roles 1920–1970.* New York: Oxford University Press, 1975.

——. *Women and Equality: Changing Patterns in American Culture.* New York: Oxford University Press, 1977.

Eleanor Flexner. *Century of Struggle: The Women's Rights Movement in the United States.* New York: Atheneum, 1974.

Gerda Lerner. *Black Women in White America: A Documentary History.* New York: Vintage, 1972.

———. *The Female Experience: An American Documentary.* Indianapolis: Bobbs-Merrill, 1977.

———. *The Majority Finds Its Past: Placing Women in History.* New York: Oxford University Press, 1979.

Midge Mackenzie. *Shoulder to Shoulder.* New York: Knopf, 1975.

Ann Oakley. *Woman's Work: The Housewife Past and Present.* New York: Random House, 1974.

Karen Peterson. *Women Artists: Recognition and Reappraisal from the Early Middle Ages to the Twentieth Century.* New York: New York University Press, 1976.

Index

307